JACOB L.

Talmon

Mission and Testimony: Political Essays

The Editor and Press acknowledge the support of
the Talmon Fund at the History Department
of the Hebrew University of Jerusalem

JACOB L.

Talmon

Mission and Testimony: Political Essays

Foreword by **Isaiah Berlin**

Edited by DAVID OHANA

Brighton • Chicago • Toronto

2 4 6 8 10 9 7 5 3 1

First published in Great Britain in 2015 by
SUSSEX ACADEMIC PRESS
PO Box 139, Eastbourne BN24 9BP

and in the United States of America by
SUSSEX ACADEMIC PRESS
Independent Publishers Group
814 N. Franklin Street, Chicago, IL 60610

and in Canada by
SUSSEX ACADEMIC PRESS (CANADA)

British Library Cataloguing in Publication Data
A CIP catalogue record for this book is available from the British Library.

Library of Congress Cataloging-in-Publication Data
Jacob L. Talmon : mission and testimony : political essays / foreword by Isaiah Berlin ; edited by David Ohana.
pages cm
Includes bibliographical references and index.
ISBN 978-1-84519-741-4 (pb : alk. paper)
1. Talmon, J. L. (Jacob Leib), 1916–1980. 2. Jewish historians—Israel. 3. Jews—History—Historiography. I. Ohana, David, editor.
DS115.9.T35J33 2015
956.940072′02—dc23

2015006455

Typeset & designed by Sussex Academic Press, Brighton & Eastbourne.
Printed by TJ International, Padstow, Cornwall.

Contents

Acknowledgements

All chapters in the Political Essays section are copyright © The Estate of the Late Jacob L. Talmon or are in the Public Domain, except where rights holders are alerted below.

The Ordeal of Sir Lewis Namier – The Man, the Historian, the Jew. reprinted from COMMENTARY, March 1962, by permission; copyright © by Commentary, Inc.

Mission and Testimony – The Universal Significance of Modern Anti-Semitism, from *The Unique and the Universal* by J. L. Talmon, published by Secker and Walburg. Reprinted by permission of The Random House Group Limited.

The New Anti-Semitism, September 18, 1976. Reprinted by permission of *The New Republic.*

The publishers apologize for any errors or omissions in the above list, and have made substantive efforts to locate rights holders. The publishers would be grateful to be notified of any corrections that should be incorporated in the next edition or reprint of this book.

A Tribute to My Friend

Isaiah Berlin

I am glad of this opportunity of saying a few words about Jacob Talmon, to whom I was bound by many years of warm friendship. I first met him when he came to see me in Oxford in, I think, 1947, on the suggestion of his then teacher, Professor Harold Laski of the London School of Economics. He wished to discuss movements in eighteenth-century Western thought which, in his opinion, had not been correctly interpreted by most writers on the subject. I realised, before the end of the first hour, that I was listening to an original thinker, a very lively talker, with interesting ideas resting on a solid basis of erudition, that he was imaginative, warm-hearted, passionately anxious to convey his vision of the French thinkers of the Enlightenment and the political consequences of their ideas. I pressed him to stay for longer than he had intended, and he readily agreed. We spent the rest of the day discussing what afterwards became the central theme of his most famous book, *Totalitarian Democracy*, and since my ideas were tending in the same direction, I found that talking with him was highly stimulating and intellectually delightful.

The sympathetic accord established between us on that first meeting remained undisturbed from then on. The major thrusts of his investigations went into two basic yet parallel directions. His first effort was to trace authoritarian and then totalitarian socialism, initially among parties and factions of eighteenth- and nineteenth-century France and elsewhere in Europe. Inevitably his scholarship turned to the post 1917 Communist régimes. But above all he bent his mind to the parallels he revealed between the thought of Rousseau, Robespierre, Saint-Just and their conceptions of liberty and fraternity. On the one hand he uncovered the role of revolutionary élites in the social order for which they were fighting, and on the other, the theory and practice of Marx and Marxists in contradistinction to those of liberals and socialists of a more libertarian kind. All this was undoubtedly his major achievement, and earned Talmon a world-wide reputation as a new and important analyst and historian of social and political ideas and movements in the last two centuries. As often happens with path-breaking work, his book was greatly praised and vigorously attacked; as might have been expected, it survived its detractors, and is today regarded as a work of permanent value. In this work and in others, Talmon freely acknowledged his debt to teachers and friends from whom he learnt, but by whom, it seems to me, he was not greatly influenced – R. H. Tawney, Lewis Namier, E. H. Carr, Karl Popper – with some of whom he remained in touch. He referred relatively seldom to his teachers at the Sorbonne in Paris or in Jerusalem – thus he recognized the scholarship of Professor Richard Koebner, but found his approach unsympathetic, a feeling that was, I suspect, reciprocated.

Zionist Lay Nearest Talmon's Heart

He followed his first, and most important book with subsequent volumes dealing with the continuing conflict of social ideas in nineteenth-century Europe, conservative, liberal, socialist, neo-Jacobin, Marxist, anarchist, syndicalist, nationalist – a vast gamut of doctrines and parties, all of which left some impression on social and political movements among the Jews, most of all, of course, on Zionism, which lay nearest Talmon's heart and affected nearly all that he thought and did. No matter what his theoretical interests were, or the topics on which he was lecturing or writing, his deepest concern was with the Jewish people, its history, its religious, moral and social values, its place among the nations, its future in Israel and the Diaspora; it was this last that utterly preoccupied him: he remained a genuine and unwavering liberal during the more than thirty years of our friendship, in the sense in which Keynes and Bertrand Russell and Graham Wallas were liberals; for all his Polish and Israeli background, perhaps because of it, it was classical liberalism of the English type that colored Talmon's Zionism, as well as his ideals of academic purpose and conduct and his intellectual and moral goals. He was something of a hero-worshipper, but he was not blind to what seemed to him his heroes' blemishes; thus he vastly admired Weizmann, but thought him too distrustful of Jewish capacity for self-government (he changed his opinion later in life, when he grew more pessimistic about the wisdom of Israeli governments). He admired Ben Gurion (whose biography he had at one time thought of writing) for his political courage, both in his policy against the Irgun Zvai Leumi and his lonely stand after the Six-Day War, but he thought him too unbending, aloof and hard-hearted. He deeply admired Namier's genius as a historian, but deplored his conservatism and distrust of ideas (Namier, in his turn, respected him and was attracted by his energy and his imagination, but thought him too sentimental). He liked E. H. Carr and admired his independence, but deplored his view of history and his excessive anti-liberal bias. He admired Tawney's character and humanity, but his socialism was too Christian to be fully acceptable. He responded to Laski's personal kindness and brilliance, but thought him thin and superficial.

I spoke above of Talmon's concern for the Jewish nation. This anxiety was always present in all his essays on Jewish topics, scattered in journals, and from time to time collected in volumes of essays both in English and in Hebrew, and translated into other languages. In one of the last letters that he wrote me, after saying how glad and relieved he was to have completed his *magnum opus* for publication after so many years of painful labor, he said that he contemplated writing a book on the history of the Jews in modern times, that is, from the eighteenth century onwards. He added that he could not make up his mind, since a pattern is always implicit in the work of a historian, whether he is conscious of it or not, whether this history was to be conceived as a progressive development towards a great flowering – the creation of the State of Israel – or conversely whether the pattern that would emerge would be a long-drawn out, pathetic story of frustration, culminating in a self-created national ghetto, self-centred, self-absorbed, unwilling or unable to understand its objective position. This despite the fact that such an understanding alone could open the door to the beginning of a normal relationship with the rest of mankind.

His Political Commitments

Personally he was a generous, kind, warm-hearted, utterly decent man – spontaneous, affectionate, passionately concerned with the rights and needs of others, above all the need for just and decent relationships between human beings; that, and a love for the Jewish people as such, in all its manifestations, colored all that he did and was. Politically this naturally entailed opposing what seemed to him the fast-growing chauvinism and methods of violence, however historically intelligible, in Israel, and supporting a humane and realistic liberalism. He had never shared the belief of *Brith Shalom* or *Ihud* in the possibility of a unified, harmonious Jewish-Arab state in Palestine. He thought the cultures were too different and the memories of bitter conflict too deep – the wounds could be healed only by separation. He was a convinced opponent of *Likud* and spoke out against its policies publicly with force and eloquence in Israel; he did not do so when he was abroad, since he thought that it was improper to appeal to a public that was in any case none too sympathetic to Israel, when it was less easy though more useful to do so at home. He was bitterly opposed to the policy of the settlements on the West Bank, and thought that the prospect of ruling more than a million Arabs in these territories, whatever rights they might be accorded, could only lead to an ultimate explosion that would put the survival of the State at great risk, and in the meanwhile would corrupt the political morality of the Jews of Israel; hence his admiration for Ben Gurion's call to return the territories in 1967, which he thought both brave and wise. His was one of the few clear and independent voices which spoke out against policies that seemed to him insane and suicidal as well as immoral.

The Man Himself

He was profoundly patriotic, without being nationalist; realistic without being cynical; and he was guided in public and private life by an unerring moral instinct without any trace of self-righteousness. His dominant wish was to tell the truth. He wished to live as a free man and scholar in a free country. He had no political ambition and no craving for power. He was emotional, had a low boiling-point, tended to be moved often to enthusiasm and indignation, hope and despair, and spoke out, as he did, with controlled passion, when he felt he could not decently remain silent. He despised duplicity, cowardice, self-protective caution, and hated fanaticism and blind, irrational faith, and perhaps died when he did because he had not the gift of insulating himself against painful awareness of morally worrying public issues. His honesty and the warmth of his nature endeared him in all the seats of learning that he visited – Oxford (he came here often, and was always welcomed in all the colleges of which he was a member), in Paris, at Wassenaar in Holland, at the Rockefeller Villa Serbelloni in Italy, at the Princeton Institute, at Stanford, in New York, and at the research center in South Carolina which invited him to return whenever he felt so inclined. He liked human beings, and was very life-enhancing. Despite his growing ill-health, he lived life fully. He was a very nice, very honorable man, to whom I was bound by ties of warm friendship. His death is a severe loss to his university, his country, the Jewish people, and the world community of scholars. Jerusalem will never be the same for me nor, I feel sure, for many others. *Zikhrono livrakha.*

Jacob L. Talmon: The Historian as an Intellectual

David Ohana

Why have revolutionary movements which sought to recreate man led to his enslavement? Why has the hope of total liberation and the attempt to realize these lofty expectations resulted in their reversal? Why did youthful dreams of the equality of man end with the shameful reality of gulags and labour-camps? Why did aspects of the eighteenth-century philosophy of the Enlightenment and the nineteenth-century political ideologies pass from the zenith of theory to the nadir of reality in the twentieth century? How does one explain a noble ideal realized through an evil action?

The underlying theme of the historical investigations of Jacob L. Talmon, which were a continuous attempt to solve these conundrums, was the secular Messianic urge of modern man who presumed to mould with his own hands both this world and the world-to-come within this world. The modern revolutionary ideologies translated the old religious yearnings into secular, political concepts. Religion was laicized and became history, the kingdom of heaven was exchanged for the kingdom of man, and transcendental salvation was transmuted into Promethian passion.

Talmon's work was basically concerned with one essential question which he formulated in his first book, *The Origins of Totalitarian Democracy*, the first of a trilogy: namely, why did the Messianic vision, which was the active motivating force of the revolutionary ideologies, move in a short time into "unmitigated tyranny and serfdom"? It seems, he said, that there is a "curse on salvationist creeds: to be born out of the noblest impulses of man, and to degenerate into weapons of tyranny."[1] The Messianic dialectic continued to trouble Talmon in the second book in the trilogy, *Political Messianism*: Why, does it [political Messianism] somehow always turn from a vision of release into a snare and yoke?"[2] In the third and last part of the trilogy, *The Myth of the Nation and the Vision of Revolution*, Talmon once again enunciated the dialectical "code" of Messianism from its "promise of a perfect direct democracy to assume in practice the form of totalitarian dictatorship."[3]

Talmon devoted his life to solving the riddle of secular Messianism. Political Messianism, which he saw as a secular religion from the eighteenth century onwards, sought to efface the contradictions and tensions in modern secular life between the individual and the community, between freedom and equality and between unity and particularity. It sought to achieve this by political means through the creation of a harmonious utopia in history. The secular Messianic conception was based on a certain idea of the nature of man. It wished to create men not "as they are but as they were meant to be, and would be, given the proper conditions."[4] The political and pedagogical shaping of modern man has been the common aim of ideologies of both left and right from the time of the French Revolution.

One of the basic forms of the Messianic idea assumes that the end of the human race will resemble its beginning. According to this view, when man started out he lived in harmony. In the course of time this harmony was disrupted for one reason or another, but in the future history promises an inevitable return to a peaceable garden of Eden in which all oppositions will be eliminated and all contradictions resolved in a final and decisive manner. The quasi-religious cast of the secular philosophy of the eighteenth century decreed that human contradictions are the outcome of man's sinful history and will finally be swallowed up in the womb of a new and harmonious history.

Messianism is essentially a belief in the perfection of man at the end of days, in a decisive and radical improvement that will take place in the condition of humanity, society and the world, and in a final and complete resolution of history. Unlike the cyclical conceptions of time in classical and eastern cultures, the Messianic conception of time envisaged a revolutionary change of order leading all at once to the Messianic future, or a linear progress of time from the imperfect present to a better state. This was an entirely new and utopian scheme, though it was sometimes viewed as a return to a golden age in the past (a "restorative utopia", to use Gershom Scholem's expression, as in "restore our days as of old").[5]

The idea of the perfection of man at the end of days lies at the heart of the Messianic conception.

Judaism and Christianity had different approaches to Messianism and consequently to the idea of redemption. The various currents in historical Judaism saw redemption as a manifestation which takes place in the public sphere and in the arena of history, while Christian theology with its stress on sin and atonement saw it as the personal salvation of the individual. Christianity, in Talmon's opinion, was essentially hostile to all movements of political Messianism because they declared that they had come to replace it. Their preaching of national or universal redemption and their vision of history moving towards a redemptive climax in which all social contradictions would be resolved in one revolutionary act was in contradiction to the Christian conception of history as a process of decline.[6]

What differences did Talmon find between ancient Messianism and modern Messianism? The religious Messianic movements and manifestations of ancient times ended with the abandonment of society and the creation of exclusive sects; the Messianism of our time seeks to bring about a revolution in society. The Christian revolutionaries owed allegiance to the Lord of the Universe and refused to recognize the rule of man; modern Messianism recognizes only human reason and seeks to achieve universal happiness within history in the here and now. The Christian revolutionaries, apart from the Calvinists and Anabaptists, recoiled from the use of force; secular Messianism tries to reach the absolute by all possible means. The dichotomy of the heavenly kingdom and the worldly kingdom facilitated the spread of religious Messianism; the monism of secular Messianism is free from this religious dichotomy and from spiritual inhibitions and demands an immediate on-the-spot settling of accounts.

Judaism was not originally a Messianic religion. Only gradually did the Messianic faith cease to be a marginal concern and gain a central position during the darker phases of Jewish history in Israel and the Diaspora. The Messianic hope became a refuge from exile, from religious persecution, from destruction and oppression. The Messianic faith represented a hope of national or universal redemption which appeared in particular historical situations. Zvi Werblowsky described Jewish Messianism as a multi-storied building to which many spiritual, universal, cosmic, philosophical and mystical levels had been added, and each floor changed the character of the previous floors. The tension between Jewish existence and Jewish Messianism resulted in moments of historical movement towards Messianism and movement away from Messianism.[7]

Talmon sought to emphasize, elucidate and illustrate the Jewish presence in general history, revealing the Messianic principle in Judaism and its contribution to universal history. He saw the Jewish idea of Providence overseeing history and moving it towards a redemptive solution as nurturing the revolutionary potential of the radical end-time movements which sought to achieve the kingdom of God within history.

Jean-Paul Sartre who, like Talmon, passed away in 1980, acknowledged in his final interview that Judaism's special contribution to the world was Messianism:

> What intrigues me is the objective which every Jew adheres to consciously or unconsciously, and which ought finally to unite mankind. It is an end in the social and religious sense, which is only to be found in the Jewish people. For me, Messianism is something important which only the Jews conceived of, which can also be used by non-Jews for additional moral purposes. What do we expect from a revolution? The disappearance of the present society and its replacement by a juster society . . . This idea of the final end of a revolution is Messianism, so to speak.[8]

This perception of Sartre's bears a surprising resemblance to that of another Frenchman, Henri Saint-Simon, about a hundred and fifty years earlier. Talmon traced the beginning of political Messianism to Saint-Simon and to the Saint-Simonian movement and its Jewish members. Saint-Simon, the first socialist prophet and the figure whom Michelet called "the most audacious thinker of the nineteenth century," was the person who identified the vision of the redemption of mankind with the Jewish Messianic message:

> The chosen people of God, which received revelation before the appearance of Jesus, the people which has spread most widely over the whole world, has always felt that the Christian religion, founded by the Fathers of the Church, was incomplete. This people has always maintained that a great age will arrive, to which they have given the name of Messianic, an age when the religious doctrine will be set forth in the most universal terms of which it is capable, when

> it will govern the actions both of the temporal and of the spiritual power, and every human race will have the same religion and the same organization.[9]

Although major Jewish thinkers were not prominent in the philosophy of the Enlightenment in the seventeenth and eighteenth centuries, it prepared the way for the Jewish Haskalah, for the Emancipation and for a renewed interest in ancient Jewish prophecy, with its universal content. Talmon said he could not "imagine European socialism without the prophetic-Messianic ardour of its Jewish prophets and of the Jewish members of the Saint-Simonian movement, Karl Marx, Ferdinand Lassalle and others."[10] Marxism's point of departure was not formal socioeconomic analysis but a "faith that moves mountains in the mission of history as a message of redemption." What motivated Marx was " the compelling thrust of a vision of a final resolution of the drama of history in the future, with a providentially predetermined realization of justice."[11] "In Marx, Lassalle, Rosa Luxembourg and the other Jewish revolutionaries, the ancient Jewish dream of a general redemption which would happen all at once took the form of a classless society based on absolute justice which would come about in a single apocalyptic reversal."

Jewish Messianism, Talmon concluded, provided the Western world with a very powerful underlying element which was one of the special characteristics which distinguished it from the other great cultures. The vision of Jesus's return to the world at the end of days was derived from it. It formed the inspiration of apocalyptic and millennary movements throughout history, and in a different sphere paved the way for the idea of an infinite progress towards socialism and the expectation of revolution as the final redemptive stage of history.

Shortly before his death, Ya'akov Talmon was chosen by the Committee of Scholars as one of the twenty greatest historians of the twentieth century. Together with him were chosen historians such as Arnold Toynbee, Johan Huizinga, Fernand Brodel, Lewis Namier, Henri Pirenne and others. In an appreciation of Talmon's work, they wrote: "One cannot read his books without being deeply impressed by the true and frightening picture he paints for us – a picture of the secular Messianic religions. His historiography is a convincing apologia for human liberty, and it belongs to the liberal-conservative tradition which had political theoreticians like Locke,

Montesquieu, Burke, Constant, Tocqueville, and in our time Karl Popper."[12]

In this essay, Talmon is depicted as the outstanding representative of the historiographical tradition beginning with Edmund Burke and Hippolyte Taine, which saw the French Revolution as the first modern manifestation of a dialectic whereby values become distorted on being translated into power. We read: "Talmon has contributed three new principles to this tradition. First, he traces the mechanism through which the loftiest ideals degenerate into cruel despotisms when an attempt is made to put them into practice. He then indicates the way in which this mechanism operated in the three types of revolutionary ideology which have come into being since 1789: Jacobinism or radical liberalism, socialism and nationalism. Thirdly, he shows that the roots of twentieth-century totalitarianism (one thinks of Lenin's Russia and Hitler's Germany) can be traced, in the final analysis, to particular aspects of eighteenth-century political thought. Unlike some contemporary historians – Peter Gay, for instance, who sees the Enlightenment as entirely positive – Talmon also recognizes less pleasant aspects of the heritage of the Enlightenment. According to Talmon, the Enlightenment bequeathed to us not only the idea of the constitutional state representative of the authority of the people but also some political sophistries which have been misused to provide 'legitimation' for most of the worst régimes humanity has known. We should not be surprised at the fact that Talmon has devoted his entire life to investigating the totalitarian régimes and disputing with them." The writer of the essay ascribes this to Talmon's Judaism and his life-history. As a child in one of the *shtetls* which were wiped out during the Holocaust and as someone who was already acquainted with antisemitism before the Holocaust, Talmon could not, he thinks, remain indifferent to a matter of such importance.

In a memorable though neglected personal confession, Talmon described the biographical origins of his intellectual attraction to studying the Messianic idea:

> I began as a member of "Hashomer Hatza'ir" in a small *shtetl*, in an atmosphere full of longings, caught in a cross-fire from two sides: the Messianic fire from eastern Europe and the fire of Zionism from Eretz-Israel. When I reached bar-mitzva age I had an attack of religion, or, if you will, I began a search for God. I finally left "Hashomer Hatzair", and unfortunately, after a time I broke off my relationship

> with the Ruler of the Universe because, when I read the prayer of the Eighteen Benedictions I felt that I did not believe it and could not endorse it. This caused me to adopt a certain position which perhaps has been responsible for my interests, my spiritual image and my outlook.
>
> I do not believe that in matters of outlook, beliefs and ideas we are concerned with algebra – that is, with formulas. We are concerned with the mass of desires, affinities, searchings, guilt-feelings – the whole aggregate which makes a person a living personality . . . The dilemma of the wanderer from the spiritual point of view is: a man who is a member of "Hashomer Hatza'ir" leaves it because of his search for God. He later leaves God because he disagrees with him. On the one hand one has a sense of one's own value and a desire to express oneself, and on the other hand one has a longing to abandon oneself. On the one hand one has a desire to be indispensable and unique, and on the other hand feelings of guilt and shame that one is different from others, that one is proud and rebellious.
>
> From that time onwards I felt I had to combine the two, the urge to break away and the desire to carry on. I was seized by the Messianic "bug": the obsession, the "dybbuk" of the Messianic idea of redemption which I hoped would one day resolve these contradictions.[13]

Talmon now began to investigate whether the "dybbuk" of the Messianic idea which took hold of nice boys and was emasculated at the Moscow trials was something immanent, beyond a specific historical explanation:

> I have never been a communist, but I always felt that I had to justify the fact that I was not a communist, because in my *shtetl* I saw boys – some of the best – rotting away in prison and destroying their lives. They endangered themselves more than we Zionists. The challenge was very strong. But then the Moscow trials of 1937–1938 took place, and everyone who thought a little said to himself: how can this be? If these people are guilty, then the whole revolution was something which had to be completely obliterated, and if they are innocent, it was those that did this to them who were the criminals. This thought led me to a structural investigation. Perhaps this did not reflect a particular historical situation, a specific combination of circumstances; perhaps it was something inherent. Perhaps it reflected a retribution, a nemesis, to use classical terminology.[14]

Echoes of these autobiographical reflections may be found in his analysis of the Jewish Messianic heritage which in the case of many Jews was expressed in a special sensitivity to social problems. At the end of the nineteenth century, the Jews' option of choosing between left and right reached eastern Europe. In contrast to the situation in the west of the continent, the millions of Jews who lived there experienced economic hardship, national and social discrimination and the oppressive régime of the Russian czars. "This atmosphere gave rise to Messianic longings and a readiness for revolution, a desire to overthrow the whole existing structure, and belief in the possibility of moving all at once from a world that was entirely bad to one that was entirely good. In no class or people was the response to the Messianic revolutionary message as fervent and enthusiastic as among the Jews of eastern Europe. The young people who had become unbelievers overnight suddenly felt spiritually liberated. They had a feeling that 'today the die is cast', that they were engaged in a mission that no power could withstand, and had an expectation that redemption was at hand, an imminent Day of Judgement. Because the Jews had served as a scapegoat for the evil czarist régime, the belief took root among them that a total revolution would immediately solve all problems, including the sufferings of the Jews."[15]

This situation led Talmon to probe the Messianic dialectical enigma as it existed in the Soviet Union:

> How did it happen that after forty years of a régime in which such gratifying hopes had been placed and to whose victory and success the Jews had made such a huge and decisive contribution, a régime which inscribed on its banner the slogan of the liberation of every human being and tribe . . . how did it happen that after only a single generation this régime unleashed a campaign of persecution against Jewish writers, prepared a programme of mass-expulsion, fomented an antisemitic atmosphere and adopted a hostile policy toward the State of Israel?"[16]

Talmon is an incorrigible unbeliever in the Messianic super-narrative, whether nationalist-romantic or Marxist-bolshevistic. The conclusion he came to was that the events in the Soviet Union revealed the true character of the communist régime. If these events cast doubt on the view common among believers that the Soviet Union was the vanguard of the world revolutionary camp, Talmon did not see this as a historical accident but as the outcome of a development whose seeds had been sown from the beginning. "In this respect the Jewish issue cannot be separated from the general problem."

The main reason for the degeneration of the communist-Messianic idea was Promethean *hubris*:

> When man has unlimited power and feels he has a mission and preaches a gospel of total redemption, how can he fail to see his selfish and ambitious thoughts as the thoughts of the Lord of history and his feelings of hatred and rivalry as the absolute truth? When the powers of the government become too great for the governed to rise up forcefully against it, the result is nihilism.
>
> The attempt to realize ideals is emptied of content and becomes a power-struggle between rivals.[17]

An outlook in which the end justifies the means permits the relativism of values underlying all dictatorships: "Dialectics are always used to prove that evil practical means are necessary and appropriate tools from the perspective of a general *a priori* scheme and are therefore objectively good."

> These observations are not made with any satisfaction but are occasioned by reflections on the tragic phenomenon of the degeneration and defilement of great human ideals in the course of their realization – a phenomenon of which history is full.[18]

Talmon feels empathy with the disillusioned Jewish intellectuals in the Diaspora who swore an oath of allegiance to the revolutionary left, but finds the best Jewish thinkers among the chief spokesmen of the anti-Messianic current in both humanistic and sceptical liberalism: Raymond Aron in France, Isaiah Berlin in England, Lionel Trilling in the United States. "Have they too been burnt as Jews by modern political Messianism?"

It is not surprising that Talmon was also among the thinkers and historians of anti-Messianic liberalism that sought the inner logic and the explanation of the totalitarian mentality on the right and left. These two types of totalitarianism were based on the idea that there is a single truth and that it finds expression in politics. The left decreed the deterministic supremacy of matter and saw class as the motive-force of revolution; the right believed in the decisive importance of blood and race and saw the nation as the motive-force of history. Both ideologies were rooted in philosophies of history which were explained in terms of class-warfare or the warfare of races and peoples. Both ideologies were rooted in a Manichaeian conception of history: because both of them claimed to possess the sole truth, both believed that anything that brought that goal nearer was acceptable and good and anything that hindered it was evil and corrupt. And the Jews, for their part, were ground to dust between the two camps.

Talmon saw the obsession with a "satanic" Jewish presence everywhere as reflecting a view of the Jews as an anti-race. The Messianic idea nourished by a belief in the unity and brotherhood of the human race was the focus of the attacks of the nationalist and racist right.[19] All arrows were aimed at Messianic Judaism which created the revolutionary universalist idea of the singleness of the human race. If one continues Talmon's line of thought one can go further and say that the people that brought the Messianic idea into history was now spewed out by history. Jewry, which sought to promote the Messianic phenomenon which meant the triumph of absolute good – the perfection of the world – was now reviled as the embodiment of absolute evil.

Christian antisemitism permitted the Jew to exist for generations as a degraded witness, but the anti-Messianic antisemitism insisted on murdering the bringer of good tidings, the people identified with the Messianic idea. Talmon saw the Holocaust as the murderous crossroads of the historical encounter between Jewish Messianism and the "bastard" Messianism embodied in Hitler.[20] The Jews, the eternal people, represented for the Nazis the idea of the unity of all races and universal brotherhood. To kill them meant killing those who gave the world the universalistic commandment: "Thou shalt not kill." "Judaism was an ideal and at the same time a disturbing nightmare, both a souce of inspiration and a stimulus to aggressive impulses." The Jewish uniqueness which embodied the gospel of the unity of mankind was attacked by those who inscribed on their banner war against the unity of mankind and saw the Jews as the enemy – as well as the yardstick – of their deterministic-racist gospel. The apocalypse of the Holocaust was an attempt to murder the Messianic idea and its representatives.

And this was the tragic paradox of the Jews in modern times, that the existence and success of many of them was in Talmon's view associated with the ideology of unity, although historically they found it difficult or were unwilling to abandon their uniqueness.[21] In the Soviet Union as well, the Jews embodied the original Messianic spirit of the Bolshevik Revolution (the disproportionate numbers of Jewish communists and revolutionaries is evidence of this), and for that reason there too they were the first victims of the revolution which went astray and became a bureaucratic dictatorship in one country. The dialectical distortion of Marxist Messianism found its full expression in the Soviet Union. Its first devotees, the Jewish revolutionaries, recalled by their presence the original Messianic Marxist-communist spark which had been distorted beyond recognition. For better or for worse, they were the litmus-paper of the revolution; they were its vanguard and also its victim.

Talmon found the same dialectic in the rise of nationalism. Nationalists said: "We are not like *them* (the people of the majority or the ruling nation); we are different from them, we must show in what our difference consists." In the nineteenth century there was a tendency among some national movements to find their special quality in the universal Messianic idea, or, that is to say, in the special mission of each nation in the plan of world history. The "Messianic peoples", to use Talmon's expression, developed general visions: Mazzini's vision of the "Third Rome", Fichte's doctrine of the nation, Mickiewitz's concept of "Poland as the Christ among the nations," and, among the Jews, Moses Hess's theory of Jerusalem as the vanguard of the nations.[22] Herzl, however, the prophet of modern Jewish nationalism, avoided making a metaphysical or metahistorical connection between the national revival and the workings of universal history.

It is perhaps against this background that one should see Talmon's long drawn-out debate with Arnold Toynbee which lasted from 1956 until after the Six-Day War. Toynbee attempted to discover the laws whereby the great structures he called civilizations rose and fell. In the last volume of his monumental work *A Study of History*, the English historian condemned the Jews for not only wanting to be the bearers of the message they received at Sinai but also seeking to exist as a people in modern times and even to be political nation.[23] Because he saw the combination of peoplehood and religion in Judaism as an expression of contempt for other peoples, Toynbee opposed anything which strengthened the existence of a Jewish nation. His great complaint against the modern Jews – that is to say, against Zionism – was that they had absorbed the bad qualities of Western civilization. The West, in his view, had always been aggressive and had drawn its Messianic inspiration from the Jewish concept of a chosen people. The paradox of his position is that he condemned the idea of a chosen people yet expected the Jews to behave as only a chosen people could! The climax of Toynbee's attack was when he said that in the Day of Judgement the sins of the Jews against the Arabs would be found to be greater than the sins of the Nazis against the Jews: "The spectacle of any Jews, however few, following in the Nazis' footsteps is enough to drive a sensitive gentile or Jewish spectator almost to despair." Talmon never tired of refuting Toynbee's "Messianic errors" one by one. The first time he did so was in a lecture he gave in Beit Hillel in London at a meeting on the three hundredth anniversary of the resettlement of the Jews in England at which the chairman was Lord Herbert Samuel and whose subject was "Jewish History and its Universal Significance."[24]

Talmon, for his part, was careful in all his writings to refrain from attaching any metahistorical or Messianic significance to Zionism and the founding of the State of Israel: "Some people see the founding of Israel as the fulfilment of Jewish history, a kind of recompense for all the problems and suffering, but there are others who see it as a major deviation from the path of that history. A scientific historian puts himself in danger if he slips into the area of metaphysics and speaks of the 'true character' or 'authentic spirit' or 'preordained direction' of a two thousand year-old history in its metamorphoses through periods, civilizations and regions so different from one another."[25] At the same time, he drew attention to the role of the Jewish model in the development of Europe, whether it was the religious war of the "people of God" in Bohemia and Moravia or the Spanish campaign against the unbelievers over the ocean. It was the Jews, he said, who gave the idea of election to the world. However, "The politicization of Jewish Messianism was the result of foreign influences, as is clearly shown by the fact that all the historical declarations of Zionist philosophy were made following the triumphs of national movements."[26] Thus, Rabbi Alkalai advocated Jewish settlement in the Land of Israel under the inspiration of the Greek War of Independence and the rise of Serbian nationalism, Hess's *Rome and Jerusalem* was written under the influence of the unification of Italy, Lilienblum called for a Jewish revival following the Hungarian national revival, and Pinsker's *Auto-Emancipation* was written against the background of the founding of the Kingdom of Bulgaria. One therefore cannot understand the roots of Zionism without understanding the mutual relationship between the Messianic self-perception of many Zionist circles, which wished to establish a "restorative utopia" in their historic homeland, and the political-Messianic intellectual climate of the national movements in Europe.

The Zionist movement was of its time, wrote the historian Anita Shapira, and consequently reflected the same general outlook as formed the psychological basis of the various different Messianic political movements. The spiritual climate in which Zionism was born was full of the quasi-eschatological fervour of movements which strove to establish the kingdom of heaven on earth, whether it was a universal kingdom which would realize the brotherhood of man or whether it was derived from the secular-Messianic movements of its period.[27] Moreover, "Scratch the empiricistic surface of a Zionist leader a little and you will discover a quivering Messianic faith which breaks forth in moments of crisis or in moments of what Talmon called 'historical breakthrough'."[28]

In the poetry of the Hebrew culture of Eretz-Israel there were different manifestations of the role of Messianism in the Zionist enterprise. On the one hand, one had the utopian idealism of the pioneers'self-perception as builders of the future, and on the other hand there was the tendency to be carried away by thoughts of "anticipating the end" and the use of violence. These two characteristics were embodied in the contrast between the symbolist school of thought of the socialist poet Avraham Shlonsky and the Messianic and apocalyptic outlook of the school of thought of the nationalist poet Uri Zvi Greenberg.[29]

According to Talmon, Zionism's vision of redemption and its revolutionary quality was a product of secularization:[30]

In the history of the Jews since they became a people, was there ever a time, asked Talmon, when they perceived themselves as having a general responsibility and being "a light unto the nations"? The young Zionists from eastern Europe, for example, who initially responded enthusiastically to the socialist vision, intended to build an ideal society in Israel, but it is doubtful if it was possible to practice the ideals of socialist Zionism for any length of time. The pioneers of yesterday became the bosses of today. In this historical situation there again appeared the contradictions which had been obscured in the changing reality: the stronger and purer the idealism had been, the more likely was it to become hypocritical and reactionary. Talmon was sceptical concerning the possibility of translating the vision of political Messianism into reality, and he was drawn to the thinker Reinhold Niebuhr who had put forward a dialectic of political power in which its realization was in the final analysis bound up with the tragic destiny of the human race.[31]

In the period succeeding the metanarratives of modernism (nationalism, fascism and communism, whose decline Talmon lived long enough to foresee), a sceptical attitude to Messianic politics became common, and Talmon explained it as being among other things a reaction to the political theories derived from Hegel. Hegelianism exalted impersonal idealism and the centrality of collective values. The origin of the dialectic of ends and means is to be found in Hegelian philosophy: the state or some revolutionary element seeks to realize a historical mission by force, like a bulldozer crushing beautiful flowers in its path (to use Hegel's imagery). This historical relativism and relativism of values was a source of inspiration and a temptation to all the political-Messianic movements of the left and right which declared they were the oracles of history, the vanguard of their nation or class, and hence had the right and duty to push the waggon of history forward and to throw on the trash-heap anything which stood in its way. The political thinking of the Jews in the past was not unduly preoccupied with these problematics because they did not become real for them until the birth of Zionism. "Many people," wrote Talmon, "are still unable to think in terms of the new dialectics which began when we rose from the status of an apolitical minority-group to the level of a member of the family of sovereign nations."

"Is it by chance," asked Talmon, "that Italy, Germany, Russia – the countries in which the universal Messianic ideal found its loftiest expression – became in the end the seat of the most perverted and corrupt régimes of all: fascism, Nazism and Stalinism?"[32] On the other hand, he found the case of Israel encouraging, for even if it was not ideal or a full realization of the vision, it was not so distorted as to be beyond repair. Talmon explained this by saying that Zionism is a unique phenomenon, a movement special of its kind with regard to its reality, its place and its significance.

In the intellectual debate which took place in the nineteen-fifties in Israel on the nature of Zionism, the State of Israel and the Messianic vision, Ben-Gurion and Talmon had a special place because of their personal interest in the subject and because of the complex discussion which took place between them on this matter.

Ben-Gurion never tired of sermonizing on the Messianic vision of the people of Israel. For him the Messianic motif, which was a kind of mobilizing myth in the building of the young nation, had no religious content or transcendental significance but was thought to exemplify a suitable moral ethos: the call for settlement, the enlistment of youth, the comradeship of the different sectors of society, the development of the arts and sciences and the strengthening of the army. In the nineteen-fifties, Talmon already had a reputation in the country and abroad as a historian of the secular Messianic phenomenon and as one of the outstanding intellectuals in Israel. The encounter between the representative and spokesman of political Messianism in Israel and the trenchant intellectual critic of that phenomenon was fascinating yet at the same time impossible.[33]

In the exchange of letters between Ben-Gurion and Natan Rotenstreich which took place from January to April 1957, Ben-Gurion gave a detailed account of his concept of Messianism, encompassing the "spiritual heritage of the Jewish people, the partnership of all sections of the Jewish people and the Jewish and universal vision of redemption."[34] He thought that "the Jews of Yemen, Morocco and Iraq came to the country out of a historical consciousness and not out of 'Zionist' ideology." The State of Israel came into being "through the power of the Messianic vision." In the philosophy of history he developed, Ben-Gurion emphasized the ancient Hebrew foundations of the people and country, and thus his outlook reflected the discordance between Messianism and Canaanism: "What we have done in this country is to leap above Jewish history." In a personal testimony, he wrote: "It may be that the Messianic vision did not reverberate in the heart of Pinsker and Herzl, but in the heart of the Jewish masses as I remember them in childhood it reverberated strongly. When I was a child of ten I heard them speaking of a Messiah who had appeared in Vienna and whose name was Herzl." He found the basis of the great vision of Jewish and human redemption in the Jewish prophets. The Messianic mission was not for him a metaphysical idea but a sociocultural-moral vision; it did not signify the end of history but the process of its redemption; there was not a Jewish side and a human side to the Messianic idea: it was all Jewish and all Messianic. Ben-Gurion, who translated the Zionist ideology into the Israeli reality, thought that the Jews had three affinities which made them a people: an affinity with the land, an affinity with the language and an affinity with the Messianic vision of redemption. Ben-Gurion's point of view represented an activization of the Messianic vision – which in its theological source had been passive – through the return of the Jewish people to history and to its homeland. And Ben-Gurion concluded in a philosophical or even religious vein:

> If God is man's faith in the absolute, in the elevated, in the creator of all and in the loftiest concept of mercy, justice and love, then the elevation of man is the aspiration to resemble God, as far as that is possible. And if that is the 'kingdom of God', then the Messianic vision is a striving towards the kingdom of God on earth. This striving has no end, for one may draw near to the kingdom of God but I fear one may not reach it, for it is a concept of the infinite.[35]

Three years later, Talmon wrote to Ben-Gurion as follows:

> I am glad that the time has finally come, with the publication of my new book *Political Messianism*, when I am available for the task which your colleagues Nehemiah Argov of blessed memory, and Shimon Peres – may he be granted long life – asked me to perform three years ago, and that is to prepare a comprehensive work which will give a thorough account of all existing first-hand sources for the story of your life against the background of our action and turmoil-filled period, and for your role in the drama of the revival of Israel and the renewal of its political independence.[36]

As Ben Gurion's prospective biographer, Talmon asked for all sources to be made available to him – the diaries and letters without exception. He further asked to be able to talk freely with Ben-Gurion, and to have the principle of historical research fully respected. If there were any disagreement concerning the publication of certain facts, Talmon proposed the arbitration of a committee composed of the President of the Hebrew University of Jersusalem, the President of the Supreme Court (or the Minister of Justice) and the Speaker of the Knesset (or the State Comptroller). Talmon accepted full responsibility for seeing that the book was published. Ben-Gurion responded positively to these requests, but he added a proviso which was finally decisive in Talmon's decision to reconsider the idea of writing the book: "All the material in my archives will be at your disposal on condition that you do not publish anything which in my opinion is harmful to security or which is injurious to people's honour."[37] Talmon was of course unable to agree to this condition, and in his last letter to Ben-Gurion hinted at what had motivated him in the first place to decide to write the life-story of this "political Messiah": "One cannot carry out the mission of reconstructing the most important period in the history of Israel since the Second Temple, at the centre of which stands a major historical personality, without being promised in advance access to all documents without exception, and without full guarantees that the historian will have complete freedom to give his verdict in accordance with the dictates of his professional conscience."[38]

The paths of the statesman and the historian crossed once again in the Lavon affair. Talmon was one of the main intellectuals that signed the "Intellectuals' Open Letter" published at the end of 1960. He associated himself with the call of his friends in the university who wrote: "There can be no greater danger to a democratic régime and its values than a contemptuous attitude to criticism and a scornful attitude to one's adversary. And the danger is all the greater in a society which is still in the process of forming its political and social régime."[39] About a week after the publication of this declaration, Talmon answered the question of an interviewer from the newspaper *Ha-boker* concerning the danger which a totalitarian democracy would represent for Israel:

> Great importance must be attached to the fact that although Zionism was a Messianic ideology because it developed before we had means of political coercion and as a result of voluntary effort, it formed a tradition of variety whose main expression was the coalition-structure which was passed on as an inheritance from Zionism to the State, with all its qualities and defects.[40]

About a month later, Talmon expressed his fears more directly in his article "The 'Affair' – Is It a Crossroads?," in which he warned against "a totalitarian state in which the Head of State is also the head of government and also the leader of the party."[41] He said he was worried that a dangerous duality might develop between the formal government apparatus open to public scrutiny and a quasi-clandestine source of covert activities and intrigues. Yet, despite these harsh criticisms, he added: "The historical greatness of Ben-Gurion has been shown in the power of decision he has revealed in fateful and critical moments like the eve of the declaration of the State, the affair of the Altalena and the Palmach, the withdrawal from Sinai and the different educational systems." He gave the

Israeli leader his due: "Mr. David Ben-Gurion will find his place among the half-dozen outstanding figures in the chronicles of the people of Israel from the time it became a people. There are few statesmen whose historical vision has been so accurate and have so often been justified by events. But as often happens to statesmen of vision, a day of reckoning comes – for the gods are jealous – and the man makes a fatal error. Ben-Gurion's fatal error was his behaviour in the Affair." In Talmon's opinion, Ben-Gurion was "not only a politician and a statesman but a visionary able to see things in a historical perspective of generations." However, he called upon the prime minister to resign: "The greatest service this statesman can do for his people is to resign and allow social forces to regroup." This was not the last time that Talmon was to call on a prime minister of Israel to resign. The last article he wrote, "The Country is in Danger," published some three months before his death, ended in a similar way with a call to Menachem Begin to step down: "A time comes in the life of a statesman when he has to weigh up if in changing circumstances he is still a trail-blazer or whether he has become an obstacle in the path of the nation."

Ben-Gurion responded in his own way. In his article "In Defence of Messianism" published some five years later in reply to an article by Shlomo Avineri, he wrote:[42]

> Mr. Avineri is a strong opponent of the messianic concept. He seems to have learned it from J.L. Talmon, Professor of Modern History at the Hebrew University in Jerusalem, who was publishing three volumes condemning the "political messianism" of the leaders of the French revolution: he sees in the Messianic doctrine the origin of the political totalitarian outlook.

Ben-Gurion ended the article with the following words:

> The fears of Professor Talmon and his students or friends that a messianic faith leads to despotism and dictatorship are the result of a mistaken and misleading reading of history. The French Revolution was a blessing for humanity. And without the Messianic faith, the last three generations of our people would not have done what they did.

What was the difference between Ben-Gurion's Messianic outlook and the Messianic vision of Gush Emunim? Talmon, of course, was opposed to both of them, but in contrast to Ben-Gurion's secular Messianism in which he discerned elements of pragmatism such as the emphasis on the return to history, he saw Gush Emunim as a political theology and an escape from history in which politics was subordinated to a religious group. The members of Gush Emunim, in the words of Talmon, "depicted the victory in the Six-Day War as the birthpangs of the Messiah and the beginning of redemption and saw the conquest of the territories as the finger of God, so that the vision of 'renewing our days as of old' and God's promises were coming true in their entirety."[43] In the "restorative utopia" of Gush Emunim, religious Messianism and political Messianism came together.

The Messianic process of the return to Zion in modern times was not seen as existing only on the national level of the ingathering of the exiles and sovereignty over the land, but as a vital moment in the cosmic redemption of the world and all it contains. This, according to Aviezer Ravitzky, was a new version of the idea of progress from the school of thought of Rabbi Abraham Kook.[44] Gush Emunim's source of inspiration was in fact Abraham Kook, in whose Messianic conception the universal principle and the national principle were combined: "The physical upbuilding of the people and the embodiment of its spirit were one and the same thing, and it was all fused with the construction of the universe."[45] This Messianic interpretation of the State of Israel also gave a meaning to the Holocaust, for just as this disaster was unprecedented, so the redemption that followed it would also be unprecedented: the Messianic redemption would be as great as had been the descent into the satanic realm. Talmon, however, was amazed that "the death of more than a million infants who had not sinned was supposed to be the Jewish people's punishment for its sins, for what sin could justify such a punishment?"[46]

In the "deterministic Messianism" of Gush Emunim there was a radicalization which was expressed in the change from the "historical necessity" of Rabbi Abraham Kook to the activization of history and "anticipation of the end" of his son Zvi Yehudah Kook. This radicalization represented a shift – and also a decline and falling-off – from the universal metaphysical-cosmic dimension of Messianism to the particular national-Israeli dimension. What some saw as the glowing image of the Messiah was seen by others as the threatening image of the anti-Messiah. If the national-religious outlook saw the founding of the State as "the beginning of redemption" and the conquest of the territories in the Six-Day War as the redemption-process in full spate, the *Haredim* (ultra-orthodox Jews) viewed the founding of Israel as an anti-Messianic manifestation.

Talmon interpreted Gush Emunim's Messianic "anticipation of the end" as an obsessive desire to see the end of history within history. With regard to this, Israel Colet declared: "The lack of substance which Talmon found in history – dialectics and irony – did not make him go outside it, either to philosophical simplification or to religious completion. He preferred the sufferings of Job to hymns of praise."[47] Shlomo Avineri, however, saw things differently: "If there had not been in his personal past an element of religious tradition from which he freed himself after his boyhood, it is possible that in the evening of his life he would have sought an answer to the distress of modern times in turning to religion, to the transcendental."[48]

Uriel Tal looked at Talmon's complex attitude to religion and the Jewish Messianic phenomenon.[49] Tal gathered together his statements about totalitarian manifestations in Judaism and said that Talmon discerned two different mystical approaches: political Messianism, which sees historical events as the fulfilment of mystical concepts, and the point of view that one should be cautious and prudent in social matters as God alone is an absolute authority, and thus one should not meddle in social and political affairs. Both approaches accept *halakha* as an authoritative binding authority. The devotees of political Messianism claim that the only difference between the Messianic era and other periods is that one is once again free of political servitude: it is the beginning of the redemption in which Messianism will be realized on a world-wide scale. This belief reduces symbols to the level of reality: thus, stones and pieces of land are no longer symbolic of something holy but are sanctified objects in themselves. As against this, the other school of thought maintains that *halakha*, as understood by the Jewish people throughout history, freed it from exaggerated ecstasy and from a mystification which could hinder the realization of lofty ideals such as striving for peace. This school of thought is characterized by ethics and consideration for others as against the militancy of the school of active Messianism. "Peace and truth within your gates," in the words of the prophet Zechariah, are viewed as the basis of the values of ethics and democracy. In the sayings of the Sages there is a specific commandment to seek wisdom, which will eventually lead to the coming of the Messiah. This approach avoids political romanticism based on personal religious experience and rejects the sanctification of politics.

In this last generation, there have been various and ever more penetrating commentaries on the concept of the "Messianic idea." Moshe Idel criticizes the expression "Messianic idea" coined by Gershom Scholem, and writes as follows: "The literature concerning Messianism is so various, and has been written over a period of two thousand years by people belonging to such different societies in so many different places that the expression 'Messianic idea' does not mean much to those who seek a deeper and more specific understanding. In place of this expression it would be better to use some such expression as 'the totality of Messianic ideas.' In other words, in Messianic debates certain Messianic themes may be identified which meet and come together in various forms with various changes and interpretations."[50]

Gershom Scholem himself reflected on the price the Jewish people had to pay for the Messianic idea it bequeathed to the world:

> The Messianic idea is not only consolation and hope. Every attempt to put it into practice tears apart and creates chasms, each of which leads from its manifestations 'ad absurdum.' There is something wonderful about life lived in hope, but at the same time there is something unrealistic about it . . . Thus Judaism, through the Messianic idea, had to live a life *in suspenso*, hanging in the air. One can perhaps say that the Messianic idea is the true anti-existentialist idea. If we understand it precisely, there is nothing real, concrete or successful about a person who is not redeemed. There will always be something defective about him. This is the greatness of Messianism but also its basic weakness. Jewish 'existence' is filled with a tension which is never really dispelled. It burns and is never consumed. When it breaks forth within our history, it is cursed, or, one can say, impatiently dismissed as what is called 'false Messianism.'"[51]

Scholem wrote his famous article, "Redemption Through Sin," in 1937,[52] and Talmon gained the inspiration for his first book in the years 1937–1938 at the time when the Moscow trials revealed to the world the bitter reality of what was happening in the Soviet Union.[53] Scholem and Talmon were contemporaries and witnesses of the transformation of communism in the Soviet Union from a vision of egalitarian and universal redemption into a bureaucratic and nationalistic despotism. The major scholar of the history of religious Messianism and the major scholar of the history of secular Messianism both widened the scope of their investigations – the first extending them into the history of Sabbatianism and the second into the French Revolution – and both reached a similar conclusion: both recognized, as Scholem put it, "the profound truth relating to the dialectics of history . . . of the historical process whereby the fulfilment of one political process leads to the manifestation of its opposite. In the realization of one thing its opposite is revealed."[54] The two great Israeli historians of ideas plumbed the depths of one of the most fascinating and at the same time tragic manifestations of "*la condition humaine*": the human challenge of bringing the heavenly city down to the vale of tears, and the price that men have to pay for their Messianic passion.

Talmon saw Scholem's field of expertise, Sabbataianism, as a historical precedent which contained a warning for the future. He said he feared being "swept into illusions and a longing for deadening narcotics." "I am very frightened," he declared, "of the time when we sober up and experience Sabbataian disillusionment with all that that involves."[55] Exactly ten years later, Talmon repeated this warning in his final article, addressed to Begin: "Are we perhaps seeing a sign of rejection and tragic inability to live with the fact of the Holocaust and the reality it left behind it, an inability to adapt to them and, as a result, an estrangement from what Freud called the principle of reality and a flight to a world of illusion, to mythological ways of thinking and feeling, of which the classic example is Sabbataianism?"[56]

In the history of Sabbataianism, Scholem showed what could happen to the comforting Messianic idea when put to the test of reality. Speaking about this, Talmon, according to Yehoshua Arieli, remarked on the confrontation and opposition which arises in any attempt to impose a conceptual framework on a given reality: "This dialectical discrepancy between an outlook, a vision and image and reality constantly increased in the age of ideology and became even worse with the advent of comprehensive schemes for a total change of the human reality in accordance with a Messianic vision."[57] Karl Popper's observation that "attempts to create a heaven on earth inevitably create a hell," captures his meaning perfectly. Hedva ben Israel adds: "Messianic beliefs come into being with lofty intentions, but they are under a curse and always degenerate into tyrannies.

Like all exclusive religions, they cannot take opposition, and hence the terror with which they are inevitably accompanied."[58]

Many intellectuals have thought about this discrepancy between the idea and its realization. When asked how he would define an intellectual, Talmon replied: "An intellectual is a man who doesn't sleep at night, and not for the reason you imagine." The interesting thing about this definition is what it does not say: it avoids the widespread supposition that an intellectual is a moral person who defends absolute values or is an arbiter of truth and justice. It is a completely neutral definition. There are intellectuals who do not sleep because they are troubled by disturbing dreams about curtailments of human freedom, and there are intellectuals whose sleep is disturbed because they have sinister visions of human engineering and power-structures. Sleepnessness can come from fear of despotism, but also from a fear of liberty. This is what Talmon implied by his remark, in the spirit of the insight of his spiritual mentor Alexis de Tocqueville on the dual legacy of the Enlightenment: it created popular democracy but also totalitarian-Messianic democracy.[59]

In contemporary post-modernist thought there is a common idea that the intellectual is no longer committed to the task of being an adviser to the masses or a critic of ideologies, but that his function is to provide tools for analysis. The intellectual has ceased to be the representative of truth and justice who gives voice to the repressed consciousness. He has to lay aside the universal truths of the Enlightenment and cease to direct the public's attention to revolutionary principles (which was Sartre's definition of the intellectual). Michel Foucault thinks that the intellectual has to focus on specific struggles and lay bare the discourse on power, power-structures and the will-to-power. The intellectual is now defined as someone who lays bare problems: he is an indefatigable subverter of basic assumptions whether utopian, ideological or scientific, and this is achieved by means of genealogy – a search for the roots of ideas and concepts. Instead of being the agent of political ideologies, he now dissects them without mercy and treats them with suspicion. His subversion of Messianic illusions, utopian dreams and ideological visions is effected through his dismantling of the mechanisms of hegemony.[60] Talmon's criticism forestalled the postmodernist intellectuals, although he cannot be ascribed their relativistic conclusions.

In Talmon's historical work and intellectual investigations, the Messianic mechanism was laid bare with a searching critical gaze, with irony and with a deep awareness of its price. He subverted the Messianic meta-narrative but at the same time showed a certain empathy for the phenomenon and its actors, in the absence of which it would have been difficult for him to reveal the secret of the Messianic spell. One can extrapolate from the Nietzschean dialectic of the apollonian principle which organizes and makes order and the dionysian principle which is creative and chaotic, a mutual relationship between the Messianic-harmonic principle and the destructive principle. Scholem already perceived that "all radical Messianism, if taken seriously, opens up a chasm in which through an inner necessity antimonian outlooks and anarchic moral attitudes accumulate."[61] Similarly, Talmon, in the words of Yehoshua Arieli, "perceived the danger in comprehensive Messianic ideologies which provide legitimation for an abrogation of every existing barrier against chaos and validation to every atrocity for the sake of the objective."[62] Talmon revealed destruction as the other side of redemption, the apocalyptic ruin from which a cleansed and reformed world was supposed to spring forth.

In Messianism there is a discrepancy between the absolute and the complete and the attempt to achieve it which involves the destruction of all that is not part of it; the hope of redemption is fulfilled at the cost of the elimination of all incompatibilities in human existence. Talmon discerned three such incompatibilities: that of liberty with equality, that of private property with the organization of the collective, and that of the freedom of the individual with historical determinism.[63] The Messianic ideologies wished to reconcile these differences. Talmon, however, reached the conclusion that the differences still remained as they were:

> My opinion and belief is that the Messianic expectation of a resolution of these contradictions, the belief in a critical period in which redemption is at hand, has been the common denominator of Marxism and the other movements of the revolutionary camp from the days of the French Revolution. Thus, any supporting superstructure of references to Hegelian philosophy or economical, historical or other proofs are only a rationalization of this lofty and profound expectation."[64]

The radical solution to human divergencies, generally bound up with an existential crisis, is to carry out a political experiment in unification at a suitable historical moment when all prohibitions would be lifted and all contradictions resolved in a single revolutionary act. The subordination of a variety of narratives to a single narrative is only possible through coercion and rape, through violence expressed in revolutions and wars. The attempt to put a secular Messianism into practice, far from resolving the disharmonies, increases them, creates new dissensions and leads to an automatic chain-reaction of the imposition of force, counter-violence and so on. Talmon hoped that a political thinker would arise "who would put an end to this yearning for a final and decisive resolution of all contradictions and differences in society in a situation of perfect harmony."[65]

Secular Messianism provides an opportunity to exit from history, but it does so within history itself. The transcendence which until modern times was embodied in religious redemption and personal salvation was secularized into Messianic political ideologies which hoped to bring about the end of history within history. In many ways, Talmon anticipated the postmodernist intellectual climate which subverted the great Messianic metanarratives.

What in fact is the mutual relationship between the historian and the intellectual? The historian looks at the past from the perspective of the owl of Minerva the goddess of wisdom, which descends from its flight only in the evening, at the end of the historical process. The intellectual, for his part, operates in daylight, in the course of the historical process.[66] As an intellectual, Talmon could only point to the dissensions and contradictions in his own time; as a historian, he saw the comprehensive dialectical process of secular Messianism. The intellectual in Talmon drew upon his understanding as a historian to illustrate how universal history could provide good and bad exemplars for Jewish life. The exposure of the dialectics of secular Messianism in European history provides insights and critical perceptions which can illuminate the tensions of Jewish history in the present. Talmon was an intellectual and historian who in his essays and studies sought to decipher the enigma of the present together with the cunning of history.

Notes

1 Jacob L. Talmon, *The Origins of Totalitarian Democracy*, London: Secker and Warburg, 1952, p. 253.

2 Jacob L. Talmon, *Political Messianism, the Romantic Phase*, London: Secker and Warburg, 1960, p. 16.

3 Jacob L. Talmon, *The Myth of the Nation and the Vision of Revolution: The Origins of Ideological Polarisation in the Nineteenth Century*, Berkeley: California University Press, p. 3.
4 *Totalitarian Democracy*, p. 3.
5 Gershom Scholem, "Toward an Understanding of the Messianic Idea in Judaism", *The Messianic Idea in Judaism and Other Essays*, New York: Schocken Books, 1971, pp. 35-66.
6 Norman Cohn, *The Pursuit of the Millennium*, New Jersey 1957; R.J. Werblowsky, "Messianism in Jewish History", in H.H. Ben-Sasson and S. Ettinger, eds., *Jewish Society Through the Ages*, 1971.
Joseph Klausner, *Ha-rayon ha-meshihi be-yisrael* (the Messianic Idea in Israel), Tel Aviv (Hebrew).
7 Zvi Werblowsky, "Introduction", *Meshihut ve-eskatologia – kovetz ma'a-marim* (Messianism and Eschatology – A Collection of Articles), ed. Zvi Beres, Zalman Shazar Center Publications, Jerusalem, pp. 20–24. (Hebrew).
8 Jean-Paul Sartre and Benny Lévy, *Hope Now: The 1980 Interviews*, trans. A. van den Hoven, Chicago: Chicago University Press, 1966, pp. 107–108.
9 F. M. H. Markham, ed., *Saint-Simon – Selected Writings*, 1952, pp. 85–86.
10 Talmon,"Jews Between Right and Left," *Ha-aretz*, 25. 9. 1957 (Hebrew); see also Talmon, *Ahdut ve-yihud – masot be-hagut historit* (Unity and Uniqueness – Essays in Historical Thought), Shocken, Jerusalem and Tel Aviv, , pp. 246–275 (Hebrew).
11 Talmon, "Prophets and Ideology: the Jewish Presence in History," *Ha-aretz*, 24. 9. 1976 (Hebrew).
12 F. R. Ankersmit, "Jacob Talmon," (Historici van de twintigste eeuw, 15), *Intermidiar*, 12th May 1980, pp. 59–67. See especially: special issue: "Jacob Talmon and Totalitarianism Today: Legacy and Revision", guest editor Arie Dubnov, *History of European Ideas*, June 2008.
13 Talmon, "Socialism and Liberalism," *Min ha-yesod* (From the Foundations), 1962, pp. 32–33 (Hebrew).
14 Ibid., pp. 33–43.
15 Talmon, "Jews Between Right and Left," *Ahdut ve-yihud*, pp. 263–264.
16 Ibid., p. 264.
17 Ibid., p. 267.
18 Ibid., p. 274.
19 Talmon, *The Myth of the Nation and the Vision of Revolution*, p. 551.
20 Talmon, "European History as the Background to the Holocaust," *Be-eidan ha-alimut* (In the Age of Violence), Am Oved, Tel Aviv, pp. 265–293 (Hebrew).
21 Talmon, "Documentation and Evidence – the Universal Significance of the New Antisemitism," *Ahdut ve-yihud*, p. 280.
22 Talmon, *Political Messianism*, pp. 229–292.
23 Arnold Toynbee, *A Study of History*, vol. XII: *Reconsiderations*, Oxford University Press, London 1961.
24 Talmon, "Arnold Toynbee and His Relationship to the Jews," *Ha-aretz*, 5. 9. 1956 (Hebrew); "The Exchange of Letters Between Professor Arnold

Toynbee and Professor Y. Talmon following the Six-Day War," *Maariv*, 4. 8. 1967 (Hebrew).

25 Talmon, "The Six-Day War in a Historical Perspective," *Be-eidan ha-alimut*, p. 297 (Hebrew).

26 Ibid., p. 298.

27 Anita Shapira, "Zionism and Political Messianism," *Ha-halicha al kav ha-ofek* (Going Towards the Horizon), Sifriat Ofakim – Am Oved, Tel Aviv , p. 13 (Hebrew). See also three articles in the collection *Meshihut Ve-eskatologia* (Messianism and Eschatology) (Hebrew): Michael Graetz, "Secular Messianiam in the Nineteenth Century as a Path of Return to Judaism," pp. 401–418; Israel Kolet, "Zionism and Messianism," pp. 419–432; and Shemuel Almog, "Messianism As a Challenge to Zionism," pp. 433–438.

28 Shapira, ibid., p. 18.

29 Hanan Haber, *Be-shevi ha-utopia – masa al meshihut ve-politica be-shira ha-ivrit be-eretz israel ben shtei milhamot ha-olam* (Captives of Utopia. Essay on Messianism and Politics in Hebrew Poetry in the Land of Israel Between the Two World Wars), the Centre For the Ben-Gurion Heritage, publishing house of the Ben-Gurion University of the Negev, Jerusalem (Hebrew).

30 Talmon, "The Country is in Danger – Open Letter From the Historian Yaakov Talmon to the Historian Menahem Begin," *Ha-aretz*, 21. 3. 1980 (Hebrew).

31 Talmon, "The Six-Day War in a Historical Perspective," p. 343.

32 Ibid., p. 231.

33 See especially Micael Keren, *Ben-Gurion ve-ha-intellectualoim – otzma, da'at ve-karisma* (Ben-Gurion and the Intellectuals – Strength, Knowledge and Charisma), Ben-Gurion University of the Negev, Jerusalem, pp. 21, 65, 73, 74, 150, 162 (Hebrew); Shlomo Aaronson, *Manhig ha-renaissance she shaka'* (Renaissance Leader Who Foundered), The Centre For the Ben-Gurion Heritage, Ben-Gurion University of the Negev, Jerusalem, pp. 344, 362–364, 380 (Hebrew); Yehiam Weitz, "The Intellectuals' Involvement in the Lavon Affair," *Zion* year 64,3, and especially pp. 367–370 (Hebrew).

34 "For a Clarification of the Matter: Exchange of Letters Between David Ben-Gurion and Natan Rotenstreich," *Hazut*, 3, ( ), pp. 16–29 (Hebrew).

35 Ibid., p. 29.

36 Letter of Talmon to David Ben-Gurion, 3. 6. 1960, Ben-Gurion Archives (Hebrew).

37 Letter from Ben-Gurion to Talmon, 6. 7. 1960, Ben-Gurion Archives (Hebrew).

38 Letter of Talmon to Ben-Gurion, 20. 12. 1960, Ben-Gurion Archives (Hebrew).

39 "Intellectuals' Open Letter," *Ha-aretz*, 30. 12. 1960 (Hebrew).

40 "Interview of the Week With Professor Ya'akov Talmon – the Agency For the Development of Democracy in Israel" (interviewer Joseph Evron), *Ha-boker*, 6. 1. 1961 (Hebrew).

41 Talmon, "The 'Affair' – Is It a Crossroads?," *Ha-aretz*, 17. 2. 1961 (Hebrew).

42 David Ben-Gurion, "In Defence of Messianism," *Midstream* XII (March 1966), pp. 63–68.

43 Talmon, "The Country is in Danger."
44 Aviezer Ravitzky, *He-ketz he-megulei u-medinat ha-yehudim – meshihut, tzionut ve-radikalism dati be-Yisrael* (The End Revealed and the Jewish State – Messianism, Zionism and Religious Radicalism in Israel), Sifriat Ofakim – Am Oved, Tel Aviv 1997, p. 174 (Hebrew).
45 Ibid., p. 199.
46 Talmon, "The Country is in Danger."
47 Israel Colat, "Unity and Uniqueness – Ya'akov Talmon's Reflections on Jewish History," *In Memory of Ya'akov Talmon*, the Israel National Academy of Sciences and the Hebrew University of Jerusalem, Jerusalem, p. 63 (Hebrew).
48 Shlomo Avineri, "Ya'akov Talmon the Thinker," *In Memory of Ya'akov Talmon*, p. 20.
49 Uriel Tal "Totalitarian Democratic Hermaneutics and Politics in Modern Jewish Religious Nationalism," in *Totalitarian Democracy and After*, International Colloquium in Memory of Jacob L. Talmon, The Israel Academy of Sciences and Humanities, the Magnes Press, the Hebrew University, Jerusalem, 1984, pp. 137–157.
50 Moshe Idel, "Messianic Ideas and Zionistic Ideas," in *Ha-tsionut ve-ha-hazara le-historia – ha'aracha me-hadash* (Zionism and the Return to History – A Reassessment), eds. S. N. Eisenstadt and M. Lissac, Yad Ben-Zvi, Jerusalem , p. 73 (Hebrew).
51 Shemuel Ram, ed., *The Messianic Idea in Israel, Study Day in Honour of Gershom Scholem's Eightieth Birthday*, Jerusalem, The Israel National Academy of Sciences, p. 262.
52 Another example of the association of Soviet communism with a form of Messianism in the past is given by Gershom Scholem in connection with the book *Thomas Mintzer and the Theology of Messianism* (1921) by Ernst Bloch. Scholem writes that it is "a book of propaganda for the pairing of chiliastic religiosity with modern political communism, written after the bolshevik revolution." Scholem, *Shabbetai Zvi ve-ha-tenua ha-shabbata'it be-yemei hayyav* (Shabbetai Zvi and the Sabbetaian Movement in His Lifetime), I, Am Oved, Tel Aviv , p. 80, note 2 (Hebrew).
53 Talmon, *The Myth of the Nation and the Vision of Revolution.*
54 Gershom Shalom, *Parashat ha-shabta'ut* (The Sabbataian Episode), a series of lectures recorded by Rivka Schatz, the Hebrew University, Jerusalem, Jerusalem , p. 1. Quoted in Avraham Shapira, "*Mavo*" (introduction) in *Gershom Shalom, retzifut u-mered – Gershom Shalom be-omer u-be-siah* (Gershom Scholem, Continuity and Rebellion, Gershom Scholem's Speech and Discourse), assembled and edited by Avraham Shapira, Am Oved, Tel Aviv, p. 23 (Hebrew).
55 "Israel's Image in the World," address by Talmon at the *Ma'ariv* symposium, 9. 1. 1970.
56 Talmon, "The Country is in Danger."
57 Yehoshua Arieli, "Ya'akov Talmon, His Historical *Oeuvre*," *In Memory of Ya'akov Talmon*, pp. 21–39.
58 Hedva ben Israel-Kidron, "Ya'akov Talmon – the Investigation of History

as the Solution to the Troubles of the Time," *In Memory of Ya'akov Talmon*, p. 15.

59 David Ohana, *Ha-tchuka ha-promite'it – ha-shorashim ha-intellectualim shel ha-me'a ha-esrim me-Rousseau ad Foucault* (The Promethean Passion – the Intellectual Roots of the Twentieth Century From Rousseau to Foucault), Mossad Bialik, Jerusalem, pp. 55–74.

60 Michel Foucault, "The Concern for Truth," in *Foucault: Politics, Philosophy, Culture – Interviews and Other Writings 1977–1984*, New York 1984.

61 Robert Alter, "The Achievement of Gershom Scholem," *Commentary*, April 1973, pp. 67–77.

62 Arieli, ibid.

63 Talmon, "Socialism and Liberalism," p. 36.

64 Ibid., p. 37.

65 Talmon, *Totalitarian Democracy*, p. 254.

66 "The Intellectual Versus the Leaders," Talmon interviewed by Israel Neumann, *Davar*, 1,8, 1969 (Hebrew).

Jacob L. Talmon's Political Essays

Part One

The Nature of Jewish History

Prophetism and Ideology – The Jewish Presence in History

The last hundred years have been the most dramatic in Jewish history since the destruction of the second commonwealth nearly two thousand years ago. From a situation of an almost hermetically closed sect and a marginal group of outsiders, the Jews found themselves propelled into the very heart of vast and fateful developments and historic confrontations as objects and as actors, as test cases and as victims: traditionalism and modernity, social hierarchy and social mobility, capitalism and socialism, gradual reform and total revolution, individualist liberalism and racist determinism, the tremendous ideological conflict between the two world wars, and finally the Middle Eastern crisis.

The Jews were seized by an ardent and restless aspiration to join the mainstream of history as represented by the nation-state or indeed world civilization as a whole. In many cases it amounted to a desire to become submerged by and to lose group identity in it. This seemingly irresistible drive was in due course met by a most implacable and brutal rejection, culminating in a campaign of total physical destruction, which succeeded in putting an end to the 1000–1500 year-old Jewish civilization in Central and Eastern Europe, with all its wealth, diversity, peculiarity and baffling problems.

Then came the heroic assertion of the Jewish will to live in the form of the restoration of Jewish statehood, as a nation in full control of its destinies, free to express its genius, eager to bridge across the ages to its earliest beginnings and into a future of dynamic spiritual, social and cultural endeavour. Locked up in bitter strife with its neighbours, who were backed by hostile or uncomprehending forces, the State of Israel has at the end of a series of dazzling military victories found itself, in the poignant words of a Franco-Jewish writer, in the situation of *La Juive des nations*, anxiously looking from almost total isolation to an anguished, bewildered Diaspora, instead of triumphantly carrying its banner.

In the face of these momentous events one feels the need to reexamine old questions. The Jews – what are they: a race, a religion, a nation? What is it that causes such a recurrence of patterns, raising them to soaring heights and plunging them into bottomless abysses? Why is it that a dispersed, atomized group, with a cohesion and identity in a seemingly permanent state of dissolution, becomes so conspicuous, and in the eyes of its enemies so compact, so devilishly affective and so ambiguous a force?

I would define the Jews as a community of fate – *Schicksalsgemeinschaft*. Judaism has originally emerged out of a tribal kernel with a tribal religion. It gradually developed into a nation. It then evolved into a tightly-knit exclusive religious confraternity, with the characteristics of a self-sufficient civilization with an extraordinary sense of its identity.

To account for this development we have to go back very far into history and to highlight a fact of crucial significance.

Of all the cultures and peoples conquered by Alexander the Great and then the Romans, only the Jews escaped absorption by the Hellenistic and Roman civilizations, and managed to preserve their own identity. It was the victory of the Maccabean revolt, in a sense an uprising of backward fanatics, which secured the survival of Judaism, while enabling it to incorporate a good deal of Hellenistic influence. This paved the way to Christianity, and thus accorded to a nation that dwelleth alone a role of incalculable universal significance.

What made it possible for the Jews to resist assimilation was the all-pervading consciousness of having come into the possession, long, long ago – and they alone of all nations – of a terrifying truth: of the idea of the total transcendence of God. Unlike the deities of Greece and Rome, who were supermen, residing in nature, the Jewish God was the Creator, the Father, the Ruler of the Universe, the regulator of history, supreme judge, the source of all truth and all goodness.

No less important was the fact that the revelation was made not solely to a few wise or holy men, nor was the covenant concluded with a priestly leadership, but with a whole people, which was proclaimed the "people of God," a "holy nation," a "community of priests." The religion was made to embrace and hallow the totality of life as a seamless web, with no distinction between service to God and human pursuits, faith and science, religious precepts and human individual or social morality, church and state, theory and practice. The Jewish religion becomes real when practiced as a way of life by society as a whole, and not by individuals. There is no suggestion of it being sustained in different ways by the perfect, an *ecclesia docens*, and by the imperfect, an *ecclesia discens*. In pre-exilic Judaism, it is not the individual who is rewarded or punished by God in afterlife, but the community and the generations are the recipients of both grace and retribution. It is nevertheless as an equal and active member of the chosen people of God and as one of the bearers of the sublime mission that the individual assumes his tremendous dignity. The behaviour of the community and its leadership is measured by the treatment it metes out to its component members, by the principle of justice. The leadership, the powers that be, are always being tested as to whether they are acting rightly towards God and His people. Power has no purpose other than service to God and the community. The question of its legitimacy is under constant scrutiny, because the real and sole sovereign is God. Remember the shock of Samuel, when the children of Israel came to ask him for a king to be like all the other nations. The scrutinizers are the prophets, who hold no power, no official position, do not form an organization or church, and if it needs to be added, have a critical attitude towards the priestly caste, towards ritualism and temporal authority. Their sole authority is the personal moral one.

The absolute character of the Revelation relieved the faithful of the task – indeed to some extent seemed to forbid them – to engage in a search for additional truth in philosophy and the sciences, which was so marked a feature of Greek civilization. Hence also the Jewish obsession with just conduct and justice in general, the horror of transgression, fear of sin which contrasts so starkly with the Greek openness of spirit, the lively curiosity, the desire for variety of experience. The obstinate refusal of the Jews to assimilate, their incomprehensible pride, were taken by the peoples of the Hellenistic and Roman empires as an expression of hostility towards mankind. Their resistance to worshipping Caesar as a god smacked of perverse rebelliousness. The Jewish horror of graven images and the facelessness of their god gave rise to suspicion that the Jews had much to hide, and to the absurd stories about the Holy of Holies in the Temple spread by Tacitus and other pagan writers.

The early gentile Christians were thus already conditioned to view the Jewish rejection of Christ and the crucifixion in a particular way.

Widespread and intense hostility, bitter tribulations and disasters befalling a people so permeated with a consciousness of having been exalted by God for a special mission, engendered prophetic messianism. That grand vision saw History as a chain, consisting of such links as choice, sin, punishment, trial, atonement and redemption. Through it, the Divine scheme would be consummated in the final denouement of all contradictions and conflict. In a time of greater ease in Zion, the ultimate shape of things assumed a universalistic and a deeply humane image of all nations coming together to worship the Lord. In an hour of great stress, painful humiliation and impotent rage conjured up pictures of a frightening punishment meted out to the heathen and of a signal recompense bestowed upon the suffering remnant of Israel.

There was another factor which contributed to the preservation of Jewish identity. The wonderful heritage of the classical Greek *polis*, with direct participatory democracy at its basis, was lost upon the vast expanses of the Hellenistic Empires. The compact, sharply contoured individuality of the *polis* became unviable in them. Bureaucratic despotism severed the unity of private and public pursuits. With the communal cohesion gone, man became a citizen of the world, thrown back upon his own inner light, with his gaze turned when not upon it, to cosmic verities and the idea of natural law as an unattainable ideal.

The abyss between the educated few and the uncouth masses assumed the character of class distinction. The esoteric minority engrossed itself in metaphysical quests and rarified morality of a universal, individualistic and increasingly more pessimistic nature, away from worldly and social responsibilities. The general populace was left with ritualistic religion, mystery cults and magic. While the sense of community was being lost in the Hellenistic and then Roman Empires, it was growing in strength and intensity in the Jewish and Judeo-Christian communities and was powerfully cemented by a vital practical religion.

A seemingly obscure sectarian development occurred at this point which is hardly known to people outside Judaic scholarship, namely the emergence of the *minyan*, the ten-man congregation of worshippers in the Diaspora. The prayers held by it replaced the animal sacrifices in the Temple of Jerusalem. With that ritual went also eventually the centrality of Jerusalem and the centralized religious regime. The ecclesia of the faithful came into existence wherever worshippers congregated, communed and evoked His Name. It is difficult to imagine the triumph of Christianity without the communal traditions and organization focused on the synagogue.

Whereas the Hellenized and Latinized pagans owed nothing to the Jews, the new converts to Christianity could not deny that their creed was an offshoot of Judaism. This immense ambiguity charged the Christian–Jewish relationship with a burden of neurosis, which has been weighing upon both, but of course mainly the Jews, ever since.

There developed among the Christians a complex attitude combining indebtedness, even awe, with still more hatred and contempt, and consequently malaise and feelings of guilt. Countless millions never ceased to behold with their eyes of the spirit, the Passion, but they were also being told of Abraham, Moses and Isaiah, and made to sing hymns to Zion and Jerusalem. St. Bernard de Clairvaux branded the Jews as Cain, and taught the believers to treat him accordingly, but not to kill him because the stigma on his forehead was an eternal witness to the triumph of Christianity. It may be said, all the same, that up to the late seventeenth century all political thought and much of the political history of Western Christendom were glosses upon the biblical story of Samuel-Saul-David. It was the example of the prophets that made the Church claim the mission and the right to struggle to bestow a moral dimension upon power. And whatever the excesses and perversions of which the Church became guilty in the process, it was the dualism of Church and State that preserved for a long time a measure of liberty in the West.

By the time of the Reformation the Jews had been expelled from most countries in Western Europe, but in the Wars of Religion the Calvinists of Holland and the Puritans of England and Scotland, as previously Jan Hus in Bohemia, proclaimed themselves heirs of the Maccabees fighting the wars of God against idolatry and graven images. And the Spaniards fought on all the battlefields of Europe and carried the cross over the seas as the chosen messengers of the Almighty. This Judaic sense of a special religious mission was by then clearly spilling over into national consciousness and into a pride in national destiny. If in the earlier days the Jewish ingredient helped to join disparate primitive tribes into a single Christian civilization, it was later the Judaic myth of the chosen people that became one of the mainsprings of incipient nationalism.

The position of the Jews as an ostracized, nonconformist

minority determined their special role in the economy of Europe. It has long ago been observed that as a marginal group, with no roots and no close ties and no reputation to lose, aliens are usually driven by discriminatory and restrictive legislation or even by their own penchant to choose occupations and pursuits which the long established shun as discreditable or as too novel and too risky. In medieval Europe the Jew was the alien par excellence. He also evoked sinister associations. His special inferior status and at the same time higher culture, his great, often enforced mobility and his international connections drove him into trade and money-lending. Here we can observe a pattern which was to recur throughout the ages and in different places. The Jews filled a vacuum and assumed a pioneering role in the earlier Middle Ages. As soon as that role had been fulfilled and non-Jews became ready for and interested in the pursuits which were previously engaged in only by the Jews, the pioneering role of the Jews took on the appearance of an usurpation by despised alien exploiters. Thus, in the later Middle Ages Jews were expelled from Western Europe. They were then admitted – indeed, invited and welcomed – into the then-underdeveloped part of the Continent, Eastern Europe, where urban life was only in its beginnings. It served the purposes of the Polish *Szlachta* and the Hungarian nobility and gentry not to let a native bourgeoisie emerge. The Jews were no rivals to be feared. So it happened that up to this century the Jews were in large parts of Eastern Europe the only urban population. This incidentally also explains why they did not assimilate, but remained a civilization apart: the nobility was too high, the peasantry too low. When the emancipation of the serfs in the nineteenth century sent millions of landless peasants and impoverished gentry into the towns, they met there the Jews and bitter competition ensued, which was made the more virulent as the Poles, Hungarians and others were gripped by a militant defensive-offensive nationalism, one of the planks of which was the formation of a national bourgeoisie. The rivalry ended in Auschwitz.

The scheme sketched here applies with greater force to the vastly important issue of Jews and capitalism.

In order to prove his thesis on the role of the Protestant spirit in the rise of capitalism Max Weber chose for his point of departure the Hebrew wisdom literature. Werner Sombart credited the Jews with the direct and active parenthood of early commercial and financial capitalism, in view of their prominent part in international and colonial trade and international banking. Some two hundred years earlier the English essayist, Addison, called the Jews the hinges and hooks of world economy.

In the wake of the French Revolution and the spread of the idea of human equality, the onset of secularization combined with the beginnings of the industrial revolution to release volcanic Jewish energies. The Jews woke up once more to a great hour of opportunity and assumed a pioneering role as hinges. In certain parts of Europe they became the sole or leading forgers of the links in the international capitalist economy – banking, the stock exchange, commodity production, chain stores, the press and news agencies, mass entertainment.

Those groups in general society which were bewildered, offended or even hurt by these vast changes and grave new problems, and were unable to understand and to reconcile themselves to the workings of a modern economy, singled out the Jews as the authors of the confusion and its main beneficiaries. From *pariahs* they rose overnight to the position of *rois de l'epoque* (Toussenel). The images of Judas Iscariot and Shylock were at hand to suggest deep plots and dark machinations. Karl Marx himself spoke of the Judaization of Christendom.

At the beginning of the twentieth century, the high priest of racist anti-Semitism, Houston Stewart Chamberlain, son-in-law of Richard Wagner and oracle of Hitler, labelled the nineteenth century as "the Jewish century," in the same way as the sixteenth was Spanish, the seventeenth French, and the eighteenth English.

While contributing so much to the emergence of modern capitalist civilization by being through their peculiar situation among its pioneers, the Jews also assumed the old mission of prophets towards it. The philosophy of the Enlightenment, which came too early for Jewish emancipation, had on the one hand paved the way for Jewish emancipation, but on the other reduced considerably or even condemned the Jewish dimension of the European heritage as the fountainhead of Christian fanaticism and superstition. But by denying the workings of Providence, and the hope of reward and punishment in an afterlife, rationalism reopened the question of the ancient prophetic puzzle, "Why do the righteous suffer and the wicked prosper?" "Shall evil reign freely?" The rationalist answer was the religion of progress, and the vision of an inevitable, preordained denouement of the drama of history in an ultimate reign of perfect rationality, harmony and justice. This was the Prince of Denmark of the socialist idea of a total revolutionary transformation which hypnotized so many Jews in the last two centuries.

The earliest prophet of modern socialism, Saint-Simon, explicitly and emphatically linked his own vision with the Messianic expectations of the Jews.

> Le peuple de Dieu, celui qui avait reçu des révélations avant l'apparition de Jésus, celui qui le plus généralement répandu sur toute la surface du globe, a toujours senti que la doctrine chrétienne, fondée par les Pères de l'Église, était incomplète, il a toujours proclamé qu'il arriverait une grande époque, à laquelle il a donné le nom de Messianique, époque où la doctrine religieuse serait presentée avec toute la généralité dont elle est susceptible; qu'elle règlerait également l'action du pouvoir temporel et celle du pouvoir spirituel, et qu'alors toute l'éspèce humaine n'aurait plus qu'une seule religion, qu'une même organisation . . .

". . . an essentially pacific organization of society," in which "all men will treat each other as brethren." Saint-Simon identifies the mounting structural crisis of European society of his day and the approaching preordained solution "which no force on earth can prevent," with the Old Testament prophecies. His Jewish disciple Olinde Rodriguez feels a direct call to face the crisis of political and moral reorganization, because of the tradition of Moses which, as he says, he carries in his blood. His Jewishness had caused him to become a savant and an industrialist, and it had thus given him a special insight into the power of the capitalists as well as into the defects of their morality. D'Eichthal, another Jewish Saint-Simonist, speaks of "the language of the prophets, the word of truth" which he derives from his race.

In a striking passage from the pen of Rosa Luxemburg, the high priestess and martyr of universal Messianic revolution, and extreme devotee of dialectical materialism, I find confirmation of the view that the primary *spiritus movens* of Marxism was not the view on capitalist economy arrived at inductively, but the compulsive hold of a vision of an ultimate denouement of the drama of history in a vindication of providential justice. It was – Rosa Luxemburg says – the conception of the socialist final goal that conditioned and determined Marx's theory of capital, his teachings on the rate of profit, on the inevitable collapse of the capitalist economy, in short the whole of his economic system. "Precisely and solely because Marx *a priori* approached the capitalist economy as a socialist . . . was he able to decipher its hieroglyphs; and because he made the socialist standpoint into the point of departure for his scientific analysis, was he – *vice versa* – able to prove socialism scientifically."

In other words, the overpowering force of the postulate gave cogency to the grandiose structure in all its parts and components. It was the "Red Rabbi" Moses Hess (and the Pole Cieszkowski) who provided Marx with the vital link in the evolution of his doctrine: that it was not enough to understand and criticize reality. The weapon of dialectical philosophy makes it possible and imperative to change it. As a Jew, Hess was barred from active politics. His sectarian religion never recognized the legitimacy of the distinction between theory and practice, because it had never made the doctrine of original sin its own. This is why Hess was never able not only to accept, but even to comprehend the idea of the eternal and inescapable dichotomy between the knowledge of what was good and the impotence to do it, between what should be and what is, the world of pure ideas and defective reality, private and social morality, politics and ethics, facts and works – as the essence of the human condition. No genuinely revolutionary disposition is in the last analysis possible as long as that resignedly fatalistic attitude persists.

"Because I not only know," writes Hess in a letter to Herzen, "what I want, but also want what I know, I am more of an apostle than a philosopher – the social revolution is my religion."

"So long as Christianity has not yet become the truly universal religion . . . true entirely and solely to its Founder, striving for the salvation of man in the fullest and most humane sense, will the Jew be unable to espouse it."

It has been suggested that it was this frame of mind that was behind Marx's prophetically relentless and wrathful unmasking of all pretense, self-deception, rationalization and mythologization of egoistic motives, covering up the root of all evil – cupidity. It was then, the deep-seated resentment of age-long injury and persecution, coupled with the malaise experienced by men who had torn themselves away from an ancient, closed tradition, but had not succeeded in becoming integrated or were not admitted into society at large, that made existing reality appear to them provisional and transitory, heading towards some fundamental change which will inaugurate a stable, rational and just reality.

This apocalyptic or Messianic mood suffered a grave setback in 1848. In the years after, capitalism, instead of breaking down, went from conquest to conquest. Attention was then diverted from social problems to the revival of oppressed or partitioned nations and their emergence as powerful nation-states. It was the rebirth of Italy that turned Hess into a Zionist: the resurrection of Athens and Rome was to him a sign that Jerusalem too was about to rise. Restored Israel was destined to realize and to offer to mankind a living example of a society incarnating prophetic righteousness.

By the end of the nineteenth century, the devotees of universal revolution woke up to the fact that their myth was being dangerously challenged by another myth, that of the nation. The Revisionist heresy, which was proclaimed by Eduard Bernstein, another Jew who could not be prevailed to let sleeping dogs lie, was at bottom a symptom of the victory of the myth of the nation. Bernstein caused irritation in the official leadership of social-democracy in Germany by driving home the fact that while the party was employing the old Marxist revolutionary slogans, it had long ceased to act according to, or to believe in the Marxist diagnosis, which Bernstein himself had indeed found disproved by social-economic developments. The gap between pretence and reality would not let Bernstein rest. Not only did he insist that capitalism was not showing signs of collapsing – the exploitation of the workers was not growing worse, and the middle class was not sinking into the ranks of the proletariat. He narrowed the sights of socialism to the frontiers of the nation-state and its particular realities and traditions. He jettisoned thoroughly the very core of revolutionary universalism, the dialectic, the vision of a universal all-determining force – capitalism – unfolding fully and then collapsing in an inevitable revolutionary upheaval. Inevitability was replaced by Bernstein with appeal to reason and to fairness. Proletarian dictatorship was rejected for the sake of gradual reforms by parliamentary consent. Social democratic parties were no longer to be sections of the indivisible universal labour movement, but the left wing parties in the political spectrum of the single nation.

Stung to the quick, Rosa Luxemburg, Parvus-Helphans, Trotsky, later Lenin and other true believers set out to revitalize Marx's early Messianic revolutionary universalism by a restatement of the issue between capitalism and socialism in global terms, and to revive Marx's old conception of the permanent revolution. Far from the nation-state having become the decisive reality, they proclaimed, it had lost all its independence to the imperialism of the superpowers.

The alleged supremacy of free democratic parliaments had become a mockery in the age of vast capitalistic interests manipulating from behind the scenes political parties, public opinion and the press. With monopoly capitalism spreading everywhere, the unified world was becoming polarized into a global capitalism and a universal proletariat. The inevitable armed collision of the imperialist powers was destined to trigger off a world-wide uprising, in which the colonial proletariat would stretch out its hand to the uncorrupted parts of the European working class movement. The first capitalist state to snap, undermined by internal rebellion, would be the weak link in world capitalism, Russia. The victorious Russian revolution would then throw the torch of revolution into the West. The roused socialists of the West would in response hasten to help backward Russia to make its way to socialism by a short cut.

Some of the earliest prophets of this version of the universal and permanent revolution in Germany were Jewish emigrés, refugees of persecution from Poland and Russia, to whom the revolution had become the unearthly fatherland, which had no particular location and no territorial borders. Gentiles like Karl Liebknecht, Klara Zetkin, Franz Mehring, even Lenin, were soon assimilated by the imperalistic racists to the Jews, in the spirit of the device that, if you have several adversaries, identify them all with the most vulnerable one.

As early as around 1800 German counter-revolutionaries argued that the very concepts of natural law, social contract, the rights of man, were all imported from France to weaken and overcome the natural resistance of the German national organism to the intrusion of an alien element. At the end of the century, Charles Maurras employed the same argument, except that the universal values were proclaimed by him to have been a Jewish import to France from Kantian Germany.

In the bizarre dialogue between Hitler and his mentor, Eckart, of the early 1920s, the Jews are no longer depicted only as solvents of social cohesion and national tradition, as eternal exploiters, poisoners of the race, and distorters of creative authenticity and integrity. They are presented primarily as the historic inciters of the inferior mobs against the superior national elites: Moses in Egypt, the prophets in Judea, early Christianity, Calvinists, Puritans and other radical protestant sects, the French revolution, liberals, democrats, socialists, finally the Bolsheviks – they all form a single chain "From Moses to Lenin" (the title of the published dialogue).

There occurred a convergence of the anti-Semitic race theories with the philosophy of Nietzsche, that bitter adversary of anti-Semitism, but thinker whose attitude to historic Judaism was most complex and ambivalent. It raised the confrontation between imperialist racism and revolutionary, prophetic Jewish universalism to the level of a grandiose encounter.

Some late nineteenth-century anti-Semites, like Drumont and Schönerer, proclaimed anti-Semitism "the greatest achievement of the century . . . the main prop of national thought" – an answer to Marxist socialism and dialectical materialism: Blood took the place of matter. Racial modifications substituted changes in modes of production. Jewish exploitation replaced class struggle. The elimination of Jewish power and influence was to constitute the real social revolution, the confiscated Jewish wealth being designated to serve, like the confiscated ecclesiastical and monastic property in the past, as the lever of a social-economic transformation.

Nietzsche then supplied the vision of the ultimate struggle between the priestly Judaic morality of the weak, the envious and the resentful on the one hand, and the ethics of the strong, overflowing with vitality, driven by an elemental urge for life and power on the other. Nietzsche prophesied that that titanic struggle between Judea and Rome was reaching a shattering climax. All the heirs of Judaism, in the first place Christianity, so bitterly loathed by Nietzsche, but also democracy, liberalism and socialism shared the basic common faith in a Theodicy: at the end of the days, God's ways will prove just – through a final resolution of contradictions, conflict, injustice, a universal reconciliation and the inauguration of perfect harmony. This was the consolation of the timid and the deprived. Nietzsche was possibly the first European thinker with the unprecedentedly cruel nihilistic courage to deny any hope of a Theodicy. He was joined by all the racists in substituting for the search for objective truth and the resolve to realize equitable justice, the eternal will to power, the cultivation of the superior specimen of man and race through the school of rivalry, struggle, war and conquest.

There is no proof, but it is highly probable that the young Hitler read the dazzling section on Jews in Nietzsche's *Dawn of Day*, in which the philosopher announces that the Jews had already crossed the Rubicon, and the twentieth century will decide whether they would become the martyrs of Europe or lose it, as they lost Egypt over three thousand years earlier. Nietzsche goes on to say that on top of the wonderful qualities which the Jews had acquired from their age-long training in self-control and in their struggle to survive they were now – through intermarrying with the best blood in Europe – becoming equipped to supply Europe with a superb elite, which will bestow immeasurable blessings upon the world. We can only imagine the effect which this prophecy on the alternative of Jewish mastery and the disappearance of the Jews, and the portrayal of the Jews as the core of the master race of the future was calculated to have on Hitler.

Strange and frightening are the dialectical ironies of history.

The gigantic twentieth-century confrontation between the various heirs of the Jewish prophetic tradition and defiantly resurgent paganism ended in the defeat of the latter. But in the process, the European part of the people of the direct descendants and of the living standard bearers of the ancient message was all but annihilated. The remnant of Israel sought a safe refuge in the ancestral land which was its cradle. But there it became locked in bitter conflict with the Arab world, itself in the throes of a national awakening and feeling all the more aggravated by the ill-timed late return of the old claimants, as it was viewing the general exit of Europe from Asia and Africa.

There occurred a baffling reversal of alliances. The fatherland of universal revolutionary socialism, which Jews did so much to create, evolved into as rigid and oppressive an establishment as only triumphant Messianism can become, and into the successor to the interests and compulsions of a Great Power. As such it came up against the phenomenon of prophetic Jewish nonconformism and dissidence. The Jews assumed the character of an indigestible and resistant element and its originally pioneering role appeared now as an unduly privileged status held by a minority, suspected also of sympathy for the United States, the heir to the Old Testament Puritan tradition, the seat of the largest Jewish conglomeration in history, and the strongest rival of the Soviet Union for world mastery.

Yesterday's victims of racist imperialism, the Third World, China, India, for whose liberation Jewish revolutionaries had fought with such ardour, were stone deaf to the magic sound of "Zion" and

"Jerusalem," and unreceptive to any feelings of awe before the uniqueness of the Jewish fate. The Bible was to them a closed book and the Jews had no place in their history. The New Left in the West was hypnotized by the facile theory of the two camps: that of imperalism and that of the oppressed peoples fighting for national liberation. The young revolutionaries of the New Left could no longer see the millions of wretchedly poor and oppressed Jews of Eastern Europe who had ceased to exist, while beholding in the West the Jewish communities which looked prosperous and influential. There emerged thus the myth of an American-Zionist-imperialist camp and it took the place of the myth of the Judeo-Bolshevik-Masonic international conspiracy of fifty years earlier, and to add insult to injury, Zionism, the Jewish movement of national liberation, was branded as racism. Western Europe was neutralized, torn between a sense of commitment to the people of the prophets and the irresistible pressures of vital economic interests in the Arab world, which from barefoot nomads of the desert had changed almost overnight into the masters of the life blood of our industrial civilization.

Israel has been reduced to the situation of a besieged city or a ship buffeted by one of those violent storms which have been assailing us throughout our long history. The Jewish historian becomes a kind of martyr in his permanent and anguished intimacy with the mystery of the Jewish fate and the Jewish survival. Whether he be Orthodox in belief or has discarded all religious practice, he cannot help but be sustained by a faith which can neither be proved nor disproved, that notwithstanding all the present torment and mortal threats, Israel will one day be spritually significant and, in conjunction with the Jewish Diaspora, spiritually effective in the world.

History would somehow make no sense otherwise.

Originally published in *The Jerusalem Quarterly*, Number 3, Spring 1977. This essay originated as a lecture delivered at a meeting at the Sorbonne, presided by its president, Professor Alphonse Dupront, in March 1976, on the occasion of the Hebrew University of Jerusalem's fiftieth anniversary.

The Nature of Jewish History – Its Universal Significance

I am very mindful of the honour which has been accorded by the invitation to inaugurate this annual lecture, intended as this venture is to serve as an annual platform for re-examining and redefining important aspects of Jewish existence and endeavour within a wider context. It is a great pleasure to all of us, and a source of deep pride to me personally, to have Lord Samuel preside at this occasion.

I can still remember when as a child in one of those small towns on the wind-swept plain of Northern Poland I heard for the first time the name of Sir Herbert Samuel. What magic, what aura surrounded that name of the *Naziv Rishon B'Yehudah*, the first governor of Judea, for us there, in the atmosphere of those days, so heavily charged with Jewish Messianic exaltation and dreamy Slavonic romanticism, full of fervent hopes and awful forebodings.

When I learned that Lord Samuel would grace this gathering, I could not help reflecting on the difference between the formative experiences which were present to shape his view of history in those spacious sunlit days of the late Victorian age, when history seemed to have only one direction – upwards to a broader humanity – and the apocalyptic shadows and convulsions which have accompanied my own generation from the moment we began to sort out the picture of the world to ourselves.

The events of the last decades have indeed given a powerful stimulus to historic speculation on a grand scale. Many a historian has been liberated from the inhibiting fear of venturing out of his microscopic preoccupation with this text or that document, and more than one has been driven to re-examine the basic assumptions of history.

Our age shows signs of becoming one of the great history-minded periods. One looks back for comparison to the time which followed the French Revolution and the Napoleonic era and which saw the flowering of the modern science of history. The student's mind wanders back to that hour, two thousand five hundred years earlier, when by the rivers of Babylon the survivors of a national catastrophe evolved the first vision of a universal historic drama. And there is no reason to apologize for drawing an analogy with the twilight of the Roman empire, when St. Augustine was reinterpreting the Judaic conception in reference to Rome and Christianity.

In all those ages the experience which shook men and set them to speculate was the baffling contrast between human intentions and expectations on the one hand and results on the other. In our own time a war to end all wars, and to make mankind fit for democracy, was followed by a structural crisis in world economy and by a defiant attack of one of the most advanced powers on values hitherto held to be self-evident and to form the essence of civilized achievement. Then came a world war of inconceivable atrocity.

As in previous history-minded ages, the brooding over the examples of man's daring and the lessons of his failure is also in our own days ensuing in vast systems designed to prove man to be dominated and wholly determined by the working of such impersonal forces as providential schemes of salvation, dialectics of history, or the law of historic cycles. The preordained evolution of these is held to reconcile the problems of freedom and fate, choice and chance, and to resolve the dilemmas of seeming chaos and integrated purposefulness, of deterministic laws and man's salvation.

The horrors of our time, which appear especially perverse through the mixture of sheer sadism with twisted idealism and which seem more frightening than any before through the unprecedented technical means at man's disposal, have led some to suspect that the age-long dams holding back man's savage instincts have begun to crumble, and that our civilization has become so entangled in contradictions that we have lost grip on our destinies altogether. Historians like Professor Butterfield have thus been anxiously trying to sort out guilt from predicament, sin from error, falsehood from self-deception, and revive for us the sense of the essentially tragic condition of man and history.

Under the impact of the great shift of balance which is now taking place between shrinking Europe and the two leading non-European powers at the head of the two conflicting ideologies, and between the West and the emerging civilizations of Asia, Professor Toynbee, Professor Koebner and others have come to see the encounter of civilizations, within the scheme of universal history, in a completely new light.

I. Historic Revision

Jews have been caught in the very heart of the whirlwind of contemporary history, and the vast transformations taking place in our time have already recast the scheme of Jewish history to a point where even the least imaginative can see that an era has gone for ever and a new epoch has opened. It is time to try to take our bearings in this new situation. What are its data? What kind of history is likely to be written from our new vantage point?

The first obvious and determining fact is the demographic changes; the centre of gravity in the distribution of Jewish populations has shifted decisively to the West, above all the United States of America. This entails so much more than mere redistribution of numbers. It means that Judaism as an integrated civilization has ceased to exist in Central and Eastern Europe, and that outside the new centre of Jewish cohesion, the State of Israel, the large majority of the Jewish people is now broken up into groups and individuals living most of their lives within non-Jewish patterns of existence. This raises the difficult question of the distribution of significance and emphasis between the old-type Diaspora, the Western dispersion, and Jewish political and spiritual nationhood in Israel. As far as the West is concerned, we are faced with the questions – What are the legitimate subject-matter and scope of the Jewish historian altogether? What are things of Jewish significance?

The second point is the need to submit to the test of events the interpretation of Jewish history offered by the various philosophies such as Western liberalism, Jewish nationalism and salvationist Marxism.

Finally, the question arises as to the place and significance of Jewish history within the scheme of universal history, from the vantage point of the new view of world history which is at present emerging as a result of the shift of balance between the West and the rest of the world.

To what extent may the Jewish historian apply the same criteria to three areas – the Eastern European Diaspora (embracing also all pre-1789 Jewish history), the modern Western dispersion and the State of Israel? Are the three parts so interrelated as to form one history?

There were up to recently two tests and standards of judgment: one was primarily applicable to the West, and was concerned with the measure of civic equality and equality of opportunity accorded to Jews; the second valued above all thickness of Jewish texture and richness of Jewish content, and could therefore see great glory even in circumstances of political oppression and squalid poverty. The latter view, as represented for instance by Simon Dubnow, portrayed Jewish history as being motivated by the urge for autonomous institutions and full Jewish self-expression through them. The Western Diaspora would hence appear only as a shadow of real Jewish existence, only as an extension and dry limb of the great Eastern-European trunk. Clearly, this philosophy has received a death blow from Nazism as well as Communism. Jewish autonomy in the Diaspora is likely to appear to the future historian as a phase in, and not as the aim of, Jewish history, and the roles may well come to be reversed in his eyes so as to turn Eastern European Jewish civilization, almost incomprehensible to him, into a prehistory of the Western dispersion.

Zionist Interpretation

How far have the Western liberal and the Zionist ideologies been vindicated by historical developments? While the gloomiest of Zionist prophecies have more than come true in regard to the hopelessness of the Jewish position in Eastern Europe, Western Jews' confidence in the liberal fibre and democratic institutions of their countries has withstood the test of Nazi infection. Jewish statehood was achieved perhaps sooner than many expected, and through a concentration of efforts which astonished most observers. But on the debit side, Hitler's annihilation of millions of potential Israelis and the ban on Jewish emigration from the Communist countries has not been balanced by any appreciable flow from the West. As things stand at present, the State of Israel may be said to have gathered in the remnant of Israel from Central and Eastern Europe and from the Oriental countries, while the Western Diaspora, though powerfully affected by the emergence of Israel in respect of imponderables, has come to comprise the large majority of Jews, without any visible difference in their status and ways of living having been brought about by Israel.

If this be the shape of things to come and stay, the approach of some Zionist students to Jewish history will have to be considerably modified. In the first flush of Zionist enthusiasm, and exercised by murderous anti-Semitism on one side and the disintegration of Jewish communal cohesion on the other, they were only too ready to portray the two thousand years of the Diaspora as one long preparation for the return to Zion. The most vital factor was to them the never-quenched Messianic hope, the highlights of the drama, the sporadic outbreaks of Messianic movements. Institutions, economic pursuits and spiritual developments were assessed as instruments of national survival in the midst of universal hostility and disintegrating influences. Jewish history in this vision reached its climax in the great acts of martyrdom, *Kiddush Hashem*. Ultimate redemption, in brief, appeared to give meaning to all the past generations, and in more recent times the Western Diaspora was looked upon almost exclusively as a reservoir of aid and sympathy for the Jewish national effort in Palestine and around it.

This strenuously dynamic conception, which is wholly dominated by the category of becoming, will have to give much greater force to the inertia of mere being. The poetic truth vibrating in the former vision may have a higher reality. The historian must however be careful to take each generation for granted as living its own life here and now and not merely in preparation for some final consummation.

Our formulation of the relationship between Israel and the Western Diaspora should not be taken as implying independent and different laws of development for each. Such a view amounts to a denial of the oneness of the Jewish people and of the unity of Jewish history. There may be some people in the Western dispersion who, out of faint-hearted apprehension of being accused of double loyalty, claim that the State of Israel is to them just another little state, with this difference that most of its inhabitants at least nominally profess the Jewish religion. There have also been some cocksure Israelis who proclaimed that the sovereign State of Israel, a normal country like any other, stands in no exceptional relationship to Jews outside its borders. But, even if there were no religious and cultural ties, that attitude would still be completely at variance with reality. It is just not true that Israel and the Diaspora are becoming so dissociated in the consciousness of Jews and Gentiles as to do away with the deeply ingrained habit of associating all Jews everywhere in a common responsibility.

The general constellation is of such a nature that should one of those calamities with which Jewish history is punctuated overtake the Western Diaspora, above all American Jewry, the State of Israel would be shaken to its foundations. Should, on the other hand, the Jewish state be engulfed by a catastrophe, the legal status and economic position of Jews outside may not be visibly affected at once. But the blow to their self-confidence, the loss of the vicarious prestige which Israel had bestowed upon them in the eyes of the world, the general disenchantment, would be too great to be survived for long.

Marxist Doctrine

The Marxist salvationist claim should be examined from the point of view of the basic fact of joint Jewish responsibility, and, to use a very modern and so-to-say specialized expression, guilt by association.

The Dreyfus affair, the persistence of various forms of anti-Semitism, and above all the eruption of Fascism and Nazism shook the hopeful liberal expectation that the general progress of humanitarian sentiments and of democratic institutions would inevitably put an end to that anomaly in the Jewish situation. Then orthodox Marxists would come forward and claim that true human brotherhood could be made real not by mere political devices and preaching but only through the eradication of those social-economic evils which feed social and racial conflict.

Now a Jewish historian who holds the view that Jewish history is not a phenomenon *sui generis*, but that its evils flow from and would be automatically cured by a general scheme of things, must make clear to himself what his values are: whether he is interested in merely improving the lot of the individual Jew or whether he cares for the survival of historic Judaism.

Totalitarian Messianism postulates an all-embracing exclusive doctrine, which is held to offer a binding view on all aspects of human life and social existence, including religion, ethics, the arts. This is not a setting congenial to Jews, who are nothing if not nonconformists, pursuing a path of their own. Insofar as it feels itself to be a Church militant surrounded by the City of the Devil, a totalitarian Communist system cannot tolerate groups of its population maintaining contacts with some international confraternity and having a kind of foreign policy of their own. Jewish life, however, shrivels in the absence of free channels through which ideas, aid, sympathy and that general sense of kinship can flow. It can prosper only in an open society.

Most Communists admit now that Jewish life in Russia has for long been in a state of atrophy, and proclaim total assimilation to be a desirable end to Jewish separateness. The disappearance of any distinct status is surely the realization of the ideal of complete equality. This may not be an untenable view, but it places its holder on a plane where discussion is no longer possible. He has taken himself out of Jewish history.

It is becoming increasingly more difficult to defend the view that, although it has emasculated Jewish life, the Soviet system has liberated the Jewish individual from the burden of collective responsibility. Like all other evils, the doctors plot, the execution of Jewish writers and other symptoms of anti-Semitism are placed at the door of Joseph Stalin. But that evades the fundamental issue.

It used to be said with enormous self-assurance that the enthronement of socialism would not merely do away with social oppression and racial animosities, but was bound to inaugurate the reign of fully scientific and objective laws of social development, with human arbitrariness and individual or group perversity entirely ruled out. If we are now to ascribe such terrific effectiveness to the personal arbitrariness of one man, we are surely thereby denying the foolproof scientific determinism of the system as such. We open the gates to those psychological and other influences which remain, as it were, only affected but are not uprooted by social-economic factors. And it is indeed these forces which are at the core of what has been called the Jewish problem.

Of course, a sociological phenomenon cannot be stated simply in terms of other people's reactions. However unjust and twisted such reactions may be, we have to go back to the irritant itself. What is that irritant in the Jews which evokes this wicked or at least irrational response? It has been suggested it was the fact that everywhere they were aliens. I would say the fact that they are different and that others are unwilling to take their existence and rights for granted. Even in America, where in a sense all are aliens, and no racial group, except the Red Indians, may claim to be the original owners of the place, Jews seem so often to be considered in some ways still more alien than all the other aliens.[1]

Some historians, impressed by dialectical materialism, lay great store on the peculiar social-economic structure of the Jews. A little reflection will reveal that, while no doubt the abnormal and top-heavy social-economic structure of the Jews contributed not a little to make their position more vulnerable, it was ultimately itself an outcome of the initially exceptional character of the Jews. Jews were different and were regarded as different, and therefore went – and were driven – into special occupations. They will be caught by fate in similar ways in most different circumstances. At the end of the last war, for instance, the Soviet troops were bound to appear as saviours in the eyes of the Jewish survivors in Eastern Europe emerging from the forests, bunkers and caves. The Jews had every reason to collaborate eagerly with the new regimes, and were in a position to offer cadres of trained personnel and even leadership. Then the Stalinist drive against cosmopolitanism found its target in Jewish intellectuals and Jews in general, while the resurgence of Poles, Hungarians and others against Soviet Russian domination is calculated to hit the Jews as collaborators with Stalinism. Abnormality, insecurity, ambiguity, absence of full and unequivocal matter-of-factness and recognition – these are the rocks in the midst of which the boat of Judaism – not excluding Israel – may perhaps never cease to steer a course. Thus the refusal of the Arab states to recognize Israel looks like a counterpart of the Western-Christian treatment of Jews as late-comers and aliens.

The Subject-matter of Jewish History

If the future historian of the Jews is to have before his eyes only two extreme cases – the full-blooded nation of Israel, and those countries in the West, in which Jewish life has lost its cohesion, where the Jew lives most of his life within non-Jewish patterns, where religious observance has often been reduced to a minimum or has ceased altogether, and Jewish learning has assumed the character of a philological and antiquarian interest, and where communal activities do not amount to more than care for synagogue and cemetery, charity balls and youth clubs – how is he to sort out his material and to define his subject-matter?

We have to ask ourselves at this juncture: Since 1948, what is a Jew? A person professing the Jewish faith? A member of the Jewish race? Is the criterion consciousness of and willingness to share a common Jewish fate, or the fact that others – Jews or Gentiles – consider you a Jew? Debate on this issue has always been bedevilled by the fact that in Central and Eastern Europe, with its mixture of races and religions, and its social cleavages running parallel to linguistic differences, the term nation or nationality has always had a racial connotation. In the West the criterion has always been citizenship, one's passport, or, to use Ernest Rénan's famous definition, "*la nation, c'est le plébiscite de tous les jours.*" A person is what he feels and votes to be: German-speaking Alsatians are Frenchmen, if they desire to share the fate of France. There is a well-known story of a German social-democratic leader of Jewish extraction being entertained soon after Hitler's rise to power by a group of Fabians in London. When commiserated on the fate of "your German Jews," Dr. X corrected his host by saying that he was not a Jew. "I am sorry," murmured the confused Englishman, "but I was under the impression that you were Jewish." "Well," answered Dr. X, "if you adopt the racial criterion, then indeed I am a Jew, because both my parents were Jewish. But you know, as early as 1923, I sent in my letter of resignation to the Jewish community in Berlin." "Oh, I see now" – replied the not over-subtle *goy* – "you mean to say, Dr. X, that Jews are a club."

We all know, on the other hand, of pious Jews who in argument would deny to a non-observant Jew the very right to call himself Jew, but who would greedily appropriate any quarter-Jew once he had won a Nobel Prize. Such a person would on occasion get into trouble by grabbing as a Jewish *chazan* a church organist, because he wrote an opera on the highly edifying Judaic motive of Samson and Delila; for who but a Jew could penetrate so deeply into the spirit of that God-fearing couple?

I believe that from the vantage point of our time Jews are to be defined as a community of fate. They are a product of history, which crystallized around an extremely tenacious kernel or nucleus of race and religion, and like any living product of time and circumstances has very suffused contours.

Grave objections may at this point be voiced by those who hold religion to be the full essence and sole test of Judaism. I would call such an attitude doctrinaire. It may be theoretically, not to say theologically, correct. It is historically false. It may have been theoretically quite wrong for Jews not to have remained exclusively members of a religious confraternity. But they did not. And so many secular elements have been evolved from or added to the religious core as almost to swamp it. This is however a universal phenomenon. Not so very long ago any ordinary European felt himself to be first a faithful son of his Church and only after that a member of his nation. Furthermore, immemorial traditions of self-government and a unique social position within the community of Christian nations throughout the ages made Jews in Europe from the start into a community of a much wider scope than a religious sect, not to speak of the national tradition from antiquity. It is sometimes amusingly incongruous to hear people, whose Judaism has been watered down to the most tepid sort of Deism or general humanitarianism, accusing Zionists and others of falsifying through their nationalism the true original spirit of Judaism.

The purely atomistic approach claiming for the individual the absolute right to define himself is inadequate. All canons of science are violated by treating the individual Jew as a primordial entity, outside the patterns evolved by centuries of Jewish existence, as a community apart, with its intricate and so exacting religion, its intense self-consciousness, the restricted geographical background and the discriminatory legal framework, with the similarity of the few occupations open to its members, and the periods of violent persecution. In brief, a Jew may be a Jew in spite of himself. A sense of chivalry makes us recoil from a person denying his Jewishness as from someone who deserted a beleaguered city or a ship in distress.

Should we therefore conclude that the Jewish historian must pursue any Jew who has deliberately or imperceptibly severed all or most of his visible links with Judaism – or never had any – wherever he goes and whatever he does? What are the associations of such a person which come within the purview of Jewish history? A peer of Jewish ancestry winning the Derby – is that an event of Jewish significance?

Furthermore, history is not a collection of individual biographies but of collective social patterns. In most cases we treat the individual, while not forgetting everyone's ultimate uniqueness, as a sample of a group, a type or a pattern.

How are we, once Jewish cohesion has loosened so drastically, to isolate those thin threads which weave themselves into some Jewish collective pattern distinct from the so much more tangible non-Jewish patterns? How are we to detect in the behaviour and actions of seemingly unconnected individuals features significantly Jewish? To what extent are we justified in summing these up as a Jewish contribution or ingredient?

We are in this respect confronted with that supreme difficulty which Dr. Weizmann used to call Jewish "ghostliness." The world is too small to contain them, and they are said to possess all the wealth of the earth, and yet, when you strain every nerve to pin them down by a definition, they elude you like a mirage.

It seems impossible to lay a finger on anything tangible and measurable in the Jew's Jewishness; yet an ailing, all-devouring self-consciousness comes like a film between him and the world. Not bothered with when things are normal and prosper, he is seen as ubiquitous, all-powerful, sinister when blame is to be laid upon someone. I believe the links holding Jews together are – to use the words of Edmund Burke – as invisible as the air and as strong as the heaviest chains, and the Jewish ingredient to be as imperceptible to the senses, yet as effective in results, as vital energy itself.

But these things are too subtle for the historian's techniques and such crude instruments as quantitative measurements of Jewish participation in trades and professions, or data on attendance at synagogue and contributions to charities. Jewish impulses and reactions, attitudes and sensitiveness, Jewish patterns of thought and feeling, and Jewish modes of behaviour call for the intuition of the artist, and can indeed be only intimated by symbols, conjured up by poetic incantation, and conveyed by the art of the novelist. We shall try presently to isolate some of them by concentrating on recurrent and what may be called typical phenomena in Jewish behaviour and activity.

II. Jewish History within Universal History

We come now to the second part of our paper, and shall from now on concern ourselves with the Jews within the scheme of universal history as it is being in these days recast by the change of balance between the West and the Asiatic and other civilizations.

In the vision of history of Western-Christian civilization, the Jew occupied a vital or at least a unique place. To the multitudes of Eastern and South-Eastern Asia Jews are an unknown, incomprehensible and negligible quantity. The Jew in the West may be persecuted, reviled, despised, expelled and massacred. He was indissolubly connected with the central event in the history of Christendom. But he constituted a tremendous problem. He embodied a great mystery. Immense effectiveness was ascribed to him, for good or evil. He appeared a factor of significance out of all proportion to the numbers involved.

We have a long, terrible and bloodstained account with the Christian West. I venture, however, to say that already now the rise of non-European powers is beginning to make the record look somewhat different and less straightforward than in the not-too-distant past. For one thing – no Jewish historian, whatever his evaluation of the various factors involved in the restoration of Jewish statehood, can ignore the fact that Zionism would never have had a chance of success if centuries of Christian teaching and worship, liturgy and legend had not conditioned the Western nations to respond almost instinctively to the words "Zion" and "Israel," and thus to see in the Zionist ideal not a romantic chimera or an imperialistic design to wrest a country from its actual inhabitants but the consummation of an eternal promise and hope. No Jewish associations impinge upon the Far Eastern civilizations. Their record is clean of anti-Semitism, but it is also empty of Jews.

If, now, world history is to be written in the future not as the history of the West, with non-European peoples treated as candidates for Western civilization and objects of European tutelage, but as the story of the relationship between various civilizations, of which our own is only one among others, what place are the Jews likely to find in that new universal scheme? As a "light to the nations," their role is bound to appear smaller. On the other hand, the stronger and clearer emphasis on the peculiar character of each civilization, resulting from the juxtaposition of several civilizations, is calculated to bring into starker relief the special Jewish ingredient in Western history.

Toynbee and the Jews

Everyone must at this juncture be turning his mind to Professor Arnold Toynbee. I think it will be relevant and helpful if I pursue my argument from now on in reference to Dr. Toynbee's views on Judaism and its history.

I believe that the lack of respect and the air of irritation, if not downright hostility, which mark Professor Toynbee's approach to Jewish history, stand on a par with his violent reaction to Europecentrism, and that both are derived from a deep sense of guilt towards the colonial peoples and a corresponding collapse of European self-confidence.

Among the terms most frequently used by Toynbee and the phenomena most strongly condemned you will find pride, hubris, egotism, self-centredness, self-idolization, self-assertion. Ultimately the whole centuries-long relationship between the West and the East is made to appear as one of sustained aggression by insatiable avarice against essentially contemplative and pacific civilizations. Church militant, European nationalism and racialism, modern imperialism, acquisitive capitalism, and also in some of its aspects revolutionary conquering Communism are only phases and versions, as it were, of the sin of pride. Far from having its cause in intellectual or spiritual superiority, the victory of the West over the East and other non-European peoples is due to one single factor – technological mastery. The Western absorption in techniques and their utilization goes to show that Western man was much less anxious to know the truth than he was eager to turn discoveries and inventions into instruments of self-aggrandizement and dominion. The Chinese fathomed some of the mysteries of science long before the Europeans, but they had no interest in utilitarian application.

The sin of pride carries with it its own punishment. Hubris prepares its own undoing. Greed, expanding and conquering, brings about irreconcilable social cleavages and antagonisms within expanding society, and bitter resentment among the conquered and the subdued races. The internal proletariat, alienated from the body politic, meets the external proletariat of the enslaved nations in a feeling of common resentment. Together they evolve a system of values – a new religion – to serve as a counterpart to the values of the conquerors, and to act as a sublimating compensation for the enjoyments denied to them. Dominant society, which has waxed fat and sluggish and has succumbed to the malaise of the satiated, is sucked up from within by the new religion and simultaneously destroyed by the combined blows administered from within by the internal proletariat, and from without by the external proletariat. Western civilization, having reached this stage, can be saved only by a new universal religion, based on a synthesis of the four great creeds – Christianity, Islam, Buddhism and Hinduism. The universal religion will redeem it from the cancer of aggressive egotism by enabling it to achieve blissful reconciliation with the eternal order of things.

What place is assigned by Dr. Toynbee to Judaism in this vast scheme? He appears to be tracing back the original sin of the West, self-centred aggressive pride, to the Judaic idea of the chosen people. There seems to be some inconsistency at first sight between Toynbee's belittling of Judaism and his attributing such effectiveness to the Jewish example. A closer examination resolves the contradiction. If you call somebody conceited, you imply a definite discrepancy between intrinsic value and claim, just as, when you are saying that somebody has always had luck, you mean to suggest that his achievement is not really due to merit.

Original Hebrew society with its peculiar beliefs and ideas was according to Toynbee only a parochial, marginal community within a much wider Syriac civilization. Judaic religion was evolved in the encounter between the Syriac exiles in Babylon and the proletariat of Mesopotamia, just as again Christianity came into being in the meeting between the Jews oppressed by Rome and the proletariat of Hellenistic-Roman society.

The mystery that it was the tribal god Yahweh, and not his so much more powerful rivals within Syriac civilization, who came to be accepted as the One God of the Universe is explained by Toynbee by the all-devouring jealousy of Yahweh, who would not brook any other gods and would incite his believers to destroy all idols and break all images.

Obsessed by its tribal exclusiveness, Judaism failed to seize the chance of becoming a universal religion which incipient Christianity offered it, but rose against Rome in a nationalist uprising and was crushed. Its role was thus played out. The two thousand years of Jewish history since represent the lingering-on of a dead fossil, without any further growth. The Jewish response to the challenge of exile and persecution consisted in the maintenance of a hermetically closed and most intricate ritualistic framework, and in the diligent accumulation of great financial power.

At the end of this long period of fossilized existence, Zionism marks another outburst of tribal arrogance. Yielding to the essentially Western passion for archaization, the Jews, instead of keeping their hopes fixed on miraculous Divine deliverance, launched an attack on the Arab inhabitants of Palestine, expelled them, and set up a statelet, which in its crude, aggressive roughness combines all the disagreeable features of a garrison and the Wild West.

Imbibed by the Christian West, the Judaic spirit acted as a most potent evil factor in the history of Western civilization. The intolerant militant exclusiveness of the Church – a primary Judaic legacy – was in due course transformed into the self-idolization of parochial nationalisms, such as those of England and France. Taught by the example of Joshua's extermination of the pagan Canaanites, Puritan settlers felt no qualms in annihilating the pagan Red Indians, believing themselves to be the heirs of the Jews who were promised to inherit the earth, European imperialist nations went out to conquer the non-European races. Having turned their backs on the One God, they abandoned themselves completely to Mammon: they applied all their energies to the perfection of the means of accumulating wealth and of reaching the highest degree of rational utilitarian efficiency. In brief, the West underwent – in the words of Toynbee – a process of Judaization.

At the other end of the scale, socialism and Communism are nothing but a metamorphosis of the Judaic apocalypse; only the final consummation is again not left to the intervention of the Almighty, but transposed into the result of a violent uprising of men, accompanied by a terrible upheaval.

What has the Jewish historian, coming from general history, to say to all that? How will he define the Jewish ingredient in Western civilization?

There seems to me to be every justification for the view that there is a distinct Jewish ingredient in Western civilization, and through it in universal civilization, and that it must be sought at the central core and within the lifelines of the totality of Western civilization. This is the measure of the paradox – an essentially marginal group, said to be the most clannish of all communities, the Jews have in their tribal seclusion in Palestine as well as in their world-wide dispersion, as a spirit and as flesh and blood, played a powerful part in making a collection of tribes, communities and countries into a civilization. Needless to add that they were not alone in the field and their influence has not invariably been beneficial.

We would search in vain in the existing world or European histories an the analysis and evaluation of the Jewish ingredient. Biblical and Second Temple history is implied by them to belong rather to theology and Sunday School. If, for completeness of record, they give a chapter on ancient Israel, the fortunes of the Israelites are normally made to appear as an incidental and episodic affair. Postulating the State as the unit of history, the existing universal histories have no room for Diaspora Jewry as an identifiable entity. Jews are mentioned only incidentally in connection with trade and usury, religious persecution and emancipation, modern anti-Semitism and the Palestine mandate. It is very characteristic that H. A. L. Fisher devoted a special passage to Jews in the Introduction to his *History of Europe*. He simply did not know where to put them in the body of the work.

Universal history as the story of forces, patterns, series, trends, "according to the time and degree in which they contribute to the common fortunes of mankind" (in the words of Lord Acton) and not as a heap of stones – nations – remains still to be written. All recognition to Professor Toynbee for his pioneering venture and for asking the right and truly important questions.

I shall not belabour the obvious: that Judaism was the parent of Christianity, and that therefore almost the whole of Jewish history till Christ and through the first centuries when Christianity received its shape, either within the Jewish community or through debate with Rabbinic Judaism, and spread through the channels and instrumentality of the Jewish communities along the shores of the Mediterranean – that all that period of Jewish history is a vital chapter in world history, parochial and unimportant as tiny Jewish Palestine may have appeared to men at about the beginning of the Christian era. One can well conceive of a future Israeli historian undertaking the history of Western Christian civilization as the story of the Judaic kernel in its encounter with Greek philosophy and art, the mystery religions of the Orient, the institutions and laws of the Roman Empire, the Germanic traditions and the facts of European economy.

The Idea of the Chosen People in Western Civilization

I shall take up only the one point which Professor Toynbee thinks to be distinctly Jewish, and to form the most effective Jewish ingredient – the idea of the Chosen People. I agree as to its paramount importance. But for altogether different reasons from those of Dr. Toynbee, I think that Western civilization, and thus universal history, would not have been the same without it.

To Dr. Toynbee the whole concept signifies merely tribal exclusiveness and a conceited claim to radical superiority. He omits the attributes of "a holy nation," "a people of priests." I believe that the uniqueness of ancient Judaism did not consist so much in the monotheistic conception, traces of which we can find among neighbouring peoples, or in the moral precepts, the counterpart to which we encounter in Greek philosophy and the teachings of the Stoa, as in the idea of a whole people recognizing as its sovereign God alone. The laws under which it lives are not dictated by a ruler, are not derived from the will of the people, are not a utilitarian contrivance. Hence what Matthew Arnold called the Jewish passion for right acting as distinct from the Greek passion for right seeing and thinking as an instrument of knowing, experiencing and dominating the world around.

Now this is the secret of the victory of parochial Yahweh over Helios, god of the sun, Ammon-Ré or Marduk-Bel, and indeed over the Hellenistic philosophies like the Stoa. Not, as Toynbee says, the devouring jealousy of Yahweh, but the total and one-sided absorption of a whole people – not a sect of the chosen, or a monastic order – in the service of an impersonal idea. The teachings of other Near Eastern religions were more tolerant and more open to light and sweetness, and left very many things outside their scope. That is why they failed to revolutionize history. The Hellenistic systems are incomparable in their broad humanity, but they were addressed to and absorbed by individuals as counsels of personal perfection. Not conclusions of close discursive reasoning, but the living model and the all-absorbing passion, proved effective. From that point of view, Toynbee's attempt to blunt the sharp identity of the Judaic source by pointing to a wider Syriac context of ideas and beliefs is hardly relevant.

That which distinguishes mature Christian civilization from other civilizations is to be sought not so much in particular tenets of Christianity, to which parallels of some kind may be found in other religions, but in the fundamentally and peculiarly Western relationship between Church and State. There was no example of it in antiquity, and none to my knowledge in Islam or Eastern Asiatic civilizations. And this ingredient is substantially Jewish. The Church means in this respect the universality of believers and not merely the hierarchy. The members of the *ecclesia* are actuated by a consciousness that as a "holy nation" and a "people of priests" they belong not to the earthly state alone but to a community of transcendental laws and aims. The permanent tension between the Church and State, while neither proved able to absorb the other, is to my mind the source of the essentially Western obsession with the problem of the legitimacy of power. It is not enough that the law is promulgated by the authority who is recognized to have power to legislate. King, Parliament, the sovereign people, even Pope and Council, must all the time show their credentials to divine or natural law. Natural law of course is of Hellenistic-Roman provenance. Yet it is fair to say that if it had not been amalgamated with divine law it would have failed to become the formative influence it became. One should not underestimate the other factors which shaped Western ideas of state, law and justice, such as the Germanic traditions, feudalism, the guild system, the changes in methods of production. Yet I believe with Lord Acton that none of these was as effective as the Church and State tension, the greatest and most important receptacle of ideas and controversies, the one which, as it were, enveloped all the others and gave the general tone.

When political theorists of the West spoke of Oriental despotism, what they meant was that the Orient did not know the problem of the legitimacy of power. Power to them was a datum, a fact of nature, an elemental, amoral force given and to be taken for granted, like sunshine and rain, storm and plague. It need not always be evil and tyrannical, it may be highly beneficial. But it is given, it is there, and we have to bow to it.

Now it is this tension between Church and State, based on the idea of a chosen holy people, that gave the history of European nations its highly dynamic quality in comparison with the early stagnation of the non-European civilizations. Thanks to the Judaic concept the Papacy never could and perhaps never really wished to reduce the body of lay believers into mere receivers of grace through the instrumentality of sacramental mystery and miracle. The task of realizing the Kingdom of God was never restricted to the *ecclesia docens*. It always continued to rest on the whole body of believers. Hence the sense of dignity and awful responsibility of a Christian nation. It could not easily accept an evil King, any more than a corrupt Pope. For Christianity could never quite be reduced to a matter of personal ascetic discipline and unworldly holiness and divest itself of all responsibility for this world on the ground that its Kingdom was wholly of another world. It was thus bound to feel the permanent challenge to realize its high calling here and now. If this be true of the Catholic Church at all times, it is especially true of Calvinism and the Puritans in Britain and America.

Nationalism

There is, I submit with Dr. Toynbee, a direct line from Church militant, permeated with the Judaic idea of a holy nation of priests, to modern nationalism, with its ideology of the chosen people. We are only too painfully aware in this twentieth century of the terrible ravages wrought by nationalism run wild. Yet it would be wrong for the historian to forget that, in its first flush in the first half of the nineteenth century, the national idea was, in the mouth of a Mazzini, and indeed even Fichte, not to speak of the Polish Mickiewicz, a prophetic clarion call to spiritual regeneration. Far from proclaiming tribal war on neighbours thought to be inferior, it imposed a special mission, a particularly strenuous obligation, on one's own nation within the scheme of mankind's endeavour to achieve higher things and universal freedom. It is indeed most strange to read today Fichte's boast that the German nation, the Urvolk of Europe, would not demean itself by joining the general bloody scramble for territories and colonies, and would take no part in the squalid game of political and mercantilist rivalry. The only true original nation in Europe, since all others had their thoughts and feelings shaped by an acquired language, Latin or German, the Germans were destined to maintain, with brows furrowed and hearts held at the highest pitch of concentration, a special communion with eternal values. Everyone is familiar with the religious Messianic overtones of Mazzini's philosophy of nationalism, with such slogans as "God and the people," "nationality is a mission," "nation means sacrifice," with Mazzini's conception of patriotism as a counterpart to selfish utilitarianism and moral self-indulgence, with his vision of a federation of free peoples, each with its mission, under the inspiring guidance of *Roma terza* – Rome of the people – the first Rome having been that of the Emperors, and the second that of the Popes. Mickiewicz, like Mazzini, consciously drew on Biblical ideas and imagery in describing Poland as the suffering Remnant of Israel, destined to atone for the sins of other nations and redeem them through her own self-reliance.

Self-surrender and Self-assertion

Professor Toynbee wrings his hands over the horrors brought about by modern nationalism and its evil offspring imperialism, seeing in them nothing but irredeemable evil, pride and hubris, in such crass contrast to the quietist broad tolerance of the Eastern religions and civilizations.

It seems to me that in his self-prostration before the East and his self-flagellation as a Westerner, Dr. Toynbee has missed a truth of awful import, a mystery of tragic grandeur: the ambivalence with which the whole of the Western achievement is charged from the start. It is an infinitely tragic fact that great good is somehow always mixed up with terrible evil, that the worst seems always to be the degeneration of the best, that some Hegelian *List der Vernunft* – trick of Universal Reason – complicates in a sardonic manner the yearning for self-surrender with the craving for self-assertion.

Professor Toynbee is filled with reverence for those Eastern civilizations whose religions are a syncretistic synthesis of various, and often heterogeneous, strands, and are ultimately the concern of the individual only, and whose Churches know no intolerant militancy.

He is attracted by those vast conglomerations of men who are not primarily political animals at all, and whose passions for power are held back by the highly developed capacity for contemplative communion with the invisible world, and the attainment of that peace which passeth understanding, for which we all are straining in vain, and of which only very few chosen in our midst ever catch a glimpse.

Nearer home, Dr. Toynbee selects the Ottoman Empire for special commendation. That was a system in which radical, linguistic, religious communities lived as Milets side by side on a completely non-political basis. He is not troubled by the fact that the Turkey of the Sultans was a byword for despotism and corrupting bribery; that even the Ulema, the supreme Moslem Court of experts in Islam, was most of the time unable to restrain the cruel vagaries of personal despotism; that in such a regime there could be no individual rights and no corporate consciousness and self-respect; that only a palace plot or the assassin's dagger, and at a lower level bribe and flattery, were any defence against the pure arbitrariness of brute power; and that consequently complete stagnation froze all cultural endeavour and spiritual vitality. In the vast empires, in which there is no political life and no popular passions, the individual may at times reach as very high degree of personal unworldly perfection. But it is at the cost of the vitality and the moral advancement of the body social.

It is a curious thing that a man so sensitive to any sign of arrogance and pride, and who over acres of self-analysis recording his visitations makes such tremendous efforts to be humble, should at the same time be so fascinated – as Dr. Toynbee is – by colossal dimensions, the mighty barbarian conquerors wading in blood up to their knees, building sky-high pyramids of the skulls of their slaughtered foes. Professor Toynbee again and again calls England and France parochial, puffed-up little countries.

I hope it will not appear impertinent if a person born in a place where there was not even a railway, where no one had ever heard of plumbing, and water had to be fetched in buckets from a well half a mile away, and who chose to live in a country with no territory but only frontiers, and frontiers permanently ablaze at that, were to tell Professor Toynbee that there is no shame in belonging to England – a piffling little country, and no stigma in belonging to Europe – a dreadful sort of province.

The finest flowering of culture never occurred on the vast

expanse of steppe and desert, but in tiny, overcrowded, noisy and proud communities, such as Athens, Jerusalem, Alexandria, Florence and Amsterdam. Why damn vitality by calling it arrogance? The truth of the matter is that in such an ambitious undertaking as the "Study of History," embracing all ages and all civilizations into one system, with the help of tidy schemata, sweeping generalizations and quantitative measurements, there can be no understanding for the unique phenomenon, the local idiom and the particular concatenation of data and circumstances, no eye for the exquisite miniature, and nothing of that "feel" for the specific situation, limpid and throbbing with real life, which comes from long meditation and loving immersion.

The Jewish Ingredient in Industrial Civilization

In the last two centuries Western history indeed became universal history. The non-European civilizations sunk in a state of languor or atrophy had their fate shaped by the expansion of Western capitalism, which turned the whole world into one economic and cultural unit, till in our own days the essentially European ideologies, nationalism, democracy and Communism stimulated the Asiatic and African peoples to seek self-determination and ways of self-assertion.

I start by agreeing with Dr. Toynbee that in forging the various instruments for the unification of the world by the West, the Jewish ingredient played the role of a powerful catalyst. Jews as living men, and not merely the Jewish spiritual legacy, moved up into the focal region of world history in the nineteenth and twentieth centuries.

One need not belittle the part of Jews in maintaining international trade almost alone in the early Middle Ages, in serving Christian scholarship as interpreters and transmitters of ancient wisdom from Arab translations and in acting as a lever in early urban colonization. Whether you call them rapacious usurers, or bankers, as one calls the more respectable, because richer, Christian Medicis and Fuggers, Lombards and Templars – whether the Jews went into the business out of their own choice or because all other avenues were closed to them – they kept up for centuries a rudimentary credit system in Europe. Nevertheless, I rather hold the somewhat chilling view that, with the exception of Spain, Holland and Poland, the history of most European nations would not have been very significantly different had there been no Jews – but only the Judaic heritage – in Europe between the Crusades and the nineteenth century. They had been expelled from a number of countries for most of that time and the living ghetto commanded too little respect to be of actual immediate influence on a society so highly stratified as European society was for centuries.

It was given to the Jews to affect the structural framework of universal history again in the last hundred and fifty years.

I believe it would be legitimate for the universal historian to call the age since the French and Industrial Revolutions the era of industrial civilization based on contract. This formulation takes account of the two most salient features of the period – industrialism and democratic growth. Furthermore, it implies that capitalism and the various forms of socialism and communism are only two poles of the same development, and not phenomena on two different planes. It then postulates a type of spiritual-cultural superstructure evolved by the essentially universal and cosmopolitan character of industrial civilization. The main point to be borne in mind in this formulation is the transformation from a society based on status and on more or less rigid patterns into a society based on contract, in other words, on individual and social mobility. This meant an entirely new situation for Jews, one of unlimited possibilities.

Our thought and formulations need to take full account of nuances in order not to overstate our case. None of the early inventors was a Jew, and there were to my knowledge hardly any early captains of industry among identifiable Jews. Werner Sombart's attempt – as a replica to Max Weber's thesis about the Puritans and the rise of capitalism – to make the Jews of the seventeenth-century bearers of early capitalism has long been discredited. Yet it is true to say that in the building up of the sinews of the modern international capitalist economy the part of the Jews, especially on the continent, was that of pioneers and catalysts *par excellence.* International credit, banking and exchange, joint stock companies, telegraphic news agencies, railway networks, chain stores, methods of mass production and mass marketing, the media and the organization of mass entertainment, experimentation in new techniques, in brief the lifelines of a universal economy, were in so many cases laid and set working by Jews who thus played, in the words of Addison, the part of nails and pegs in the world economy.

The abstract, rational nexus holding together concrete, disparate detail was more quickly and easily grasped by people with a long training in intellectual speculation and in the art of assessing the data of a situation and its distant consequences. Not place-bound, the emancipated and detribalized Jew was unhampered by routine and conservative attachments, and his international connections helped him to build or to force the hinges of new artificial frameworks. It is in the nature of a marginal community, especially one living in metropolitan centres, like the Jews, to acquire the refined sensitiveness of an exposed nerve, and to be the first to sense the trend and shape of things to come. Hence the proneness and courage to experiment. Emancipated formally, but not really and fully admitted as equals, lacking the prestige of lineage and establishment, while eager for a place in the sun and restlessly ill at ease as people in ambiguous situations are, the Jews would throw all their energies and pent-up intensity into the two levers of power open to them, economic activity and intellectual prowess. Centuries of disciplined living and sober calculation would prevent ambition from dissipating itself in a haphazard, chaotic manner. Vitality would be turned into a strictly rational and well-regulated instrument of power designed to obtain maximum results at the lowest cost.

Revolutionary Messianism

As to the Jewish ingredients at the other pole of industrial civilization, revolutionary Messianism, I have come to the conclusion on somewhat closer study that it was to a large extent the Jewish Messianic vision of history that made the Industrial Revolution appear not merely as another crisis and another bad spell but as an apocalyptic hour leading to some preordained final *dénouement*, and that the social protest of its victims no longer took the character of another desperate, elemental *jacquerie*, but became a part of the preparation for a Day of Judgment, after which justice and peace would come to reign supreme, and history would as it were only begin, with all conflicts and contradictions resolved.

The earliest prophet of socialist transformation in nineteenth-century Europe, Saint-Simon, quite explicitly links up with the Jewish Messianic expectation. The Jews, who were the leading spirits in his extremely fascinating and influential school, most emphatically voiced their conviction of carrying on the perennial Messianic mission of Judaism. Their future city of universal perfect harmony was to be guided by technicians and bankers, who were at the same time to be artists and priests, and was to be founded on a universal religion of humanity, *Nouveau Christianisme*, with the old division into State and Church, matter and spirit, freedom and duty, personal and general good, theory and practice done away with for ever. It is very significant that the Jewish Saint-Simonists, the Rodrigues, Pereiras, d'Eichthals should in the course of time have become the architects of France's industrial and financial revolution and of much of Europe's industry and banking.

The deep, ingrained experience of history as the unfolding of a pattern of judgment and as the realization of a design of deliverance makes the Jew almost incapable of taking history for granted as an eternal meaningless cycle. Time must have a stop. History must have a *dénouement.* At the same time the lack of roots in a concrete, given tradition, with its instinctive certainties and the comfort of smooth, almost automatic procedures, combines with the absence of experience of practical government to turn many a Jew into a doctrinaire and impatient blueprint addict. Where there is a prophetic temperament, as in the case of a Karl Marx, there comes forth relentless denunciation. A terrific, fiery over-simplification reduces all, human laziness and thoughtlessness, the weakness of the flesh and the heterogeneity of impulse, peculiarity of tradition and complexity of situation, into nothing but greed, falsehood, hypocrisy – all part of a kingdom of the devil – to be replaced in the imminent future by a kingdom of God. Suspended between heaven and earth, rejected and unadmitted, tormented by the humiliations, complexities and ambiguities of his situation, many a young Jew threw himself with the deepest yearning and passion into the arms of the religion of revolution.

We all know the inhumanities of capitalism at the height of its imperialistic expansion, and the perverse denial of traditional morality, man's freedom and dignity which accompany the attempts to satisfy the Messianic longing for salvation by a totalitarian system. This erosion of ideals has no particular relevance to Jews *qua* Jews. For it is rooted in the tragic condition of man as such, in the essential ambivalence of things human and social, the Christian would say – original sin. It is at the same time not to be denied that the surplus of intensity among Jews, peculiar to a marginal minority in constant need of justifying its separateness by self-assertion, has its own polar ambivalence: besides idealistic self-dedication to causes and things of the mind, there is a particularly harsh, shrill and unscrupulous style of Jewish self-seeking.

Cosmopolitan Culture

We come now to the Jewish ingredient in the universal or cosmopolitan culture, characteristic of industrial civilization based on contract instead of status, and sustained by media of mass communication.

It is one of the commonplaces of Jewish apologists to emphasize the fact that Jews have enriched the life and culture of every country in which they have lived. Yet – a not very comforting thought – I do not believe that the culture of England, France, Italy and even pre-nineteenth-century Germany would have been very significantly different, had there been no Jews in those countries. Modern universal civilization is, however, unthinkable without Marx, Freud or Einstein, who have moulded the consciousness of modern mankind.

Isaiah Berlin has given an acute explanation of the contrast between the superb achievements of Jews in the sciences and music, and their rather inferior showing in literature. Jewish writers have excelled in biography and the biographical novel – Maurois, Zweig. They have been highly stimulating on the human situation as created by the complexities and dilemmas of contemporary life – Arthur Koestler, Arthur Miller, Ilya Ehrenburg. They were helped in that by their psychological acumen, which came to their race from the age-long need to adjust itself to others, as well as by their being simultaneously in the very heart of metropolitan nerve centres, and at the same time detached, while over-sensitive. Yet, while being highly communicable and often stirring and provocative, their writings do not represent great literature. It is not enough to be able to penetrate – even lovingly – into the inner springs and hidden recesses of men and societies. Vigour and intimacy come to the novel from the subtle, almost unconscious and automatic associations which are not acquired with the help of the algebraic language of science but imperceptibly lived within a specific ancient tradition. This is why Yiddish literature had such vigour as well as warmth.

The literature produced by Jewish writers in various languages in centres like old Vienna, where Jews very often formed the nucleus of the most advanced and cosmopolitan vanguard as producers as well as consumers, served for all its lack of greatness as a barometer and stimulant of universal significance.

The passionate patriotism of a Disraeli, a Walter Rathenau, a Léon Blum had perhaps greater intensity and depth than the devotion of an ordinary British, German or French Christian statesman to his country. It was conditioned by an agonized yearning for something romantically idealized which was not a simple datum to be taken for granted. It had a deeper and more articulate understanding of the national tradition and its peculiarities than was the case with a "normal" leader to whom this tradition acted in the form of spontaneous reflexes. And it was always more universal, or more imperial (as in the case of Disraeli) in its awareness.

Far from giving support to any doctrine of race in the biological sense, our terms of reference have been throughout the latter part of the argument a spiritual legacy and facts of history and social psychology on the one hand, and the individualistic mobility of industrial civilization on the other.

The fortunes of Jews under Hitler may in this respect rank as a focal point of twentieth-century world history; not merely because of the enormity of the crime perpetrated and the suffering inflicted, with the help of scientific long-term planning and execution, or because the mass violation of the sanctity of human life was calculated not to stop with the Jews but was bound to undermine the most vital foundations of our civilization and open a general race slaughter. Hitler's racialism signified an attempt to reverse the main trend of modern Western civilization, and to return from individualistic contract to deterministic patterns of race, caste and tribe, through a denial of the unity of mankind. It is no accident that Nazism found it necessary to reinterpret the whole of history as a permanent life-and-death struggle between Nordic Aryanism and the Jewish spirit, attributing to Jews a significance and effectiveness which the most extreme Jewish chauvinists would not dream of claiming.

The marginal situation of the Jews, turning them into an exposed nerve of exceptional sensitiveness, enables them to act as pioneers, but makes them also the first victims of any storm or disease. People mean this when they call the situation of the Jews a barometer of the health and balance of a society and age. This marginal situation coupled with the extreme metropolitization of Jews, i.e. their apparently irresistible tendency to congregate in vast cities and around central and highly sensitive arteries of social organization, results in Jews being so often swept into the very heart of a national and international upheaval. It is tempting to speculate on the part played by the exploitation of anti-Semitic instincts in Hitler's rise to power and the fascination he exercised outside

Germany, as well as on the contribution to Hitler's downfall made by a Jewry driven to desperation.

Israel and the Diaspora

Our theme has been Jewish history from the point of view of universal history. Although the Palestine problem has been one of the focal points of international politics, and albeit that little country of strange destinies is once more a centre of world attention, it is still too early to say whether the extraordinary fact, so heavily charged with symbolism, that the return of Jews to Zion coincides with the general retreat of Europe from Asia, is going to have greater significance than the establishment of just another little state among the many new independent states which have come into existence in this internationalist twentieth century.

In Professor Toynbee's violent condemnation, Zionism appears as an integral part of Western imperialistic rapacity, made effective by technological superiority and shabby American electioneering intrigues. The music of Messianic hope kept alive for two thousand years, the saga-like quality of the return to Zion, the historic perspectives and vistas opened by the event – in the words of Sir Winston Churchill an "event in world history to be viewed in the perspective not of a generation or a century but in the perspective of 1000, 2000 or even 3000 years" – the element of awful tragedy in the fact that the restoration of Jews to Israel had to be effected through a terrible conflict with the Arab world – right against right – fail to strike a chord.

We have instead the silly, ignorant nonsense about Jews taking over the Western heresy of archaization; the tasteless, sermonizing reproach for not trusting to God's miraculous deliverance, and for demeaning ourselves to such unworthy and petty things as State, flag, army and postage stamps; a selective method of presenting facts, which amounts to telling an untruth, for instance, failure to mention the United Nations decision, representing world conscience, on partition, or to refer by a single word to the invasion of Palestine by five Arab armies. We then get the horrifying comparison of the treatment of the Arab population by the Jews with the extermination of six million Jews by Hitler, and finally the crowning sanctimonious blasphemy in the prophecy that on the Day of Judgment the crime of the Jews will be judged graver than that of the Nazis.

There are one or two pointers to the universal historian meditating on the future of Jews within the scheme of world history. There seems to be something almost providential in the way in which the two new centres, Israel and the United States, were established just on the eve of the catastrophe which put an end to a history of some 1500 to 2000 years of European Jewry. There is also a striking analogy between the present relationship between Israel and Anglo-Saxon, especially American, Jewry, and the relationship at the time of the Second Temple between Jewish Palestine and the Jewish communities along the Mediterranean in the Roman Empire on one side, and the Jewish conglomeration in Mesopotamia on the other. It is a fact of very great importance that English has come to be the language of the majority of the Jewish people.

The problems of the Palestine/Mediterranean axis were very similar to the problems of the Israel/Anglo-Saxon axis today, including the annual United Jewish Appeal, the problems of assimilation, mixed loyalties and so on. The encounter of Judaism and Hellenism, and the synthesis of the two in the Alexandria of Philo paved the way for the triumph of Christianity. Is it too fanciful to suggest that New York of today may be destined to play the part of Jewish Alexandria in the twentieth century? There is much food for speculation in the fact that tiny Israel on the troubled eastern shore of the Mediterranean has a kind of counterpart in the most vital country in the world at present, and one which seems to be destined to set the tone in the days to come.

If it was given to the Jews to make some mark on world history it was not because, as someone said, God was kind to the Jews in scattering them among the nations, but because they had fashioned their real contribution in their own country – the Judaic heritage – and were dispersed only after they had been moulded into a unique phenomenon.

No historian, I believe, can be a complete rationalist. He must be something of a poet, he must have a little of the philosopher, and he must be touched by some form of mysticism. The sorting out of evidence, the detective skill in discovering inaccuracy and inconsistency are of little help when the historian reaches the hard residue of mystery and enigma, the ultimate causes and the great problems of human life.

The Jewish historian becomes a kind of martyr in his permanent anguished intimacy with the mystery of Jewish martyrdom and survival. Whether he be orthodox in his beliefs or has discarded all practice, he cannot help being sustained by a faith which can neither be proved nor disproved.

I believe that notwithstanding all the vexations and horrors, squalor and bloodshed, seeming impasses and entanglements caused by emergency and inescapable necessity, all so reminiscent incidentally of the times of Ezra and Nehemiah, Israel is one day going to be spiritually significant, and, in conjunction with the Jewish Diaspora, spiritually effective in the world.

History would somehow make no sense otherwise.

Published by the Hillel Foundation, London, 1957. The lecture was delivered at the Gustave Tuck Theatre, University College, London, on October 17, 1956, under the chairmanship of the Rt. Hon. Viscount Samuel.

Note

1 It will be said the State of Israel will break this perennial law. Marshal Bulganin's violent ultimatum to Ben-Gurion, with its dark but explicit threat to "the very existence of Israel," was an eloquent comment on this very problem. The Soviet leader would never have used such terms in a note to another small and young state, Lebanon or Libya. Jewish rights to Israel are not taken for granted. One is reminded of the famous words of General Bonaparte to the Allied representatives on the non-recognition of the French Republic by the old monarchies – "France is like the sun, she needs no one's recognition, she is there in blinding splendour." Tiny Israel needs recognition more than any other political entity in a world in which the existence of a state is – in international law – proved solely by the fact of its recognition by other states. At a deeper level, we are led to conclude, Israel is still part of the problematic ambiguity attaching to Jewish existence everywhere and at all times. This is fate. And the historian need not be ashamed to use a word so heavily charged. The fate of a nation, like that of a person, may be the working-out of the traumas of early childhood, in short the outcome of some basic decisive experience. The belief that they are a chosen people, coupled with the fact of exile, produced a traumatic twist in the Jewish psyche which made the Jews impervious to the assimilating influences of Hellenism and Rome. They could hardly be absorbed by the amorphous barbarians in whose midst they found themselves in the early Middle Ages. Not only were they the bearers of a higher and more ancient civilization, by then they were also burdened with the charge that they had killed Christ.

The Jewish Intellectuals in Politics – New Factors in an Ancient Tradition

I happened to be visiting California at the height of the McCarthy scare, just at the moment when the Oppenheimer case exploded and I stumbled upon a leading article in one of the Californian newspapers characteristically entitled "What is an egghead?" I was reminded of the article when my quest for a definition of an intellectual in the established dictionaries of our time failed me. All they had to say was that "intellectual" appertains to the intellect, which appertains to reason, which again appertains to the faculty of thinking and understanding, and so on.

Indeed, the Californian leader writer was more helpful. In calling Robert Oppenheimer a classical sample of an egghead, the author defined the type as a man who may be most brilliant in some specific and limited field, lacks entirely in common sense, and yet, in his arrogance, sets himself up as judge over everything, refusing to accept and bow to the general consensus of his ordinary fellow men, to a point of becoming self-willed and dangerous to society.

By implication the writer was calling upon society to "erase this infamy" in the name of democracy. Yet, we have been accustomed to associate the breed of intellectuals with service to human causes, defence of moral values, and devotion to the ideals of freedom.

It is no accident that the dictionaries fail to refer the term "intellectual" to the role of intellectuals in society and politics, which concern us here, and would not, of course, demean themselves to deal with the egghead.

This only goes to confirm the rule, which has been observed by historians, that all the "isms," which the intellectual species has appropriated – despotism, imperialism, liberalism, conservatism, socialism, communism, fascism – have started as emotive and polemical terms, war-cries or terms of abuse. Then came the scholars and set themselves to analyse them, and weave systematic patterns around them, till they were gradually raised to the dignity of scientific terms.

To start with, then, I would define as intellectual a person who is worried by general problems. It is not so much bookish learning, intellectual curiosity or dialectical skill that single him out, as a preponderance of reason and analysis over instinct, feeling and will; a penchant for abstract, generalised thinking at the cost of realistic and empirical sobriety and attention to concrete detail; an obsessive preoccupation with the question of ends and means coming between him and the objective.

The intellectual is conditioned to operate with scientific modes of thought, to look for the general and the recurrent; he has a liking for neat classifications, while politics, like life, is untidy, messy, replete with exceptions, and each case in it is ultimately unique. Hence the natural inclination of the intellectual to be a doctrinaire and to miss the peculiarity of the given situation, and to kick against the inexorable limitations and compulsions of the concrete set of circumstances. At the same time, the intellectual has too refined a critical sense to accept cut and dried solutions, to reduce all colours and shades to black and white, right and wrong. He pauses to analyse and to weigh, and this intellectual preoccupation becomes to him an end in itself.

In his intense awareness of historical precedents, the intellectual is often so hypnotised by them that, instead of applying himself to the matter at hand, he is all the time comparing himself to men in similar situations in the past; he is not doing, but acting a role.

The faculty most vital to the politician is the will and the ability to take decisions, and not critical insight; the power to reduce complex issues to their simplest elements, and not a comprehensive all round view, taking in all shades and nuances. Ultimately politics is a struggle for power; let us be charitable and add – the power to realise ideals and carry out policies.

The road to power is a warpath upon which the aspirant has to get the better of other contenders, and that competition is not a simple battle of wits or a dialectician's match. The political world is not a world of reason. Without an insatiable thirst for power, a very thick skin, a conscience which is not too squeamish and not too fastidious, a self-assurance that borders on arrogance, and indeed a ruthless capacity to inflict pain, a man may never get to the top.

Where the end is so ardently desired, the means must be willed. The intellectual, even if he is able to brace himself for all the gruelling tests, so often collapses half way at the awful realisation that, after so much trickery and compromise, half truth or sheer lying, degrading makeshifts and cruel wounding of susceptibilities, the fruit when reached will be too sour, and everything all round too corroded and rotten for real and fundamental repair; and radical betterment is the intellectual's dream.

Not all have the nerve to act on the Hegelian device that in this world good and evil, sublime impersonal idealism and cruel selfish passion are inextricably mixed up, and History has willed it that great (and evil) men, like Napoleon, driven by demoniacal urges and pursuing consciously nothing but personal aggrandisement should nevertheless, in spite of themselves, carry out beneficial designs, and jog mankind along with them on the path of progress; and that the flower of fine human values should blossom forth amidst wreckage and squalor, blood and mud, once the hurricane has subsided and the sun has rekindled the dew with blinding splendour.

Now, when saying intellectuals, one finds oneself almost inadvertently adding Jewish intellectuals. The other day at high table in Oxford a very eminent president of one of the great American universities was trying to explain to his insular co-diners the workings of American society.

"Oh well," he said, "the New York intellectuals, but they are all . . .," and catching sight of me, he suddenly had a fit of coughing. He had forgotten, when warming up to his subject, who was sitting opposite him.

While it is, of course, not true that every intellectual in America or elsewhere is a Jew, we must take it for granted that almost every Jew active in public life is an intellectual, except indeed – for good reasons – in England.

There is a grain of truth in the definition which I heard from a brilliant international Jewish intellectual, of the complete intellectual as a person who had forgotten his Hebrew. It is no accident that of the three figures with whom James Joll deals in his book *Intellectuals in Politics*, two were Jews – Leon Blum and Walter Rathenau – while the third, Marinetti, was never an active statesman. The founder of Futurism only served as an inspiration to Fascism.

In a sense the intellectual in politics is a modern phenomenon, as are Jews and Jewish intellectuals in politics. In earlier days statecraft and politics were the business of those whose birth had destined them for it: kings and aristocrats. Legists were employed by rulers to explain the law and to draft decrees, and theoreticians were in the background, their view heeded and made use of when considered helpful.

Politics were a kind of husbandry to princes, and they had hardly any room for ideology. Of course there was a Church based on most fundamental and rigid principles. Churchmen were almost by definition intellectuals, and they had at the same time to guide the destinies not merely of an enormous complex of power, interests and institutions that were the Church, but very often also to assume responsibility for the affairs of the secular State directly, or to influence them indirectly.

But there is one vital difference between the clerics of the past and the clerics of the modern age. The former constituted not merely a class, but were bound by a most cohesive body of doctrine and subject to a most tightly knit organization. The modern intellectual belongs to no estate, and even after joining a movement, party or group, feels bound by no ready-made programme. He would accept no orders conflicting with his conscience. He recognises ultimately only one superior – his own judgment. This is his strength and his weakness.

Another difference has to be borne in mind. The role of the intellectuals has not been the same in countries with a long and unbroken tradition of parliamentary government and freedom of expression, as in countries which have never known them, or lacked them for most of their history, and developed them only in recent times.

In oppressed nations, like the Italians and the Poles in the nineteenth century, or in Tsarist Russia, to a large extent even in France, where illiberal foreign or native governments prevented any form of free political activity, poets, writers, thinkers, scholars, artists – in brief, intellectuals – became the mouthpiece of the nation. The people looked to them for inspiration, guidance and example, and often comfort and solace.

This is why those intellectuals – a Mazzini and a Herzen, a Mickiewicz and a Michelet, indeed a Fichte and a Treitschke – became prophets, to an extent to which even John Stuart Mill or Carlyle, Cardinal Newman or Ruskin, never were in England.

Moreover, in those circumstances, the role of the intellectuals grew identified with struggle against oppression and injustice, and for human rights and national freedom, liberty of expression and the dignity of labour. In other words, to be an intellectual meant to be a progressive, a humanitarian, just as in a certain propagandist sense in our own day, it means to be a fighter for peace, an enemy of imperialism and a crusader for racial equality.

The politics of the intellectuals in those times and in the countries in question were not concerned with practical immediate issues, nor with responsibility for taking decisions and choosing between pressing alternatives. Men were preoccupied with principles, ideals and visions, blue-prints and sweeping short cuts. They were propelled by resentment and anger, were filled with longings and hopes, and in the case of the Russian intelligentsia, they groaned under a bad guilty conscience.

Very often mystical poetry became the real fatherland. National history and mythology were a substitute for a State Constitution. A journal like Herzen's *Kolokol*, and later *Iskra*, was in a way the forerunner of a regime and the formulation of doctrine, and doctrinal disputes were pursued with a passion and abandon which the conflicts between parties and classes in a country like England had never known.

This was an ambiance made for Jews, and the Jews were made for it. For centuries they were a closed sect on the margin of society. Their very existence in a hostile world was not a function of natural conditions and concrete circumstances, but the triumph of a will which ignored them or in an unyielding effort succeeded in overcoming them.

Their constitution was a Law given to their ancestors millennia earlier, and while living under heavy skies and in countries of green pastures, they would with compulsive, relentless stubbornness refer every action, every minute of their lives, every experience, to a written constitution, codified against a background of parched rock and desert.

Although they owned not a square yard of land, never touched a plough, and often could not distinguish between wheat and barley, they would spend their days studying the laws of the Shemita (the seventh Sabbatical year), and the prescriptions about harvest gifts to the poor in the country of their ancestors. Entirely dominated by a distant past, there beckoned to the Jews from the indefinite future a vision of sudden release and total redemption. In brief, they lived entirely in the past and in the future.

Finally, while having a certain form of secular self-government, their real leadership was that of scholars and men of the Book. With this mentality and habits of mind, the emancipated Jews found themselves almost overnight atomised and unattached.

In the early days, emancipation meant of course an end to Jewish clannishness. It implied being like everybody else, entering the great society of free and equal men, who recognise neither class nor sect, no differences of birth or creed, status or place of origin. That was more true on paper than in life, and the Jews for obvious reasons took those promises much more seriously than the gentiles.

Social stratification, classes and groups remained pretty real, and the Jews found entrance into them very hard, and even after forcing their way into them were made to feel very ill at ease. And so, naturally, the actual was not accepted by them as real, and that which was becoming, destined to be, the should-and-would-be of the doctrine and the vision assumed the character of the natural and the real.

Alienation combined with a prophetic tradition, deep sympathy for all victims of oppression and injustice, placed the Jewish intellectual well to the Left in the camp working for change, and dreaming of some final preordained, salvationist dénouement. He was always in this a few paces ahead of his fellow-workers.

The problems of the Jewish intellectual in politics may thus be defined as that of an encounter between outsiders and organic entities; between the urge for change and forces of conservatism; between rational resolve and the recalcitrance of matter.

The first name to spring to our lips when our question is asked, is of course that of Karl Marx. Yet it is doubtful whether he could be regarded as typical of the Jewish intellectual in politics. For one thing Marx was so exceptional and extraordinary a phenomenon that he was a world to himself. It is no use comparing him to others, or trying to measure others up to him.

And then, when all is said and done, Marx's real contribution was made from the British Museum Reading Rooms, at a time when he deliberately cut himself off from all party activity and contacts with the emigré revolutionaries in England after 1848. His activities in the obscure revolutionary conventicles on the eve of the 1848 revolutions, and as editor of the *Neue Rheinische Zeitung* in 1848–9, and later his role as leader and wire-puller in the First International, however effective, do not make his life the life of a politician.

Karl Marx was an extraordinary mixture of a monumental power of systematisation, which succeeds in inter-relating and integrating all disparate facts, data and aspects with a relentless passionate urge to unmask all pretence and hypocrisy, and reduce vast complex issues to first elements of morality, so as to provide the grandiose vision of a total breakthrough from darkness to light, from bondage to freedom. One need not apologise for trying to detect in all this the workings of a prophetic and Talmudic tradition.

Romantics and Revolutionaries: the Zionist Movement and the State of Israel

The two outstanding Jewish intellectuals in nineteenth-century politics are Lassalle and Disraeli, two great spellbinders whose meteoric careers and fabulous personalities will never cease to fascinate, and besides whom the Laskers, the Bambergers, the Gabriel Riessers, Cremieux, and others, look like pale insignificant figures. And although one became the founder of the German working class movement and its fiery tribune, and the other won undying fame as the founder of the reformed Tory party and Prime Minister of England, the two indeed have much in common and *mutatis mutandis* embody the same problem. They both took their respective countries and movements by storm, indeed forced themselves upon them.

Both had exceptionally colourful personalities. They were great romantics, with a penchant for striking poses and taking up attitudes that repelled their more restrained and more puritanical contemporaries as sheer exhibitionist charlatanism. Theirs was the egotism of a climber which suggests the unscrupulous opportunism of the adventurer.

That the behaviour of Lassalle and Disraeli, especially in the early part of their careers, would not stand the test of dignified rectitude would be hard to deny. The point, however, is that restrained, modest behaviour would have taken them nowhere. They would never have climbed out of the insignificance of journalism and the authorship of glossy novels.

A Lord Derby or Prince von Hohenlohe could afford to behave like a gentleman. He was already there; he had no need to climb. A Jewish boy from Breslau and son of shopkeepers, used to bazaar haggling, and a debt-ridden literateur without even a university degree, had an enormous amount of climbing to do, and had to resort to all kinds of tricks, stunts and even scandalous actions in order to attract attention, and then do the impossible in transforming the feelings of revulsion, distrust and contempt they evoked into recognition, appreciation, respect and love.

"At last I have got to the top of the greasy pole" – Disraeli is reported to have murmured, when he received the call from the Queen to form a government. There is something quite monumental in this seemingly cynical exclamation.

It seems to me that in his repellent confession that he hated nothing more than Jews and intellectuals, and had the misfortune to be both, Lassalle, who as a boy dreamt of being a Judah Maccabeus to his suffering people, was expressing the same sentiment of guilt-ridden resignation that in order to become known he had to resort to such theatrical stunts as becoming the defender and saviour of a wronged lady of aristocratic birth, turning her family troubles into a *cause célèbre* which shook Germany, and inciting accomplices hypnotised by his personality to commit criminal deeds for this romantic cause.

Disraeli a little earlier was raising eyebrows and giggles with his trinkets and rings, and dumbfounding some and thrilling others with his savage, vicious attacks on Sir Robert Peel, a man of deep integrity and sensitiveness who after infinite heart-searching changed his convictions. The very fact that neither of the two young Jews chose the party which would have been natural for them to join, a bourgeois liberal party, is also significant. They would not take on the colour of their surroundings or merge into them.

Well, why did they not both stay in the station which their birth had assigned to them? They were both passionately conscious of their intellectual superiority. Disraeli's letter to his sister on his first visit to the House of Commons saying that he was sure he could do better than any and all of the speakers he had listened to, has parallels in Lassalle's correspondence. And that was an age which believed in careers being open to all talents.

Both were, however, genuine idealists. Their hankering after aristocracy and their love of pomp and circumstance was probably the expression of a longing for that "drapery of life" above squalor and shabby dealings.

The contribution of both, the conservative and the revolutionary, was in initiating change and innovation, and not in simply weaving the thread of tradition. The Tory party had to make peace with the nineteenth century, but it needed an outsider, sufficiently detached, a visionary not bound by routine and habit, to effect the transformation of an aristocratic coterie into a mass party, to replace defence of vested interest with a nationalist-imperialist ideology, and to turn irrational conservatism into great poetry.

The depth of Disraeli's idealism is revealed in his proud single-handed struggle for Jewish equality, in the teeth of the bitter opposition of the whole Tory party, and it was he, the Tory, who coined the famous phrase about the two nations. He spoke with moving compassion of the sufferings of the submerged half of the nation, and swept almost by ruse the hordes of "heavy, stupid country gentlemen" into voting for a Reform Bill that gave the working classes parliamentary representation.

He remained feared, distrusted, half-loved, half-hated, shrouded in his private world of fancy in which the immemorial antiquity of the Jews, a priestly-princely Hebrew ancestry, and the chosenness of a race destined to rule the world were strangely blended with medieval tournaments of the Young Tory romantics, visions of a natural landed aristocracy making common cause with the robust people of England against the selfish heartlessness of the middle classes, and the grey prose of the machine age.

Already his contemporaries had noticed that Disraeli was, with all his dazzling gifts, an indifferent administrator. Once he had solved for himself the intellectual problem posed by an issue, he lost interest in how the case was then dealt with in practice – typical of the intellectual.

In the two years of his agitation before Lassalle fell in that absurd romantic duel at the age of 42, he had revolutionised German politics, creating a labour movement and first mass party in Germany out of nothing.

Lassalle saw his own role as that of a leader lifted above the mass of followers, to be obeyed blindly and acclaimed. To what extent Lassalle was not really part and parcel of his movement is best shown by the astounding, secret negotiations he conducted with Bismarck, without the knowledge of any of his collaborators.

He was a young man in a hurry, and he had the conceit to believe that he could outwit the crafty Junker leader, use him and the Hohenzollern monarchy for his purposes, and then bestow upon the German working classes as a single-handed achievement a dominant role in the German nation, and thus realise simultaneously his two great aspirations: the emancipation of the proletariat and the unification of Germany under the aegis of a populist ideology.

In their days Disraeli and Lassalle, as well as those mainly liberal and progressive Jewish members of the Reichstag or deputies to legislative assemblies in other countries, were isolated individuals, and although one could detect similar features in their views and conduct, there was no contact between them and they formed no recognisable or effective groups.

In the last two decades before World War I and in the turbulent years of revolutionary ferment from 1917 onwards, Jewish intellectuals in Central and Eastern Europe emerged as a most vital and distinct element with a corporate identity, in the movements of the Left.

They played a role of universal historic significance in preparing the minds of the public and the organisational cadres for the future breakthrough. Then when the war cataclysm brought down old established structures, their furious zeal and disciplined energy were a mighty factor in erecting new frameworks. Of these some remained, others were swept away by the counter-revolution.

All the characteristics of the role of Jewish intellectuals in politics stand out in the starkest relief at that historic juncture. In the first place, the astonishing phenomenon of the Jewish revolutionary who hastens from country to country to help the cause of revolution: Rosa Luxemburg, Yogiches, Karl Radek, Parvus-Helphand, Kurt Eisner and Gustav Landauer, and also many less well-known idealists.

They never stopped to ask themselves by what right a Polish Jewess, like Rosa Luxemburg, comes and plunges into an internal German quarrel and tries to upset a national tradition of centuries, or what business had Kurt Eisner, a Prussian journalist, to proclaim a socialist revolution in Catholic monarchical conservative Bavaria?

Their answer was that their fatherland was the Revolution which had no frontiers; their country was mankind or the proletariat. Bela Kuhn in Hungary, Borodin in China, Radek in Germany, and Zinoviev everywhere; not to speak of Trotsky in Russia – what other race had even remotely experienced universalist Messianism with the same intensity?

There is a shattering report in one of Rosa Luxemburg's letters from prison to a Jewish friend: "Why do you pester me with your Jewish sorrow? There is no room in my heart for the Jewish troubles."' And she goes on to speak most eloquently of the suffering of the Chinese coolies and of the Bantus in South Africa. Twenty-five years later, after the Germans had occupied it, there was not a single Jew left alive in Rosa's native Zamose, which was also the hometown of J. L. Peretz.

The expectation of an imminent world-wide breakthrough cost practically all the Jewish revolutionaries their lives, and enabled

Hitler, and others before him, to offer "proof" of a world-wide Jewish conspiracy to subvert all existing regimes and enthrone Jewish Bolshevism. There can be no doubt that Hitler's and Stalin's campaign of destruction against Jewish intellectuals has made a recurrence of this internationalist phenomenon virtually impossible – ever.

Few Jews could ever again master enough ideological self-assurance to make them totally oblivious of their own Jewishness, national peculiarities in other peoples and the age-long attitude of gentiles towards them. It is also hard to believe that after the communist International has disintegrated under the impact of nationalism, universal ideological Don-Quixotism would still be practised on any scale.

As a leaven, the Jewish element was able to be immensely effective. As a constructive factor of stability in ordinary times, its possibilities were limited from the start. No one offers a better example of this than Leon Trotsky.

A man of extraordinary gifts, as speaker and writer, sophisticated and flamboyant, with a highly analytical mind, yet capable of quite irresistible enthusiasm and energy, prepared to jump into fire for the Revolution, on condition that the whole world looks on, he played a decisive role in the Russian Revolution's initial breakthroughs.

Although at heart opposed to the Brest-Litovsk peace terms, he took upon himself the gruelling but spectacular task of leading the Soviet delegation in the negotiations with the German and Austrian ministers and generals.

With incredible energy and ruthlessness, he then threw himself into the gigantic task of building up an army out of a totally demoralised and hungry population, which only the day before was incited by him and his friends to desert, throw away rifles and run home in order to stop an imperialist war and "plunder the plunderers" – and then he led them to victory.

And yet this colourful, dazzling hero, with a career and achievements more fabulous than imagination could evoke, had no chance whatsoever to vanquish the drab, pedestrian, wood-chopping Stalin in the struggle for power, once the hour of heroics was over, and things had to be thrashed out among equals around the committee table and in intrigues in corridors.

Trotsky's thrusting energy, his arrogant sense of superiority, his impatience with detail, his contempt for the slogging and plodding along of bureaucrats, made him ill at ease, caused him to fumble, to wound many a susceptibility and often make himself, in his Don Quixotic ways, quite ridiculously wrong.

It is no accident that as the Soviet regime grew more stabilised, and bureaucracy and routine took over, Jews gradually dropped out completely from Soviet political leadership. The same phenomenon may be observed in the Popular Democracies after 1945.

In times of revolutionary stress or periods of rapid change, the malaise of the Jewish intellectual, suffering from isolation, becomes a source of strength. Discomfort is transformed into a furious élan of release. It renders the Jewish intellectual peculiarly, often pathetically (considering his gifts and idealism), ineffectual in more ordinary circumstances. This is illustrated by the careers of three eminent Jews in three different countries – Walter Rathenau, Leon Blum and Harold Laski – in the period between the two wars.

Rathenau seemingly had everything to make him one of the happiest of mortals. He inherited enormous wealth, succeeded his father as head of one of the greatest and most advanced industrial empires in Germany, consorted with all the famous men of his age, had vast literary and artistic culture, and wrote books on philosophy, economics and current affairs.

Yet he was so isolated a bachelor, in spite of enjoying the affection of relatives and the warm respect of friends, and so wretchedly unhappy, that the assassin's bullet which killed him for daring to become the Foreign Secretary of Germany, was a release.

Rathenau never wanted what he had and could have, but always hankered to be somebody else, and to have something that he could not have. He at first refused every offer, including office, and always ended by reluctantly yielding, and considering himself a martyr, which he was eventually to become.

As a Jew and rich man, he suffered from intense masochistic self-hatred, and the thought of his Jewishness never left him for a moment. Hence, his ulcered self-consciousness, and the craving for recognition and affection, which had the opposite effect he wanted on those whose love he so overpoweringly solicited. Of a Semitic, or rather negroid, appearance, in spite of his very tall stature, he envied the blond and blue-eyed, and would wax lyrical about the Wagnerian splendours of the authentic German mythology.

One of the pillars of German capitalism, he never tired of preaching against materialistic purposefulness, luxury, and the soullessness of the machine age, and of calling for the cultivation of the spirit and the arts as ends in themselves. A democrat and humanitarian, he hated trade union politics, and designed schemes of a corporate organisation of industry, which combined a strong dose of Fascism with an ultra-modern use of technology.

At the end of the First World War, he was put on the list of criminals whom the Allies wanted to put on trial, and before that Rathenau passionately opposed General Ludendorf's call for a ceasefire. Yet he was destined to be decried as traitor for his efforts to come to an accommodation with Germany's former enemies and for being the first Western statesman to make a pact with Soviet Russia (on terms favourable to Germany).

Rathenau never had any party behind him, just as he never was absolutely sure what he wanted, never discovered his own identity, if he had any, and never ceased to look back – not forward.

Leon Blum and Harold Laski were both men of very great talents and socialists of the highest devotion, whose logic was that of the Revolution, but whose humanity had been deeply disturbed by the horrors of the Bolshevik Revolution. Their lively imaginations and quick sympathies often made them understand only too well the position of their opponents and this would often make them halt questioningly rather than proceed decisively.

In an ice age, with French Communists self-righteously and viciously abusing him as a "social-Fascist," and the French Fascists clamouring "better Hitler than Blum," Leon Blum's Popular Front government got bogged down by the Spanish non-intervention issue. All his instincts were against deserting the Spanish Republicans; he abhorred the negotiations with the Nazis, and he was intensely unhappy to have to resort to ambiguous and lame formulae in polemic with his own ardent followers; but he was a helpless hostage.

Leon Blum's term of office will be remembered by little more than a few measures favouring the workers, but Blum's nobility of character and courage as a Jew and Frenchman, under the Nazi occupation and at the Riom trial will remain a profound inspiration.

While Blum was fundamentally a man of letters, with no craving for power, a politician almost in spite of himself, the scholar Laski was a frustrated politician. He loved power, or rather the substitute for it in the form of influence on the hearts and minds of men by word of mouth and pen to the point of even spinning yarns in order to compel attention, and by confidential advice to those in the seat of power.

Consciously or unconsciously he at the same time feared power. He was, for instance, never willing to stand for parliament. He wanted to be effective as one of the decision-makers, but he could not abandon his role of critic and prophet. He loved to be in the inner council, but, as Lord Attlee pointed out the other day, he could not abstain from making indiscreet speeches. Although he always topped the list of candidates to the Labour Party Executive, he was never on terms of real intimacy with any of his colleagues, and of course was never really accepted by the masses of the Trade Union movement as one of them.

Laski was no more sure than were others about what he loved more, socialism or the British Constitution, which of course did not save him from losing a famous libel case – incitement to violent revolution. But then Laski's generous heart, unbridled imagination and torrential oratory often led him to rhapsodise for its own sake.

Completely ineffectual as Laski became when Labour obtained power, he certainly affected the course of history by moulding that generation of Britons in the grim 1930s, who after 1945 built the Welfare State, and more still in powerfully influencing swarms of students from Asia and Africa, many of whom stand today at the helm of independent countries.

It is time to ask about the role of the Jewish intellectual nearer home in the Zionist movement and in Israel. The Zionist movement was a movement started by intellectuals. One may say that Herzl's original approach was that of an intellectual. He strove for an international charter, a juridical definition, before engaging in any practical activity in Palestine, in fact discouraging any such efforts, without a political settlement first.

The founder of political Zionism envisaged the transformation of Palestine into a Jewish State and of the Jewish settlers into a new nation as a kind of sudden leap. He seems to have sincerely believed that persuasive argument would be enough to get the benevolent attention of the great Powers focused on the Jewish question and to make them act almost disinterestedly to solve a great human problem. Millions of Jews would then simply pack up and throng to the ships placed at their disposal by their millionaire brethren. Herzl's intellectual enthusiasm remained for long oblivious to inertia, obtuseness, ill-will and the general messiness of politics. No wonder that the waspish Achad-Haam poured ridicule upon *Altneuland*, preferring a spiritual centre, and the sceptical Weizmann spoke of "dunam to dunam, and cow to cow."

But, of course, Zionism was an intellectual movement for deeper reasons. It was deeply anchored in a strenuous conception of Jewish history and aspired not merely to be a colonisation venture, but was motivated by a vision of an ideal society, spiritual rebirth and universal mission.

The doctrinal aspect was no less important in Zionism than in the socialist movement. It is impossible not to admire and at the same time not to shake one's puzzled head at the tremendous intellectual effort made by socialist Zionism to reconcile dialectical materialism, class war and revolutionary universalism with uncompromising devotion to the ideal of the ingathering of the exiles and a revived Hebrew culture. What a difference between the vigour and wealth of, say, the thinking represented by Borochov, Syrkin, Berl Katznelson and the utter poverty of political thinking in Israel today. Practitioners discourage too deep a probing into fundamental issues. Even after the establishment of the State kibbutzim would split and old comrades would come to blows on the interpretation of the phenomenon of Titoism or social realism in the arts.

The position of the intellectuals in present-day Israel represents something of a paradox. They simply do not count as a force in the Jewish State. The outgoing Knesset numbered only one university teacher among its 120 members. While you will find here and there a writer or professor associated with one party or another, no intellectual is to be found in the leadership of any single party.

It has been one of the disappointments of Zionism, and, if Israel be entitled to claim to serve in this as a laboratory to mankind, to the world at large, that the dream of a society in which a worker labouring with his hands would still be able and willing to take an active part in intellectual life and even in the creative arts, has proved a pious illusion. Moreover, with the Oriental Jews having in fact taken over all the "dirty jobs," even to a large extent, and to the chagrin of veteran idealists, in the kibbutzim as wage labour, the European chalutzic elements have moved up to a managerial position and the intellectuals have become a very distinct and far from privileged group.

What are the reasons for the absence of intellectuals from the political life of the Jewish State? It could be said that there is no room there for professional intellectuals, since in a sense all Jews are intellectuals and every party operates with an elaborate ideology.

The Israeli intellectuals cannot afford the detachment which characterised the Jewish intellectuals in the Diaspora. Yet, it is not difficult to discern an element of alienation in the attitude of the uncommitted. Being too strongly aware, in some cases of being part, of the great currents sweeping the world, they are not quite able to take the plunge and become totally identified with what is going on in their own little country. Moreover, as hinted earlier, realities have played havoc with earlier visions of a perfect new heaven and new earth.

More important are other causes. The harsh and cruel limitations circumscribing the freedom of choice and manoeuvre of a tiny, besieged State, and the inexorable determinations inherent in such a concrete situation, have a sobering and damping effect on intellectuals. So many walls arise on all sides; the Arab refugees, Arab intransigence, Soviet obdurate unfriendliness, the Chinese wall, the communal and religious issues and many other intractable problems. To this we have to add the stranglehold of tightly organised, highly disciplined parties led by professional politicians.

Their dominion is so all-pervasive that even the most forceful pronouncement by a most highly respected private individual will be of no lasting effect, and intellectuals get easily discouraged. Hence their mood of frustrated opposition and protest, which has found expression in the hostility to Ben-Gurion in the last few years.

The only time that the intellectuals asserted themselves as a distinct group was some five years ago when the Lavon affair blew up, and the professors of the Hebrew University of Jerusalem took the initiative in launching a movement of protest against Ben-Gurion's handling of the case. The lively public response astonished the professors themselves, and the demands addressed to them to continue to act as a group as well as the courting of some of them by the various political parties showed that the country was hungry for leadership and disappointed with the politicians. Also the deep traditional Jewish respect for learning lent effectiveness to the intellectuals' stand.

Yet the awakening of the professors and intellectuals proved an ephemeral episode. They made no attempt to maintain themselves as an entity. In a sense the "Min Hayesod" group grew out of that movement, but in spite of the momentary attention it attracted, the venture seems to have been stillborn and to have no future.

Ben-Gurion's own attitude to intellectuals is very ambivalent. The prophet and teacher in him lifts him above the here and now, and his Jewish veneration of learning causes him to flirt with Spinoza, Plato, Bible studies and Buddha. In his unsophisticated and uninhibited enthusiasm he would often stamp heavily, philosophising where angels fear to tread. The vindictive cat among the pigeons that he is, makes him speak with contempt of "intellectuals," when they voice opinions not to his liking, or scrutinise his obsessions with critical acumen.

It is to be feared that the electoral orgy of venomous vindictiveness which is taking place this summer in Israel will estrange the intellectuals still further from politics, confirming them in their despairing contempt for and horror of politics as something too degrading for a true scholar and scientist.

For years we have been observing at the universities in Israel a trend which should please us, but is becoming in fact a source of worry to us: the students with the best brains and finest character run away from politics and aspire to be only scholars or scientists. This may mean that the worst will go into politics.

A Jewish State run by smart executives, and streamlined for maximum efficiency above all, will no longer be a Jewish state. One man with an idea is worth more than a hundred men who have only interests, said John Stuart Mill. Throughout the centuries the Jewish people was led by spiritual leaders and scholars and not by resourceful politicians.

To strike a more hopeful note, it may well be that the state of flux into which Israeli politics have run in the last year, after long decades of stagnation, will, in spite of the momentary disarray, issue in an atmosphere which will be more conducive to a reappraisal of the deep problems of Israel by minds freed from the iron casts of congealed shibboleths. We may still see in the near future a wave of "teach-ins" in the Israeli institutions of higher learning. Thus a new factor may emerge to link up with a very ancient tradition.

First published in the *Jewish Observer and Middle East Review*, Vol. XIV, No. 39, September 24, 1965.

Jews between "Right" and "Left"

Our generation has witnessed so much ideological confusion that the baffled spectator no longer seems able to arrive at a precise definition of Right and Left, and the traditional criteria for progress and reaction no longer seem adequate. Jews appear most perplexed of all because so many of their cherished assumptions have been belied by events, so many certainties have proved to be no more than wishful thinking.

The distinction between Right and Left originated in the parliamentary assemblies of the French Revolution. Parties which defended the *status quo* were seated on the right wing of the amphitheater, while those which agitated for change took their places on the left side. The division into Right and Left was unknown before the French Revolution, since there were no representative bodies or political parties in the age of absolutism. In countries where assemblies of the Estates had existed without interruption from the Middle Ages, distinctions were not based on ideological differences in the modern sense of the word.

Similarly, the division into Right and Left is not part of the original British parliamentary traditions, and again for a technical reason. In the British House of Commons the party in power sits to the right of the Speaker, the opposition party sits to his left, the two facing each other. It would be an anachronism to consider the division of Tories and Whigs in the eighteenth century as a confrontation of conservatives and radicals.

The accidental origin of the division into Right and Left was, however, soon forgotten, and the terms came to designate two opposing world-outlooks. For a long time the Jews adhered to an axiom formulated by republicans in France a century ago: *Pas d'ennemis au gauche* – "There is no enemy on the Left." And its corollary, consequently, was that all evil originates on the Right. The conceptions of Right and Left current among politically conscious Jews were steeped in the myth of the Revolution, and the political nomenclature and associations of several generations of Jews reproduced the well-known patterns of Left ideology and expression. The fear of being identified with the Right is so great among Jews that in Israel today parties regarded normally as rightist have refused to sit on the right-hand benches of the Knesset. As Gustav Flaubert once put it, "The bourgeois – that's always the other fellow." It is very doubtful whether even a sophisticated Israeli can shake off the image of the Right as the defender of privilege, the exploiter of labor, the chauvinistic, anti-Semitic vanguard of reaction bent on diverting the attention of the masses from social injustice. The Left, on the other hand, is regarded as a movement for the redemption of man, the liberation of peoples, and for the equitable distribution of goods through the social ownership of the means of production. The Left and anti-Semitism are of course seen as mutually exclusive terms.

A re-evaluation of these shibboleths must begin with an examination of the premises of Right and Left at the moment of their emergence, during the period of the French Revolution. A survey of the historical development of each camp will inevitably raise this question: to what extent does the old distinction between Right and Left still hold good in general, and for Jews in particular?

The Left believes in the natural goodness of man. In line with its optimistic view of life, the Left strives to provide man with the widest opportunities for self-expression: freedom, rights, security, and access to whatever enriches life and enhances individual dignity. It is confident that man will make good use of these opportunities. Naturally, the Left cannot deny the existence of evil, the prevalence of aggressive instincts and anti-social conduct; but it argues that these are the consequences of repressive institutions and laws prompted by the doctrine of the natural depravity of man. By such means, man's naturally benign instincts were frustrated, and his healthy energies distorted and diverted to anti-social violence and corruption. Given freedom and self-expression and an absence of inhibiting social arrangements, man's natural propensities will spontaneously produce harmonious social patterns. The contradiction between private interest and the general good will be resolved, the opposition between freedom and necessity will disappear, and the separation of the ideal and the real will lose all meaning.

For the Left, the past is a wholly unreliable guide to the present and future, based as it was on pernicious beliefs and unjust laws. Thus the Left asserts for each generation the right to declare its independence of the past, to re-examine its inherited values and to order its life in accordance with its own understanding and needs. Man must be his own legislator and every generation its own master.

The Right has a deep-seated suspicion of humanity. Believing that man is evil, weak and corrupt, the Right is afraid of man as his own master. His natural desires require a tight rein. For once his evil impulses are let loose, society sinks to the level of internecine warfare, and life becomes, in Hobbes' phrase, "solitary, poor, nasty, brutish and short." It is therefore essential that authority comes from above, ultimately from God and immediately from his surrogates on earth: from a priesthood which interprets His teachings, from royalty which rules by His grace, from an aristocracy which combines superior qualities and the traditional skills in the art of ruling. On a more abstract level, the Right insists that there is need for such impersonal checks as religion, tradition, ancient usage, established institutions and fixed ordinances.

The Left sees in religion a device employed by exploiting and repressive forces to convince the masses of their irremediable weakness, sinfulness and utter dependence upon the powers that be. This is the basis of the execrable distinction between the kingdom of heaven and the kingdom of earth, between spirit and matter, between the ideal and the real. This basic distinction permanently stifles the hope that man can ever attain a just social order on earth.

The doctrine of original sin is the mainstay of the Right. Society, like the individual burdened with a "complex," is unable to act in accordance with what reason teaches it is good. Man cannot be redeemed by his own efforts but is dependent on divine grace. Without the fear of God there can be no order among headstrong and rebellious children. Such wayward creatures would never be able to develop and abide by the principles of right reason and morality without the aid of revealed religion.

The optimistic Left regards the heritage of the past as an incubus; the pessimistic Right sees it as a life-preserver. For the Left, the ways of the past are obsolete, outdated encumbrances; for the Right, the very survival of these traditions proves their usefulness and legitimacy, while the new has yet to prove itself. The Left condemns existing institutions as evil but extols man as good; for the Right it is the institutions that are good and man that is evil.

The Right believes that the world and its goods are finite; for the Left they are infinite. In the former's view, the quantity of material goods available for distribution is limited. If these goods were divided equally, no one would receive more than a pittance, and the result would be utter impoverishment, general barbarization, the end to civilization. Hence it is preferable to perpetuate inequality and with it a system whereby the many toil for the sake of the few – for it is these few who preserve the patterns of civilization. Modern technology, with its promise of limitless production and plenty, was seized upon by the Left as a decisive argument against this doctrine of inequality. It follows that the Left believes in social-economic revolution and, in effect, challenges each generation to begin its political experience with a fresh slate of institutions. The Right, on the other hand, not only denies the justice of revolution but even its possibility. It is convinced that in the last analysis revolutions are illusory.

The Left enthrones the individual as the first and ultimate entity and end of society. Society is the product of a social compact; it is assembled or dismantled in accordance with the conscious resolve of rational beings. Nothing is hallowed merely by reason of its existence. Tradition possesses no sanctity which can compel us to render reverent obedience. To promote the individualist goals of society – the freedom, happiness and dignity of the individual – it is permissible, even obligatory, to overturn ancient institutions and to set up, consciously and deliberately, a new social structure that will realize those goals.

The Right refuses to see in the individual an independent entity capable of choosing its course rationally. It would deny to the current generation the right to determine its own path without reference to the past. The Right accords greater power to the dead than to the living. It holds that the human personality is shaped by collective, impersonal forces reaching into the dim, distant past. The attributes of our character are preponderantly the product of heredity. The language we speak is not our creation: we received it, and it molds the very processes of our thought. The usages we observe have been developed by past generations. Climate, terrain and other geographic factors determine our existence to a far greater degree than do our own conscious calculations. The irrational, instinctive and reflexive elements in our lives are of far greater moment than the rational and conscious ones. Just as there are no short-cuts or sharp discontinuities in nature, so total revolution as the result of deliberate, rational calculation is inconceivable. Development is gradual: this is a law of nature – from the seed to the embryo, from the suckling to the child, from the lad to the man.

In the light of this analysis, revolution can only be a change of leadership. Whatever innovations may be introduced in outward forms, the distinction between rulers and ruled is firm and immutable. A total change in the nature of man and in the laws of society, which grows out of man's nature, is inconceivable.

It is not hard to deduce from all this that the Left tends toward universalism, whereas the Right is normally nationalistic. The Right regards the individual as a function of a collective historical entity, the nation. And the nation is a natural phenomenon, the product of history, and not a mere human contrivance. Contrariwise, in the Left's hierarchy of values, rational man, a reflection of universal reason, is assigned the superior role; distinctions of race and tradition are, by comparison, insignificant. From this to the denigration of national boundaries and the glorification of universal unity, or at least the unity of the international proletariat, is but a short step. So for the Left, quarrels between nations are not inevitable; instead, it attributes them to the competition for power and profit among rulers or ruling classes whose rivalry sows dissension and strife among peoples. The Right, on the other hand, accords supreme value to the nation and claims that competition between nations is innate and inevitable. Thus the fate of the individual is indissolubly bound up with that of his country. The Right therefore directs its attention chiefly to foreign affairs and treats problems of the domestic economy as ancillary to foreign policy. The individual's well-being is a function of the nation's economic progress, which is, in turn, dependent upon national security and the nation's standing in international rivalries.

How does one respond to the disparate appeals of Right and Left? The aspirations of the Left elicit warmer sympathy, but the major premises of the Right possess greater depth. Generous impulses throb on the Left; a sense of tragedy informs the Right. One will often find on the Left a naive optimism that borders on folly; on the Right, there is much narrow rigidity and obfuscation. To the former, all things seem easy and possible; to the latter, no change seems feasible or worthwhile. The two extremes do approach a common center: on the Right, the arrogance of callousness to the underprivileged and lowly; on the Left, the arrogance of fanaticism that claims exclusive possession of the whole truth.

If in the light of the foregoing analysis we examine traditional Judaism as a spiritual and historical phenomenon, it becomes clear at once that in essence Judaism savors strongly of the doctrines of the Right: the overriding injunction to God's Chosen People to walk in the ways of their fathers; the absolute validity of tradition; the preservation of national identity as the supreme duty; and, as its corollary, the unremitting and obstinate resistance to external assimilatory pressures. The Jew's Judaism is recognized as a fact which determines his fate, and therefore the allegiance he owes to the national-religious entity is the most categorical of all imperatives. Where could one find a more striking example of the dominance of the dead over the living, or of the precedence of the historical community over the individual's right to self-determination?

To be sure, the revolutionary élan of Zionism powerfully projected the resolve that the Jewish people shape its destiny with its own hands rather than remain the plaything of an inexorable fate and of malignant forces. But more deeply rooted, and more decisive still for the success of the Zionist movement, was the powerful consciousness of the unity of Jewish history and of the Jewish people throughout the ages and throughout the world. Neither the Jewish predicament in Galuth nor the idealism and courage of the pioneers of Zionist settlement; neither the achievements of the Yishuv nor the valor of the Israeli Army would alone have sufficed to gain the world's recognition of the Jewish right to Palestine. That recognition was gained – the fruit of two thousand years of Bible reading in the Western world – because of the general awareness of the unbroken continuity and identity of the historical phenomenon of Judaism.

Despite the kinship of the spirit of Judaism and the doctrines of the Right, the historical circumstances attending the birth of the modern age made the Right the enemy of the Jewish people, and the Left its ally. The ruling classes – the feudal nobility and the Church – invoked historical tradition. The Left – mainly the liberal bourgeoisie and the petty bourgeoisie that followed its lead – raised the banner of abstract natural law and the rights of man. The Right spoke in the name of the past and of existing realities, for these were the props of its authority. The revolutionary Left saw only abomination in the dead hand of the past, and so it resorted to principles of abstract reason. But historical tradition, the past, and existing institutions were fetters on the body and soul of the Jewish people. As a result, the Jews inevitably linked their aspirations to the abstract principles of the revolutionary camp.

(Parenthetically, this ideological commitment of an awakened Jewry involved the Jews in a fundamental contradiction between the abstract, universal principles of natural law and the uniqueness of the historical Jewish entity; between full civil rights for the Jewish individual and the preservation of the national identity. That contradiction has remained unresolved from the days of Moses Mendelssohn to the Bund and Hashomer Hatzair.)

It was only natural that the Jews should do so. Conservatives took the Jews as the particular object of their hatred. The awakening of this universally despised people particularly incensed the privileged classes; it struck them as a vivid and decisive sign of the overthrow of all order, the rank growth of plebeian effrontery, the desecration of traditional standards and sanctities. For the clergy, equality for the Jews represented a flagrant assault upon the Christian character of the state. Thus, situated on a battleground where the Right attacked them and the Left defended them, the Jews had no choice but, as an elementary matter of self-preservation, to adopt the rationalist and utilitarian credo of the Left. Furthermore, they had no reason to revere the medieval-feudal past. The romantic myths of medieval chivalry, the traditions of Christianity, and the symbols of nationhood represented to them only the stigmata of a long, drawn-out, and bitter experience of violence and oppression. Finally, the Jews were able to avail themselves quite early of the new instruments of power – commercial opportunity, economic enterprise, financial resourcefulness, industrial diligence – which the rising bourgeoisie had forged to supplant the traditional roads to influence: ancestral, religious authority and feudal privilege.

United in the face of the common enemy in the first days of the French Revolution, the anti-feudal Left soon split into opposing camps. With the final collapse of the feudal-clerical reaction in France after the revolution of 1830, Right and Left came to connote the struggle between the conservative bourgeois liberals and the revolutionary social or socialist forces of the Revolution. It is important to remember, however, that both components of the new political constellation continued to maintain the belief in the ultimate perfectibility of man and the progressive advance of society toward the final goal of social harmony.

The moderate bourgeois liberals feared the political millenarians who sought to take the kingdom of heaven by storm. The radicals genuinely believed that total salvation – a society based upon absolute equality and social harmony – was just around the corner and that only hard-hearted, stupid and selfish reactionaries barred the way to its realization. As the trustees of posterity, they considered themselves duty-bound to those who, because of stupidity or wickedness, impeded the course of History. It was incumbent upon them to confront the timid, the unimaginative and the backward with a *fait accompli*.

In reaction to the violent determination of the millenarians, the moderate elements developed a pragmatic conception of politics as a process of trial and error. Politics for them came to mean a technique for dealing with immediate, concrete conditions; the fulfillment of the Messianic social dream was postponed to a distant point in the future, to be approached only slowly and gradually. So the liberals found themselves unwitting disciples of the conservatives. The concrete past, the particular national tradition, the unique individuality of each nation – these came to possess a far more potent appeal to them than the revolutionary imposition of some abstract conception of the ideal society.

The Messianic Left – so the Liberals argued – stands condemned by its use of force at the very outset of its mission. Its object is to liberate the individual from all personal dependence and to create a society of absolute equality, and it ends by imposing uniform patterns of thought, conduct and property relations. The price of equality is freedom. Those who see themselves as agents of historical necessity, executors of the will of History, presume to know the will of the people better than the people themselves. They seek to achieve a revolutionary *fait accompli* and postulate the ultimate liquidation of all their opponents. But is this not, then, a return to the old division between rulers and the ruled? Does this not reflect a contemptuously manipulative attitude toward their fellow-men, as though they were either children or malefactors?

The primary meaning of freedom is indeed the removal of chains; but the imposition of abstract freedom is yet another, newer form of pernicious constraint on man. For in the last analysis, man is a creature of habit, warmly attached to the living substance of his concrete situation. Man loves what he is accustomed to more than he desires innovation; he is by nature more of a conservative than a revolutionary. You cannot save an individual by forcing him to conform to an ideal pattern; on the contrary, you strip him of the concrete substance which constitutes his special and unique individuality.

The chief point at issue was economic – the role of property in the rising social order. Liberalism sought to free man from the pressures and constraints of feudalism, to assure freedom of gainful occupation to every individual. Liberal economic theory mirrored Liberal psychology: just as the natural desires of man attain a state of equilibrium when given free rein, so man's freely competing economic enterprises will produce a proper equilibrium between supply and demand, between the interests of producers and consumers. Against this, the socialists argued that if man's economic security was not assured, all abstract freedoms and rights, however solemnly proclaimed, were nothing but a snare and a delusion. In their view, laissez-faire and the social inequality it engenders are tantamount to the subjection of the weak and the poor to the will of the rich and the powerful, whose sole interest is to exploit those who possess nothing but the labor of their hands.

It is the duty of government, Liberalism taught, to protect freedom. It is the duty of government, the socialists cried, to ensure man's survival. While the liberals condemned the despotism of kings, they were no less fearful of the violence and terror of the Left. Hence their concern with ways of limiting the power of government. The socialist challenge to the state to assure the survival of each of its citizens by assuming control of the means of production and distribution appeared to the liberals to open the door to slavery. It was not difficult for the socialists to reproach the liberals with being more concerned with the privileges of inherited property than with freedom. This privilege was particularly irritating to the socialists, for it was the only one that remained after all other hereditary privileges had been swept away. There was no rational principle to justify it. Its isolation now only made it all the more conspicuous and vulnerable; to the socialists this single privilege seemed a disguised restoration of all the others.

The liberals did indeed agree that private property was the key to their entire system, but in this they saw a decisive argument for its retention. All the other freedoms – of thought, expression, belief, movement, etc. – were vague and indefinite things, but the guarantee of property was something substantial, and hence a buffer against encroachments on the other freedoms. If it were abolished, all the other freedoms would remain lifeless abstractions. The government which could seize all means of production would become an all-powerful Leviathan whose citizens would be reduced to the status of slaves.

It was in this context that the question of the nature of man was raised anew. In the view of the liberals, social security and absolute equality achieved through the abolition of private property would deprive man of every incentive to exert himself. If he has no prospect of improving his situation, of excelling, of bequeathing the fruit of his labor to his children, why should he labor at all? Under such conditions, productivity would drop drastically, a general decline of vitality would ensue, and we should all find ourselves reduced to poverty. The Left responded by projecting a new image of man. The man of the future would act on motives to which contemporary man is indifferent: satisfaction in one's work, love of one's neighbor, commitment to an ideal of justice.

This discussion was of course powerfully affected by the implications and consequences of the Industrial Revolution. Its advent on the morrow of the French Revolution, in the atmosphere of messianic expectation which the latter aroused, was regarded by contemporaries not as an age of rapid technological development, but as an apocalyptic turning-point. Immediately beyond lay the imminent dénouement of the messianic drama which all men were solemnly obliged to hasten along. The extreme hardships created by the Industrial Revolution appeared not as a crisis of readjustment to unexpected and rapid changes, but as the apocalyptic travail of a new world about to be born.

Some historians are eager to prove that the evils of the early part of the Industrial Revolution have been considerably exaggerated, since they were accompanied by certain decided advances. For example, prices of many commodities previously beyond the means of the workers were considerably reduced. Nevertheless, whatever the objective situation may have been, the measure of suffering is always in the end subjective. The fact was that the worker of those days who had learned the lessons of human dignity and human rights from the French Revolution was not inclined to accept poverty as a permanent expression of God's will. And he greeted with growing restiveness the glaring contradiction between the potential abundance promised by the new technology and the immediately evil consequences of the Industrial Revolution. This contradiction was cast into even sharper relief in the light of the revolutionary doctrine that the welfare of the individual is the supreme goal of the social contract. The doctrine was belied by the reality: man had become chained to the machine or had been made superfluous by it.

For a time Liberalism yielded to the mood of hard-bitten conservatism and accepted the pessimistic views of Malthus and Ricardo. According to their teachings, the constant growth of population coupled with the fierce competition of industrialists in various countries inexorably results in the iron rule that the workers' pay can never exceed the minimum necessary for bare subsistence. Workers who demanded pay increases, shorter working hours, or the abolition of children's and women's labor failed to understand that these reforms would hit them first and hardest, for they would be followed by industrial paralysis and unemployment. There were, in fact, entrepreneurs who did not regard unemployment as a disaster, for they believed that poverty serves as a goad to exertion and unemployment provides a constant reserve of labor force. In one sense, the selfishness of the capitalists was more callous than the attitude of the feudal lord to his serfs, for the impersonal character of industrial relations precluded the patriarchal solicitude that was occasionally to be found in the seigneurial system.

The liberals of the Right maintained that the system of private property and freedom of economic initiative was the only safeguard of the perennial values of civilization. Though it was unhappily true that the masses suffered heavy burdens, any attempts to upset the prevailing economic order were bound to lead to chaos. The order of Creation cannot be altered by utopian dreams; similarly, it would be criminally insane to sabotage the operation of so complex a structure as the industrial system by experimenting with fanciful theories. The clamor of the discontented poor for a free and equal vote was tantamount to a demand for a social revolution. For after they had won a majority of votes, the masses would divide property among themselves, causing disaster to the national economy and the collapse of all civilization. In these circumstances, there was no choice but to deprive the poor of the franchise and to institute restrictive measures against anarchistic and communistic agitation. Thus the liberals desecrated the most sacred article of their creed – the right of the individual to determine and defend his own fate at the ballot box, in the press, through political assembly. It was this betrayal which led Karl Marx to declare that the bourgeois state is not a national government, but an instrument of bourgeois exploitation, and its administration – the executive committee of the exploiting class.

But Marx's formulation remained true only for a short period. Developments of his own day soon removed the sting from his words. The speedy victory of the revolutionary forces of 1848 over the old order was quickly followed by the not less easy victory of the bourgeoisie over the revolutionary socialist movement. In the democratic elections held in 1848, the conservative instinct of the agrarian masses prevailed over the revolutionary aspirations of the urban workers. To its surprise, Europe discovered that unrestricted franchise was not a preliminary to revolution, but rather a support for conservative forces. The bourgeoisie, which had been haunted by the specter of revolution and which, at the beginning of 1848 had thought itself doomed, now breathed freely again, and with its self-confidence restored, bourgeois liberalism became more generous.

The second half of the nineteenth century witnessed the triumph of the free, equal and universal franchise, and an increasing series of social reforms. The opening up of new markets in various parts of the world for European manufactures, the vastly improved means of communication, and the invention of new technical processes brought remarkable prosperity. An incidental result of the triumphant Industrial Revolution was the alleviation of many of the evils it had spawned at the outset. The first victims of capitalist manufacture, those artisans and craftsmen who had fought bitterly for their precarious independence against the Leviathan of mass production, were finally absorbed by the economy. Living conditions improved. Factories were located in spacious buildings, and measures were taken to prevent accidents on the job. General prosperity, the pressure of enlightened public opinion, the awakened conscience of some of the industrialists, and a better understanding of their own long-range interests – all these factors led the manufacturers to realize that the advantages of long working hours were deceptive and that a shorter work-day ensured higher productivity. They perceived that the labor of women and children would eventually undermine the vitality of the labor force of the next generation. And they came to understand that trade unions were not necessarily a conspiracy to impose the will of the workers by violence, but an instrument for regulating labor relations – that collective bargaining was not an arbitrary restriction on the freedom of contract, but its true expression.

By the second half of the nineteenth century, Marx's prognosis for Western Europe had been proven by events to be mistaken. The doctrine of the father of "scientific socialism" was based on conditions that obtained only in the first half of the century – the economic development of England, German philosophy, French political life.

Its political program was wholly a response to the events of 1848 – and that, only to their external and immediate consequences. Marx had predicted the progressive impoverishment of the masses as a result of the concentration of the means of production in the hands of an increasingly small number of owners. Instead, the proliferation of stock companies and credit organizations extended capitalist ownership to wide strata. The upper echelons of labor became bourgeois. Workers who were elected to public office attained influence, and the success of trade unions and their political organizations gave the lie to the dogma that the workers were slaves and that their country was their enemy, not their homeland. In 1914, the workers of all countries remained staunchly patriotic and rejected the banner of international proletarian solidarity and revolutions.

In this corrected perspective, the nineteenth century in the West emerges not as an age of revolution but as an epoch in which the revolution was tamed. The gradual but unmistakable realization of the authentic and fundamental aspirations of the Left did not result from the success of the revolution, but from the fact that it never took place. True progress in the extension of freedom has no greater enemy, no more formidable obstacles, than an atmosphere of emergency. Such an atmosphere is the inevitable concomitant of the revolutionary situation; it is stimulated by the fanatical resolve in preparing the revolution, by the fear of those against whom it is directed, and once it has been achieved, by the strenuous efforts to maintain it against enemies from within and without. Seen in this context, West European democratic socialism is clearly a synthesis of social messianism and empirical liberalism, rather than the heir of messianic radicalism alone.

At the close of the nineteenth century the revolutionary specter wandered eastward.

In the struggle between bourgeois liberalism and the various forms of socialism in the nineteenth century, the interests of the Jews of Western and Central Europe lay with liberalism. The Jews belonged to the upper or middle bourgeoisie. They had reason to feel uneasy about the proletariat and avoided contact with it. Because of their place in the social structure, they tended to adopt the liberal outlook, which viewed life as a field for adventure, an aggregate of opportunities. Liberalism protected the Jew at once from the disabilities imposed by the *ancient regime* and from the encroachments of socialist plans for the nationalization of the means of production.

The Jew of the West sought not security from hunger, but an opportunity to rise in the social scale. The recurrent crises of the laissez-faire system did not frighten him; he saw them as so many opportunities. In a general atmosphere of adventure and initiative, the Jews were given virtually official encouragement as pioneers and entrepreneurs. They were able to make significant contributions to the expansion of capitalist economy in the West and to exert a powerful influence on the industrialization of more backward countries. It is not often remembered that early socialist propaganda, including the writings of Marx himself, portrayed the Jew as the high priest of the cult of the golden calf. The Rothschilds and other Jewish financiers were credited with pulling the strings of the modern capitalist state – "the kings of the age," the Fourierist Toussenel called them.

Yet European socialism would have been inconceivable without the prophetic and messianic elements represented by the Jewish Saint-Simonists, Karl Marx, Ferdinand Lassalle, and so many other Jews. What made Marxism a gospel for millions was not its keen analysis of economic determinism, but its vibrant, compelling faith in History as a drama of salvation. Despite the claim that it is only an analysis of objective trends, Marx's doctrine of self-alienation derives its true effectiveness from the prophetic denunciation of the dehumanizing subjection of men to the products of their own hands, from the passionate protest against the fetish of the cash nexus which reduces man to a mere instrument of production and corrodes all higher values, aims and sentiments. No canon of logic or law of history, but an *a priori* Messianic vision of ultimate redemption informs Marx's major prediction: the stage of capitalism – monopolistic concentration on the one hand and mass pauperization on the other – must inevitably become the apocalyptic moment of proletarian liberation. There is no logical necessity for the seizure of all means of production to be followed by their transformation from fetters into instruments of true human self-expression and freedom.

It was the Jews, Moses Hess and Karl Marx, who channelled the theological-philosophical speculations of the Young Hegelians onto the path of social analysis and social protest. This they accomplished by their insistence that critical speculative reason, when reduced to mere contemplation, becomes a helpless accomplice of the evils of reality. Neither social harmony nor man's emancipation from the tyranny of fetishes – whether of religion, metaphysics or money – was possible without the abolition of private property and of the destructive selfishness that feeds on it.

The salvationist universalism of Marxism was in no small measure influenced by the fact that its Jewish prophets were so much less tied to particularistic traditions and allegiances than their Gentile fellow-citizens. For as Jews, they had only recently broken away from their Jewish heritage without having become integrated or even accepted into the national life of their countries. Marx's ardor in unmasking hypocrisy and self-delusion, in exposing sentimental beliefs as selfishness or mental indolence re-echoes the prophetic wrath of an Amos or Isaiah, but also shows incomprehension of the genuineness of ingrained habit, irrational attachment, idiomatic peculiarity and complex involvement. Everything is reduced to basic ethical concepts. What in a lesser man would have remained turgid preaching became through Marx one of the most effective prophecies in human history.

The Jewish Saint-Simonists quite consciously and explicitly proclaimed their socialist creed to be a modern version of the mission of the prophets of Israel. They secularized and universalized the traditional Jewish concept of "a kingdom of priests and a holy people." In its new form, this ideal was to serve as a corrective to the iniquitous Christian doctrine that sanctioned the distinction between the kingdom of Heaven and the kingdom of earth – between private morality and personal holiness on the one hand, and the ethos of power politics and social-economic amorality on the other. All nations were to become transformed from armed camps poised for battle into a united humanity working for the conquest of nature.

The prophets of socialist universalism did not, of course, remain within the fold of Judaism. For the Jewish Saint-Simonists, their Messianic message was a way of shaking off the incubus of Judaism without, as Heine put it, suffering the indignity of baptism as the price of admission to European society. Both Marx and Lassalle (who in his youth had dreamed of playing the role of Judah Maccabaeus), became enemies and denigrators of Judaism. (Moses Hess was a unique phenomenon in his age, with his messianic synthesis of socialism and Zionism.)

On the other hand, the two most distinguished nineteenth-century Jewish figures on the Right, Benjamin Disraeli and Adolphe Crémieux, bore their Jewishness proudly. This was no accident. For once Liberalism had lost its messianic fanaticism, it no longer insisted, as it had in the Napoleonic era, on assimilation as the price of equal rights. The liberals refused to tie their political opinions to a universalistic and rigidly exclusive world-view. In contrast to the harsh dogmatism of the Messianic movement, Liberalism created a more favorable atmosphere for the individual Jew to pursue a course of his own. And among Jews of the liberal-conservative outlook, the Messianic Jewish heritage found expression in their highly developed sensitivity to social evil and their extensive philanthropic activities. It is not unlikely that Disraeli's bold, original attempt to associate traditional British aristocratic conservatism with a policy of social reform – to some extent in opposition to middle class liberalism – was in some way connected with his Jewishness. At the same time, it should be noted that this brand of anti-bourgeois, social-minded nationalism in Imperial Germany and Austro-Hungary assumed a strong anti-Semitic character.

At the close of the nineteenth century, the center of gravity of our problem shifted to eastern Europe. In contrast to the situation of their co-religionists in the West, millions of impoverished, downtrodden Jews in eastern Europe suffered vicious oppression and persecution at the hands of a tyrannical regime. Czarism in Russia pursued a systematic policy of oppression of national minorities as well as of the masses of Russians themselves. Out of an hysterical fear that the entire social-political structure would collapse if a single brick were disturbed, the Czarist regime conducted a relentless war against any and every aspiration for even the slightest change in the status quo. A tyrannical order which allowed no outlet for self-expression, which permitted no safety valve for the anger and frustration of its subjects, unwittingly stimulated revolutionary passions and messianic yearnings. Innumerable devotees of the religion of revolution lay in wait, harassing the enemy state to which they felt no allegiance, and ready to break into the open on the Day of Judgment when a wholly evil world would be transformed into a wholly good one.

The Messianic tidings of revolution nowhere found a more enthusiastic response than among the Jews of Eastern Europe. No other national or social group – not even the masses of peasants whom the Industrial Revolution had suddenly uprooted and cast into a maelstrom of new and bewildering social problems – experienced with the same intensity the trauma of breaking with historical continuity and tradition. Countless Jewish youths, often enough yeshiva students who had become secularized overnight, experienced the revolutionary revelation almost as a visitation bringing in its wake sudden release and redemption. They were knocking at the gates of Paradise. The intense preparation for the hour of grace, the sense of being swept on irresistibly, the anticipation of imminent redemption, the vision of the Day of Judgment when the proud would be humbled and the lowly exalted – all those aspects of the new dispensation made many of the noblest hearts in Israel exult.

It is no exaggeration to state that the very rigidity and harshness of the Marxian doctrine, the dialectical casuistry peculiar to it, and the quasi-neurotic adherence to the minutiae of a written code so characteristic of Marxists – were calculated to exercise a special fascination for the heirs of countless generations of Talmudic students, hair-splitting exegetes and ritualistic bookkeepers. Moreover, the uncompromising Marxist distinction between the progressive proletariat and reactionary capitalism could readily serve as a secularized parallel to a concept familiar to ex-yeshiva students – the sharp cleavage between the Chosen People and the other nations. Since the Jews were the classical scapegoats of the Czarist regime and since, at the same time, all forms of evil appeared to be interconnected, there arose the conviction that only a total revolution could solve all problems at once, including the Jewish problem. Finally, the impact on East European Jews of the rise of anti-Semitism in Western Europe, climaxed in the Dreyfus affair, was sufficient to disillusion many moderate Jews with liberalism and to throw them into the arms of revolutionary messianism.

How shall we explain the extraordinary transformation that has occurred in the course of these last forty years? What has happened to that revolutionary regime which so many Jews had hailed as the fulfillment of their most cherished messianic hopes, to whose victory Jews had made such a great and perhaps decisive contribution? A regime that had borne aloft the banner of freedom to all men and races, had made anti-Semitic propaganda a punishable crime, and for a time had even shown readiness to foster some form of autonomous Jewish cultural life, launches an extermination campaign against Jewish writers, plans mass Jewish expulsions, encourages the growth of anti-Semitism, adopts an implacably hostile and insulting policy toward the state of Israel, and gives its unconditional support to feudal forces, dictators and adventurers sworn to the annihilation of Israel. How did this happen? Is it a mere accident? An error due to the lack of understanding on the part of short-sighted politicians? Are these only external appearances, unrelated to the true inner nature of the regime and its historic universal mission of redemption?

Can there be any doubt by now that these developments are symptoms which can tell us a great deal about the fundamental nature of the Communist regime? And an objective acknowledgement of their significance is bound to puncture the illusion, so dear to the remaining faithful, that the Soviet Union is the vanguard of world revolution moving inexorably toward its ultimate culmination. Indeed, it is no exaggeration to assert that the Jews are a test case for the evaluation of the nature of the system as a whole. The Communist experiment may be judged on this one count: did it succeed in removing from the Jewish heart and from the Gentile mind that type of "Jew-consciousness" which has always determined the status of the Jew in the Diaspora? Has the special standard of judgment for the Jew disappeared, regardless of whether he chooses to merge with the larger social environment or prefers to be identified as a member of a distinct and separate cultural-national-religious group?

Unbiased observers generally agree that this Jew-consciousness has not only not vanished, but is actually gaining stronger hold in Russia. Attitudes toward the Jews in the Soviet Union, we are reliably informed, are colored by suspicion, contempt and hostility. Many grim anecdotes tell the same story. An Oxford professor visiting Russia asked a Soviet scholar whether Freud is taught there; a grimace accompanied the reply: "Another Jewish invention!" Another Soviet scholar teaches that historical religions may be classified as fertile or barren creeds, the principal example of the latter type being Judaism. Anti-Semitic expressions and proverbs have come into vogue again in Russia – and proverbs, jokes and anecdotes are a sure index to the workings of a people's unconscious mind. Nikita Khrushchev's notorious outburst last year – that there is an excessive number of "Abramovitches" in Poland – is only one instance of anti-Semitic sentiments current in the U.S.S.R.

Staunch Soviet sympathizers and naive partisans will doubtlessly trot out their stock argument: these deplorable things are vestiges of the past which the new Soviet education has not yet managed to erase completely. But it is much more likely that this phenomenon, instead of being a mere vestige, is a persistent component which, after having been more or less dormant for a while, is now reasserting itself with increasing virulence. It may be taken as a historical rule that in a revolutionary period, national unity is at its peak at the very beginning of the triumphant revolution, in the first flush of enthusiasm and victorious élan engendered by the collapse of the common enemy. At that moment, people seem to rise above the old patterns of prejudice, selfish interest and fixed habit. But with the emergency gone, they revert to the habits and prejudices inherited from past generations. The fatal mistake of revolutionary dogmatists is to confuse transitory enthusiasm with "a new heart and a new spirit," a momentary outburst of altruism with a permanent ideal order.

Thus, for an instant, the high ideological tension of the Revolution, coupled with terror, was able to suppress the outward signs of anti-Semitism; it may be that even inner aggressiveness toward the Jews was somewhat blunted and inhibited. But as the state of emergency receded, it became clear that little had changed. The experience of revolutionary comradeship and pride in Communist achievement were too feeble to blur the boundaries between "Jew, Gentile and Greek."

Psychological trends in society go hand in hand with social changes. The decisive fact that shaped Soviet society was that the Soviet leaders lost faith in the efficacy of the appeal to the people's commitment to socialist ideals. This forced them to fall back upon the traditional stimuli of the stick and the carrot as incentives to greater effort: promises of higher wages and threats of retaliation. Gross inequality in income and social status was the inevitable result. Thus, open competition ("socialist emulation") dealt a fatal blow to the official doctrine of equality in the common endeavor. In a competitive system, whether or not it is called socialistic, Jewish talents and proclivities inevitably assert themselves, the distinctive separateness of the Jewish group entity becomes the more conspicuous, and so the Jews are left all the more open to contumely and discrimination.

The emergence of social inequality and the growth of the competitive spirit are rooted in more profound changes than those already alluded to. The political development of the Soviet Union reflects the bitter dilemma of a regime controlled by an exclusive élite. Let us for the moment disregard the rightist character of this phenomenon and view it from an internal Soviet vantage-point, as it were. In this context, the élite is not a ruling class in the accepted sense, but the quintessence of the general will, a sort of Urim and

Tummim of history. In order to merit so exalted a position, the élite must pass the most rigorous tests, demonstrate absolute purity and remain always on a superhuman plane.

But like any élite, the Soviet leadership became a clique. When men combine limitless power with a sense of their unique mission of universal regeneration, it is all too easy for them to mistake the promptings of their ambition for the voice of History, to rationalize their hatred and envy into Truth. Moreover, the very nature of unlimited power attracts to the regime self-seeking, power-hungry, sadistic men. The inevitable response of the masses to the unmistakable deterioration of the élite, the caretakers of their destiny, is disappointment and contempt. With every possibility of revolt cut off by a regime that possesses all the instruments of military and political coercion and controls all the means of production and distribution, the resultant mood of the people can only be apathetic and, in the end, nihilistic. The sustained selfless effort to enthrone an ideal of righteousness gives way to a struggle for power among those in a position to compete for it. There is no choice of weapons in this battle. On the contrary, the dominant code renders the question of ends and means virtually meaningless. For a dialectic is always at hand to prove that any specific means, however repugnant to common sense or abhorrent to natural human instincts, is, within the larger context of the *a priori*, all-embracing scheme, not only acceptable but indispensable – and thus objectively good. Surely, "socialist legality" cannot fail or err, since it is the manifestation of the inexorable evolution of a preordained historical pattern, the goal of which is absolute justice. In such an atmosphere anything can be contrived and explained away, including a Jewish doctors' "plot" and a plan to exile Soviet Jews to the far North.

From one point of view, the root of the Jewish tragedy in the Communist world is to be found in the failure of the abortive revolutions outside Russia in the immediate post-World War One period, and in the subsequent confinement of Communism within the borders of one country. In this process the beginning of the general degeneration of Communism can be discerned. For in the very course of silencing Trotsky and destroying all other opposition in the Party, Stalin became the victim of his own success. He was compelled to go on showing that he was right in decreeing that revolution must be limited to one country. This was the origin of the attitude that treated Communist parties outside Russia as satellites taking orders from Moscow. Stalin's obduracy led to the suicidal policy of the German Communist Party on the eve of Hitler's accession to power. The principle was that no Communist Party outside Russia may succeed by its own strength. Furthermore, Soviet Russia imagined herself surrounded by enemies bent on her destruction. Thus, the defense of the Revolution and of the encircled motherland became inseparable causes. With the Nazi invasion of Russia, the spark of nationalism grew into a great flame. And after the Second World War, the country's nationalistic temper found a special irritant in the existence of the Jewish community – a distinctive people, acutely susceptible to influences of a universal character and possessed of a vague sense of kinship with some international confraternity.

The ironical dialectic of the Soviet system has been given special impetus and wider extension by the death of Stalin, and more particularly by Khrushchev's campaign to destroy the Stalin myth. The Communist movement as a whole was shaken to its foundations. Despite nationalistic deviations in the workings of Soviet diplomacy, Stalin's personal dictatorship symbolized the monolithic character of the world Communist movement. Official doctrine recognized only one universal Socialist revolutionary camp, headed by the Soviet Union. It regarded national differences and local deviations as irrelevant or merely apparent. Moreover, the phrase, "Stalin, the genius of Socialist science," reflected the belief that Soviet development under Stalin's guidance was not the result of trial and error, like the history of other countries, but the actualization of objective iron logic, immune to personal arbitrariness, error or accident.

Khrushchev's abrupt revelation that Stalin had violated all the canons of socialism and had completely distorted the progress of the U.S.S.R. by his tyrannical willfulness was a traumatic blow from which world Communism has not yet recovered. It virtually destroyed the fundamental belief in the "scientific" nature of the Soviet system. The way to political empiricism was opened. Freedom of conscience in interpreting the divine revelation was implicitly admitted in the new slogan that each people has its own road to socialism. The kind of evolution foreshadowed by Tito, and for which analogies can be found in the fortunes of past revolutionary ideologies, gathered momentum and grew into an avalanche in Poland, Hungary and other countries. People's adherence to their nationalistic sentiments proved infinitely stronger than the attraction of a universal messianic faith.

The Jews were the first victims of this development. They constituted the principal instrument of Stalinist centralization in all the satellite countries. At the end of World War II, many Jews – whether liberated prisoners of concentration camps or former partisans emerging from forests and hideouts – received the Red Army as saviors; these Jews put all their talents and devotion, their considerable organizational skill and pent-up energy, at the disposal of the Red regimes. Without these cadres, the new governments might not have been able to maintain themselves, for the non-Jewish intelligentsia largely refused to cooperate either because of their hatred for the Soviets and all their works or because they doubted the durability of the new regimes.

(This phenomenon has a parallel in pre-war history. The peculiar interstitial position of the Jews frequently led them to forms of cooperation with the majority nation or with the racial group representing higher culture in plural societies. In the German areas of Poland, for example, the Jews assimilated themselves to German culture; in the Ukrainian areas of Poland, however, the Jews spoke Polish.)

After Stalin's death and particularly after the Khrushchev speech, when the forces of national unity in a country like Poland reasserted themselves, and the Polish intelligentsia decided to cooperate with the new anti-Stalinist government of Gomulka, they found many of the key positions in the hands of the Jews, who had been willing or unwilling protegés of Stalin and Stalinism.

The conclusion suggested by this analysis places in grave doubt the entire romantic, mythological scheme of apocalyptic socialism anchored on the Soviet Union. The partly-naive, partly-arrogant image of the inevitably triumphant camp of world revolution led by the Soviet Union is no longer relevant.

In the perspective of history, the last forty years of Russian history will, I believe, receive their real and abiding significance from the mighty industrial revolution that swept the country and made tens of millions of its peasants and workers literate. As a result of this industrial revolution, Russia has become one of the two great world powers, America's rival in the struggle for world domination. Socialism is hardly relevant to this vast transformation, either as a stimulus or as a goal. For socialism is not to be defined by productive power or technical efficiency, but by its social and human content.

Soviet sputniks and guided missiles, received with envious and fearful admiration by the rest of the world, may have proved Soviet destructive power greater than that of the West; a Soviet professor may receive a much higher salary than his counterpart in the West, and he may have two automobiles at his disposal; the number of students in Soviet institutions of higher learning may exceed the number in America; a Soviet worker may even eat a larger slice of bacon each morning than does a British miner. But all these achievements are irrelevant to the main issue of socialism.

It has often been said that the success of the Bolshevik Revolution in industrially backward Russia was in flat contradiction to the Marxist prognosis. We may say now that the very success of the industrial revolution in the Soviet Union cuts the ground from under the Communist regime. The revolution of October 1917, impossible a century earlier, was able to make the enormous strides it took precisely because Russia had experienced neither a Renaissance nor a Reformation, neither an era of Rationalism nor one of bourgeois liberalism. The impetus of her advance was in direct proportion to her backwardness. The price Russia had to pay for her industrial revolution was greater than that of any other country. In part, this was the result of Russia's enormous backwardness and of her Messianic exaltation; in greater part, perhaps, it stemmed from the exceptionally harsh and inhuman manner in which Russia has traditionally effected constructive changes in her history; nor, finally, should the state of siege in which the Soviet Union found itself for many years be overlooked in this connection.

At the end of forty years, a new generation of intelligentsia has arisen. Russia is no longer in danger of being strangled; on the contrary, it has become a threat to other countries. Dictatorial centralization, terroristic methods of repression and austere living conditions have outlived their usefulness. Dictatorship is no longer justifiable. The new generation will not tolerate it, not least because of its intense Russian national pride.

At the end of forty years we may attempt to assess whether, or to what extent, the Communist regime has rendered irrelevant the complex of historical laws and data that have determined the nature of the Jewish problem for centuries. Has the Soviet regime succeeded in eliminating the exceptional features of Jewish existence? Has it placed the problem on a new plane? Or, to put it differently, is Communism still of any special relevance as a factor likely to affect the Jewish destiny in a manner at once new and salutary?

In posing this question, we must remember that the Jews were not simply a passive object of the Soviet regime, but a very important and active force in the rise and victory of Communism in Russia and the satellite countries. The Jewish role in the rise of Communism is of a distinctly universalistic character; it is comparable to the part played by Jews in the expansion of liberal capitalism in the first half of the nineteenth century, and in the spread of Christianity in the Roman Empire. There is no doubt that they have left their imprint on the history of the Communist lands, not merely as individuals but as a group with distinct and unmistakable qualities of intellect, character and temperament. It was only natural that they represented universalism within Communism, rather than its national version in each country. In other words, the Jews contributed importantly to the institution and growth of Muscovite centralization.

As the nationalist trend gained ascendancy over revolutionary universalism, and as a new intelligentsia arose within each dominant nationality, there began a process of removing the Jews from key positions. It may be said that we are now witnessing the close of a great chapter, saturated with Messianic hopes, rich in achievement, but also filled with disappointment and drenched in blood: the Jewish part in the rise of Communist rule in the twentieth century.

Let us turn now to the question of the Jews as an object of the system. On the assumption that the Jews, by their own desire or by historical necessity, are fated to remain a distinct entity of mutually responsible components, it is obvious that a liberal regime is infinitely preferable to a totalitarian system. Even if the latter has no anti-Semitic tendencies, it imagines itself to be in a perpetual state of siege and demands complete submission to a monolithic pattern of thought and belief. By its very nature, it cannot be expected to permit the Jews to preserve their separateness or to maintain their ties with world Jewry and their sympathetic interest in a foreign state, Israel. Severed from world Jewry and from its historical continuity, subjected to the incessant pressure of an exclusive ideology, the Jews are in no position to maintain their social and spiritual cohesion.

In its earliest years, the Soviet state provided certain favorable conditions and allowed for special institutions for the maintenance of a distinct Jewish culture. Nevertheless, Jewish cohesion in Russia began to disintegrate fairly soon and specifically Jewish vitality ebbed away. Still, this was not sufficient to obliterate Jewish individuality altogether, and as Russian nationalism steadily grew more powerful and more pervasive, the Jews remained unassimilated. They were neither a clearly defined and separate nation like the many other nationalities of the Soviet Union, nor an organic and inseparable part of the Russian nation. Thus the Jews came to stand out increasingly as a foreign body, a dangerous and aberrant element. And once a totalitarian state – in complete control of the levels of power, the organs of propaganda and the means of production – decides upon hostile policies towards its Jewish subjects, the Jews are doomed, powerless to resist or to appeal to public opinion.

It is clear that Communism is no longer relevant in any new or constructive way to the question of Jewish survival. In fact, recent events have demonstrated that it can be decidedly dangerous. By now this should be clear even to those true believers who were convinced that the Jewish national and social renascence was inseparably aligned with the interests of the Soviet Union as the natural leader of all peoples seeking redemption. For these dreamers, the victory of the revolutionary camp meant the automatic abolition of the barrier between Israel and its neighbors, the end of imperialist-feudal plots to sow dissension between Israel and the Arab peoples. One cannot help recalling, in the light of current Soviet policy in the Middle East, the well-known statement made some years ago by a leader of Hashomer Hatzair: "Should the Red Army, in its pursuit of the imperialist enemy, cross the borders of Israel, it will not be treated as an aggressive force. . . ."

History has disproved the assumption that the only enemy is on the Right. All categories have become so confused in recent decades that it is doubtful whether there is any point in continuing the traditional distinction between Right and Left. We have seen a nationalist tyrant, the murderer of Jews and socialists, swept into power by the votes of millions of workers. We have seen a nation, fearful of change and seemingly paralyzed by its archaic attitudes, galvanized by revolution into a satanic dynamism. We have seen a country, supposedly in the last stages of decadent capitalism, become transformed by a regime characterized by state control of the means of production and far-reaching social legislation. And then we have seen the "partisans of progress and redemption" suppress a revolt of workers and students in a neighboring state, with the help of tanks and slogans taken from the classical vocabulary of blackest reaction: "Death to the foreign propagandists and foreign agents who confuse the minds of the people." "Discipline and obedience." "Law and order." Was the right of self-determination, a holy principle of the Left, crushed by the necessities of a global revolutionary strategy, by the objective dialectic of Communism on the march – or by the national interests of Russian power?

This essay has not been written in a spirit of *schadenfreude*. It grew out of brooding over the tragic mystery of the degeneration and corruption of high ideals in process of realization – a recurrent phenomenon at every stage of history. There is tragedy too in the disenchantment of those Jewish intellectuals in the Diaspora who put all their faith in the revolutionary Left and whose devotion to its Messianic message filled their lives with meaning. On the other hand, it is perhaps no accident that the best contemporary Jewish thinkers are among the leading proponents of an anti-messianic, humanistic, skeptical liberalism: Raymond Aron in France, Sir Isaiah Berlin in England, Lionel Trilling in America. Were they, as Jews, frightened by modern political messianism? Or do they, because they are endowed with an acute Jewish sensitivity, feel more intensely the meaning of our age and the lessons of its history?

At closer scrutiny, the leftist orientation of many Jews appears to be motivated less by an optimistic than a pessimistic outlook: the despairing view that Jews can hope for justice only in a perfect society, but are doomed in any imperfect system. This, of course, means to court certain defeat. Deterioration and corruption being the fate of all things in an imperfect world, the worst is usually the corruption of the best. There is nothing more soulless, cruel and virulent than the hypocrisy and callousness of an exclusive salvationist creed turned power machine. And the effect of this sort of thing on believers is quite disastrous. One still remembers the agonized cry of some Jewish leftists at the time of the Slansky trial and the Soviet doctors' plot that "socialist justice cannot err." Some of them went on to condemn the demand for freedom of *aliyah* from the "popular democracies" as arrogance toward the builders of socialism. They created the impression that Israel, and Jews in general, must somehow display some special or higher merit in order to forestall or soften the displeasure of Communist leadership. Far from expressing the human or national self-assurance of the emancipated, this attitude reveals a deep Jewish inferiority complex.

The future attitude of Jews to the Left will be affected not only by disenchantment with the Communist message, but by a major demographic fact: the bulk of the Jewish people now lives in countries whose traditions and institutions developed through trial and error processes and which have never been deeply influenced by universal Messianic ideologies. The same countries happen to be multiracial immigrant communities, in which none can claim superior rights or treat others as strangers on sufferance. It was to a large extent the malaise of the unintegrated and unaccepted that fostered among Jews an addiction to utopianism and doctrinaire abstractions and a feeling that they had to prove themselves exceptionally deserving to merit human and civic rights. There are signs that the concrete nature of the immense problems facing Israel is producing new and more realistic attitudes among the younger generation; and the leftist trauma is being dispelled by the cold, hard impact of events. Diaspora Jewry must also strive to be accepted for what it is: at once a distinct component of the society in which it lives, requiring no special justification for its distinctness, and a part of a universal confraternity. By being just what history has decreed them to be – a phenomenon at once unique and universal – the Jewish people as a whole, Israel and the Diaspora together, cannot help fulfilling a role of universal Messianic significance.

First published in *Midstream*, Summer 1958; a translation from Hebrew, *Ha'aretz*, September 25, 1957.

Suggestions for Isolating the Jewish Component in World History

Several months ago, I saw a brief news item about a young American Jewish historian who had written an essay on the treatment of Jewish history in Soviet textbooks. In his study, the author pointed out a startling intention on the part of the Russians to ignore the existence of Jews in history or at least to belittle their historical importance and show them in an unfavorable light.

Reflecting upon that short item, my mind went back to a related problem, a broader and more basic one which has interested and troubled me for many years.

The general historian whose field is the vast canvas of the human situation and who is at the same time a committed Jew, will naturally find his attention arrested by the Jewish aspects of his subject matter, particularly by the uniqueness of the Jewish phenomenon within the context of universal history and by the question of the mutual exchange of influence between Jews and general history. The more I study general history and ponder its problems, the greater my awareness becomes of the Jewish presence in it, and the deeper seems to me the mystery of its uniqueness and of the startling contradiction of a people that is a "nation dwelling apart" on the one hand, and so essential and effective a component in world history, on the other.

I can feel this without joining the ranks of those who see the Jewish people as a paragon that surpasses all others in its wisdom, as the sole and eternal source of morality and justice, ever pure and righteous, the perennial lamb among wolves. My entire historical perspective, whether concerned with world history or with Jewish history in its confrontation with universal history, is imbued with ambivalence, with the two levels of meaning and value that Sigmund Freud perceived so profoundly as a Jew.

How do the textbook writers of the western world treat the role of the Jews and the place of Jewish history in general history? The fact is, the Jews are barely mentioned in their works. By historians I mean, of course, neither committed theologians nor sworn racists, but objective investigators of the past who, to the best of their ability, seek the truth for its own sake, whose object is a balanced picture and whose attitude is a liberal one – scholars with minds open to all historical phenomena and discoveries, who are ready to endow each phenomenon with the significance it deserves.

Non-Jewish historians do not really know how to treat the Jews, and so they barely mention them. They do not know where to place Jewish history or how to handle it within the scheme of world history or even of their own national history. When dealing with ancient times, they see the Jews crushed and ground fine between the millstones of mighty empires – Egypt, Assyria, Babylonia, Persia, the Hellenistic Empires, Rome. As a religious phenomenon, the Jews, according to general historians, belong to the realm of theology, comparative religion, and Biblical and New Testament research. As popular reading of the Bible wanes and the religious experience weakens or even vanishes, the history of Israel, as the history of a religious experience and a religious law, is bound to be relegated to the domains of anthropology or comparative literature. The historical role of the Jews will be diminished in comparison with those of the classical civilizations of Greece and Rome, because the Jewish experience appears narrow, constricted, and one-dimensional, compressed and bequeathed only in a Book, while these two mighty civilizations sport rich and many-faceted political, social, cultural, and artistic façades.

As far as later periods are concerned, the major difficulty in Jewish history for general historians revolves around the question of categorization. For generations the accepted historical framework has been the nation-state; but from the destruction of the Second Commonwealth, Jewish history ceased to be the history of a nation-state. If it is viewed as the history of a religion, the problem arises as to why such a sect, which shifted as it were to the margin of world history, should merit more concern than the Baptists or the Quakers or the Moravian Brothers. Indeed, in their incipient periods such sects appear as striking examples of revolutionary new phenomena emerging in the midst of some great spiritual ferment. But once their stormy, precedent-breaking Sturm und Drang phase passed and they settled down as quietistic groups enclosed within their own narrow bounds, the world at large lost interest in them.

As for the influence of the Jewish spirit in history, Gentiles claim that the Book which enshrines it in all its grandeur has become a common heritage. The descendants of its authors are no longer needed to maintain the influence which emanates from it, or to ensure to it a special direction. Furthermore, theory has it – as expressed by Toynbee and accepted by not a few in the non-Jewish world – that after their initial creative period, the Jews became fossilized and incapable of further creativity.

The role of the Jews as cultural intermediaries between Greek philosophy, Moslem culture, and medieval Christianity rates only an aside. Liberal historians then only reluctantly and guardedly dwell on the economic role of the Jews in international trade and in the development of public credit, because they hesitate to offend Jewish sensitivities by too much emphasis upon usury, interest, financial matters, etc. However, there is a more profound reason for this reticence. A liberal historian, friendly to Jews, once said to me: "I see no reason to single out Jews, since I see them as fundamentally no different from other citizens, except for their religion and tradition. I hesitate to play into the hands of anti-Semites by treating the Jews as a special phenomenon and as a foreign stock." The great personalities of Jewish descent, such as Spinoza, Disraeli, Marx, Ricardo or Franz Kafka, should be seen, in his view, as part of the culture from which they derived and within which they worked, members of a nation-state or of humanity, and only incidentally members of the Jewish race or descendants of the Jewish religious tradition.

When writing his important *History of Europe*, H. A. L. Fisher, the noted English historian, did not know how to handle the Jews, but felt that he must recognize them in some way. He found a solution all his own; he relegated them to the Introduction. After "giving them their due" and devoting one page to them, he was done with the Jews as such and did not refer to them again in the body of his thousand-page book.

It is interesting that in recent decades a new term has been coined, "Judeo-Christian," a term which is particularly prevalent in America. This expression and the time of its appearance are another demonstration of the way new historical categories emerge within a certain socio-cultural atmosphere, as a function of contemporary problems and preoccupations; for it was born of the encounter of American Judaism and Anglo-Saxon Protestantism in the "melting-pot."

Certain Jewish historians, trying to demonstrate the outstanding role of Jews in history, have written books which are, in effect, no more than digests of Jewish names upon which fortune has beamed, lists of notables who became famous in the world of business, banking, politics, social service, music, theater, sports or other fields, regardless of whether they were fully Jews, half-Jews, or even apostate. If the man received the Nobel Prize, he is ours.

In my statements on the Jewish component in world history, I am referring to Jews not as individuals but as a corporate identity. I am deliberately avoiding such terms as "ethnic group" or "religious sect." I have in mind a way of life, and patterns of thought, feeling and behavior – in short, mentality. If such a collective Jewish spirit exists, how can it be identified? How can its characteristic manifestations be isolated and its impact on its surroundings verified? These questions are being asked on the assumption that the encounter between Jews and the non-Jewish world has differed fundamentally from the confrontation of either the Bulgarians, the Dutch or the Japanese, for example, with world history. Furthermore, I have deliberately chosen the term "world history" or "universal history" rather than "history of nations," because my concern is not with one nation or another with whom the Jews came into contact, but with world history as an entity in the cultural sense.

I will not consider the Far East, since I know nothing about it, though my knowledge of it is sufficient for me to maintain that, from a Jewish standpoint, it is a blank page. I will also pass over Islam, because of my lack of competence in this complex area. My concern here is not only with the spiritual influence of Judaism, but with Jews as a living factor, both active and activating, a stimulus and irritant to others as well as the object of the doings of others. For the form in which the Jews were such objects is of vast significance not only to the Jews themselves, but to all those whose activities bore upon the Jews. Often victims of the actions of others, the Jews also became the touchstone for the conduct and deeds of the latter and the mirror enabling them – and impelling them – to define themselves in opposition to the Jews or in comparison with them.

Which elements in world history clearly and distinctly bear the Jewish imprint, and how can we identify them? First, there must be proof of a direct and continuous connection or of an intensive encounter that left ineradicable traces in the non-Jewish environment. Second, it must be established with certainty that the impact left by this connection on western Christian culture has no parallel in other cultures.

Matthew Arnold's well-known essay, "Hebraism and Hellenism," seeks to prove that all the products and values of western culture are of either Hebrew or Greek origin, and to depict the entire history of western civilization, from ancient times, as a constant tension between these two components, the Jewish and the Greek. The Jewish spirit, according to Arnold, is based on an extreme limitation of the self, on adherence to a single exclusive, all-embracing principle of life. The purpose of life is not self-realization by experimenting with as many and varied forms of life as possible, not variegated and yet well-balanced self-expression, but the perpetuation of the living Torah and the spinning-out of the thread of tradition. The Jew is forever accompanied by the fear of the Lord and the horror of transgression. He feels bound by the commandments of "Justice, justice, shalt thou pursue" and "Thou shalt proceed on the righteous path." Because of this, he shuts his eyes to whole spheres and qualities of life, especially the aesthetic, which are considered distractions, or temptations leading man astray, even to sin.

In contrast, the Greek spirit is characterized by an extreme openness, an insatiable intellectual curiosity, and a responsiveness to everything offered by the world of the senses. To the Greeks, life is an endless adventure, and self-realization is its objective; the harmony of experience, thought and conduct, the harmony of the true, the good, and the beautiful is the ultimate – and attainable – goal. Whereas the severity of the moral commandment informs all the life of the Jews, a consciousness freed from all restraint and restriction is the *alpha* and *omega* of the Greeks. If we turn to the distinction drawn by Isaiah Berlin in a completely different context, we find the Jew comparable to a hedgehog and the Greek to a fox. One is withdrawn within himself, encased in his armor, stubborn and tense; the other, eyes always roving, nostrils flaring, searches tirelessly – and from this comes the flowering of science, philosophy, and the arts in Greece.

But that very limitation, it seems to me, that self-enclosing, that exclusiveness, is the secret of the effectiveness – not the superiority – of the Jewish component in world history. We will not deal with the obvious, the well-known, and the non-controversial, such as monotheism or the moral teachings of the prophets. We will concentrate on that which seems ambivalent and equivocal to our critics, namely Judaism as a tribal religion and as a theocratic system. These two organically related elements were thorns in the side of many well-wishing non-Jews.

It can be assumed that all the ancient religions, including the Greek and the Roman, were at their inception tribal; each tribe had its religion, each nation its gods. These religions were bodies of laws which shaped the fabric of life in all its aspects, with no distinction between religion and state, between church and society, between the commandments of the Gods and the orders of the king, between religious morality and the principles of social conduct. However, Greek distinctiveness was swallowed up within the Hellenistic empires, and Rome, starting out with its tribal religion, became a world empire. These originally tribal religions found themselves in constant contact and friction with many other different religions. As a consequence, not only did each religion lose its distinct identity, and become part of a syncretism which blurred differences, but also the proliferation of religions, the dilution of the compactness and the sharply contoured identity of each of them deprived religion of the character of a doctrine which regulates the whole of existence. Life became divided into religious, cultural and socio-political spheres. While the mighty Empires developed into cosmopolitan despotisms, religion became mere ritual to the mass of the people, and the cultural and social elite exchanged its religious faith for abstract philosophy, at once individualistic and universal, such as Stoicism and Epicureanism.

Only a slight connection remained between the religion of the masses and the philosophy of the enlightened on the one hand, and the concrete existence of the individual and the affairs of state on the other. This polarization in the realm of beliefs and ideas had far-reaching consequences in the social-political sphere: not only did tribal unity and distinctness disintegrate, but the consciousness of collective fate vanished among the component parts of society, and very little was left of a sense of partnership between the despotic rulers and those whom they ruled. The distant Caesar in Rome was raised to the dignity of god and saviour and the official worship of this Caesar-god became the cement which unified the varied and remote lands of the empire. The homeland of the enlightened, however, was now the universe and the temple of their religion the heart, while the concrete world around was merely a shell and of peripheral concern.

Concrete reality lost its justification as it were, and after the loss of the sense of common endeavor, no concept of community, of congregation, could take root. There was no longer a collective personality, conscious of its identity and historic continuity, of a common share in aspirations, institutions, symbols, myths, traditions and hopes and visions – in brief of all those things which make a multitude of human beings into a people, a nation, a community. Thus were created the conditions and climate which enabled Christianity to offer itself as an other-worldly heavenly homeland and a creed encompassing all of humanity.

The Jews were the only group which remained tightly knit. Their life was given unity and made tremendously real and meaningful by the identity of thought and conduct, and by the fact that the bearer of this idea of unity was the community and not the individual believer. The rise of the synagogue, the house of prayer and the Minyan, the congregation, as substitute for or coeval with the unique national shrine, in the wake of the destruction of the first Temple and the dispersal, was of momentous importance. To the extent of my knowledge, this form of *communitas*, of congregation, is not to be found in any other religion or civilization up to the modern period.

Of course, the world of the Middle Ages derived its inspiration from non-Jewish sources as well – from memories of Greece and Rome, from Greek philosophy, from Roman legal precedents, and from the traditions of the Germanic tribes, and indeed Christianity identified itself in emphatic opposition to Judaism as a universal creed. But what Christianity took over from its mother-religion – the idea and institution of the community and congregation – was the most effective and decisive instrument of its phenomenal success. The Greek heritage was filtered through the Jewish communal religious patterns. The abstract starkness of Greek philosophy and ethical teachings needed concretization and institutionalization, which only such "Jewish" channels as the practical commandments, religious symbols, popular imagery, above all the congregation, could supply. In short, to become an effective, living force, Greek philosophy had to be theocratized and absorbed into a single totality, woven into a fabric with no seams. Thus the classical values were transformed from precepts for the educated into the common heritage of all.

Basic and crucial as the distinction has been in Papal Christianity between the *ecclesia docens* and the *ecclesia discens*, between the hierarchy that teaches, administers the sacraments, provides leadership, and transmits grace, and the ordinary believers, that is, the passive recipients, the masses, the Catholic Church of the Middle Ages never lost the tradition of *universitas fidelium*, according to which the totality of believers constitutes a congregation, with a corporate identity, a group personality, in short, the *corpus Christi*, the mystical Body of Christ. This religious community is identical with the people, one people, despite differences of class, descent, and legal and social status. Through the example it transmitted, through its continuous influence on the countless millions who read the Scriptures, chanted "Jewish" hymns, recited Jewish psalms or listened Sunday after Sunday to the preacher standing in front of the congregation and speaking of the God of Abraham, Isaac and Jacob, of the righteous or the wicked of the Chosen people before its birthright was taken away from it by the new true dispensation, Judaism remained a living influence of unrivalled effectiveness.

A paradoxical dualism characterizes the encounter of Jewish history and world history through the ages. On the one hand, the Jewish heritage was the mortar which unified scattered disparate tribes of different languages and traditions – with little or no culture and hardly any contact between themselves – into "Christendom," in other words into that Western civilization which was for centuries dominant among the civilizations of the world. On the other hand, the Jewish example of a holy community helped so many congeries of tribes to unite into nations, first by enabling them to gain a collective consciousness as a congregation of the faithful, or as a national Church situated in a given territory and living under the same sovereign. The notion of the "national" Church was the prelude to the consciousness of national identity.

All the history of political doctrines and controversies and much, if not most, of the political struggles throughout the Middle Ages and the Renaissance, perhaps until the end of the seventeenth century, could be summed up under the title: "The Adventures of the Biblical Story of Samuel, Saul, and David." This story was the mirror, the code of law, and the source of inspiration to all the protagonists in the theoretical and political struggles as well as to those observing and reflecting upon them.

This idea of congregation acquired greater reality under Protestantism than it had ever possessed in the life of the Catholic nations. The idea of universal priesthood did away with the exclusive elitism represented by the Catholic Church hierarchy, with its monopoly over the administration of the sacraments. The Protestant congregation was a congregation of believers in the manner of the Jewish community. Calvin's congregation in Geneva, the Massachusetts Bay Colony, and John Knox's followers in Scotland identified themselves with a proud and militant consciousness as heirs to that Jewish tradition. It made no difference whether the king or the elders stood at the head of the congregation. In the absence of a priesthood which stood above and apart as a vessel of grace, all were members of a peoplehood of priests and constituted together a holy nation. Every one of them felt called upon to make the community into a congregation of saints and to guard it from profanation. With the disappearance of the magical and sacramental elements from the Protestant creeds, all emphasis was placed not merely on faith, but on a strict code of behavior, on moral conduct, and of course on the study of Scripture; in some cases preference was given to the Old Testament.

It is quite legitimate to see in the militant congregation of the faithful at the time of the wars of religion the matrix of modern nationalism. I am referring not just to the sense of collective identity of a highly organized and embattled sect, with its strict and all-embracing code of behavior, but more so, to the proud consciousness of embodying and actively asserting a religious mission which animated the English Puritans, the Dutch Calvinists, and others, to fight the wars of the Lord, destroy the images and idols, spread the word of God, and purify Christianity. In the Catholic camp, it was Spain that proclaimed its mission to carry the cross over the ocean and to defend the pure Catholic faith on the battlefields of Europe. The fifteenth-century Czech followers of Jan Hus, Queen Elizabeth in England, Cromwell and Milton, all identified themselves as the Maccabees of the modern age, warring against idolatry and the profanation of God's name, and fighting for freedom of conscience and the glory of the Lord. The soldiers of God, the members of the holy nation, were hardly bothered by the conceptual difference between the community of the faithful and the people chosen by God. Modern nationalism – that which preceded the French Revolution – was in short born of a sense of destiny which was primarily religious. It is incorrect to maintain that the nation was created first and then sought a destiny for itself; it was the concept of the elect which gave birth to national consciousness.

As hinted at the beginning of this essay, these developments were loaded with ambivalence. While they stimulated the growth of the idea of the rights of man (at first the rights of the believer) and of democratic popular sovereignty, they goaded nations into waging wars and embarking upon campaigns of conquest. They inspired feelings of individual responsibility and self-respect among men and often strengthened the bonds of social solidarity, at the same time that they bred arrogance, aggressive sentiments, and rapacious designs.

In the Protestant lands, the congregation of the faithful developed its brand of secular nationalism, to a considerable extent under the influence of the idea of progressive revelation. Zealous to comprehend the word of the Lord, and to interpret it truthfully – each individual according to his conscience in order to save his own soul, and all together in order to realize together the way of life of a holy congregation – some of the Protestant believers, especially in the American colonies, gradually concluded that it was wrong to limit divine revelation to one hour alone at the dawn of mankind, as though everything had been revealed then and from that time onwards the Divine presence and prophecy had departed from the believers forever. The divine presence continued to reveal itself in every age and to every generation, even though no longer by means of signs and wonders, miracles and symbols – as it had been wont to in ancient days when wishing to vouchsafe truths to a mankind in a state of childhood or early adolescence. The means of imparting divine wisdom and assistance were now abstract ideas, concepts, scientific discoveries, and philosophical truths, as befits generations which have grown up and matured. As for the Catholic countries, the transformation from congregation of the faithful to secular nation took largely the form of a revolt against the religious message and its bearer, the established Church allied to the throne and part of the feudal order; the classic example is France of the eighteenth century and the Revolution.

The immediate result of eighteenth-century rationalism and the secularization of society that followed it was the displacement of the Jewish component by the Greek, the Roman and other components. However, this elimination of the Jewish influence was only temporary, because in the great secular religions – the salvationist ideologies which drew their sustenance from rationalist thought and the ideas of freedom – the Jewish component again became a powerful inspiration, the focus of a new all-embracing system of values, and the fulcrum of vast historical happenings.

The polemical thrust of iconoclastic French rationalism was primarily directed against superstition and prejudice, religious fanaticism and religious persecution. In this regard, the Jew figured as the primary and eternal victim of persecution, of religious intolerance, and of aggressive and benighted fanaticism. Man would now be seen no longer as primarily a son of the church, but as a human being endowed with reason. He would no longer be regarded as a member of a tribe dominated by history, but as a creature born a *tabula rasa* neither with any predetermined gifts bestowed by divine grace, nor with evil penchants, the sign of God's wrath. Every person was now held to be perfectible and able or even destined to reach perfection, with the help of proper education and reformed social institutions. This conviction made the persecution of the Jew and his inferior status appear as the classical example of the old evils, which had to be wiped off the face of the earth. This conviction was represented by Gotthold Ephraim Lessing and Rousseau, in the first place. But there were those who could not or did not want to forget or let others forget that Judaism was the progenitor of Christianity. Voltaire and d'Holbach were genuine Jew-haters. But one did not have to be obsessed by anti-Semitism in order to condemn the Jews as the begetters of Christian distortions: it was easier to attack and defame Christianity by casting aspersions on Biblical Judaism and mocking the faith and customs of the Jews. It was an effective way to revile Christianity among its children: "Just see the source from which it all sprang." Furthermore, the Jews were not protected by any censor; the Jew thus absorbed the blows intended for another.

However, this attitude grew much more ambiguous following the rise of the theory so well highlighted by Prof. Hertzberg of the profound and eternal conflict between the Greek heritage and the Asiatic (not yet Semitic) world, of which the Jew was the representative and concrete and ever-present embodiment. The Greek spirit personified all sweetness and light; the Jewish was all darkness, narrowness, and fanaticism. However, their basic assumptions prevented the eighteenth-century thinkers from departing from as well as arriving at racial determinism. For every man was to them the product of his environment, of education, and of social arrangements, and he was destined for perfection through the workings of progress. No judgement could be passed against an entire race or against an individual of a certain race because of what they were by accident of birth.

The anti-Semites among the rationalists did come near to modern racial anti-Semitism by claiming that the accursed religion of the Jews had so thoroughly corrupted them that they were beyond remedy in their degenerate state. They would not however ask themselves the obvious question: had an evil religion brought the Jews to such a path, or had the Jews, a rotten race to begin with, engendered such a repugnant creed out of their inborn evil?

I would put stress on the ambivalent influence of the Enlightenment on the position of the Jew. While as such it tended to liberate the Jew as a human being and a citizen, the anti-religious rationalists among the eighteenth-century *philosophes* succeeded in undermining and, to a considerable extent, in destroying the feeling of awe that non-Jews had for Judaism, a feeling connected by countless threads with the central mystery of Christianity, regardless of the spirit of rejection and distaste which contemporary Jews aroused. Only a few, such as Montesquieu, and in part Rousseau and Herder, were capable of developing empathy for Jewish attitudes and even feelings of reverence for Judaism as an indestructible and venerable phenomenon, which has withstood the ages, the natural decay of nations, bitter persecution and universal contempt. For the majority of the writers of the period the Jews were too close, too prosaic and often too obstreperously disturbing (e.g.: Voltaire's debts to Jewish moneylenders) to exercise the kind of fascination that distant tribes and the noble savage were capable of. The Jews appeared a strange tribe, bewildering, stubborn, and repellent in their conduct, their zealous adherence to weird and absurd customs, and their tribal solidarity.

The Jewish component became the test case in the confrontation between the two forces which were set in motion by the French Revolution, and between which, one may say, history has been swaying for almost two hundred years now – the aspiration to achieve universal unity and the desire to retain historic uniqueness.

The first derives from a fervent faith in the strength of man's conscious resolve to shape a rational and unified pattern of existence based upon the oneness of truth, the universal and eternally valid principles of justice and morality, and the objective trends in science, technology, communications, economy, which appear to create a world that is one. The second accords higher and indeed decisive significance to the strength and reality of such basic deterministic factors as natural conditions, blood, geography, climate, as well as religious and historical tradition. It claims that these powers are immeasurably stronger than all the abstract ideas and rational decisions of men who aspire to form their lives anew in accordance with universal blueprints or prearranged models. In constituting concrete, living, historical data they are the manifestation of authentic identity, original and unique selfhood.

Although at first glance it is possible to identify the rationalist approach with the universalist ideologies and to link determinism with nationalism, the doctrines of nationalism were in fact divided into two schools. The first is based on the conscious determination of men to constitute a unified nation and sustain national unity for the purpose of preserving common values and attaining common goals, with no reference to blood, descent and religious faith – e.g. the U.S.A. The second regards the nation as the function of blood, soil and history. The first sees the nation-state as a mere fragment of the one great robe of humanity. The second regards each nation as a unique entity, a law unto itself.

Precisely because of their marginality as a group, the Jews became the touchstone and measuring stick of these two different attitudes – the tendency towards oneness on the one hand, and the self-assertion of the unique on the other. Furthermore, the fate and status of the Jews tended to go a long way towards defining the nation in the midst of which they lived, to indicating whether it was a society based on a freely concluded social contract – theoretically, at least – between individuals-atoms or a living indivisible organism, with a distinct life over and above the existence of the individual men who form its component parts.

The believers in an open society, a democratic state, the rights of man and the principle of the equality of all citizens, could not feel they had achieved their aims so long as Jews were not accorded equality and their entry into the ranks of equal citizens was not guaranteed. To the guardians of the fortress of uniqueness, the free access of Jews to all positions signified the end of the "Christian state," the granting of Jewish emancipation marked a rejection of time-hallowed traditions and the destruction of a peculiar way of life and of authentic and original identity. Their penetration into the spiritual sanctum of the nation was a breach of the walls, a profanation of the pieties evolved through the centuries, an emasculation of the primary drives and a dilution of the original authenticity of the spiritual life of the race. However, these schools of thought were – for opposite reasons – united in their aversion to Jewish separatism.

Even liberalism found it hard to come to terms with the existence of a separate Jewish entity drawing its inspiration from national memories and hopes, while claiming and indeed enjoying full civic equality and active membership in the national body politic. Liberalism was therefore inclined to belittle the reality and significance of Jewish separatism and to hope for a speedy disintegration of Jewish communal cohesion. For Jewish separatism was calculated to serve as a potent argument against the two main tenets of the liberal *Weltanschauung*, individualism and universalism. To the determinists, the "living apart" of a religious ethnic group for so long and with such tenacity on the one hand, and the instinctive aversion of the majority nations to them as unassimilable and indigestible aliens on the other, served as proof of the correctness of their basic ideas on race, the uniqueness of each nation, and the irrelevance or even pernicious character of abstract universalist ideologies.

It is quite legitimate to argue that the relative success of Jewish emancipation west of the Rhine and its failure east of it were the result of the success of the ideas of the Enlightenment in the West and their defeat in Central and Eastern Europe; and that to the extent Jewish emancipation as it were gave reality to the victory of liberalism in the west, while in the east the refusal to grant Jews equality signaled and highlighted the failure of liberalism in that part of Europe, and indeed made it inevitable. One is at the same time permitted to put more emphasis upon numbers – the proportion of Jews in the respective populations – or on the time-lag factor in social-economic development. Be that as it may, in historical perspective the difference in the evolution of the Jewish situation in the various parts of Europe (and, it can be said, in the world, if the New World is included along with western Europe) is a fact of momentous and compelling importance.

What was said earlier about the role of the Jewish component in the Middle Ages holds true for the modern period. If by his very existence, the Jew became a challenge to the nations of Europe to identify themselves – to define themselves and the nature of their national consciousness – it would be difficult to exaggerate the role of the Jewish component in the trend towards universal oneness in both the sphere of concrete action and the realm of political thought and social vision. We are faced here with a series of paradoxes. The Jewish protagonists of this trend were very eager to cut themselves off – and at times even formally – from the Jewish community, vehemently condemning Jewish isolationism. Every one of them acted in this respect in his individual capacity, since a corporate endeavor to disintegrate was ruled out by definition. Nevertheless – and this is the heart of the matter – in spite of themselves and as if to mock their own firm intentions, all these escapees from Jewish clannishness into the wide world, where there were to be no Jews, Greeks or gentiles, but men, behaved as if in accordance with rearranged patterns that demonstrated a distinct corporate identity. In a way tragic to themselves, they would thus confirm their enemies in the view that blood, heritage, tradition, and history were more potent than the decision of the individual to set precedents for himself and begin completely anew. This object-lesson was, as hinted before, generalized by the enemies of Jewry into an all-embracing philosophy with which to afflict and finally seek to destroy Judaism.

We all know Werner Sombart's exaggerated description of the role of the Dutch Jews in the rise of early capitalism during Holland's golden age in the seventeenth century. The Netherlands were then the metropolis of a world empire, Amsterdam the banking center of the world, and its Sephardic Jews, according to Sombart's version, held in their hands the strings of world trade – especially the monetary transactions. Thus, they were able to convert the world into one market and prepare the funds for the capitalist investment of coming generations, in the various parts of the globe. About the same time, Max Weber advanced his famous thesis about the impact of the Calvinist-Puritan mentality upon the rise of capitalism, especially the ethical values of Old Testament Judaism as they were imbibed by Protestant sectarian Bible readers of the Psalms and Proverbs. The rational calculus, the precise book-keeping, the sober assessment of ends and means of early capitalist enterprise was made to appear by Max Weber as stemming from the book-keeping which the Jewish and the Calvinist believer engaged in when dealing with the Almighty, in observing or failing to observe His commandments and in searching for confirmation that he is one of the well-beloved of God, success being regarded as proof of belonging to the elect.

The eighteenth-century English essayist Addison compared the Jews to hinges and hooks, items useless in themselves, but without which no house could be built. Whatever the exaggeration in Sombart's and Weber's assessment of the role of the Jews or the Jewish component in the economic evolution of Europe and the world in the earlier centuries of our era, there can be no doubt as to their enormous importance and effectiveness in the nineteenth century. In certain spheres the Jewish component may then appear as even decisive. It was largely the Jews who in one way or another, directly or indirectly, linked together various and distant parts of the world and fused them into one market by supplying the abstract, anonymous, and universal sinews and veins. Jewish banks regulated the flow of gold; Jewish financiers and entrepreneurs built the trains that joined provinces, countries, and whole areas of the world; and Jews pioneered the tremendous modern network of mass communication. They were the founders of the first news agencies and many of the modern newspapers, which not only distributed news throughout the world, but molded a collective consciousness and shaped world public opinion, and bred a sense of a universal common endeavor, interdependence, indeed interest.

The great mobility of the Jews led to their concentration in capitals and large cities. There they shook off their traditional way of life, freed themselves from the compulsive habits and narrowness of provincial conservatism. The metropolis aroused their natural curiosity, stimulated their penchant for innovation, experiment, speculation, and risk. Jews were most conspicuous in the vanguard of all new pioneering ventures, and bold experiments: the railroads, fashion, psycho-analysis, nuclear physics, and the mass entertainment industry. It was as if the entire world had become their stage and homeland. They sought to supply man's necessities – whatever they were, wherever they were – cheaply, quickly, and in ever larger quantities. Hence, the major role of Jews in the trends towards standardization: in setting up chain stores, in stimulating public demand and satisfying it. The law of ambivalence again: the Jews have rendered immense service to the process of the democratization of modern society, but they have also had their part in the vulgarization of culture in the age of the masses. Through their concentration in metropolitan arteries and in the most sensitive nerve centers they became very powerful, but also conspicuous in a very vulnerable way.

As large as the role of the Jews was in the history of one nation or another, it can be said that the history of England, France and even Germany (prior to the twentieth century) would not have been significantly different if Jews had been absent from it. It is difficult, however, to imagine modern civilization without Marx, Freud, Einstein, Proust and Kafka. The outstanding contribution of Jews was to our civilization as such, rather than to this or that national culture; its focus was universal human values – on the one hand man per se created in the image of God, on the other hand the great human condition of men aggregated in society. The work of two outstanding creative and innovative Jews in our generation, Claude Lévi-Strauss in anthropology and Noam Chomsky in linguistics, is a most paradoxical and instructive example from this point of view. Modern racial theories derived much of their sustenance from the wonder-inspiring phenomenon of language and from the preoccupation with the bewildering variety and strangeness of thought and behavior among distant and primitive tribes. The fact that every language was a kind of unique miracle, that there are no two identical languages, that they were not created by the conscious and planned effort of individuals but grew and developed mysteriously of themselves, and were passed on from generation to generation like a natural force that erupts or grows without being consciously imitated and systematically guided but nevertheless blossoms into a marvelous structure that has rhyme and reason, cohesion and logic – all this seemed to speak strongly in favor of the uniqueness of every race and ethnic group and against the concept of the oneness of mankind. Whether it was their conscious intention or not, Lévi-Strauss' and Chomsky's achievement is geared to lay bare a kind of primal universal human logic behind the most bizarre and seemingly irrational and capricious expressions of tribal culture, folklore, ritual, legend, myth, saying and proverb, and to reveal a single basic structure of all human speech.

If the role of the Jewish component looms large in having shaped patterns of thought and forged the means for creating a world that is one, the impact of Judaism and Jews was even more potent in the growth of the vision of a world that is one into a passionate Messianic religion, embraced by the keenest idealists and by immense multitudes all over the world. The contribution of individual Jews and groups of Jews to the movements which propagated the salvationist message has been incalculable.

The Jewish concept of a Providence hovering over the chosen people, guiding history in general and directing it towards some salvationist denouement, in contradiction to the cyclical conceptions of history as eternal and aimless repetition, without any ultimate goal, held by the other great classical civilizations, has been the inspiration of the Christian view of history. The revolutionary potential of this vision has manifested itself from time to time in radical millennarian movements which sought to realize the kingdom of God by casting down evil and restoring Christianity to its early purity where there were no master and slave, rulers and subjects, mine and thine, coercion and punishment. The conservative view, which saw evil in the life of man and society as a punishment and atonement for man's original sin, and as a necessary stage on the way to the kingdom of grace, acted as a curb on this radicalism. It made effective use of such safety valves as the promise of reward and threat of punishment in the next world where all souls would stand equal before the heavenly Judge, and the vision of redemption at the end of days.

The decline of religious faith caused men to look for another vision of history which would give meaning to their pilgrimage on this earth. If there was no heavenly tribunal before which all mankind would be judged on an equal basis, the problem of the righteous who suffered and the wicked who prospered acquired acute urgency. It had to be resolved here and now. Thus there arose the vision of history as a continuous and sustained progress towards salvation on this earth. All of history came to be depicted as striding inexorably towards some preordained denouement, to be followed by a state of perfect social harmony. Here was a promise not limited to the salvation of the individual's soul alone, but an all-embracing one, giving indeed pride of place to social justice throughout the land and the realization of the ideal of community, where there would be no distinction between the individual interest and the good of the many, between freedom and equality, between private morality and political conduct, between theory and practice.

For two hundred years this faith has been stirring the hearts of millions and has progressively encompassed all the tribes and nations throughout the world. Since the eighteenth century the world has been teeming with prophets, thinkers, standard bearers, groups of fighters, conspirators and schemers, mass parties, which have been lying in wait and preparing themselves for the day of total

Revolution. In this camp the Jews played a tremendous role, and in certain ways and situations, even a decisive one. They were driven by an intense, stormy, sweeping Messianic urge, a burning faith fortified by a sustained intellectual effort on the one hand, and by boundless dedication to the practical organizational tasks for realizing revolutionary goals on the other.

The Messianic faith was in their blood. They were unable to take evil, oppression, the lawlessness in society for granted and make peace with them, or to accept meaninglessness in history as inevitable, eternal, preordained; nor could they subsume under that vision of utter resignation their own suffering fate. They were irresistibly fascinated by and riveted to the vision of universal salvation. It seemed also such a wonderful answer to their own predicament, to their personal anguish and that ambiguous estate of escapees from one tradition who are not admitted to any of the other established traditions. And so the Revolution became their homeland, a universal and boundless kingdom, with no local focus or political borders. To say it once more, it became a sheet anchor to those of our people who had abandoned or severed their connection with the ancient and all-encompassing heritage of their own people, but were not able, did not succeed, or were not permitted to adhere to another culture. They could now embrace as passionately convinced crusaders a lofty creed without the sense of self-denial or hypocrisy, of betrayal or humiliation that attached to apostasy. There were no revolutionary internationalists among gentiles whose universalist passion could compare with that of Karl Marx, Rosa Luxemburg, Trotsky, Karl Radek, Zinoviev, and the Jewish prophets of the New Left in our own time.

The violent reaction against modern universalism which began at the end of the nineteenth century transformed anti-Semitism from a matter affecting only the persecuted Jews and their persecutors into a problem of universal significance and a touchstone of the radical tendencies in modern history – indeed, in history *tout court.* The Jew, intractable and recalcitrant, the chosen of the Lord and, at one and the same time, the murderer of the Savior, never ceased as such to disturb and provoke Christianity. The great debate between the church and the synagogue not only served as a vehicle to vent anger, hatred and contempt for Judaism; it also furthered the crystallization of the identity and essence of the Christian faith. The major expulsions and Jewish migrations then had their far from negligible effect on the course of world history. It is sufficient to recall – as hinted in an earlier context – the impact of the expulsion from Spain, of the Marranos' underground existence, and of the migration of the exiles and some of the Marranos to Holland and the Turkish Empire, upon the shifting of the centers of international trade and economic-political power. However, as was noted, only around 1880 did anti-Semitism acquire its full significance as a momentous factor in world history.

All the forces which viewed the ever faster and ever more radical pace of change in technology, economy, society, state, beliefs, ideas, and style of life, which was initiated by the encounter of the Industrial Revolution and the French Revolution with mistrust, fear or downright hostility; all the entrenched interests which were adversely affected, or feared that they would be harmed or even effaced by raging modernization; all the bearers of ancient prejudices and conservative habits that were disturbed and disrupted; all those with deep-seated attachments to the old customs, local peculiarities, historic symbols; all those who had grown so used to the exercise of dominion that they would be shocked by any refusal to obey and respect them unquestioningly; all the frustrated groups and individuals to whom the success of others, especially newcomers, is a source of irritation and scandal – all of them overcame in the last third of the nineteenth century their timidity and sense of resignation and defeat, sank their differences and joined hands in a defiant uprising against the force which they came to regard as the author of all the alarming changes, the only or chief profiteer of the distress and ruin of the old established, "solid" and "decent" elements – the Jewish Revolutionary.

It was the Revolution that brought the Jews out of the ghetto and propelled them into the center of the world stage. They were its main beneficiaries, and – to continue the train of thought – they had evidently brought it forth. It was bewildering and disturbing to see a pariah suddenly grow so successful and ubiquitous and so he became identified in many envious or merely confused eyes with all the new evil things they disliked and feared. At the beginning of the nineteenth century the anti-Semitic reactionaries in Germany claimed that the concepts of the rights of man and human equality, the ideas of universal natural law and popular sovereignty, were Jewish imports, brought over from France in order to weaken and overcome the natural resistance of the German national organism, with its instinctive mechanism of self-defense, to the penetration of aliens – namely the Jews. Similarly, at the end of the nineteenth century, Charles Maurras was to claim that these same ideals were brought to France by Jews from Germany as a weapon for breaking down the fences which the French nation had erected throughout the centuries. At the beginning of the twentieth century, the high priest of world anti-Semitism, Houston Stewart Chamberlain, labeled the nineteenth century the "century of the Jews," comparing the alleged preponderance of Jews at the time to that of the French in the seventeenth century, that of the Spanish in the sixteenth century, and that of the English in the eighteenth century.

All the tendencies towards universal oneness, which worked to break down barriers between countries, nations and languages – such as capitalism, liberalism, democracy, socialism – were made to appear as symptoms of the Jewish virus which causes the disintegration of the individuality of historic ethnic entities. Moreover, while ardently preaching to others the unity of mankind, the blurring of differences, and the equality of all beings, and condemning and mocking all conservative attachments and racial and national separatism, the Jews themselves clung desperately to their own tradition of a nation dwelling apart, and refrained from intermarrying with outsiders. Therefore, their universal teachings, the anti-Semites concluded, were nothing but a ruse whose purpose was to lull the nations into listless inattention, to undermine their self-assurance and destroy their compact unity so that the Jews could dominate them all. Thus arose the myth of the Jewish world-wide conspiracy to debauch, debilitate and subdue the nations of the world, the foundation of *The Protocols of the Elders of Zion.*

Anti-Semitism was elevated to being the pivot of a social ideology, a philosophy of history, indeed a *Weltanschauung* which claimed to refute and replace the world-view that was bequeathed by the Enlightenment. Furthermore it developed a dialectic and a momentum which inexorably led to a total and defiant denial and rejection of Christianity. The new race theory claimed that there was no class war between exploiters and exploited within one and the same nation as Jewish Marxism taught. Jewish finance capitalism, as distinguished from the allegedly productive gentile variety, was the exploiter of all the nations and all the classes within them. The class struggle was thus nothing but a Jewish contrivance, and both Jewish and non-Jewish socialists were, knowingly or not, agents of Jewish capitalism. The true socialist revolution would be realized not through the dictatorship of the proletariat but through the overthrow of Jewish domination.

From a threat to the well-being of the national organism, the Jews became the mortar of a kind of universalism in reverse; of the anti-Semitic International which at its congresses proclaimed war on the destructive influence of the Asiatic element in and upon Europe. In their endeavors to refute the basic assumptions of universalist liberal rationalism the theoreticians of racial anti-Semitism sought support in Darwin, Nietzsche and others. In place of the oneness of mankind they put the primacy of race. The phenomenon of eternal struggle for survival was made by them to appear much nobler than the yearning for peace and harmony and reconciliation. The ideal of equality was contemptuously rejected in favor of the urge for self-expression and self-assertion by the strong and the select, each in a manner uniquely his own. The search for objective and universal truth – held until then in veneration as the supreme ideal – made way for the challenge to cultivate the qualities of the warrior. The morality of self-restraint was condemned as a rationalization of envy and the token of a fear of life – that dangerous adventure – and as a symptom of decaying vitality. In brief, the whole ascetic tradition in ethics was declared to be the cunning invention of the weak, the inferior, the unsuccessful, the fearful, and the botched – more precisely, the product of a priestly Jewish conspiracy in ancient days. Christianity, rationalism, liberalism, democracy, socialism, and above all, communism – all derivations of the Jewish spirit – were the instruments of – or the stages in – the uprising of the degenerate rabble against the racial and social elite: In the words of Hitler, "From Moses to Lenin."

Thus it came about that the myth of the Jews as the head of the world conspiracy against Germany hatched at the Versailles Conference at the close of the First World War, camouflaged as an endeavor to secure permanent peace among equal nations under the aegis of the League of Nations, found willing listeners among millions of Germans, and enabled Hitler to take a step, at the very start of his career, that symbolized in a most defiant manner the nature of his regime, a regime of revolt against those values which for one hundred and fifty years had been considered sacred, self-evident, and irrevocable. The Nuremburg Laws rescinded Jewish equality by a stroke of the pen in the name of the philosophy of *Blut und Boden*. The principle that man was born free to achieve self-realization through his own efforts – the pivot of our modern society based on contract – was thus replaced by the ancient conception of society based on status, or worse, on the inexorable primitive determinism which treats man's fate as already decided in his mother's womb, with no possibility of escape. The war against "Jewish" Bolshevism made possible the next stage – Auschwitz – which sounded a warning to all mankind as to the extent to which racism might challenge the sanctity of human life in an age of total race war, gas chambers and the hydrogen bomb.

During the second half of the twentieth century, the context of the Jewish component in history underwent a drastic and bewildering change. Contrary to the ardent early Zionist desire to solve an international problem – the Jewish question – by removing the persecuted and homeless from the international cauldron and converting them into a separate nation dwelling in security and recognized and guaranteed by international public law, the Jewish state and its immediate vicinity have become a focus of world events, a touchstone for international alignments, one of the most sensitive points in the very heart of the global power system, whose fate – who knows? – may decide who will rule the earth, and whether civilization will survive at all. Despite the preferences of many, and to the chagrin and horror of most, the political confrontation in our region has assumed a distinct ideological complexion. At the same time the danger to the state of Israel has unified the Jewish people. The proud and anguished support offered by world Jewry to embattled Israel and the uneasy and precarious alliance with the U.S. are again interpreted by the enemies of Judaism as evidence of a world Jewish conspiracy. But whereas in the not-too-distant past the enemies of Israel spoke of the Jewish-capitalist-communist-cosmopolitan camp, in our own time, we hear of the Zionist-imperialist-American plot.

At the head of the anti-Jewish camp stands that very Soviet Union to whose rise the Jews have made such a vital contribution, in formulating its ideology, playing a crucial role in the planning and execution of the October Revolution, and making possible, through their fervor, diligence and technical and organizational skill the establishment of a revolutionary regime in a country in ruins surrounded by countless internal and external enemies. In this regard, the drama that began almost two thousand years ago is repeating itself: the tidings that came forth from the midst of the

Jews are spreading and conquering many nations, but they, in turn, have become merciless enemies of the progenitors of their faith. What has occurred in recent years in Russia, Czechoslovakia, and Poland confirms a principle of Jewish history which Rosa Luxemburg recognized when she bitterly referred to a Jewish-Polish proverb in a letter to her Jewish friend Yogiches: "When in need they turn to the Jew – then when the Jew has done his job, they reward him with a kick."

The first great hours of revolutionary exaltation tend to blur all differences between the victorious fighters and engender an orgy of universal brotherhood. When the early wave of enthusiasm inevitably subsides, and the mounting difficulties and the greyness of the days make the world look much less changed than it was thought, people begin to return to their former habits and prejudices of hundreds of years, and become again conscious of the differences and different interests which divide them. After the doctrine of socialism in one country was proclaimed, and still more, when the motherland of socialism was invaded by the Nazis, resuscitating deep-rooted feelings of Russian patriotism, it became more and more evident that the Jews had remained Jews, and that the gentiles are gentiles. Early in the Revolution, when the old bureaucracy and professional intelligentsia had refused to collaborate with the new regime, or could not be trusted by it, a disproportionate number of Jews came to occupy leading positions, because they were eager, trustworthy, capable – or because Petlura's pogroms left them with no choice but to defend the new order. In the meanwhile, a new Russian generation had grown up, well trained, without the reservations of the older generation of intelligentsia, and indeed in need of jobs. This in itself limited the dimensions of the Jewish component. But this new generation also strove to limit it even further, at first inadvertently, and in the course of time, quite consciously and with the help of reasons of principle.

As has been the case with all victorious Messianic revolutions, the Soviet system degenerated into an authoritarian establishment. The Jews appeared to the leaders of the latter as intellectual nonconformists, as eternal cosmopolitan rebels, furthermore as suspects because of their profound sympathy for Israel and their ties with world Jewry.

The rulers of Russia are genuinely fearful that the example of the Jews asserting their separate identity and ardent desire to leave

Russia for Israel may stir up the other national minorities, encourage the underground movement of intellectuals and opponents of the regime, and split the communist movement throughout the world. Once again Judaism is being proclaimed a disruptive element, a solvent, the carrier of the germ of decomposition and revolution. But in how ironic a situation!

The phenomenal success of the Jews in the New World, to which the center of weight of the Jewish dispersion has shifted after the Holocaust, and which regards as its destiny the conscious and voluntary amalgamation of all races, nations and religions in one national association, has given rise, at the present, to problems which are both old and new at the same time. When liberalism was at its height, especially in America, the impressive achievements of the Jews appeared to themselves and to their liberal sympathizers as confirmation of the principle that success was the natural reward of talent in a regime of equality of opportunity. The blacks in America (and members of the lower strata in communist-controlled countries) are now putting forward claims which are at variance with the liberal principle of *la carrière ouverte aux talents*, namely demands for special privileges as compensation for centuries of oppression and discrimination which had prevented them for so long from enjoying equal opportunity in the race for success. The edge of this demand, which is voiced loudly by the blacks in America and by their white supporters in the New Left, is directed against the Jews, inasmuch as they are a stratum, which, despite past oppression, has succeeded, thanks to its talents and diligence, in scaling the social ladder with dizzying rapidity.

Similarly, the State of Israel has been placed in an ambivalent position in the eyes of the awakening races and civilizations of Asia and Africa. Even though the teachings of Marx, the Jew, have been a source of inspiration to millions of inhabitants of Asia and Africa, there is no awareness of the Jewish component and its historic role among the millions of the Far East, India, and Africa who do not know the Bible and have had no contact with Jews. As the relative weight of China, Japan, India and the other countries of the Far East and Africa increases upon the world scales, the relative importance of the Jewish component is bound therefore to decline, and its dimensions to shrink correspondingly. While Western civilization may regard the State of Israel as reparation for the countless injustices which the Jews had suffered at its hands, the non-European races are free of a sense of guilt towards the Jew and are not even able to comprehend the uniqueness of Judaism and of the Jewish claim to their ancient homeland.

It is difficult to expect that the extraordinary success of the tiny State of Israel in its struggle for existence against the millions besieging it should not remind them of the success of the white conquerors in their endeavor to dominate the colored races. We cannot take lightly the image of the State of Israel and of Judaism as a whole which is continuously being impressed upon the minds of countless millions in Asia and Africa at this moment. We should take cognizance of the fact that for hundreds of years the position of Jews throughout the world was determined not by what they were and what they did, but by the image which others developed of them: let us recall the impact of Shylock, created by Shakespeare, who never in his life met a Jew.

Not a few of our people in the Diaspora are influenced by the description of the State of Israel by its enemies on the Left as an imperialist aggressor. They are haunted by simplistic, outworn images of the division of mankind into the "children of light" and the "children of darkness," and by the idea that it was the destiny of the Jews to carry high the banner of the international camp of the fighters for freedom and progress. Their minds are torn, and many of them are driven to self-hatred. The signs are multiplying that as a result of the far-reaching changes in the setting of the Jewish component in world history, the State of Israel and the Jewish people with it are now being hurled into one of those great historic gales that burst upon us from age to age. What the shape of things will be when the storm has abated no one can as yet tell.

First published in *Midstream*, March 1972.

Part Two

From Anti-Semitism to the Holocaust

Mission and Testimony – The Universal Significance of Modern Anti-Semitism

The fate of the Jews during the last two hundred years is indissolubly connected with issues which form the very core of the condition of modern man. Jews played so important a role in modern history, not because they had a mission to carry out (though this aspect should not be belittled), but because it was their fate to serve as a testimony, as a living witness, a touchstone, a whipping block and symbol all in one.

I

If the French Revolution may be considered as the beginning of an era that has not yet come to an end, we can view the 1880s as the beginning of a historical wave – with anti-Semitism as one of its motive forces – which may, for all we know, not yet have been brought to a halt in 1945. Jewish emancipation in the French Revolution was an offshoot of the triumph of rationalism and the idea of the rights of man. More than that, it sealed the complete victory of these values, since the Jews were a marginal case. The anti-Semitic rage that erupted in Europe eighty years ago was not a by-product, but the point of departure and focus of a vast political and ideological movement. From its Archimedean point of anti-Semitism that movement was driven on to repudiate everything affirmed by humanist rationalism, and indeed everything taught by its parents, Christianity.

The tragic paradox of the Jews in modern times has been the fact that their existence and success have been dependent upon the triumph of the idea of oneness as represented by liberal democracy and socialism, while the very phenomenon of Jewry is an unparalleled demonstration of the enormous power of the element of uniqueness. The Jews did not want and could not escape the fact of their uniqueness; the general community would not and could not be made oblivious of it.

The liberal state which accorded full rights to its Jewish citizens on the same basis as to all others, including freedom of economic pursuit, a share in the running of the nation's affairs, took its stand on the theory of a social contract concluded between men of reason. Racial origin, religious affiliation, social class, and all those deep but elusive differences, rooted in and exemplified by habit and custom, reflex and prejudice, instinct and frame of mind, disposition and manner of reasoning, which separate and isolate men, were considered irrelevant when compared with the forces of conscious deliberating reason. On the other hand, the texture of the liberal state was limited from its very inception to a legal framework. Outside it, the citizen was free to follow his own judgment. Such a regime was ideal for the Jews: but to their misfortune it never even came into being. Liberalism came to the fore partnered with nationalism. The universalist principle of common citizenship replaced the feudal structure based upon class and caste distinctions, but the new national brotherhood strove after homogeneity which would mark it off from all the other national communities.

From the very day when the nation-state appeared on the scene of history it began – as does every vital institution – to develop an ethos of its own by trying to enrich and deepen its own contents. Every nation went out of its way to stress its own uniqueness based on blood, common memories, common symbols of a remote past in which the Jews had no share and which very often only served to remind them of past persecution, and to emphasize their status as aliens. Even during the honeymoon of emancipation after the victory of the French Revolution, the slogan was coined: "Everything for the Jews as individuals, but nothing for them as a nation." And if the Jews were unfortunate enough to be irrevocably committed to the preservation of a national identity and their historic uniqueness, they would have to be expelled, for there was no place for a state within a state. Napoleon did not merely compel the Jews to forget Zion and the Messiah who, the Jews believed, would someday come to redeem Israel. He went further, planning to force the Jews to intermarry "so as to dilute their blood."

In Western Europe there were ancient nation-states with developed economies, a balanced social structure, a rich and varied cultural heritage, and small Jewish communities. The Jews soon abandoned their separate language, became assimilated to the culture of the environment, and discarded most of those religious observances which served to separate them from their neighbors.

Of course many Jews became totally assimilated. Others assumed the color of their surroundings so that they lost almost all distinctness in the eyes of their neighbors. Yet the process of assimilation was never completed. Among other factors, it was continuously disturbed by waves of Jewish migrants from the East European pale. Their arrival in the West infused new vigor into the local Jewish communities. At the same time there developed a stereotypical image of the alien Eastern Jew, an image that was transferred in the minds of many to all Jews.

II

The murderous assault did not come from the side of the conservative, feudal, and clerical forces which were opposed to equal rights for Jews because the "arrival" of the Jews was in their eyes a symbol of a libertarian repudiation of all traditional values, the overthrow of hierarchical order, and the end of the Christian state as it had existed for centuries. Nor did it come from those who in the name of national homogeneity demanded that the Jews should become totally assimilated. The attack came from men who started as devotees of the democratic ideals, but, incensed by the Jewish phenomenon, were swept from a refusal to respect human dignity in the Jew to a denial of the very idea of human rights based on the conception of human equality.

Nothing demonstrates this shift more strikingly than the brochure *The Jews and Music* which Richard Wagner published in 1850, only two years after the composer's fight on the barricades of Dresden at the side of the arch-revolutionary and anarchist Mikhail Bakunin. "There will never be true liberty for humanity so long as there are still oppressed men left anywhere in the world, however few and far between they happen to be," the young Wagner wrote. In his discourse on *The Jews and Music* so soon after, Wagner (made to feel uncomfortable by the Jewish composer Meyerbeer) dwells on the contradiction between reason that teaches men to view the Jews as human beings like all other humans – in this case like all other Germans – and the stubborn fact that the actual Jews whom he saw around him were in his eyes still German-speaking Orientals, despite the 2,000 years they had been living in Germany. This led

Wagner to speculate on which was more real: The abstract idea, pure reason, postulating the unity of mankind, or the concrete fact of group peculiarity? The unity of the human species, or racial uniqueness? What should be, or what is? Humanism was teaching men to treat the Jews in a spirit of tolerance and respect for the human personality, for all men were created in the image of God, but a primeval and spontaneous instinct found expression in hatred of the Jews. When was a man truest to himself, when engaging in ratiocination or when obeying the voice of blood? Which had a higher claim to be the truth – the logical syllogism or the intuitive response?

The implication of these questions, once posed, reached out far beyond the subject of the Jews. The very nerve center of rationalism and indeed Christianity itself was attacked here. The concept of a universal natural law was also repudiated. The individual as a creature of a reason common to all men was no longer, as he had been for millennia, the primary and most important fact. The collective group of the race became primary and fundamental. Language and art were invoked by Wagner and his followers as the conclusive proof of this primacy, because they bore the unmistakable and indelible imprint of race. These were not contrived deliberating by reason, but sprang from dark forces and hidden wellsprings.

The two pamphlets by Karl Marx on the Jewish question and its connection with capitalist liberalism, published just a few years before Wagner's pamphlet, reveal an attitude not entirely dissimilar to that represented by Wagner. To Marx, liberal-capitalist society appeared to be founded upon fraud. It had declared itself in favor of equal legal and political rights for all, irrespective of social origins and economic status. In other words, inequalities of wealth were proclaimed irrelevant, and hence beyond the limits of governmental intervention. The fraud, according to Marx, consisted in the fact that with the abolition of all other privileges – racial origin, family status, religious association – the privilege of wealth had become the most decisive social datum. In law, differences in wealth and property no longer existed, but in actual fact it was they that shaped society. In theory, the parties in a state struggled over formal principles. But in fact, hidden and "unacknowledged" interests, one may say illegitimate interests, were turning the wheels of history. That unacknowledged and illegitimate force which had become omnipotent was embodied in and symbolized for Marx by Judaism.

The liberal constitution accorded full rights to the Jews on the ground that their religious affiliation was irrelevant, and in so doing did away, as it were, with Judaism. But instead of doing away with Judaism, it enthroned it, giving it free rein, liberating it from all restraint, as it had declared status and wealth irrelevant, while in fact giving supreme power to money to dominate society. For "money" read "Jews." The liberation of mankind therefore meant the liberation of mankind from Judaism. "Following the liberation of society from Judaism will come the social liberation of the Jews themselves," Marx wrote in the concluding section of his second pamphlet. The annihilation of Judaism would bring with it the liberation of the Jews. "There is only one possible way of redeeming the Jews from the terrible curse that hangs over them – annihilation," Wagner wrote in the concluding passage of his essay on *The Jews and Music*.

Despite these passages in Marx, it would be a distortion to label him or the socialist movement of Europe as anti-Semitic. It is easy to collect many anti-Semitic quotations from the works of the early socialists such as Fourier, his pupil Toussenel, who wrote the book *The Jews, the Rulers of the Age*, and from the voluminous writings of Proudhon. Anti-Semitic opinions, which lesser socialists voiced as empirical statements, would inevitably be integrated by the great systematizer, Marx, into a cohesive weltanschauung. Yet anti-Semitism could never become an essential prop to hold up the doctrine of socialism. The primacy of the class war on a world scale runs counter to the belief in race as a factor of decisive importance. And the vision of a universal classless society is inspired by the idea of the unity of the human species. In the messianic visions of the socialist pioneers the international proletariat was destined to become humanity itself.

But if responsibility for anti-Semitism cannot be laid at the door of the socialist movement, neither should socialism be looked upon as the sworn and consistent defender of the Jews against anti-Semitism, certainly not before the end of the nineteenth century. Socialism emerged as a shield only when the modern mass movements of the nationalist Right began to steal the socialist clientèle by directing social wrath into channels of hatred of Jews and diverting it from the idea of class war. That process began about the year 1880, with the emergence of anti-parliamentary mass movements.

III

The attack on parliamentary government was launched in the years when European liberalism had reached its apex. In the 1870s constitutional regimes were celebrating their triumph in all countries of Europe except Russia. And even Russia had taken the road of reform in the 1860s. Czar Alexander II was about to grant a constitution when he was struck down by terrorists. It was also the golden age of liberal capitalism. The principle of free trade was acknowledged as the very token of the harmony of interests between nations. Every European country was overflowing with enterprise and economic activity. On the morrow of the war of 1870 Germany was swept by a frenzy of joint stock activity. New companies vied with each other in daring ventures. France changed from an agricultural country into a nation that served as a banker on a worldwide scale, financing railways in Russia and the Suez and Panama canals. In both France and Germany it was not long before wild speculation was overtaken by Nemesis. Many persons who had started with high expectations found themselves grievously disappointed and cheated.

It was the contradiction between the triumph of parliamentarism, on the one hand, and the disasters wrought by the workings of capitalism, on the other, that gave birth to the anti-parliamentarian mass movements of modern times. The masses had been led to believe in representative government and elected bodies as a panacea for all the ills and deficiencies that beset society. Representative government was seen as the omnipotent sovereign, and the people had, after all, the power to elect or dismiss its representatives at will. And so it was natural that the belief should spread that the failure of representative institutions in the fulfillment of their prime duty – the assurance of social-economic stability – was proof of some deep-seated illness. And when crises were accompanied by scandals involving politicians and statesmen, the cry went up that the people's representatives were the servants and the agents of the men at the stock exchange who pulled the strings in a plot against the innocent masses. As European society became more democratic, the parliamentary regime became progressively more threatened.

The Jews played an active and extremely important part in the development of capitalism. Emancipation had set free forces that had been lying dormant for hundreds of years. The emancipated Jew did not feel that he had reached a haven. He had cut himself off from Jewish tradition, but he had not been accepted by the society in which he lived, and many doors remained closed to him. He wanted to escape from his deprivation by intense activity in fields to which he had free access. The social mobility of the Jews exceeded that of any other group. Jews thronged to the cities which are the most sensitive arteries of any country, illuminated by publicity and public attention. When Jewish names then surfaced in public scandals, they attracted disproportionate attention.

Among the principal victims of these crises and scandals that afflicted society were the lower middle classes rather than the proletariat which had little or nothing to lose, let alone invest. The petty bourgeoisie grew impoverished while lacking any real sense of identity or cohesion as a class, for they had no organizational equivalent of the workers' trade unions and socialist parties. At the same time they dreaded the specter of sinking into the ranks of the proletariat. Nationalism, which was capable of giving them a feeling of belonging to the national brotherhood on the same footing as the upper classes, appeared as an anchor of salvation and a compass in a world shaken by upheavals. Lower-middle-class chauvinism found in anti-Semitism one of its main props. This anti-Semitism permitted many shopkeepers or artisans to feel superior to the Jewish intellectual or businessman, especially when menaced by the two "Jewish conspiracies" – international finance and international communism – both allegedly intent upon disrupting national unity. Nationalism was everywhere in ascendance.

The national sentiments which from 1870 divided the two greatest and most advanced nations in Europe, France, and Germany, put a decisive brake upon revolutionary socialist internationalism. The patriotic sentiment of the workers and their leaders proved to be incomparably stronger than international working-class solidarity. Concomitantly anti-parliamentarism with its social and anti-Semitic flavor had emerged in several European countries and, in special form, in the Austro-Hungarian Empire.

The conditions in the Austro-Hungarian Empire during its twilight period exerted the most direct and decisive influence on the shape of modern German Nazism. In *Mein Kampf* Hitler admits that all his political and social ideas were born under the impact of the political realities he was able to observe in Vienna, especially the two pan-German anti-Semitic movements; one founded by Georg von Schoenerer, the other the Social Christian movement led by the popular mayor of Vienna, Karl Lueger.

The basic problem of the Austro-Hungarian Empire, as Hitler saw it, was the bitter struggle of the German-speaking part of the population to remain the masters of the country's destiny, despite the fact that other races – and in particular Slavonic peoples – formed the majority of the country's inhabitants. A parliamentary regime based on numerical majorities, and the principle of "one man one vote" threatened the special status of the Germans in the Empire. Two alternatives presented themselves: either to dismantle the Empire and annex the German-speaking areas to Germany to form a Greater Germany, or to reject democratic parliamentary government in favor of the principle of a governing élite – in which case the party system would have to make way for government by an inspired leader. Viewed from this angle, the Social Democrats and the Jews were the most dangerous enemies. The German-speaking socialist in Austria who contended that the Czech worker was closer to him than the German bourgeois was undermining the unity of the German race. Austrian socialists found themselves reluctantly defending the unity of the Empire, while demanding wide autonomy for its component peoples, because the break-up of the Empire was calculated to be interpreted as a victory for isolationist nationalism at the expense of international unity.

The only racial group in the Austro-Hungarian Empire that was fully committed to the Hapsburg ideal of a multiracial kingdom was its Jewish population. The Jews were convinced that change in the multiracial, supranational empire, where groups and entities of all kinds were assured the right of self-expression, would be to their disadvantage. Moreover, the principal leaders of the Social Democratic party in Austria were Jews. So the conclusion could easily be drawn that there was a Jewish-capitalist-socialist-democratic plot to destroy the German race in Austria. The equality of all the citizens of the country, the principle of the sovereignty of the numerical majority, the parliamentary regime with its political parties, could be viewed as a screen laid by the Jews for their cunning schemes to liquidate racial élites. The destruction of the élite and the consequent weakening of the nation was an opportunity for the Jews to exercise their destructive tyranny without hindrance. In *Mein Kampf* Hitler singles out the Soviet Union and France as proof of the correctness of his doctrine.

Hitler's criticism of the two anti-Semitic movements of the Austro-Hungarian Empire deserves attention. He praised the pan-German movement for its adherence to the principle of race, but criticized it for its lack of social orientation and its remoteness from the masses. The chief virtue of the Social Christian movement, on the other hand, was its closeness to the masses and its understanding of the techniques of mobilizing the masses. But Hitler found it wanting in that it did not have a doctrine of race and had its loyalties divided between Germany and the Roman Catholic church. Without a racial doctrine, Hitler thought, anti-Semitism was bound to remain a tepid affair. It is no accident that a high proportion of Nazi leaders were from multiracial areas, where the Germans had played the part of a master race: Alfred Rosenberg came from the Baltic; Rudolf Hess was born in Cairo; Darré originated from the Argentine; quite a few, like Hitler himself, came from Austria-Hungary, and especially the Sudeten.

Hitler believed that the secret of political success was to concentrate on one enemy. Success in politics required the selection of a principal enemy who could be shown to embody the characteristics of all the other enemies and to arouse fiercer revulsion and hatred than any of them. In this way the principal enemy could be isolated, other rivals for power could be identified with him and held up to contempt and ridicule. The Jews presented an ideal target. Crudely understood Darwinist biologism, when juxtaposed with the interracial struggles of the peoples of the old Hapsburg Empire, created the vision of an interracial war of destruction. The words *Ausrottung*, *Vernichtung* ("destruction," "annihilation") crop up countless times in Hitler's writings, and not just as picturesque expression or vivid metaphor. Since the conflict between races was a life-and-death struggle, there could be no laws to regulate it other than the law of the stronger. Such a war demanded masses of soldiers who would fight relentlessly and, even more, a quasi-religious ideology – a weltanschauung to stir men and fire them to action by rousing their fanaticism (another word that Hitler never tired of using). That faith must be based upon a set of ideas as few and simple as possible. The creed should not be confused by complicated questions, side issues, and unresolved problems such as religion or economic policies, for the main thing was to seize power. If there was no power to act, there was no point in putting forward political programs; and once power was won, everything would come in its wake. In essence, the fight was not concerned with who was more right – we or they – but which one of us was it going to be? We personify the new faith of the master race. Our enemies are the forces of Satan.

The movement initiated in the 1880s by the German court preacher, Adolf Stöcker, offers us an insight into the transformation of anti-Semitism from traditional hatred of the Jews into the demoniacal racial mass movements of our age. German conservatives of the old school were at first attracted by the crusade that Stöcker, himself a commoner, was waging against the Progressist-Socialist heresy which denied God, the Kaiser, and the Fatherland. The campaign for the saving of souls was welcome to them, and incitement against the Jews did not particularly upset German Junkerdom: they were rather pleased by the discomfiture of the Jews. Kaiser Wilhelm I himself expressed his satisfaction with Stöcker's efforts to put the Jews in their rightful place, for he thought they had become far too impertinent. However, the Kaiser hastened to add, although it was true that the Jews had been granted too many opportunities, this was a fait accompli and these rights had been incorporated into the statute book of Germany, and he (the Kaiser) had sworn to uphold the constitution. Similar opinions were voiced in the Reichstag when a petition with a quarter of a million signatures was introduced demanding an end to Jewish emancipation in Germany.

In his youth Bismarck used to say that he would never be able to serve under a Jew or to obey a Jew, and in the debate on the German defense budget of 1879 – a date of prime importance in the history of Germany and the world – the Chancellor did not shrink from attacking his Jewish rivals, Edvard Lasker and Ludwig Bamberger of the Liberal party, by dropping hints about those who "neither spin nor sow, yet reap rewards." Although Bismarck had no liking for Stöcker, he advised his son, who was a candidate for a Berlin constituency, to use him in the common struggle against the Social Democrats and the Progressive Party (which was generally regarded as a Jewish political group). As for mass agitation engaged in by Stöcker, and in particular his appeal to the petty bourgeoisie, Bismarck declared himself indifferent as to whether or not the priest incited people against the Jews as such. The trouble, as Bismarck saw it, was that he also attacked wealthy Jews, including such men as his private banker, Gerson von Bleichröder, and it was only a step from such preaching to demagogic socialist propaganda against private property.

But Stöcker came to grief during one of his propaganda missions to England. His enemies disrupted a public meeting that he was to address in London. The incident suggested scandal to the court in

Berlin, for it was unthinkable for a preacher of the Kaiser to be mixed up in an ugly incident with the rabble of a foreign capital. So when Stöcker also became involved in a court case and was convicted on a charge of perjury, his career came to an end.

One may warrant the generalization from this episode and from others like it in several European countries, particularly the attempted seizure of power by Boulanger in France, that the victory of extreme anti-Semitic mass movements becomes possible only after the traditional Right has been completely demoralized. This is borne out by the history of Germany between the two wars.

On the eve of Hitler's rise to power in Germany, right-wing politicians such as von Papen, Hugenberg, and some Rhineland industrialists toyed with the idea of championing the "Bohemian *Feldwebel*" (as Hindenburg called him) and using him as a puppet. Paradoxically and ironically, Hindenburg was persuaded to appoint Hitler as the only way of restoring the parliamentary constitution. A coalition of Nazis and conservative nationalists would be able, he was assured, to command a parliamentary majority, and thus put Germany back upon the road of constitutional legitimacy which had been so badly battered by the governments of Brüning, Papen, and Schleicher. These, for lack of majority support, were compelled to rule by presidential decrees designed for situations of national emergency. The Nazis were in fact a minority in the first government set up on January 31, 1933. It was humanity's disaster that Hitler was swept forward on the tide of an extremely cohesive movement based on a weltanschauung.

Hatred of the Jews by the traditional Right was rather a peripheral and empirical matter than a central point in a definite ideological system. We could even term it "defensive anti-Semitism." The traditional Right recoiled from contact with Jews and wanted to set a limit to their influence. But the rights accorded to Jews were, as we saw, considered by them as part and parcel of the law of the land. The state was duty-bound to protect the life, property, and safety of its citizens, and incitement that insulted a citizen's self-respect was considered vulgar and uncouth. Stöcker himself declared that though in principle he deplored the fact that "the Jews can vote and be elected, serve as civil servants and occupy commanding posts, sit on local councils and even in parliamentary bodies, and are permitted to teach in our schools," he could not avert his eyes from the fact that "emancipation is a fact of life that cannot be ignored. There is not a government or a parliament that would consider abolishing it." He went on to say that if a conservative government were one day to put an end to Jewish emancipation, their action would be undone as soon as a more liberal regime were returned to power at a later date. "We are a nation based on the rule of law," Stöcker declared, "and we wish to stay that way." When elected *Bürgermeister* of Vienna, Lueger dismissed Jewish officials from his municipal administration, but he took the trouble to find alternative employment for every Jew who had been deprived of his job; the world was no jungle, and people cannot be deprived of means to exist.

Treitschke may be looked upon as a watershed between the traditional hatred of Jews and modern theoretical anti-Semitism. He adopted the popular cry that "the Jews are our great misfortune." His immense prestige as national historian and prophet of the Second Reich lent respectability to the slogan. It was the mocking approach of Jewish writers to the sacred values of the Teutonic race and the Prussian tradition that aroused the ire of that poet of Prussianism. Börne and Heine represented in his view an alien influence, since they tried to nourish the Germans with Western ideas borrowed from the liberal tradition and revolutionary France. To Treitschke, as to German conservatives of all hues and the various radical Christian mass movements, "*Manchestertum*" (in the sense of liberal laissez-faire) was interchangeable with "*Judentum*": both connoted selfish materialism, unconcerned with social welfare or national glory. Treitschke was shocked by a slip of the pen committed by Heinrich Graetz. Graetz had written that Gabriel Riesser, the German-Jewish politician, was *by chance* born on German soil. So, the enraged Treitschke commented, the place of birth of a Jew is merely a matter of chance! Graetz had also said that although Jews had been accorded recognition in Germany, Judaism as such had not been similarly recognized. In what capacity does Judaism seek recognition? – Treitschke asks in his polemic with Graetz. In its capacity as a nation within a nation? If that is so, the answer is a categorical "never" – "*Nie.*" If the Jews consider themselves to be a people, let them pack their bags and emigrate to the Land of Israel.

But Treitschke was not so extreme as to draw the conclusion that all Jews were foreigners and would never be able to form part of the German nation. On the contrary, he blamed the Jews for their stubborn refusal to assimilate. Yet it was only a short step from this opinion to the conclusion that the Jews would never be able to be absorbed by other peoples, and should therefore be denied the opportunity of mixing with the pure Germans. In order to arrive at so extreme a conclusion it was necessary to abandon certain restraints which neither conservatives nor anti-Semites of the type of Stöcker could easily break. It was necessary to question the fundamental assumptions of Christianity in respect of the unity of mankind, the brotherhood of men, each created in the image of God. The whole of the Judeo-Christian tradition had to be thrown overboard. There was indeed no escape from a denial of Christianity as such. Many of Stöcker's allies, such as Wilhelm Marr (who invented the term *anti-Semitism*), Karl Eugen Dühring, and others were bold enough to take this final leap.

IV

Richard Wagner inspired Houston Stewart Chamberlain, and Chamberlain became the oracle of Adolf Hitler and Alfred Rosenberg. Chamberlain, son of a British admiral, who fell in love with the Teutonic race, was the son-in-law of Richard Wagner, and the high priest of the cult of Wagnerism. In 1923 just before the death of Chamberlain, Hitler came to pay homage to the racist philosopher. After the meeting Chamberlain wrote: "My faith in the German people has never been shaken, yet I must confess that my hopes had sunk to a low ebb (in the last few years). But your visit has wrought a complete change in my mood." That was in 1923. Rosenberg's book *The Myth of the Twentieth Century* takes up the thread of Chamberlain's work *The Foundations of the Nineteenth Century*.

Alfred Bäumler, who was one of the first Nazi theoreticians in the Faculty of Philosophy at Berlin University, was advancing this set of ideas when he proclaimed that "when we shout 'Heil Hitler' to German youth, we are also hailing Friedrich Nietzsche"; he also asserted that "the theory of race was the Copernican revolution of modern times."

The theory of race is a compound of many and diverse elements: Ernest Renan's theory on the essential differences between Semitic and Aryan languages, revealing basic differences in the spirit and mentality of the two racial groups; the studies of Count Gobineau purporting to prove the inequality of the respective roles of different races on the stage of world history; the philosophy of history propounded by Chamberlain; biological evolutionism as taught by Darwin, which substitutes the principle of the struggle for existence for the older vision of a universe of natural harmony; Nietzsche's glorification of the strong natural man, impelled irresistibly by elemental forces and unhampered by pity or the whisper of conscience; Wagner's Gothic pagan Valhalla, the home of heroes larger than life.

Yet it seems questionable whether these diverse elements would ever have combined to produce such a destructive and demoniacal gospel were it not for the fact that there were Jews in Europe whose presence made it possible to demonstrate what the word *Aryan* meant. As for the other non-Aryan races, they were far away. Negroes were out of sight, and Germany had not yet come into contact with the world of the Chinese and the Japanese. As for the Arabs, no one gave them a thought. The racial theory made possible the systematization of disparate anti-Jewish notions and anti-Semitic sentiments into a coherent pattern. It raised the status of anti-Semitism to the dignity of a comprehensive weltanschauung, based on the findings of science, providing a key to the understanding of history and offering a political program armed with a ready-made guide to the art of political techniques. With the help of the theory of race, traditional dislike of the Jews on the part of those who wanted to preserve their historic national identity undiluted, and were concerned with nothing outside their own existence and purity, was transformed from a defensive reaction into a universal mission. The Jews were said to be a menace to all the peoples of the Aryan race, and the Teutonic peoples, who personified the noble virtues of the Aryan and Nordic races at their finest, were called upon to act as a spearhead in the struggle against the force which threatened to destroy the Aryan brotherhood.

Both branches of Western civilization, the Christian and the rationalist, despite other important differences, share the common premise of a direct relationship between man as an individual and humanity as a species. Differences of race, origin, language, and religion are of secondary importance in comparison with the primary fact of man's humanity. The Western tradition has always drawn a clear distinction between the human species, whose distinguishing attributes are soul and reason, and all other manifestations of creation. The destiny of man, in this view, is in the never-ceasing endeavor to gain clear knowledge of reality and achieve a social order based on harmony.

The doctrine of race negates the reality of man as man, as well as the conception of humanity as such. The oneness of humanity is regarded by the racial theory as an artificial abstraction. Such an abstraction has no real life. Life, that is to say reality, is possessed only by organic entities, in other words races.

For all its seemingly scientific basis, the doctrine of race gives rise to a kind of mysticism which expands into boundlessness. Blood becomes the real primary cause that determines the whole personality of its bearer. It is held to predetermine the character, the mentality, indeed the values and preferences, dispositions and modes of thought of everyone who has a share of that blood. Thinking is speaking with one's blood: man does not fashion his character out of his free will, with the help of his autonomous power of decision and clear reason. His place, role, actions are determined for him by the great organism of which he is part.

The universe appears in the race theory as the fullness of life, the totality of power in it. The destiny of man is not to learn and to know for its own sake, but to live, to fight, like all other creatures, for his share of that fullness of life and power – the universe. The fact of struggle is the highest reality, and the word *Kampf* is a key word in the vocabulary of Hitler and the Nazi party. The predetermined way on which every race struggles to express, assert, and realize itself, and the requirements of that strategy at the given hour and in the given circumstances, are seen as forming together the supreme and sole laws of the race. It follows therefore that it is foolish to confront any race with an objective test of validity applicable to all mankind.

In its cosmic struggle the race must be permanently on the alert, mobilized and fit for battle. Viewed from this angle, reason was not a quality that could be singled out or put above other faculties. When isolated, it was bound to become sterile, for exaggerated analytical intellectualism weakened the will and lessened the individual's instinctive self-assurance. Intellectualism was a sure sign of the weakening of the voice of the blood and man's elemental impulses. Not with ideas will the leader come to the masses – taught Hitler – nor to teach them to consider dispassionately the pros and cons of any issue. The intellect was in the service of those forces which reason had neither produced nor set in motion. Mobilization for a breakthrough demanded the coordination of all those faculties that influenced the fighting ability. The different efforts had to be guided by one single and exclusive principle so as to respond to the common impulse with the same thrill and rhythm. Totalitarianism is the companion and function of the permanent war-readiness of the race in its struggle for power. It is, at the same time, the logical outcome of the idea of organic determinism.

In according supreme significance to race, nature invested in the race the right to use its strength to the full. There was no room therefore for any respect for each other's rights, for relations based on equality or mutual consent or numerical majority between races. And the same was true within the framework of the race. Dominion and government were not matters to be decided by elections and negotiations. The leader would grasp power because his qualities, his vital powers, and sense of destiny moved him with irresistible force. For he was the supreme personification of the race. Being the most perfect creation of the evolutionary process, overflowing with love for his race, he was endowed with the special powers of the visionary and prophet so that he was able to perceive the deeper meaning of his age, to hear the steps of the race's destiny, still hidden in a nebulous future. The leader's intuition was thus hailed as the highest law; the will of the supreme commander of the race in its life-and-death struggle was proclaimed the categorical imperative.

It is difficult to establish whether it was hatred for the Jews that led to this denial of Christianity, or whether the rejection of Christianity removed all limitations from hatred for the Jews. Christians may have disliked Jews, hated and persecuted them, treated them with contempt, and held them responsible for all manner of misdeeds, Yet, they could not but stand in awe before the mother-religion and the bearer of a divine mystery, the central figure in an enormously significant part of God's scheme of history. Furthermore, the Jewish element served to emphasize the universal side of Europe's history and culture: the unity of all believers in a church universal and the equality of all believers in the eyes of their Creator, race being wholly irrelevant.

Anti-Semites such as Bruno Bauer, Chamberlain, Julius Langbehn, and Paul Anton de Lagarde, joined forces in destroying the Christian image of Judaism and denied to it its historic role. Bauer did not try to deny that Christianity had developed out of Judaism and had been born in the land of Israel within a Jewish society. But Chamberlain sought to prove that Jesus did not belong to the same race as Abraham. He was sure that Jesus had fair hair and blue eyes, and laid great stress on the fact that Jesus was born in Galilee where a considerable section of the population was Greek.

The most important of Chamberlain's arguments was the claim that Jesus and Christianity were born among Jews in order to demonstrate the tremendous difference between the irreligion of the Jews and real religion. Christianity came into being as a reaction to the caricature of religion that had its roots in materialistic Jewish racialism.

Bauer developed the historical thesis that from antiquity to the present day, the Jews had always acted as a solvent, a virus of disintegration. Modern Jewish universalism in the form of international capitalism or international Marxism was the same thing using two differing disguises, since both aimed at weakening the organic unity of the race and national solidarity.

The "stab in the back" explanation of Germany's defeat in 1918 was seized upon as conclusive proof of the correctness of the racial theory. The nationalist Right found it easy to fasten upon international Jewry its old obsession with encirclement plots by envious neighbors, especially since Jewish devotees of universal political Messianism played so prominent a part in the mounting wave of the international revolution. It could be said that it was upon the corpse of the assassinated Jewish intellectual, Kurt Eisner, the ephemeral and ineffectual dictator of the Revolutionary Republic in Munich, that Adolf Hitler began, in that Bavarian capital, his climb to supreme power. Jewish international finance was also made to bear the odium of the ravages of inflation. The Jew thus became the target of the two most powerful resentments, nationalist rage and social protest. Instead of being at odds as they had previously been, the two passions were now fused to form an infinitely more dangerous dynamite than the anti-Semitic movements a generation earlier in France, Germany, or Austria-Hungary.

"The decline of civilizations is the most horrifying and most mysterious spectacle in history" – with these words Count de Gobineau opens his *Essay on the Inequality of the Human Races.* Oswald Spengler's influential book was entitled *The Decline of the West.* Edouard-Adolphe Drumont, author of *La France juive,* wrote in a similar vein: "There is nothing more instructive than the examination of the first signs of those diseases which slowly but relentlessly weaken, pervert, and finally destroy the body of . . . society." Extreme right-wing French authors whose writings abound with hatred and incitement, such as Maurice Barrès and Charles Maurras, reach the heights of lyricism in the description of the sadness of cemeteries, death of civilizations, the disintegration of traditional and stable forms of life in towns and villages, under the impact of the industrial revolution.

These writers' dread of some approaching end, the sense of decline and degeneration are accompanied by a morbid fear of infection. Chamberlain remarked that one could be infected without coming into physical contact with the Jews. It sufficed to read newspapers to which Jews contributed, or books they wrote, for their poisonous influence to penetrate the human mind.

At the same time the writings, pamphlets, and papers of the Nazis and various other groups of fascists are teeming with expressions such as "assault," "charge," and "break-out." It is strange to note that baffling contradiction between the dread of Jews, and the fierce desire to demonstrate strength and to assert superiority.

V

The disintegration of traditional and stable forms of life under the impact of the Industrial Revolution and massive urbanization deprived man of the self-assurance of a creature of routine. The loss of traditional stability makes man increasingly uncertain of his real identity. Men have a feeling of impotence and frustration when confronted with the terrible problems brought about by the development of technology – the fruit of man's genius and the glorious vindication of his mastery over nature, and when faced with world conflict often conducted by governments chosen by the common man.

Reason has not succeeded in preventing or curing this mass distress. There has been no single clear voice of reason in the modern world. Reason has been employed to defend every possible cause, and no evil action has ever lacked intellectuals to offer a rational justification for it.

The mass movements of Messianic totalitarianism came into being as an expression of and response to the neurosis that has held humanity in its grip throughout the modern age. It has been pointed out many times that the secret of Hitler's extraordinary success as a mob orator lay in his uncanny ability to strike the most sensitive chords in the hearts of the masses. He knew how to release the most hidden passions in the masses, to liberate them from feelings of malaise and frustration, and to enable them to take part in an ecstasy of anger, hatred, and fanatical enthusiasm. There was a hypnotic effect in the permanent repetition of the same themes, while the demonstrations of strength and acts of violence were intended to create the impression that here was a force that could not be resisted, that fate had already decided, and history had already pronounced and carried out its verdict. The masses were only too happy to be raped.

The Nazis had a preference for the *Jude* in the singular rather than for *Juden* in the plural, when speaking of the Jewish people. They refused to recognize differences, to discern individual faces or acknowledge different characteristics. One can detect in this the culmination of a long trend whose dangerous potentialities were for the first time revealed in the French Revolution – the frame of mind that thinks of collective entities upon which history has pronounced a verdict of death. They are to be eliminated not for any crime committed by each of them or all of the members of the group together at that hour and in that place, but for the crime of having been born into that collective entity, be it aristocracy, the bourgeoisie, Kulaks, the Jews. The individual, his guilt or innocence, are irrelevant. The individuals are "they," specimens of a force which has to be destroyed, eliminated, annihilated.

Ironically, in the late stage of the war Goebbels would implore the Germans not to weaken, for they all shared the common responsibility, and the "Jews will never forgive us what we have done unto them and will never make any distinction between one German and another."

This frame of mind that is capable of ignoring fundamental moral distinctions was strongly enforced by those biological teachings which tend to abolish the barrier between human beings and the world of animals and plants. Formerly the bearer of an immortal soul, raised above all creation and creatures by his soul, reason, and consciousness, man had now, as it were, been integrated into the universal evolutionary process, and the fullness of life universal. As one of the protagonists, along with others in the struggle for existence, the human species, itself allegedly divided into struggling races, loses its uniqueness. Races emerge and races perish, and are wiped out from the surface of the earth. There are fine races and harmful species. And human life forfeits the sanctity that hallowed every individual soul for so long.

The absolute sanctification of the totality of life on earth in the spirit of universal pantheism is also conducive to an attitude of indifference to the life and dignity of man. For the difference between man and any other living creature has been blurred. Both are part of life universal, and the body of a man is only a temporary receptacle for that tiny fraction of life.

There is little doubt that the instinctive revulsion from taking away a human life had been greatly weakened in our day in comparison with the climate that has prevailed for some two centuries after the end of the wars of religion in the seventeenth century. If that be so, apocalyptic fears of an imminent Day of Judgment should not be lightly dismissed.

VI

The root cause of these mortally dangerous tendencies is the refusal, perhaps even inability, to take for granted the rights of man per se. Human rights, instead of being seen as natural and inalienable, are held to be a concession or a gift—to be bestowed by the masters among mankind on those others whose destiny it has been to serve the privileged, giving them a sense of higher dignity and that measure of communal cohesion which is cemented by the sight of the excluded outsiders. This assumption of a master-slave relationship is so deep-rooted that even at the historical hour of the apparent enthronement of the principles of the rights of man we see the simultaneous emergence of those rationalizations calculated to legitimate the denial of rights to entire groups without reference to any justifiable disqualification or personal guilt.

Often, of course, the outsiders, the "strangers in our midst," have been minorities and nonconformists, men of different religion or race or color. As the nonconformists par excellence, the Jews have epitomized the position of the outsider in Western societies. Yet, paradoxically, the stubborn retention of a separate identity has also been the source of their contribution to universal- ism throughout their history. Thus the Jews, though powerfully influenced by Hellenism, were not absorbed by the Graeco-Roman civilization. Conscious of being the only guardians of the tremendous message of the existence of a transcendental God, the source of all truth, the Jews successfully resisted assimilation. By remaining themselves alone, paradoxically, the Jews prepared the way for the universal message of Christianity. Nevertheless, despite its acknowledgment of Judaism as its source, Christianity denied legitimacy to the earlier religious tradition, and throughout the many centuries of Christendom's dominion over Western civilization, Jews were denied equality of rights. Consequently, the secular and universalist Enlightenment seemed to hold out to the Jews the promise of relief from religious intolerance. It soon emerged, however, that Jews were now exposed to attack from another direction, for the rationalist rejection of religion was incompatible with any religious reverance for the Jewish phenomenon, nor did its atomistic universalism allow for any raison d'être for a Jewish ethnic collectivity.

Notwithstanding their commitment to liberal individualism and their interest in social mobility, the majority of Jews neither would nor could disperse into human atoms. Nor, for that matter, was the majority community able to shed its historically conditioned view of the Jews as an indigestible collective entity. That view, moreover, had received a new stimulus from nationalism, especially its organicist and Darwinian variety. Lingering unwillingness to grant full legitimacy to Jews meant that any increased Jewish participation in the national life would be perceived as an alien invasion. And, as we have seen, that image of a compact alien force conjured up specters of an international Jewish plot to gain world mastery. The hatred and fear of the alien who had set out to dominate were now systematized and absolutized into the race theory which was to prove the fatal verdict for European Jewry.

Many Jews, especially in the poverty-stricken ghettoes of Eastern Europe, whose newly awakened sense of human and Jewish dignity was deeply offended by degrading czarist oppression and threatened by the hostility of nascent militant nationalisms, looked to the socialist revolution as the harbinger of universal equality and the liquidator of all types of oppression. In the light of the commitment and the contribution made by so many Jews to the cause of social revolution, it has come as a shock to behold the fatherland of socialism – which had originally taken a public stance against any form of anti-Semitism – now pursuing policies designed to eliminate all religious and cultural Jewish self-expression, barring to Jews the road to professional advancement, and giving free rein to defamatory public utterances. To many it must have seemed unbelievable that a Communist regime could, as did the Polish government a few years ago, resort to racist policies in the name of a "national self-respect which could not brook an undue influence by an ethnically foreign element." Should we see in this baffling volte face an example of the burden of history and of ineradicable prejudice? Is it another manifestation of the historic role of the Jews as nonconformists, dissidents? Or is it perhaps an expression of that ever-present opportunism which diverts social frustration in the direction of a vulnerable, always suspect, group of never quite fully recognized legitimacy?

The most recent, and not least baffling, episode in the long history of denial of rights to Jews centers on the embattled and isolated State of Israel. For centuries the curses of anti-Semites had been dispatching the unwanted Jews of all countries to Palestine. Finally, after almost two millennia in dispersion, the never-extinguished Messianic dream of national restoration in the ancestral land, coinciding with a worldwide drive for national self-determination, combined into an irresistible resolve to create a Jewish national home in Palestine. The search for a refuge – whether from indignities, ambiguities, or ambivalences – by a people despairing of ever being accorded full status as men and as Jews was given burning urgency. The irreversible destruction of a Jewish civilization of well over a thousand years in Central Europe transformed the land of Israel into the sole repository and heir of that civilization.

Now, however, it almost seems a part of the curse pursuing the Jews to their Promised Land that their claims should there clash with the national aspirations of another people. The right of Jews to reclaim their ancient land has been uncompromisingly rejected by the modern Palestinian Arabs, notwithstanding the asymmetry between the exclusive significance of Israel to the Jewish people and the colossal arena upon which the Arab civilization is free to unfold. It has also been the singular misfortune of the Jews that their return to their ancestral home coincided with the withdrawal of the Western colonial presence from Asia and Africa. For while the Christian nations of the West, conscience-stricken by the Holocaust, have not allowed their commitment to the preservation of the Jewish state to be entirely overcome by political and economic self-interest, the newly emerged nations of Asia and Africa – whose record is free of anti-Semitism but also empty of Jews or of any association with Judaism – fail to comprehend the unique relationship between the Jewish people and the land of Israel. They can therefore be easily blandished into joining in the condemnation of the State of Israel as an outpost of "American imperialism" and the embodiment of "racist Zionism."

So, at the very hour and from the very forum of the apparent enshrinement of the universal principle of human rights we have heard the latest version of the denial of legitimacy and rights to the Jewish people.

The case of the Jews is that of a product and at the same time a victim of history. History has been its Archimedean point as well as its prison. Its uniqueness has been the secret of its universality, and simultaneously the justification for the enmity of its adversaries. Man's stand toward history should be likened to that of psychoanalysis, and indeed also to that of the fighters for human rights: to recognize the extreme potency of the determinations, deprivations, and compulsions created by the past, and to lay them bare, while endeavoring to liberate men from their thralldom.

First published in *Essays on Human Rights: Contemporary Issues and Jewish Perspectives*, ed. David Sidorsky, 1979, Philadelphia, Pa: The Jewish Publication Society of America, pp. 336–359.

The New Anti-Semitism

In those distant days when General de Gaulle drank a toast to "the state of Israel, our friend and ally," a right wing anti-Semitic weekly in Paris, which fiercely upheld the idea of "Algérie Française," published a long article under the title "Is it possible to be a friend of Israel and an anti-Semite at the same time?" The author thought that it was. He argued that Israel was a nation of peasants and soldiers, while "the Rothschilds were neither farmers nor warriors." One cannot help being reminded of that fine distinction when hearing nowadays PLO spokesmen swearing that they are fighting racist Zionism, but have nothing against Judaism as a religion, and Jews passionately insisting that the former was only another formula for the latter.

In the pre-Holocaust period and before the Jewish state came into existence the distinction was tenable. There were then gentile anti-Zionists who by no stretch of the imagination could be called anti-Semites. Their reservations against Zionism stemmed from a variety of motives: the Zionist endeavor was a threat to the Arabs; it was utopian romanticism, and it was sure to create more problems than it would solve; the paraphernalia of statehood, with power politics and the fundamental immorality attending it could not be reconciled with the spiritual vocation of Judaism.

It has become impossible to maintain the distinction between anti-Zionism and anti-Semitism since Auschwitz and since 1948, and the honest and thoughtful non-anti-Semitic anti-Zionists in the Western world realize it. I can recall a revealing conversation in a Cambridge (England) college in the late 1950s. My host, an eminent historian and devout Christian, summed up his feelings about Zionism by saying that it had become plain to all that the Zionist idea was a grievous error, and the British involvement with it a disastrous mistake. But – he went on with deep feeling and intense sincerity that were characteristic of the man – "the Jewish state has already come into being and it is there, and it is just unthinkable for the Christian world to let it go under." I believe it was the latter sentiment that made practically all Western nations recoil almost instinctively from the motion in the UN condemning Zionism as racism, and thereby undermining the very legitimacy, not to speak of the moral case, of the State of Israel.

The word "Holocaust" does not signify only the physical fate of six million Jews, of a third of the Jewish people as they existed in 1939. It drives home the stark fact of the irretrievable and irreversible end of a vital and rich Jewish civilization spun over nearly 15 centuries throughout the lands of Central and Eastern Europe by closely knit, populous communities, with their peculiar ancient religion, culture, language, art, folkways, social-economic structures, self-governing institutions, values, aspirations and dreams. In comparison with that rich, dense and compact fabric of Jewish life, the contemporary Jewish settlements in the West present, with all their well-being, power, influence, freedom, great opportunities and cultural and social achievements, a picture of atomization and disintegration, of a paucity of authentically Jewish features and of growing assimilation. The sole heir and repository of the destroyed Jewish civilization is Israel.

Out of ignorance or out of propagandist zeal Arab spokesmen shrug all this off by wearisome repetition that the Jews are only a religious sect, descendants of an ethnic group or adherents of a philosophical system. An Israeli who since the Six Day War consistently opposed annexation of territories densely populated by Arabs and has fought tendencies in his own camp to refuse recognition to the Palestinian Arabs as an entity entitled to corporate self-expression free from alien rule, may claim the moral right to ask Arab writers to exercise a measure of intellectual integrity in this matter.

If they justly resent others telling them that they are or are not a nation, they have no business to decide for others whether they are a nation or a religion. They cannot portray the Palestinian Arabs as a nation deserving the right of national self-determination, though historically they had never identified themselves as such nor ever possessed the attributes of distinct nationhood; and at the same time deny the same right to bearers of one of the oldest traditions of mankind in their ancestral home. The Jews were aroused in the last century to political nationalism under the stress of unparalleled persecution and in tune with the spirit of the modern age, which has been stirring nation after nation, tribe after tribe to the most remote confines of the earth to demand a place under the sun as a self-governing community.

Not only the Jews wherever they be, but the Christian world as a whole, with its awareness of the peculiarity of the Jewish phenomenon, its sense of obligation, duty and guilt toward the Jews, is acutely conscious of the fact that the destruction of the State of Israel would drive a knife into the very heart of Judaism not only by decimating, and – who knows – wiping out perhaps another three million Jews so soon after the Holocaust, but also by annihilating the last remnant of the integral historic Jewish civilization. The blow to world Jewry, its pride, faith in itself and in its future would prove too heavy for it to survive as an entity, just – I hasten to add – as a disaster befalling US Jewry would sound the doom of Israel. The fortunes of Israel and the Diaspora are so linked that no wedge can be driven to separate them. The asymmetry between Israelis and Palestinians is in that respect so obvious that one hardly needs to argue that Arab civilization in the 22 independent states from the Atlantic to Iran would not in any appreciable manner be damaged or adversely affected if not a single Arab were left on the West Bank of the Jordan (which no one advocates). Much criticism may be leveled against the past policies of the Israeli government – its muddle-headed, self-centered and self-righteous obtuseness to Arab susceptibilities, its obsession with security. But there never existed an unambiguous, firm resolve to keep all the territories, forever. The government of Israel lacked the conviction, the will and the courage to decide to annex the latter, but neither did it have the strength to make up its mind and declare itself outright against any annexation. There was the doctrinal and emotional commitment to the historic Jewish right to the whole of Eretz Israel. Settlement on the land was always held as being of the essence of Zionism. The names of ancient historic places exercised a magic fascination. Above all, there was the implacable Arab hostility, the fear of indefensible borders, and the reluctance to offer ammunition to the right-wingers. There were no particular pressures from outside, and an erroneous evaluation of Arab capacity and of the winds of change in the world at large had won wide acceptance. All these combined to foster the policies of immobilism, to encourage activists in and outside the establishment to take partisan action to create settlements, and to inhibit the authorities from resolutely setting their face against it. In giving in to pressure to establish settlements across the 1967 border in strategic points or on historic sites, the government allowed the image of "the creeping conquest" to strike roots in Arab minds and to spread everywhere. Encouragement was thereby offered to extremists at home to demand a national decision in favor of the principle of total annexation.

There is no doubt that had the Arabs given the slightest token of a readiness to accept the existence of the State of Israel, the vast majority of Israelis, including those who harbor deep suspicions about Arab intentions as well as those who were finding it most difficult to "renounce" the Jewish rights to Hebron and Nablus, would have opted with enthusiasm or out of a resigned sober assessment of the data of the situation – for withdrawal from most of the occupied territories. There are also just too many thoughtful Israelis, with memories of oppression, an anguished desire to safeguard Jewish identity and authenticity and with liberal convictions and temper to envisage with equanimity the specter of a Jewish master race forcing itself upon an alien, hostile, subject people constituting some 40 percent of the population, in an age of passionate, obsessive nationalism, and in the era of decolonization. I dare say no sophisticated Arab propagandist would expect that the slogan of a single, democratic, secular Palestinian state of Moslems, Christians and Jews would be taken seriously by world opinion in the light of what has happened in Lebanon, and the fate of the Kurds and Assyrians.

Even if one discounts the bitter lessons of worldwide tensions and conflict between ethnic groups with different traditions, cultural backgrounds and social development living together, the panacea offered by the leaders of the PLO would still be totally at variance with what even the minimalists among Jews and the international community as a whole had envisaged Jewish settlement in the national home to be about: a refuge from persecution and a home for the Jewish genius to express itself in an integral manner.

I remember a conversation I had a year or two after the Six Day War with a highly cultivated Arab notable, who had a very colorful past. The man had taken the trouble to study Jewish history, the Zionist classics and even Hebrew, and he had become convinced that the feelings about their distinct collective identity were so deep in both communities that the only way of solving the conflict, healing the wounds and preventing endless misery in the future was to sever them. It is anguishing that a liberal historian of national movements feels, after 30 years of studying them, that it's necessary to endorse the view that in a world of nationalist obsession and egalitarian passion, separation was the most practical remedy for ethnic strife. Nor should the Arabs forget that an apocalyptic Day of Judgment would in all certainty mark not the doom of one side only, but that the other one would also be engulfed.

Men of goodwill on both sides should, bearing this in mind, try not to succumb, nor let others grow neurotic, under the shadow of a demonologized image of the adversary. They should also try as far as possible to spare the susceptibilities of the other side. While insisting on Arab recognition of Israel's existence, a good many Israelis would be ready not to press for an explicitness that may weigh too heavily on obsessively held principles in Arab nationalist philosophy. They would not for instance resent or begrudge to the Arabs the revised vision of their political theology, which puts its trust in time, internal difficulties, the growing indifference of the world and of the Jews across the ocean, to bring within half a century or so the demise of that nonviable, alien little state in the heart of the Arab continent. And the Jews should do all they can not to let this happen.

Jews all over the world were incensed and deeply affronted by the condemnation of Zionism as racism. There was something horribly mean and spiteful in spokesmen of what is, in their language, always named "the noble Arab race" bamboozling representatives of states, born yesterday, without even a word in their native tongues to describe the Jew, without the vaguest knowledge or understanding of the peculiar and distant roots and the worldwide aspects of the Jewish problem and the Middle East conflict, without any authentic information on what is going on in present-day Israel. No less repulsive was the plotting with Machiavellian regimes, whose cynical opportunism knows no bounds, to brand as racists the most tragic victims of racism, for whom actually the very word had been coined, and upon whom it has been practiced most thoroughly.

After all, not so long ago the words anti-Semitism and racism were almost synonymous. In the European countries the Jews were almost the only representatives of an alien race. There were no Negroes, Chinese or Arabs there. The race theory gained its mass appeal only because those to whom it was being sold could apply it there and then to Jews. It is enough to try to define racism and to sort out its data to bring home how utterly alien it is to Zionist ideology and the Jewish mentality, and indeed interests.

What is racism about? It signifies biological determinism. There was the primary ineffable and unfathomable datum of blood, which unalterably predetermined character, inclinations, reactions, ideas, beliefs, conduct to the most refined intellectual and artistic activity. "Pure" blood endowed its possessors – the race – with an unerring instinct, unreflecting self-assurance, a distinct style, and there was no more heinous thing than the mixing of different kinds of blood, especially of an inferior with a superior brand. It resulted in mongrelization, debility and degeneration. There was a Darwinian rivalry and struggle between the races for a portion of the cosmic life-force, for survival, self-assertion and power. In this eternal confrontation combative vitality was the supreme instrument, and its cultivation the highest task; and not the training of an abstract, universal intellect in order to discover objective universal truths, not moral education designed to foster a sense of justice and fairness to all. Preoccupation with allegedly universal, human, objective values had a debilitating effect on the prowess of the race, since it diluted its firm resolve and compact simplicity, and undermined its fighting self-concentration. The Jews were simultaneously insiders and outsiders, an anti-race with no roots in the soil, given wholly to abstract speculation. They were propagators of internationalism, of the idea of the equality of races, of liberalism, democracy and pacifism. They were the begetters of international systems such as capitalism and finance, and at the same time the prophets of cosmopolitan revolutionary ideologies such as socialism and of individualistic theories like psychoanalysis. They were therefore a most dangerous solvent and were a poisonous destroyer of race certainties and vigor. They fomented class cleavages, exploitation and struggles. They had always exploited the host race, and at the same time had from Moses to Lenin – in the language of Hitler – been inciting the mobs of inferior races against the national elites of the superior breeds, all that as part of an international plot to dominate and exploit the stultified and benumbed Nordic nations.

The insidious, eternal well-poisoner had to be severely segregated and eventually extirpated so that his blood and ideas no longer infected the superior breeds. What has all this got to do with Zionist theory or Israeli practice? Has anyone seen in Israel notices of separate public lavatories or separate seats in public conveyances for Jews and Arabs? Are Arabs not admitted to schools and universities in Israel? Are mixed marriages forbidden there?

What does the much publicized absence of civil marriage, which incidentally irks all liberal Jews, really purport? It is a concession to the religious minority, for whom, as for members of most religious denominations, adherence to the rite of immemorial antiquity is a matter of conscience. But at a deeper level, the reluctant consent of the secular parties to the religious rules on civic status stems from the anguished, post-Auschwitz fear that as a result of the destruction of the cohesion of Jewish life in Central and Eastern Europe, the atomized, rapidly assimilating secularized Jewish communities, in which mixed marriages threaten to disrupt all that is left of the fabric of Jewish life, are left with the synagogue as the sole focus of group identity. The people of Israel, so desperately anxious for Jewish survival and unity, must not set a bad example by lowering the barriers and facilitating mixed marriages; so say the defenders of the status quo. Mixed marriages are not forbidden in Israel. It's just that no facilities are provided for them. But there are ways to have them solemnized. They are then legally recognized. The Law of Return is, again, motivated by an anxious desire to bring Jews in, and not by a resolve to keep others out.

Far be it from me to describe the Jewish-Arab coexistence in Israel as an idyll. How could it be, in face of the terrible clash of rights, decades of war, traumatic memories, mutual fear and suspicion? The policies and attitudes of Israel, however, will stand any comparison with the treatment of Poles by the Second Reich, of the Ukrainians and Byelo-Russians in inter-war Poland, the attitude of the kingdom of Hungary toward its Slav and Romanian subjects, the fate of the Irish under British rule, not to speak of the situation of Jews in the countries of Eastern Europe – all cases of a dominant race set upon strengthening its hold, by methods which include settling members of its ethnic group in border areas inhabited by national minorities. Why has no one formally asked a UN commission to investigate the policies of the USSR in the Baltic countries designed to swamp those minorities with multitudes of Great Russians and members of other races, and to transfer large numbers of Lithuanians, Latvians and Estonians into remote areas of Russia?

As to the right of Arab refugees to return, surely not many cases, indeed hardly any, could be cited of return of refugees whom an international or revolutionary cataclysm has sent flying. Where should look for them? On the Indian sub-continent? In Central and Eastern Europe? In the vast expanse of Africa? The whole delicate and intricate fabric of life, into which nearly a million Jewish refugees from the Arab countries had been absorbed, would be destroyed by the come-back of the whole mass of Arab refugees.

The heart-searching and the malaise weighing upon many

Israelis and voiced by them publicly on the Palestinian tragedy has no parallel whatsoever in the broodings or public statements of Arabs on the fate of the Jews and the causes that have led them to establish themselves in the Jewish National Home. It is a travesty of the truth to depict the Zionists as a band of imperialists who sat down to hatch a plot to conquer and dispossess an Arab nation for the sheer love of power and spoils, out of unprovoked hatred for Arabs.

Zionism was motivated by a determination to escape the fate of being an eternal anvil to the blows of turbulent history, by a desire to find a safe refuge where the Jews could be themselves, free to express their particularity, away from the grave international, nationalist, social and revolutionary complications in which they had invariably been caught in modern times. They seem now to have landed in the very heart of the universal vortex, and to be compelled to act, to some extent at least, as instruments of grave dislocation to another people.

For 2000 years they were as a "Cain race" exposed to the never-ending barrage of opprobium and hostility of Christianity. No sooner had the reaction to Auschwitz and the common interest in warding off the dangers of neo-paganism begun to grant some relief, than Judaism found itself under a ferocious assault by Islam, with the uncomprehending unfriendliness of races and creeds of the Third World, which lacked any of the background and experiences to make them understand, let alone sympathize, with the Zionist endeavor. Judaism was beset finally with the resentment of members of historically deprived ethnic groups, who envied the rapid Jewish success in the New World.

For generations it was axiomatically believed by Jews that there was no enemy on the left – the natural defender of all the oppressed and the persecuted. Being part of a marginal, hard-pressed minority, inheriting the prophetic and the Messianic traditions together with the social and mental restlessness of town dwellers and migrants, turned many Jews into prophets, pioneers, leaders and practitioners of evolution. In the same almost Oedipal manner as happened at the time of the scission between the mother religion (Judaism) and the daughter religion (nascent Christianity) nearly 2000 years ago, the church of the religion of revolution has now risen against the people who were the begetters of their creed. The old myth of a Judeo-Marxist international plot has been substituted by the myth of an international Zionist-American-Imperialist conspiracy. It has come in response to the compulsive need to see the world divided into a camp of imperialists and a camp of peoples striving for national liberation.

In its terrible isolation, the state of Israel has become the old Jewish outlaw: the outcast, the collective Jew of the nations. A pariah people has, as it were, created a pariah state. The would-be imperialist has been reduced to beggary. It is now the barefoot nomads of the tents of Kedar who sit upon mountains of gold, hold the world to ransom through the possession of a treasure, one that fell into their lap without them having to hoe or spin, and for the life-blood of the nations they are exacting a tribute, in comparison with which the old usury of the Jews appears a miserable pittance. Indeed, they seem determined to follow a set plan to dominate the heights of world economy.

At the opening session of the Eichmann trial in Jerusalem, the counsel for the defense, Dr. Servatius, asked the eminent Judaic scholar who was presenting the historical background of the Holocaust, what was the reason for the permanence and universality of the phenomenon of anti-Semitism? Surely, there must be something in the Jews that provoked such a reaction? Jews tend to become very angry when such a question is put, and a few years ago a British scholar, certainly no anti-Semite, got into trouble when he ventured to raise the point in a review of a book on anti-Semitism in the French Enlightenment.

It all started long, long ago. Hellenism and Rome succeeded in divesting all the conquered peoples, at least their urban elites, of their native languages and cultures. The Jews were the exception, because of their overpowering consciousness of being the sole trustees of a terrifying truth – the existence of a one, omnipotent, wholly transcendental, invisible god. In the Latinized or Hellenized Roman Empire the recalcitrant Jews came to stand out as a strange, queer, incomprehensible, and uncannily frightening breed. The facelessness of their god suggested that they had much to hide, their refusal to mix was proof of misanthropy, and their resistance to Caesar-worship manifested perverse rebelliousness. The Christianized gentiles were thus already disposed to view the crucifixion, the rejection of Christ by the obnoxious people, in a predetermined way. The fact that all the Apostles were Jews was almost ignored, but Judas Iscariot was remembered as the Jew *par excellence*. To the barbarian tribes that later overran the Roman

Empire and established themselves upon its ruins, the Jews appeared as uncanny aliens, bearers of a much older and higher civilization, burdened with the murder of the Savior.

As highly problematic aliens, with no strong ties and no reputation to lose, the Jews chose or were driven by restrictive legislation into the less reputable occupations or into new ventures which the old established conservative populations were unequipped or reluctant to take up because of their novelty, their hazardous nature and their lack of that respectability which comes from sheer duration. Trade and then money-lending became almost exclusive Jewish occupations. The image of the usurer Shylock stuck to them. The Jews fulfilled a necessary and pioneering role in the urban life of the early Middle Ages. When they became expendable, and the host nations had overcome their early inhibitions and were ready and eager to take up the till then despised pursuits, the Jews were expelled from most of Western Europe. They established themselves in the Eastern underdeveloped part of the European continent as the nearly sole and at first welcome middle class, and in such countries as the wide-flung Polish Republic and the Kingdom of Hungary as the major part of the urban population.

The emancipation of the Jews by victorious liberalism, the onset of secularization and capitalist industrialization came almost at the same time to the European continent. Together they released the immense, bottled-up, volcanic forces of a purposeful race which had for ages been compelled to practice an exceptionally severe economy of energy in the very restricted fields of religious observance, study of the law and money-making. The Jews seized the new opportunities with ferocious abandon. In some countries they made their leap at a strategically crucial moment, as modernization was put on the agenda, and the gentile population, gentry and peasantry, were not yet ready to join in the race. Bewildered, powerfully affected, often inconvenienced, in many cases deprived of old status and privileges, and even harmed and ruined by the flood of change, the gentile neighbors came to identify the whole process with the Jews, and to hold them responsible for it, since the newcomers seemed to be the greatest beneficiaries thereof. They felt offended by yesterday's pariah who had overnight grown so mighty, and too big for his boots. To the impoverished nobles and dispossessed peasants flocking to towns, the Jews, whom they found there, looked like invaders who had forestalled them. There ensued a tension and conflict that came to a climax in the Nazi campaign to drive the

Jewish invaders back, and ended in Auschwitz. The same pattern may be detected in the fortunes of the Jews under the Communist regimes. After centuries of Tsarist oppression and humiliation the Russian Jews had every reason to flock into the ranks of Revolutionaries. They played an enormous part in all the Socialist parties, being before 1917 actually more numerous in the Social Revolutionary and Menshevik factions than in the Bolshevik camp. When Lenin and his followers seized power, most Jews hesitated at first to join them, having like most Russians, grave doubts about their survival. The non-Jewish intelligentsia was unwilling to collaborate with the Bolshevik authorities. Jewish hesitations were soon swept away by the terrible pogroms which broke out in the areas held by the counterrevolutionary generals and the Ukrainian nationalists. So the Jews were again placed in the role of pioneers. At first, this was held to be irrelevant, since the proletarian revolution was supposed to recognize no distinction between Jew, Greek and Gentile. When, however, the Soviet-bred cadres of non-Jewish intelligentsia came up ready and eager to play their parts, and the great patriotic war revived Russian nationalism, the Jews began to appear too conspicuous and too ubiquitous in high places.

Similarly, at the end of World War II the Polish Jews had every reason to welcome the new regime. Pre-war Poland had been a hotbed of anti-Semitism. The Red Army had saved the remnants of Polish Jewry. A social revolution was altogether overdue in Eastern Europe. So while the majority of Poles resented Russian rule most bitterly, the Jews could be trusted by the Soviets and their Polish satellites. Twenty-odd years later a racist campaign was launched by the Polish Communist party, under the official slogan coined by a party theoretician that no self-respecting nation could tolerate such a disproportionate influence by a racially alien group. And this in a regime drawing its inspiration from such "foreigners" as Marx and Lenin.

Throughout the ages the Christian–Jewish relationship has been beset by a profound neurosis. The peculiar, indeed unique concatenation of historical feelings in the Christian psyche toward the Jew: awe, sense of obligation, resentful hatred, contempt, guilt. The gentiles were thus conditioned to react to the stimuli that the Jew projected with an intensity out of all proportion. It was not, in the final analysis, the nature of the stimulus; it was the neurotic disposition that somehow made the behavior and acts of the Jew appear as a caricature. Hence the utterly contradictory accusations with which Jews have been charged: they were clannish, and then they became too obtrusive; they were cringing and soon too arrogant; they were blamed for being superstitious and obscurantists, and then for being profaners of all ancient traditions and promoters of shoddy vanguardism. They stood condemned as capitalists, and at the same time were feared as revolutionaries. No doubt, the highly ambiguous situation of the Jews, their being always exposed to some kind of blame, their existence, rights and character never being quite taken for granted as natural, obvious, the eternal fear of discrimination and persecution – all these shaped a nervous, neurotic, restless, furtive or self-assertive, at all events, an intense, exaggerated and shrill manner of responding.

Not so long ago an article in the London *Times* spoke of the paranoia of American Jews. The allegedly excessive touchiness of Jews has more than once evoked the reaction that the Jews were claiming exemptions from criticism, as if a single word of criticism was an expression of heinous anti-Semitism, and therefore inadmissible.

The Jews may exaggerate, but the reflex is far from being unjustified. Experience has shown again and again that not only was there something infectious in anti-Semitism, but that it belonged to that sort of emotion which makes one lose control, one's sense of proportion, which escalates, drags one down, unleashes uncontrollable dormant instincts: "the rush of blood." I was reminded of that when I recently read a revealing passage by an attractive and humane British historian on his experiences in World War I. "Most men, I suppose, have a paleolithic savage somewhere in them. . . . I have, anyway . . . that's the beastliest thing in war, the damnable frivolity. One's like a merry mischievous ape tearing up the image of god." What else could one say about the queer passion for destroying graves in Jewish cemeteries, or about the coarse, savage venom and spite, and the urge to sneer, insult and hurt displayed in anti-Semitic literature? At the end of the road is Auschwitz. In the Jewish reflex to criticism, and in the insistence to be spared it, there is therefore something of that which moves say the blacks and other traditionally underprivileged races in the US to claim compensating allowances for past deprivation, on top of formally equal opportunity in the present.

For generations, the Jewish question was haunting the world. The term has become "irrelevant" on the morrow of the Holocaust. Those to whom it had applied had ceased to exist. Instead, the State of Israel, which was meant to solve it, has become the problem child of the world. After displaying dazzling military valor which dumbfounded all those who had for ages been mocking Jewish cowardice, the people of Israel have found themselves in the situation of a ghetto of victors, a besieged city, an outcast nation.

Israel is caught between contradictory sentiments and commitments. It is yearning for peace. But it is confronted with an implacable enemy threatening total destruction; it is weighed down by the traumas of Munich and Auschwitz and fearful of the terrible risks involved in whatever alternative it finds the courage or is forced to choose. In a painful self-questioning mood, it is being challenged, goaded, prodded to hurry, to take the plunge into the unknown, to consent to the setting up at its doorstep of a garrison state headed by a terrorist leadership flushed with success, driven by a feeling of being on the crest of the wave and on the way to total victory. In recent weeks, the Israel–Arab conflict has been powerfully affected by two sets of events of an utterly contradictory nature, and it is impossible to leave them out without any comment: the drama of Entebbe and the ghastly, to the outside world totally incomprehensible, happenings in the Lebanon.

The former – a tale of valor which caught the imagination of the world and will be celebrated for a long time in ballad, legend and film – has acted as a tonic to Israeli morale. But it is the Israeli doves who have special reasons to rejoice. Their orientation was all along based on two props: the assumption that the Arabs were deeply convinced of Israeli invincibility and the hope that, as a consequence, Israeli moderation and magnanimity may instill some realism into Arab thinking and a readiness to make a deal. The Yom Kippur war, the grave internal problems of Israel and the courting of the Arab states by the community of nations had created among the Arabs the conviction that Israel was on the run, disintegrating, disoriented and abandoned by all. That extraordinary feat of courage, ingenuity and organization is bound to make many Arabs pause and think, especially in the light of the butchery that is going on in the Lebanon, the plight of the Palestinian refugees in the Lebanese camps, and the impasse and the defeats which threaten the PLO with strangulation from the hands of its patrons of yesterday.

The Arab leadership in the occupied territories may one of these days pick up courage to emancipate itself from the PLO and other outside agencies and organize itself to treat with the Israeli government, which on its part will then be duty bound to respond, with or without the concurrence of Jordan. In the meantime, Israel will still be scolded for its dithering behavior, for interfering directly or through its desperately anxious brethren in the Diaspora, with the policies of the great powers, for endangering their interests, meddling in their internal party politics – an unheard of thing in the United States. It is threatened with the spectre of a new wave of anti-Semitism, bullied with hints about dual loyalty, when all it wants is, after all, just to stay alive, afloat and tolerably safe, free to contribute in its own way to the wonderfully knit tapestry of world civilization and humanity's quest for a just society.

Even when all allowances are made for the part which irresolute and misguided behavior, unwise and rash pronouncements by Israeli politicians may have played in alienating sympathy, there still remains the fundamental truth that somehow the Jewish right to live and to exist on a basis of genuine equality, as a right, and not on sufferance or in return for some special excellence, is not yet taken for granted as natural and obvious by the world.

First published in *The New Republic: A Journal of Politics and the Arts*, September 18, 1976.

European History – Seedbed of the Holocaust

Never since the dawn of history had the world witnessed such a campaign of extermination. This was not an explosion of religious fanaticism; not a wave of pogroms, the work of incited mobs running amok or led by a ringleader; not the riots of a soldiery gone wild or drunk with victory and wine; not the fear-wrought psychosis of revolution or civil war that rises and subsides like a whirlwind. It was none of these. An entire nation was handed over by a "legitimate" government to murderers organized by the authorities and trained to hunt and kill, with one single provision, that everyone, *the entire nation*, be murdered – men and women, old and young, healthy and sick and paralysed, *everyone*, without any chance of even one of those condemned to extermination escaping his fate.

After they had suffered hunger, torture, degradation and humiliation inflicted on them by their tormentors to break them down, to rob them of the last shred of human dignity, and to deprive them of any strength to resist and perhaps of any desire to live, the victims were seized by the agencies of the state and brought from the four corners of Hitlerite Europe to the death camps, to be killed, individually or in groups, by the murderers' bullets over graves dug by the victims themselves, or in slaughterhouses constructed especially for human beings. For the condemned there was no judge to whom to appeal for a redress of injustice; no government from which to ask protection and punishment; no neighbor on whose gate to knock and ask for shelter; no God to whom to pray for mercy.

It is in all this that this last campaign of extermination differs from all the other massacres, mass killings and bloodshed perpetrated throughout history, such as the annihilation of defeated tribes in ancient times or in the African jungle, the slaughter of conquered peoples by the Mongols, the crusade of extermination against the Albigensians in the thirteenth century, the horrors of St. Bartholomew's Night and of the wars of religion in the sixteenth and the seventeenth centuries, the Chmielnicki pogroms in 1684, and peasants' uprisings and their suppression in rivers of blood, even the massacres of Greeks and Armenians at the hands of the Turks at various times.

The Holocaust visited on the Jews is different from all these earlier massacres in its conscious and explicit planning, in its systematic execution, in the absence of any emotional element in the remorselessly applied decision to exterminate *everyone*, but *everyone*; in the exclusion of any possibility that someone, when his turn came to be liquidated, might escape his fate by surrendering, by joining the victors and collaborating with them, by converting to the victors' faith, or by selling himself into slavery in order to save his life.

There is no doubt that even had the Final Solution not been formally decreed, tens of thousands of Jews would have perished in the war by the sword, from hunger, through epidemics, by all kinds of strange deaths. Millions of Jews would have suffered torments of hunger, infernal torture and all the degradation and humiliation possible at the hands of the Nazis and their helpers. I myself heard Chaim Weizmann's sombre prediction at the beginning of the hostilities that "in this war, we shall lose a million Jews." Ze'ev Jabotinsky, sometime before the outbreak of the war, sounded the warning that the Jews of Central and Eastern Europe must soon expect a St. Bartholomew's Night. Yet no one thought, or could have thought, of an Auschwitz.

Are we dealing here with a regression to the most primitive barbarism or with the nihilism of a later, sophisticated generation? With the outbreak of sadism or with the rabid frenzy of a perverse idealism which offers release, legitimacy and even glamor to the instincts of aggression and cruelty? What made this unprecedented deviation from the norm possible at all? The immediate and simple answer is, Hitler. There is certainly no need, nor any reason, to belittle Hitler's direct responsibility. Without him the decision to proceed with the Final Solution would never have been taken. This answer is, however, entirely unsatisfactory. Hitler depended on the consent of associates who would carry out his monstrous plans; he needed hundreds, thousands, perhaps tens of thousands of assistants at all levels, from the most highly-placed, sophisticated and "well-bred" intimates who participated in the decision making, down to the lowliest apprentice in the arts of homicide – the sadistic killer or the mindless robot.

The deviation from the traditional, the hallowed, the almost instinctive norm enshrined in the injunction "Thou shalt not kill" – nor take life without proper trial, nor kill the defenceless, nor harm the innocent – was in this case so violent and unprecedented that it is difficult to grasp how even an insane or half-sane fanatic could find it in himself not only to conceive such a plan, but to decree that "Thou shalt kill" millions, an entire nation, without evoking the immediate horrified reaction, "Why, you must be out of your mind."

How, we wonder, did he obtain the consent and cooperation of his closest associates, the compliance of the mass of executioners and the resigned acceptance of the very many who did not care or who were unwilling to get into trouble but who all knew, fully, partially or dimly, what was going on, and chose not to ask questions, but to look away?

Even an Oriental despot in bygone days would have shrunk from committing – indeed would not have been able even to contemplate – certain actions which would constitute an attack on established beliefs, violate certain taboos, strike a blow to deep-seated feelings or ancient traditions. In every period in history there have been things that people "simply will not accept," come what may; things that are so unbearable that it is better to die than be a party to them.

Fear alone cannot explain everything. Even the most arbitrary act of an unbridled tyrant is in some measure a function of the general climate, the spirit of the times, the social structure, the standard of values. For instance, the interference of the military with the political process by overthrowing the government or imposing their will by force on the nation, is utterly inconceivable in England and the United States, while it is a daily occurrence in Latin America and the Third World. In this sense one can perhaps speak of a consensus by silence, of acquiescence through indifference. Between the ruthless tyrant and the silent majority there is a quantitative difference that gradually expands into a qualitative one; this development, however, does not invalidate the basic premise, the common point of departure.

Release from awe and respect, the disappearance of inhibitions against deviant acts, does not take place overnight; it is a protracted, gradual process of dialectical development. However the transition from absence of inhibition to the actual commission of acts without precedent is not a result of structure only, but also of opportunity, of a state of emergency giving rise to storms of emotion, of a situation in which all restraint is jettisoned, of a period of danger and peril which give a certain legitimacy to acts and methods required by desperate circumstances where all other methods have failed. The sense of exceptional emergency unleashes instincts of violence and sweeps away inhibitions imposed by institutional framework, by sentiment, and by the labyrinthine workings of the subconscious mind. There is great importance in the tools and the techniques which allow such acts to be carried out with speed, efficiency and a minimum of publicity, for it is essential to confront everybody as quickly as possible with the fact that they have all become, in Goebbels' words, accomplices in a crime for which they can expect no excuse and no pardon.

We shall try to penetrate the "geological," historical, social, ideological and psychological layers from which this terrible act of *hubris*, the decision on the Holocaust, sprouted. The question that must be asked is, whether the point of departure, the core of the entire development was anti-Semitism, hatred of the Jews, and nothing else. Such a limited answer does not seem adequate to me. Even if we agree that antagonism to the Jews is an unchanging element, a primary factor, continuous and identical from Hellenistic times until today, and not merely a cluster of superstitions that erupt from time to time in waves of hostile agitation, in persecution and riots – even then we shall be obliged to recognize a multiplicity of formulations, expressions, methods of implementation, modes of incitement, types of accusation, all dependent on place, time, political and socio-economic conditions, moral and spiritual values and psychological factors. In short, anti-Semitism may be an autonomous, or, more exactly, a primary phenomenon, but one way or another it is a function of external factors. Anti-Semitism is part of a wider context.

The whole pattern of relations between Christians and Jews has from the beginning been saturated with a neurotic element on both sides, and it could not have been otherwise. Neurosis consists in the compulsive tendency to react disproportionately to stimuli as the result of a shattering experience at the dawn of youth. The birth of Christianity, its central *mysterium* and all its most decisive events tie it inextricably to Judaism.

Judaism is Christianity's parent, but Jews are at the same time deicides, the murderers of the Messiah, of the Redeemer. Christians are mankind redeemed by Jesus, but they are also the new Israel, the heirs of the election taken away from the old Israel because it rejected God's Messiah and thus God himself.

Murder within the family, the murder of a father or brother according to Freud, and murder as a consequence of incest in the view of various anthropologists, is the cornerstone of every culture, every order of values, every ethical system and code of behavior (*vide* Cain and Abel, Oedipus, Romulus and Remus). Instincts of aggression boil up to the point of murder; the participants in the act are deeply shaken and their feeling of guilt gives birth to conscience; mourning unites the family or the tribe in the cult of the deceased relative; anxiety to prevent the recurrence of a similar crime gives birth to a system of laws, ethics and taboos; the memory of the experience inspires story-tellers, poets and artists.

How much more true is all this of the murder of God. The believers in the murdered God are full of hatred and craving for vengeance against the murderers, but they can never forget that Jesus, his mother, the apostles and the apostolic community sprang from the nation of the murderers. They cannot forget that the Old Testament and everything in it, the idea of election and the prophecy of the savior who shall come at the end of days, is the prehistory, the *preparation of* Christianity, its seedbed, a preparatory stage of the true faith that could not be skipped. Gratitude acts as a brake upon hatred, but gratitude is stifled by hostility.

We shall ignore the background of Hellenistic anti-Semitism, the hatred of a strange, alien people, avoiding contact with all other peoples and exalting itself in the belief of its uniqueness and election, a nation of "mankind haters." We shall also ignore the influence of these sentiments on the final rupture between Christians and Jews, on the formation of Christian anti-Semitism and on its adoption of philosophical, ethical, social and other anti-Jewish arguments. The peculiar neurosis referred to above is wholly due to the original dichotomy contained in the affinity of Christianity to Judaism. It becomes visible not only in homicidal hostility and in the urge to persecute, but also in manifestations of a strikingly sympathetic attitude, for example, towards Zionism in its early days, in the first years after the Holocaust and in the period of the establishment of the State of Israel. This attitude stems from feelings of remorse, duty, and shame. In other words, the feelings of gentiles towards Jews are marked by an absence of balance, impartiality and ease. They gravitate between opposite poles. Amos Oz succeeded beautifully in describing the Christian's reaction to the Jew as the expression of the worst and the best in him.

The encounter between the Jews and the Germanic and Slavic tribes in the centuries following the demise of the Roman Empire added complications to this neurosis. The new masters, ignorant uncivilized barbarians, were confronted by a people of ancient culture, incomparably higher than theirs, a people with a strange faith, mentality and customs, a race shrouded in mystery and a people descended from those who killed God.

At first sight, these people were weak and helpless, but at the same time astonishingly resourceful, vital and tenacious. In the eyes of the Church, they were a permanent reproach and challenge because of their refusal to acknowledge the Savior and the fact that they were no longer the chosen people. Despised and outcast, they were, however, neither pagans nor infidels. One could and should persecute them, but it was forbidden to kill them, because with the sign of Cain on their foreheads they were living proof of the Church's victory and Israel's forfeiture of election, and therefore of the truth of Christianity. Outcasts, they do not belong anywhere; "they cannot enter the congregation of the Lord"; the warrior class is closed to them; they are not permitted to join the guilds of artisans and merchants; they are not found among peasants or serfs; their business dealings are not considered legitimate by the god-fearing masses; and they are despised by the well-born and the well-bred. They thrive on the misfortunes of others, and the very sight of them evokes the image of Judas Iscariot and Shylock.

Then comes the nineteenth century, the century in which the walls of separation come tumbling down and the Jews suddenly leap onto the stage of history. And lo and behold, yesterday's outcast is achieving phenomenal success. He climbs higher and higher, his touch is felt everywhere. Energy pent up for centuries spurts out in a torrent, sweeping away the old and changing things that had seemed as immutable as the laws of nature. He is the pariah risen to sudden preeminence, the slave become king.

The image of Judas and Shylock, of the crafty and deceitful Jew, of the heretic harboring eternal hatred for the faithful – these images are so deeply ingrained that it is impossible for gentiles to believe that Jewish achievements have been attained honestly and are the proper rewards of talent, industry and hard work. The liberals are disturbed and annoyed by the obvious discrepancy between the abstract principles of the equality of man and equal opportunity on which they pride themselves and their instinctive aversion to having live Jews in their midst. The frustrated losers from the vast revolutionary changes of the nineteenth century, as well as those whose expectations of imminent redemption by revolution have been disappointed, are bewildered when they look around and see that the Jews who previously had no place at all in society are the chief beneficiaries of modernization. Jews fatten on other people's losses and misfortunes and, they hasten to conclude, it is they who are responsible for them.

We must now trace the form, the stages, the circumstances and the time of the fateful transformation of the image of the Jew in the eyes of Europe, from God's accursed, an evil breed, a harmful force, and an embarrassing problem, to the concept of the Jew as the root and incarnation of all evil in the Manichean sense, as the source of all the evils that come together to form the one pervasive and all-encompassing evil. This transformation, in its turn, was to help change the mechanism of alleged defence against the spread of the baneful Jewish influence into the idea of the necessity and the legitimacy of a plan for a Final Solution that would put an end, once and for all, to the irrepressible absolute and eternal evil. These concepts, images and plans were to help erode, weaken and finally sweep away the inhibition before a violation of "thou shalt not kill" as soon as circumstances combined to produce a climate of emergency and of supreme danger.

Developments in European civilization and society at large contributed their share. These developments were not caused or occasioned by the Jews, but their edge was turned against them, directly or indirectly, for more or less objective reasons or because the gentiles, affected as they were with an anti-Jewish neurosis, were bound to link them with the Jews. For the obsessive Jew-haters, of course, animosity to the Jews came first for they were always on the lookout for a pretext to magnify the evil and the danger of the Jews.

One must not put racist Manichean anti-Semitism on the same level as manifestations of hatred of the Jews throughout the generations, however great the cumulative influence of the latter in preparing minds for accepting the theory of race. Oppressive Medieval edicts limiting the rights of Jews and riots against Jews as blasphemers of the living God, enemies of Jesus and the Christian nations, exploiters and even murderers of Christian children, poisoners of wells, carriers of the poison of heresy even after expulsion; the refusal, at the beginning of the Emancipation, to grant Jews equal rights because they were a nation within the nation, an alien element, a purblind growth that could not and would not open up to the enlightenment, to the winds of progress, and mend its ways and its flawed morals; the charges levelled, after equal rights had been granted, against the cosmopolitan Jews for their debilitating and perverting influence on the nation, its religion, tradition and national spirit; the propaganda of the Christian Social Party in Germany and Austria against the threat of Jewish infiltration into key positions in public life, and the disproportionate Jewish share of the national capital; the agitation about Jews controlling the stock exchange and corrupting officials and politicians during the great financial parliamentary scandals in France, for instance, the Panama scandal – all these manifestations can still be regarded as gentile "defense" reflexes.

Kaiser Wilhelm I and his protégé, the anti-Semitic preacher Stoecker, can be regarded as a case in point. They constantly warned against the increasing influence of Jews in all areas of German life, in education, law and culture in general, and stressed the urgent need to protect the artisan, the farmer and the "little man" from Jewish moneylenders and cheats and to preserve the Christian religion and the traditional German way of life from the Jewish materialist atheists. Nevertheless, the Kaiser insisted, one thing was impossible, and that was to deny the Jews their equal rights because the emancipation of the Jews had become an integral part of the German constitution, which he had sworn to preserve and defend.

It may be argued that this latter-day notion of the Jew as the embodiment of evil in the Manichean sense was only a new version of an ancient motif, belief in the Devil or in witchcraft. In both cases there appears the fear of an omnipotent and omnipresent power, a master of cunning impossible to locate but whose hand is felt in everything. I however am inclined to place the emphasis on the explicitly modern character of these Manichean ideas, which led to the Jews being stamped as a hopeless evil that must be exterminated and caused the revulsion against killing to dissolve.

As a result of the vast structural and spiritual changes in European society after the French Revolution, the Jews became the target and the victims of a sort of neo-Manicheism from both flanks, the Right and the Left. Despite the individualism, the pluralism, and mobility that characterize modern society, it has become, both in theory and in practice, a single, cohesive, interconnected entity containing many elements. Its blood circulates throughout the body without skipping a single part. Not as in the old society, poor in means of communication, where individuals and groups, social classes and entire regions were able to maintain a largely independent and separate existence, with the king as the principal symbol and embodiment of national unity.

It is not by chance that counter-revolutionary romantic ideology, especially in Germany, echoed the famous slogan "*La Republique, une et indivisible*," with the philosophy of an organic state or society, which despite the ancient label of *Standestaat* (corporate state) was wholly dissimilar to the class society of the Middle Ages.

With the increasing consolidation and unification of society the idea took hold that there is a factor of one kind that secures society's health, vigor, prosperity, harmony and justice, while some other single factor works as a poison to distort, corrupt and dissolve the bonds of society. There were those who, frightened by the vertiginous changes, and outraged by what they regarded as the putrescence consuming society, kept their eyes fixed on some idealized image of the past. Others brought up in an ardent faith in progress and in humanity's destined achievement of a free, harmonious and just society, were gripped by an impatient and exasperated hatred of that power which stood in the way and impeded the leap from the kingdom of darkness to kingdom of light, from bondage to freedom.

The eighteenth-century philosophers, such as Voltaire and Diderot, had placed the responsibility for this on intolerance, superstition and the priests; the Jacobins warned against aristocrats and their fellow-travellers; socialists denounced the bourgeoisie and capitalism; but for the champions of the idealized past, it was the French Jacobin Revolution which spawned the heresies of atheism, materialism, rebellion and anarchy eating away at society and corrupting it.

What characterizes such patterns of thought is the concept of abstract powers, ideas, desires, interests and processes being embodied in entire groups of people, and the condemnation of these groups as guilty, sinful and conspiratorial merely because they exist. In other words, there are entire classes of people whose very existence is objectively a crime and who must therefore be cut out of society's body like a diseased limb. The question of individual guilt or responsibility, of the subjective good character of the individual is irrelevant – it is neither here nor there.

An extreme manifestation of this type of thinking was the indiscriminate "absolute terror" of the anarchists of the late nineteenth century, who not only shed the blood of kings, presidents and ministers and their families, but spread death in theatres, concert halls and other places of entertainment and out in the crowded streets. Their contention was that the whole of society was guilty and rotten; that all were accomplices in the evil and responsible for the reign of overweening pride meriting punishment by death or by suffering pain at the deaths of their children, their brothers and their relatives, because none of them showed mercy for the suffering of the innocent who had been struck down by fate or damned by God.

Throughout the nineteenth century we hear ominous sounds such as these heralding trouble for the Jews. They are heard both from the Left and from the Right. The Fourierist socialist Toussenel writes a complete book entitled "Juifs, Rois de l'epoque" (Jews, the Kings of Our Time). Karl Marx produces in two separate pamphlets, his far better known – and far more shocking – definition of the Jews, variously, as the embodiment of the rule of Mammon; the bearers of the "cash nexus"; the bedrock of the entire capitalist system; and finally, the fount of the poison that consumes money-mad bourgeois society, which has regard only for price and cares nothing for value. The liberation of mankind is liberation from the Jews. Similarly, the German guardians of the traditional German virtues – resourcefulness, fidelity and honesty – identify the egoistic and rapacious *laissez faire* doctrines of the Manchester School with the Jews.

Germany's solid national distinctiveness disintegrates increasingly under the impact of Jewish ideas, imported from France – cosmopolitan ideas about the unity of mankind, an eternal natural law, the rights of the individual, the equality of all men and popular sovereignty. This what the German Romantics were arguing at the beginning of the nineteenth century. At its end the French anti-Semite Charles Maurras will be exclaiming bitterly that the viruses of Protestantism and Kantian philosophy were imported to France from Germany by the Jews in their attempt to break down the instinctive and traditional resistance of Catholic France to the infiltration of the alien Jewish element. Houston Steward Chamberlain, the racist prophet and Hitler's mentor, was to call the nineteenth century "the century of the Jews." I have the occasion to quote the breathtaking prediction of Friedrich Nietzsche whose own attitude to the Jews was highly ambivalent, but whose hatred for anti-Semitic vulgarity is beyond doubt. This prediction was not motivated by anti-Jewish intention. The Jews of Europe had reached their Rubicon, and the twentieth century will decide their fate, for "either they will become masters of Europe or they will lose it," proclaims Nietzsche.

> "I have never yet met a German who was favorably inclined to the Jews," wrote Nietzsche elsewhere, "and however decided the repudiation of actual anti-Semitism may be on the part of all prudent and political men, this prudence and policy is not perhaps directed against the nature of the sentiment itself, but only against its dangerous excess, and especially against the distasteful and infamous expression of this sentiment – on this point we must not deceive ourselves. That Germany has amply sufficient Jews, that the German stomach, the German blood, has difficulty (and will long have difficulty) in disposing only of this quantity of 'Jew' – as the Italian, the Frenchman, and the Englishman have done by means of a stronger digestion – that is the unmistakable declaration and language of a general instinct, to which one must listen and according to which one must act. Let no more Jews come in! And shut the door, especially towards the East (also towards Austria): Thus commands the instinct of a people whose nature is still feeble and uncertain, so that it could be easily wiped out, easily extinguished, by a stronger race.
>
> "The Jews, however, are beyond all doubt the strongest, toughest, and purest race at present living in Europe; they know how to succeed even under the worst conditions (in fact better than under favorable ones), by means of virtues of some sort, which one would like nowadays to label as vices – owing above all to a resolute faith which does not need to be ashamed before 'modern ideas' . . . It is certain that the Jews, if they desired – or if they were driven to it, as the anti-Semites seem to wish – could now have the ascendancy, nay, liberally the supremacy, over Europe."

In the light of what the future held in store, it is a shock to read Nietzsche's expressed desire for a fusion of the Jews with the Prussian nobility to create a new ruling caste for Europe.

> "That they are not working and planning for that end is equally certain," he admitted. "Meanwhile, they rather wish and desire, even somewhat importunely, to be insorbed and absorbed by Europe; they long to be finally settled, authorized, and respected somewhere, and wish to put an end to the nomadic life, to the 'wandering Jew'; and one should certainly take account of this impulse and tendency, and make advances to it (it possibly betokens a mitigation of the Jewish instincts); for which purpose it would perhaps be useful and fair to banish the anti-Semitic bawlers out of the country.
>
> "One should make advances with all prudence, and with selection, pretty much as the English nobility do. It stands to reason that the more powerful and strongly marked types of new Germanism could enter into relation with the Jews with the least hesitation, for instance, the nobleman officer from the Prussian border: it would be interesting in many ways to see whether the genius for money and patience (and especially some intellect and intellectuality – sadly lacking in the place referred to) could not in addition be annexed and trained to the hereditary art of commanding and obeying – for both of which the country in question has now a classic reputation. But here it is expedient to break off my festal discourse and my sprightly Teutonomania: for I have already reached my serious topic, the 'European problem' as I understand it, the rearing of a new ruling caste for Europe."

Writing in a vicious tone reeking of hatred and patrician disdain, Nietzsche's older friend and colleague, the Swiss historian, Jacob Burckhardt, had even earlier uttered dark threats against the Jews. The nations of Europe, he declared, would no longer tolerate Jewish interference in their affairs and one night there would arise a storm which would rob the Jews of all their conquests: their control of the press, their domination of the judicial system, and so on.

At about the same time, the Frenchman, Drumont, preached a solution of France's social problem at the expense of the Jews by the confiscation of the wealth which he alleged to be derived from exploitation, robbery and usurpation that had given rise to the social problem in the first place. This retribution would not only provide compensation for past injustice; it would also make Jewish property available for distribution among the French victims of Jewish exploitation and for financing national investments, public works and a system of social reform.

It could of course be argued that all this talk – along with the bloodthirsty sermons of such German Jew-haters of the time such as Marr, who coined the word "anti-Semitism" and Dühring, the influential pseudo-socialist philosopher who provoked Engels to write his famous "Anti-Dühring" – was still nothing but empty rhetoric and propaganda however vicious and vitriolic. It is one thing to say that the Jews were fated to play a despicable, harmful, even disastrous role in society. It is quite another thing to advocate a doctrine of racial determinism which seeks to settle the fate and destiny of nations from the beginning to the end of time, and legitimizes bloodshed and the taking of life.

Some of this was, however, advocated by – of all people – the populist socialists, Proudhon and Bakunin. In their teachings they went beyond the basic premises of rationality which deny any collective biological determinism and acknowledge the supremacy of reason, and the power of education and social engineering. They proceeded to a glorification of the existential situation, primary instinct, historical roots and the like, though not in terms of the purity of blood.

Proudhon jotted down some notes on the subject one day.

> "The Jews: Write an article against this race which poisons everything by butting in everywhere without linking up with any nation; demand their expulsion from France, except for Jews married to Frenchwomen; liquidate the synagogues; deny them any kind of employment, work for the abolition of their religious practices. Not for nothing did the Christians call them God-killers. The Jew is the enemy of mankind, this race must be sent back to Asia or else be exterminated . . . whether by fire or by assimilation or by expulsion, the Jew must disappear . . . the older ones who cannot bear any more children may still be tolerated. There is a task before me . . . What the Middle Ages loathed by instinct, I loathe upon reflection and irrevocably."

Darwin brought down one of the strongest barriers protecting "thou shalt not kill." For this reason alone, its great diffusion and enormous influence make it a turning point in the history of mankind. Darwinism deprived man of his uniqueness in the order of creation. Man was no longer created by God; he did not emerge from the womb of nature *ex nihilo*, a final and completed product with a soul that elevates him above other creatures, all creation his footstool. Man no longer enjoyed a direct and special relation with his all-merciful heavenly Father, who spreads the canopy of His peace over man and accompanies him in all his ways, provides him with sustenance, sees into his heart, rewards him for keeping His Commandments, punishes the sinners or visits the iniquities of the fathers upon the children.

Not any longer. Nature, it turns out, is not benevolent, it does not take care of everyone, and most important, it does not take care of the crown of creation, man himself. There is no Providence to look after man; nor can one speak of Nature as having been planned by a Creator or by some cosmic intelligence. The universe was not wrought by God, nor is it the handiwork of abstract reason. There is no order in the universe, no plan, no harmony, that could prove the concern of a Creator. Rather, it is characterized by confusion and contradiction, by waste and antagonism and by the struggle of all against all.

Such ordered harmony as does strike the eye and provoke wonder and gratitude – because it seems to indicate the possibility of progress and harmony – is in fact only the product of a struggle for existence, paid for in blood, pain, and suffering. There is no end to this desperate struggle in which the strong, the fit and the talented rule the roost, while the weak, the botched, the unfit and the inefficient bow themselves out or else become the tools of those with greater vitality, and the instruments of their will. The notion of the sanctity of life therefore has no meaning. The whole earth, man's battle-ground, is strewn with the corpses of creatures that have been obliterated because they could not adapt to or resist their betters.

Now, if mankind is not distinctive, it becomes difficult to speak of the unity of mankind. If there is no soul, then there is no reason either, for reason is the only quality that distinguishes man from the rest of the animal kingdom. Reason is but one of the tools evolved in the course of the struggle for existence, a particular expression of animal vitality.

It also becomes impossible to acknowledge objective morality, for the only purpose of morality is to safeguard existence by cementing the unity of the race in its struggle against rivals and enemies. In a Nature "red in tooth and claw," the sanctity of life is a contradiction in terms. Not only are the weak doomed to die, but the progress of the universe virtually demands their extinction or extermination, so that the fittest shall survive to employ the power that Nature has given them for the conquest of Nature, its resources and its potentialities and possibilities, turning individuals inferior to themselves to use.

We know full well the moral boost Darwinism gave the "robber barons" in the United States during the early "storm and stress" period of rampaging American capitalism – a time when "jungle" was the only word for relations between workers and employers. And we know the rationalization Darwinism provided for imperialism – nay, more, it was a hymn of praise – in its heyday at the end of the last century, especially for the Anglo-American variety. Although one cannot equate Darwinism with racist theory, it would be impossible to imagine racism without Darwin. And I am speaking here not of an indirect affinity but of a direct connection.

In the *Descent of Man* Darwin writes:

> "With savages, the weak in body or mind are soon eliminated; and those that survive commonly exhibit a vigorous state of health. We civilized men, on the other hand, do our utmost to check the process of elimination; we build asylums for the imbecile, the maimed, and the sick; we institute poor-laws; and our medical men exert their utmost skill to save the life of everyone to the last moment. There is reason to believe that vaccination has preserved thousands, who from a weak constitution would formerly have succumbed to smallpox. Thus the weak members of civilized societies propagate their kind.
>
> "No one who has attended to the breeding of animals will doubt that this must be highly injurious to the race of man . . . Care, or care wrongly directed, leads to the degeneration of a domestic race; but excepting in the case of man himself, hardly anyone is so ignorant as to allow his worst animals to breed."

Darwin states this more explicitly in a letter of July 3, 1881, where he writes: "Looking at the world at no very distant date, what an endless number of the lower races will have been eliminated by the higher civilized races throughout the world."

The idea of natural selection brought Darwin to an elitist and authoritarian view of society and the state. Thus, in his *Origin of the Species*, he writes: "I regard pure democracy as visionary as a country peopled by one invariable species. This with me is no question of what is good or bad, but of what must ever be, and I do hold that a government must always eventually get into the hands of an individual, or a family, or a class, or there is no truth in natural selection."

The doctrine of racism, especially in its German version, represents a fusion of German Romanticism and the science of biology, mainly in its Darwinist form. Neither Herder, who coined the virtually untranslatable expression *Eigentümlichkeit*, nor the other German thinkers who spread the idea of *Volkgeist*, had at first any intention of going beyond the realms of language, literature, religion, aesthetics, folklore or historical research. However, even during the Napoleonic period, the cult of exclusive German identity, personified in the ancient German hero Arminius, who rebelled against cosmopolitan Rome, spilled over into the domain of political ideas and the relations between nations.

Before long, there sprang up a whole school of thought – led by the jurist Savigny – which repudiated the idea of a natural law based on universal human reason and moral perception. In its place, this "historical" school posited the laws of nations against a background of natural and geographical factors, national character, specific traditions, *Volkgeist*, local customs and ancient myths. In short, a complete *Weltanschauung* was formulated on the basis of the rejection of the unity of mankind in so far as such unity is founded on universal reason, morality and law.

The racist doctrine constituted a spurious scientific systemization of these theories, and they paved the way for Auschwitz. Blood, the biological prerequisite of our existence, became a substance which determinates every aspect and manifestation of personality, from the structure of the skull to the minutest results of scientific research and the finest nuances of artistic expression, to say nothing of emotional predilections, character traits and patterns of behavior.

This implies that society – the community, the race or the tribe – possesses an immeasurably higher degree of reality than the individual, who has no existence apart from – nor any prospect of escaping – this all-determining, all-embracing reality. Thus scientism reaches back into the dark recesses of the most distant past and, in the case of Richard Wagner, is invested with the hypnotic halo of spellbinding religious symbolism.

Ancient legends, myths and symbols are like hieroglyphs, whose decipherment lays bare the primordial life of the soul, mode of existence and pattern of conduct. Monumental in their pristine simplicity, they assert themselves continuously anew, in one variation or another.

These primeval patterns, which spell the integrity of the soul and the immediacy, the intensity of original experience, must be protected against the pernicious intrusion of bad alien blood, against the analytical intellectualism that disrupts, debilitates, distorts and destroys original, intuitive and instinctive truth.

This primordial purity, integrity, rootedness and uniqueness fed on the apocalyptic fears that were widespread at the end of the nineteenth century, and found its own expression in the obsessive interest in the mystery of the decline of civilizations, the downfall of empires such as ancient Rome, the eclipse of great powers and the death of nations.

The mystery seemed to have been resolved, however. It was the result of the admixture of alien blood which helped to weaken the authentic instinct of survival and undermine the sense of pre-intellectual assurance.

And who is the alien but the Jew, who lies in wait for the nations of Europe, at once an outsider and an insider, foreign and familiar, preaching a system of universal values – the primacy of abstract reason, of a pure, universal morality and of the unity of mankind – and scorning the voice of the blood and of primordial instincts.

He himself, meanwhile, manifests an impregnable racial distinctiveness. A rationalist cosmopolitan, he clings to his exclusive heritage and preserves the purity of his own race. Though he may marry off his daughter to princes and counts so as to corrupt their blood, he remains forever a nation apart, although he is dispersed among the nations.

All history, to be exact, is but a series of incessant conflicts between the races, the chronicle of the rise and fall of racial entities imbued with their own authentic ideas and principles of survival. It is not the mode of production, but rather changes in the composition of human blood, that provide the motive force of history. And wars are waged not over universal truth, equal justice or abstract ideas, but for self-assertion through the accumulation of power, the demonstration of power, the exercise of power, the deployment of power.

Was this cult of power and vitality a revolutionary innovation? In some measure, it is true, this has been the way of the world from time immemorial. The way of the world, perhaps, but not its conviction – the kind of conviction one would be prepared to express in public, or even to oneself, without feeling uncomfortable, without any pricks of conscience. For beside – or rather, against – the primordial urge, had stood the system of Judeo-Christian ethics, preaching humility, meekness, reciprocity, love of man, regard for others, abstinence, asceticism, the need for truth, the claims of justice and the virtue of equality.

Then came Nietzsche, the mad apostle of naked and unvarnished truth, and proceeded to rip off all the veils of schizophrenia, hypocrisy, deceit and self-hatred that beset the dichotomy between the pagan heritage on the one side and Jewish ethics on the other, and to expose the unbridgeable gulf which separates Rome and Jerusalem.

Nietzsche hailed the Will to Power as the primary, authentic and noble urge, and condemned the ethic of asceticism as an invention of weaklings, a conspiracy of misfits and a bit of priestly chicanery designed to emasculate the strong, foster their feelings of guilt, arrest their native powers and defeat them by guile and trickery.

The Jews, according to Nietzsche, are that nation of priests that sired slave morality. All that has been done against the "aristocrats," the "tyrants," the "Masters," the "mighty" is nothing in comparison to what the Jews did to them. The Jews avenged themselves on their victorious enemies by radically inverting all their values, a most spiritual act of vengeance.

> "Yet the method was only appropriate to a nation of priests, to a nation of the most jealously nursed priestly vengefulness. It was the Jews who in opposition to the aristocratic equation (good-aristocratic-beautiful-happy-loved by the gods), dared with frightening consistency to suggest the contrary equation, and indeed to maintain with the furious hatred of the underprivileged (the hatred of impotence) this contrary equation, namely that "the wretched alone are the good; the suffering, the needy, the sick, the ugly are the only ones who are pious, the only ones who are blessed, for them alone is salvation.
>
> "But you, on the other hand, you aristocrats, you men of power, you are to all eternity the evil, the horrible, the covetous, the insatiate, the godless; eternally also shall you be the unblessed, the cursed, the damned! We know who has fallen heir to this Jewish inversion of values. In the context of the monstrous and inordinately fateful initiative which the Jews have exhibited in connection with this most fundamental of all declarations of war, I remember the passage which came to my pen on another occasion – that it was, in

fact, with the Jews that the revolt of the slaves begins in the sphere of morals; that revolt which has behind it a story of two millennia, and which we have lost sight of today simply because it has triumphed so completely."

The heirs to and followers of the Jewish legacy are the Christians, the French revolutionaries, the liberals, the democrats, the socialists – indeed, every movement of social rebellion and liberation throughout history. The war between Rome and Jerusalem has been going on for 2,000 years. But now at last, says Nietzsche, the war is reaching a stage of ultimate confrontation.

"Which of them has been temporarily victorious, Rome or Judea? There is no shadow of doubt. Just consider to whom in Rome itself you nowadays bow down, as though before the quintessence of all the highest values. And not only in Rome, but over almost half the world, everywhere where man has been tamed – to three Jews, as we know, and one Jewess (to Jesus of Nazareth, to Peter the fisherman, to Paul the tentmaker, and to the mother of the aforesaid Jesus, named Mary). This is very remarkable: Rome is undoubtedly defeated. At any rate there took place in the Renaissance a brilliantly sinister revival of the classical ideal, of the aristocratic valuation of all things. Rome herself, like a man waking up from a trance, stirred beneath the burden of the new Judaized Rome that had been built over her, which presented the appearance of an ecumenical synagogue and was called the church!

"But immediately Judea triumphed again, thanks to that fundamentally popular (German and English) movement of revenge, which is called the Reformation, and taking into account its inevitable corollary, the restoration also of the ancient graveyard peace of classical Rome. Judea proved yet once more victorious over the classical idea in the French Revolution, and in a sense which was even more crucial and even more profound. The last political aristocracy that existed in Europe, that of the French 17th and 18th centuries, broke into pieces beneath the instincts of a resentful populace – never had the world heard a greater jubilation, a more uproarious enthusiasm.

"Indeed, there took place in the midst of it the most monstrous and unexpected phenomenon; the ancient ideal itself swept before the eyes and conscience of humanity with all its life and with unheard-of splendor. And in opposition to resentment's lying war-

> cry of the prerogative of the most, in opposition to the will to lowliness, abasement, and equalization, the will to a retrogression and twilight of humanity, there rang out once again, stronger, simpler, more penetrating than ever, the terrible and enchanting counter-war-cry of the prerogative of the few! Like a final signpost to other ways, there appeared Napoleon, the most unique and violent anachronism that ever existed, and in him the incarnate problem of the aristocratic ideal itself – consider well what a problem it is: Napoleon, that synthesis of Monster and Superman."

The issue could not have been more clearly stated. On one side, there is the idea that all men are created equal, and that they are endowed with equal rights and proper universal reason. On the other side, and as a direct consequence of the denial of these same truths, there is the doctrine which claims that life in this world is worthless and meaningless except insofar as it consists in the self-realization of the elite of the strong and the powerful – a workshop for superior specimens who employ the common people as mere slavish instruments of their own will.

All religions and movements originating in Judaism have drawn their inspiration from the Messianic vision – a vision of ultimate universal reconciliation when all shall become one true community, when nation shall not lift up sword against nation and when justice shall rule the world.

Nietzsche, however, rejects this vision with angry contempt; to his mind, it is nothing but a consolation for the meek and the cowardly – the virus of infirmity and helplessness. Instead, he conjures up the vision of an eternal war that fortifies the strong, assures natural selection, and advances the select few. Racist theoreticians hastened to avail themselves of this gift of this convention-demolishing philosopher; champions of elitist inequality found in it ample support for the cult of personality.

"The universal degeneracy of mankind," writes Nietzsche, "to the level of the 'man of the future' – as idealized by the socialistic fools and shallow-pates – this degeneracy and dwarfing of man to an absolutely gregarious animal (or as they call it, to a man of 'free society'), this brutalizing of man into a pigmy with equal rights and claims, is undoubtedly possible! He who has thought out this possibility to its ultimate conclusion knows another loathing unknown to the rest of mankind – and perhaps also a new mission!" In other words, a war of annihilation against socialist egalitarianism.

All these trends of thought combined to remove the remaining barriers around the commandment "thou shalt not kill." The racist doctrine forbade contact with any Jews as the carriers of a deadly poison – going as far as Houston Stewart Chamberlain's ban on the reading of any literature written by Jews. It closed for Jews all avenues of escape from collective determinism, and assigned a cosmic dimension and a crucial metaphysical and historical significance to the confrontation – nay, the unbridgeable Manichean antagonism – between Jewry and the world, i.e. the Aryan race.

If one assumes that the distinctiveness and the cohesion of a race provide the vital impulse of its culture, then it follows that the anti-race characteristics of the Jews, as well as their cunning and their materialism, must devitalize the primal instinct of race by means of an abstract intellectualism that sows doubts, saps self-assurance and desecrates hallowed symbols. This it does with the help of an egotistic individualism that disrupts social unity, with the help of a pacifism that puts the warriors' vigilance to sleep, and through the manipulation of capitalism and socialism – both of them cosmopolitan forces that split the nation up into embattled factions.

Anti-Semitism was elevated to the rank of a substitute for, or more exactly, an antidote to, scientific socialism. Jewish financial capitalism became the exploiting class; blood replaced the modes of production as the key to history; the struggle over the seizure of power by the Jews took the place of class warfare; and liberation from the Jewish yoke was presented as the victory of a classless, nationalist society – a covenant of brothers.

When one of his disciples objected that anti-Semitism did not amount to a political program, Charles Maurras replied:

> "One of these days it will be shown that, on the contrary, it is as a function of the anti-Semitic program that all the rest of nationalist and monarchist programs will be able to pass from conception to execution."

Similarly Hitler was to declare:

> "We are confronted with a [Jewish] question, without the solution of which all the efforts to awaken Germany and bring it back to life shall be in vain . . . This is a vital question for entire mankind since the fate of all non-Jewish peoples depends on its solution."

The great role played by Jewish Marxists in the reinterpretation of the socialist canon – by tying up the success of revolutionary socialism with the looming confrontation between world imperialism and the world proletariat, especially in the nationally oppressed and socially exploited colonial countries – was seized upon by Hitler, following the Bolshevik revolution and the establishment of the Comintern, as positive proof of a global, satanic conspiracy to destroy the native national elites and thus to bring about the ruin of all gentile peoples. This, he claimed, had been the traditional Jewish strategy "from Moses to Lenin," finding its expression both in the ancient prophets of Israel, and in the new Jewish revolutionaries who incited the rabble against the elites, and provoked the inferior races to war against the superior races – all to insure world dominion for the Jews, as is written in the *Protocols of the Elders of Zion.*

Cosmological lubrications, nightmarish visions, provocative and inflammatory rhetoric – all these combined to remove ancient inhibitions, to break down existing barriers, to awaken dormant instincts and cravings. They were forged into forces of terrifying efficacy under the impact of mighty historical events: the First World War, the Bolshevik Revolution and the civil wars that followed them.

The bloody frenzy of the years 1914–18 threw humanity into a state of confusion without any precedent. First the war, then the inflation that followed it, and finally the great crisis of 1929 – which was widely regarded as the harbinger of the collapse of Western civilization – destroyed all sense of cohesion, continuity, certainty and confidence. Age-old moral constraints were swept away in the desperate rage which seized millions of people. Sacrosanct commandments and prohibitions were turned upside down by a false and distorted idealism – the violation of a precept became its fulfillment.

Defeated Germany developed the psychosis of a "nation under siege" threatened by the whole world, with the Jews as the insidious agents of that world conspiracy inside Germany itself. For by spreading their liberal-cosmopolitan-pacifist propaganda, by working inside the Socialist opposition parties, by preaching defeatism, and by degrading the symbolic national myths, the Jews stuck a knife in the back of the fighting German people. No sooner had the Reich collapsed than they appeared – these vultures preying on a corpse – as the new rulers and the chief spokesmen of reconciliation with the West and observance of the Versailles Treaty – in other words, of capitulation and slavery.

Even a humanist such as Thomas Mann, married to a Jewish woman, in his famous speech of reconciliation with the Democratic Republic, exhorted German youth to "take the wind out of the sails of the clever young Jews" who were pushing to the head of the line. General Hans van Seckt, virtual dictator of Germany in the early days of the Weimar Republic, a conservative, aristocratic officer of the old school, would say that despite differences in background, mentality and viewpoint he was able to find a common language with Ebert, Scheidemann and Noske; but in no circumstances could he talk to the Jewish journalists of the *Berliner Tageblatt* and the *Vossische Zeitung* such as Theodor Wolff and George Bernhard, for he was convinced that they never said what they thought.

Dr. Friedrich Thieme, a principal assistant of Karl Legien, leader of the Socialist trade union movement in the Weimar Republic, wrote of the well-known Jewish publicist, Maximilian Harden, in the journal of the movement: "The German people is honor bound to reject this leper. German people, you cannot sink so low as to have any truck with this Judas Iscariot . . . Germany people, do your duty!"

Even deeper was the abhorrence felt in all strata of German society for the Jewish satirical writer, Kurt Tucholsky, who certainly went to extremes in his virulent lampoons on the national mythology, German patriotic slogans, Prussian militarism and the Teutonic mentality.

There is no stronger testimony to the consent by silence and indifference – more than that, the readiness to welcome the "thou shalt kill" measures when the times comes – than the following extract from an article which appeared in 1921 in *Die Neue Zeit*, the official ideological organ of the German Social Democratic Party, on the penetration of *Ostjuden* into Germany:

> "East German Jews are mainly a proletarian population, sunk in squalor and wretched poverty, on the lowest rung of business morality . . . they are unable to enter industry . . . they are unfit for work on the soil. The great majority of them lack any sense of order or cleanliness; their clothes are full of stains and holes, their houses are unbelievably filthy . . . The memory of the Jews of Eastern Europe will remain one of the most nauseating experiences in the minds of our soldiers."

In his post-Hitler autobiography, "My First Seventy-Six Years," Hjalmar Schacht, the financial wizard who served every master of Germany from the beginning of the Weimar Republic almost to the end of the Nazi regime, cites a report submitted in 1920 by the Berlin police chief, a Social Democrat, to the Minister of the Interior, about a Jewish slum in Berlin; it reads very much like the report of a Nazi gauleiter in occupied Poland during the Second World War:

> "The district swarms with hordes of the most unsavory elements, which are dangerous not only from a criminal but also from a political point of view, since they have brought with them from their Polish-Russian homeland Bolshevik ideas which they disseminate here. Moreover, the health of our own people is seriously threatened by these immigrants. The habit of cleanliness is entirely foreign to them. Their homes are unbelievably overcrowded, crawling with filth and vermin. At the same time, they are stocked up with all kinds of food and delicatessen illicitly acquired and handed on . . .
>
> "The present acute housing shortage is needlessly aggravated, to the detriment of our native-born taxpayers, by the absorption of this mass of foreigners . . . They do no honest work, they pay no taxes, they evade every form of control; on the other hand, they seize every chance to circumvent German laws and damage, or even destroy, German property. It is entirely unnecessary to show any consideration whatsoever towards such people. On the contrary, it is more urgent than ever that, until they can be shipped back to their own country, they should be accommodated in internment camps, or better still, be rendered harmless . . ."

And now, to quote Lord Keynes, appears a lunatic who declares that he "hears voices from on high," which are in fact but the echoes of phrases he has read in the brochures of some vulgar popularizers of racist theories. But this lunatic has no longer any inhibitions whatsoever about drawing the most extreme conclusions from these theories and putting them into practice.

"Even if there had never been a synagogue, or a Jewish school, or the Bible, the Jewish spirit would still exist and exert its influence. It has been there from the beginning, and there is no Jew, not a single one, who does not personify it." Thus declares Hitler in the famous dialogue with his mentor, Dietrich Eckart. There is therefore no alternative to the physical annihilation of this "flesh and blood" substance.

Hitler's angry, violent fanaticism sweeps along the mass of impoverished and rudderless middle class. Put to shame by the well-to-do and the well-bred, fearful of being assimilated into the proletariat, the middle class is left with only one single – but the most cherished – asset: its German blood. The members of this class yearn for a strong hand to lead them, and at the same time they long for the power and the glory of treading on other nations.

Meanwhile, the German intelligentsia, their minds deformed by theories of mighty primordial forces gushing forth from the depths of the collective soul, are deeply stirred and prostrate themselves before this expression of elemental forces – this colossal natural phenomenon, this veritable volcano, the epitome of their hopes and aspirations, the quintessence of the Nordic spirit. As such, he is above the law, and above all moral codes; a man such as he cannot be held to account for the violation of legal rules and regulations. And thus it came about, as Ernst Nolte has observed, that Hitler was greeted in 1933 with shouts of joy by Germany's leading philosopher, best playwright, greatest jurist and foremost composer. But long before Hitler, the Jew had become for most Germans an enemy and an outcast, and an embarrassment even for liberals and socialists.

It would be impossible to exaggerate the contribution of the Bolshevik Revolution to the collapse of moral barriers and to the process of man's brutalization throughout the world. The Russian civil war, the GPU terror, the physical liquidation of entire social classes during collectivization and industrialization, the hideous show trials, the mass purges, the slave-labor camps, the bloody, lawless dictatorship – all these provided an example, a challenge and a license.

After the first terrorist attempts on the lives of Lenin and the two Jews, Uritski and Volodarski – incidentally, at the hands of Jews – Zinoviev, also a Jew, and then at the peak of his career as secretary-general of the Comintern, declared: "We shall liquidate not only individuals, but entire classes."

It was Zinoviev who, in a four-hour speech at an historic congress of the German Communist Party, led the German comrades down a path that was eventually to serve as a springboard for Hitler's leap to power. Zinoviev's humiliating and bitter end came in 1936 when, early one morning, the odious man was dragged, screaming and kicking, to his execution in a GPU cellar.

To the new nation-states of Eastern Europe, reborn after a prolonged period of subjection, the victory of Bolshevism seemed not only a danger to their feudal and capitalist classes; it was an even greater threat to their national distinctiveness and political independence – their sole possessions – than their traditional enemy Czarist Russia.

The Jewish leaders of the revolutionary regime in Russia and the Jewish Communists in their own countries were identified in their eyes with the Jewish masses who inhabited their cities and towns. These they had come to regard not as God's creatures, people who had lived among them for more than a thousand years, but as an alien growth, a vicious exploiter, a punishment from heaven. They were searching the whole time for some way of getting rid of the Jews, waiting for someone to save them from this mass of strangers blocking the road to a national and social cohesion, to genuine self-expression.

Poland's National Democrats, for example, insisted that the most dangerous of the four Powers that had divided Poland among them was still around. It was the most dangerous precisely because it was not an army of occupation, like Russia, Germany and Austria, but was settled in Poland and could not be uprooted. Thus the Jews became the Trojan horse of the world conspiracy headed by Poland's age-old enemy, which was now scheming to devour the infant state minutes after its rebirth.

No wonder, then, that the Polish Ambassador to Berlin, Jozef Lipsky, could applaud Hitler after hearing from him of his Madagascar plan, and declare that for such a noble service – the removal of the Jews from Poland – the Polish people would raise a monument to the Fuehrer in Warsaw. No wonder, either, that at the time of Auschwitz, the Polish underground press was capable of thanking Providence for solving a most difficult problem for the Polish people in a way that nobody could have imagined previously.

But for this Polish attitude – and without the participation of Ukrainian, Lithuanian, Lettish and Bielorussian auxiliaries – the Nazi campaign of extermination could not have been carried through; nor without the systematic dehumanization of the Jews in the minds of millions of Germans.

To them, the Jew had become, as Hitler wrote to Eckart: "a parasitic growth over the whole earth, sometimes creeping, sometimes leaping . . . sucking . . . at first the bursting abundance, finally the dried-up sap. No people in the world, not even Attila's race of murderers, would allow him [the Jew] to remain alive if it could suddenly see him for what he is, what he desires; screaming with horror, it would strangle him the very next instant."

However, there were two other necessary preconditions without which the Final Solution would never have been ordered or executed. One was the war with the Soviet Union; the other, modern technology. Only in the frenzy of an Armageddon for the rich lands of the Ukraine, coveted by the rapidly expanding master race – in the mood of a crusade for the extermination of the Communist monster, personified by the Jews and other inferior races – was it possible for the ancient cry of the First Crusade to be sounded again across a gulf of eight centuries. Since one must travel thousands of miles to kill the infidel, one should start by discharging this sacred duty at home.

After the war, neo-Nazis of all types put forward the claim that the gas chambers had been merely the twentieth-century version of the guillotine – a more effective, speedy and humane instrument for killing people. Although the *Einsatzgruppen* (Extermination Squads) carried out mass murders, using machine guns and other weapons of death, it is inconceivable that they would have been able to complete the Final Solution by this method alone. It is extremely doubtful whether they would have been able to stand the psychological strain for any length of time, even though the arch-murderers, Himmler and Globocnik, kept praising the fervent idealism and steadfast loyalty of their subordinates who, wading knee-deep in rivers of blood and climbing over pyramids of corpses, persevered fearlessly with their sacred mission on behalf of the fatherland, the nation and the race.

The historian who, perhaps unconsciously, seeks to punish himself because he neither perished in Auschwitz, nor endured hunger and torture in the bunkers, nor witnessed the death agonies of his dear ones, nor froze as a partisan in the forests of Bielorussia, nor fell in action during the Warsaw ghetto revolt – such an historian buries himself for years under piles of papers and books which represent his own personal valley of the shadow of death, and asks himself: What is the meaning of history's greatest horror within the scheme of universal history – what is its sense, its purpose, its logic?

Could the Holocaust be the conclusive proof that history moves by no law, offers no lesson, and serves no purpose? That it is merely a succession of irrational accidents, insipid banalities and gratuitous horrors? The mere inclination to accept this point of view suggests a surrender to the mentality of the perpetrators of the Holocaust. After all, they ended up where they did partly as a result of their desperate denial of a final station of redemption in history.

This heresy of theirs gave birth to the cult of power and vitality for their own sake, as a substitute for the search for truth and justice. Because they ceased to believe in eternal verities, they were ensnared by a perverted, murderous idealism which gave them absolute belief in their own superiority and in everyone else's inferiority. This is the kind of idealism that unleashes the beast in man, and turns high-flown ideas into a mere rationalization of the urge to murder.

In parenthesis, let us not disregard the modern technocratic philosophy which finds satisfaction in a job well done, and hails the challenge of solving a scientific or technical problem, regardless of the nature of the eventual uses to which they might be put.

As Aristotle wrote in his "Treatise on Government":

> "In this particular man differs from other animals, that he alone has a perception of good and evil, of just and unjust, and it is a participation of these common sentiments which forms a family and a city . . . for as by the completion of it man is the most excellent of all living beings, so without law and justice he would be the worst of all, for nothing is so difficult to subdue as injustice in arms: but these arms man is born with, namely, prudence and valor, which he may apply to the most opposite purposes, for he who abuses them will be the most wicked, the most cruel, the most lustful, and most gluttonous being imaginable."

The Holocaust put an end to over a thousand years of Jewish history in Central and Eastern Europe. It solved the entire Jewish problem – a product of special historical conditions – in that region. Are we then to conclude that every diaspora is similarly doomed? I find it difficult to accept this thesis when I think of the downfall of great powers, and of the disasters that have befallen so many nations, states and cultures in the course of history.

I recall, for example, the Tartar invasion in the thirteenth century, which enslaved Russia and cut it off from all contact with Europe for more than 300 years; the extinction of the entire Czech social and intellectual elite for several generations following the battle of the White Mountain in 1620; the years of the Polish "flood" in the middle of the seventeenth century – Chmielnicki's uprising and the Swedish invasion, which put an end to Poland's urban culture – not to mention the period of partitions which wiped Poland off the map of Europe; the horrors of the Thirty Years War, which turned a large part of Germany into wasteland and sent entire regions back to cannibalism; the bloody history of the Armenians and the Irish, and the destruction of the Byzantine Empire, Bulgaria, Serbia and the other Balkan states, by the Ottoman conquerors.

True, none of these catastrophes ended in the total physical annihilation of a whole people; but it is entirely possible that this is the end that still awaits many races and nations – maybe all of them. And the Jews will then prove to have been not the last, but the first victim of this new experiment.

Some people profess to see the Holocaust as an ineluctable stage in Jewish history – the labor pains of national rebirth, so to speak, or the price of redemption. One hears this kind of interpretation from extreme nationalists as well as from certain extremely religious Jews.

This I shall never be able to understand. I shall never be able to believe in a Guardian of Israel who claims the lives of a million children as the price of national revival. One must not confuse a metaphysical and theological question with historical and empirical statements about the role of Jewish despair after Auschwitz, the guilt feelings of the Christian world, and the fluid situation at the end of the war aiding the restoration of Jewish statehood in modern Israel. There is, of course, unparalleled grandeur in the explosion of Jewish energies and the display of an inconquerable will to live on the morrow of the most horrible bloodletting and deepest degradation and wretchedness that any people has ever experienced – in the struggle for independent Jewish nationhood.

Did those millions die a martyr's death for the Sanctification of the Name? A great many of them were killed without ever having had this feeling. Did they, then, die in vain, more of the innumerable victims of man's bestiality throughout history?

Was the Holocaust nothing but an act of degradation which can only arouse searing pain and endless horror? Or was there, perhaps, beyond the unbelievable indignity, some terrible majesty and magnificence to the Holocaust? By this I do not mean only the manifestations of heroism and courage in the Warsaw ghetto revolt and the struggle of the Jewish partisans.

Rather do I mean that in the vast perspective of history, the Holocaust assumes the grandiose dimensions of a confrontation between the two diametrically opposed world views about which Nietzsche spoke: between morality and paganism; between the sanctity of life and the cult of warfare; between the equality of all men and the supremacy of the select few; between the search for truth and the display of vitality; between the quest for justice and the discharge of instinctive impulses; between the vision of a genuine society of equals and the prospect of a society of masters lording it over slaves.

In these times of population explosion and racial struggles, when we have at our disposal all the means necessary to ensure either a Golden Age for all or the destruction of all, the future of mankind seems to depend on a choice between two alternatives: either the establishment of a genuine world community, or the outbreak of Armageddon over world domination and the rule of the strong over the weak. In other words, the awesome question is, has Auschwitz become an eternal warning, or merely the first station on the road to the extermination of all races and the suicide of humanity?

It would perhaps be appropriate to conclude with Nietzsche himself. In "The Genealogy of Morals" he says:

> "Let us come to a conclusion. The two opposing values, 'good and bad,' 'good and evil,' have fought a dreadful, thousand-year fight in the world, and though indubitably the second value has been for a long time in the preponderance, there are not wanting places where the fortune of the fight is still indecisive. It can almost be said that in the meanwhile the fight reaches a higher and higher level, and that in the meanwhile it has become more and more intense, and always more and more psychological; so that nowadays there is perhaps no more decisive mark of the higher nature, of the more psychological nature, than to be in that sense self-contradictory, and to be actually still a battleground for those two opposites.
>
> "The symbol of this fight, written in a writing which has remained worthy of perusal throughout the course of history up to the present time, is called 'Rome against Judea, Judea against Rome.' Hitherto there has been no greater event than that fight, the putting of that question, that deadly antagonism. Rome found in the Jew the incarnation of the unnatural, as though it were its dia-

metrically opposed monstrosity, and in Rome the Jew was held to be convicted of hatred of the whole human race, and rightly so, insofar as it is right to link the well-being and the future of the human race to the unconditional mastery of the aristocratic values, of the Roman values."

Nietzsche goes on to describe the long-drawn-out struggle between Judea and Rome, with its climax in the French Revolution. Hinting that the battle between the aristocratic ideal of Rome and the democratic-socialist egalitarian vision of Judea is still going on, he adds:

> "Was it therewith over? Was that greatest of all antithesis of ideals thereby relegated *ad acta* for all time? Or only postponed, postponed for a long time? May there not take place at some time or other a much more awful, much more carefully prepared flaring up of the old conflagration? Further! Should not one wish that consummation with all one's strength? – Will it oneself? Demand it one's self? He who at this juncture begins, like my readers, to reflect, to think further, will have difficult in coming quickly to a conclusion."

As to himself – Nietzsche continues in his oracular style – he has "ground enough to come to a conclusion, taking it for granted that for some time past what I mean has been sufficiently clear, what I exactly mean by that dangerous motto which is inscribed on the body of my last book, 'Beyond Good and Evil' (*Vorspiel einer Philosophie der Zukunft*) – at any rate that is not the same as 'Beyond Good and Bad'." Nietzsche would certainly have been shocked to learn that one day he would be officially celebrated as the prophet of the Third Reich.

"Now begins the last great revolution," Hitler was to write in *Mein Kampf.*

> "By wresting political power for himself, the Jew casts off the few remaining shreds of disguise he still wears. The democratic plebian Jew turns into the blood-Jew and the tyrant of peoples. In a few years he will try to exterminate the national pillars of intelligence and, by robbing the people of their natural spiritual leadership, will make them ripe for the slavish lot of a permanent subjugation. The most terrible example of this is Russia . . . But the end is not merely the liberty of the peoples suppressed by the Jew: It is also the end of this

parasite people itself. After the death of the victim, sooner or later the vampire dies too."

On the eve of his squalid suicide in the Berlin bunker the arch-murderer still had enough spirit (or madness) in mind to claim the world's "eternal gratitude" for National Socialism: "For having eliminated the Jews from Germany and Central Europe . . . who wanted war and engineered it."

Terrible and bloody are the ironies of History.

First published in *Midstream*, May 1973. The lecture was delivered at the Yad Vashem symposium on "The Holocaust and the Rebirth of Israel," in Jerusalem on April 19, 1973.

Part Three

Israel between War and Peace

For Total Peace in the Middle East

What is the secret of this fantastic victory of a tiny nation of hardly 2,500,000 over the combined military might of several countries comprising a total population of some fifty millions, which before launching the attack had stood for weeks in serried ranks on the Israeli borders ready to bound forth; of that feat of arms which – to cite the London "Times" – not merely won a series of brilliant battles, but within fifty hours changed the whole balance of power in a very large area of the world, placing the Great Powers before the necessity of a thorough reappraisal of their policies?

It was human valour. But still more so the lack of any alternative between triumph and extinction. That "no choice" situation gave valour all its irresistible intensity. Israeli valour is neither the fruit of a long martial tradition and thorough practice in waging battles, nor was it born in a climate of worship of the art of war and the man of war.

In those centuries in which Christian Europe, Islam and the Mongol Empire lived by the sword, upheld the right of conquest and conqueror, glorified the soldier as the embodiment of every fine virtue, saw in duelling the noblest assertion of the quality of honour and manliness, and in the trial by combat the conclusive test proving the stronger to be the better, the Jew stubbornly refused to admit that success was a sign of valour or strength the mark of right. In the long drawn out dispute with ecclesia triumphans as well as with the worldly powers of Christendom, all of which endeavoured to convince the Jew by words and indeed by more telling demonstration that his own defeat and the glory of his adversaries were proof that he had been rejected by God, the Jew never wavered in his belief that the suffering remnant, humiliated and mocked at, had God on its side. In contrast to the ideologies of most movements of national liberation and mystiques of national renaissance, one would look in vain for any reference to military heroism and conquest by force of arms in the writings of the Zionist prophets and teachers. Herzl envisaged the future Jewish State as a kind of neutral Switzerland; Ahad-Ha'am had no sympathy for any kind of political, and still less military, society, his thoughts being dominated entirely by the vision of a spiritual centre. Zionist mythology gave place of pride to the kibbutz, the University, spiritual rebirth, social planning, conquest of nature, but never to war and military glory. The need for self-defence was considered a lamentable predicament, and those who fell while defending Jewish settlements were proclaimed martyrs rather than heroes. It was Auschwitz that fired the Jews in Palestine with the desperate resolve to fight for their lives, without relying on others, and for mastery over their own fate, first against the British Mandatory Power and then in 1948 against the invading Arab armies, which resorted to war in order to prevent the establishment of the State of Israel, which the U.S., with the concurrence of the U.S.S.R., had decided upon. It was also the memory of Auschwitz that had made it impossible for Israelis to treat Arab threats of destruction and annihilation as rhetoric, figures of speech and metaphor. The Arab spokesmen, big and small, from the highest dignitaries, trained to weigh their utterances carefully, to the meanest scribe and soapbox speaker carried away by their own exuberance, all insisted that they meant what they said.

"The liquidation of Israel," proclaimed Nasser in one of his speeches (8.3.65), "will be liquidation through violence. We will enter a Palestine not covered with sand but soaked in blood." The order-of-the-day issued by the commander of the 3rd Egyptian division, situated in Sinai, said (15.2.56): "Every commander should prepare himself and his men for the inevitable war against Israel, with the view of realising our supreme goal, namely the liquidation of Israel and its annihilation in the shortest possible time and in the most brutal and cruel battles."

In the words of an eminent foreign journalist, "to look around to see the infinite effort that has gone into parks, museums, forests, housing, fields, into raising a new race of Jews and into creating a nation – then the prospect becomes intolerable." The Jews in Israel and the world over were also urged on by the agonizing certainty that, in view of the total annihilation of that Jewish civilization which the six million of the murdered European Jews had embodied, not merely Israeli Jews as individuals, but the corporate identity of the Jews as a people was facing the danger of ultimate extinction. The survival of the millions of Diaspora Jews, who lack that cohesion, as a living entity would have become most problematic had Israeli Jewry gone under.

The Israel–Arab conflict is of a kind quite different from those conflicts familiar to the historian, which arise from clash of economic interests, disputes about boundaries, the urge for expansion, the wish for revenge, historic memories and obsessions. Israel is the only State in the world whose neighbours do not put forward claims against it, but simply unceasingly and vehemently deny its very right to exist and are pledged to wipe it out. And not merely to abolish its sovereignty and dismantle the legal-political structure, in other words to commit politicide, but indeed – as said before – to annihilate its population, that is to say to accomplish genocide! Hence the incongruity, often almost grotesque and macabre, between the sense of urgency and despair felt by the Israelis and the long drawn out formalities of international diplomacy, the muted tones of official statements and the circumlocutions and studied vagueness and ambiguities of speeches around the green table, and above all the hypocrisies of lip service on the one hand and hidden designs which have no relevance to the matter on hand at all on the other, not to mention vilification and slander by foe and the friend of foe.

The Arab–Israel conflict is a lesson in the ineffectiveness of half-measures and legal formulae in a situation where not only is there no genuine disposition to abide by agreement and uphold the law on the part of both sides, but an absolute resolve on the part of one of the sides to prevent their working by all means.

The Armistice Agreements concluded in 1949 between the new State of Israel and the Arab countries which resorted to war in order to prevent its emergence, contained prima facie all the guarantees for peace, if not in form, at least in substance. They laid down that there shall be no hostile propaganda, no acts of sabotage, no military or para-military formations, certainly no armed intrusions or incursions by army detachments. But apart from these Armistice Agreements, there was after all the United Nations Charter which forbade in most explicit and solemn terms the use of force, overt or hidden, by one member of the U.N. against another, and both Israel and the Arab countries were all members of the U.N.

The Arab States, however, never ceased to proclaim that a state of war existed between them and Israel, which meant not only refusal to make peace and the implication that latent war was designed to flare up at the expedient moment into shooting war, and everything had in the meantime to be subordinated to that supreme consideration. It involved the policy of preventing any normalization of life in Israel, a sustained effort to sow insecurity, uncertainty, to sap its energies and waste its resources, in brief a kind of a long barrage, in preparation for the final assault.

Hence the dreary round of infiltration, sabotage, murder, arson, which, not being able to employ the same methods, Israel was compelled to answer with massive military retaliation. Single acts of sabotage and murder of partisan character attract little notice, while a raid by a military detachment across a border catches the headlines of the world's newspapers and sends the Security Council scurrying. The actions of Israel thus got all the publicity, while the provocations preceding them went almost unnoticed. While never tiring of reiterating that a state of war was on, the Arabs would at every Israeli retaliation self-righteously accuse Israel of aggression before the U.N. Security Council.

In a state of war no points of contact are possible between the sides. Hence the irrelevance of the empirical approach, so dear to Anglo-Saxon statesmanship, which sets its hopes on gradual, imperceptible sliding from a state of half-war, half-peace, into a state of full peace, from contact and cooperation in practical concrete and small things into sustained neighbourly give-and-take in all spheres. The best known attempt was the Johnston plan for the division of the Jordan waters entailing international cooperation in harnessing their power. Not to share the waters equitably, but to deny them entirely to Israel was the Arab resolve. The economic boycott, the closing of Suez and the Straits of Tiran to Israeli shipping and any shipping making its way from or to Israel and such similar actions were designed to isolate and undermine the State of Israel and maintain the conditions of siege and quarantine.

This is the context of the question of refugees. Acute as the problem in terms of human suffering is, and few Jews, sons of a nation of exiles and refugees, can be callously indifferent to this aspect of the problem, the state of war makes its solution quite impossible. The world is understandably deeply exercised by the plight of hundreds of thousands of refugees wasting away their lives in camps in pitiable conditions. One often hears the well-intentioned opinion that that was the most serious obstacle to peace, and if that tragedy were to be put out of the way, peace could easily be established.

The Arabs themselves have never said that the return of the Arab refugees to Palestine was their condition for peace. Quite the reverse. Already in October 1949, the Egyptian Foreign Minister wrote: "It should be known and well understood that in demanding the return of the refugees to Palestine the Arabs mean their return as masters of their country and not as slaves. More clearly, they envisage the liquidation of Israel." And in a more recent speech Nasser stated (26.3.64): "There have been attempts to separate the issues and present them in an imaginary way, as if the question of Israel is just the problem of refugees, and that once this problem is solved the Palestine question would be solved and no trace would be left of it. The Israeli danger lies in the very existence of Israel and in what this State represents."

If war was the objective, and the state of war could not and would not come to an end till the State of Israel had been destroyed, surely no one could blame the Israelis for believing that the demand for the readmission of refugees was motivated not just by the wish to see them restored to their homes, but by the desire to use them as an instrument and Trojan horse to disrupt Israel, first economically and politically and then militarily. The social-economic framework of the small State could not well absorb the large numbers of refugees with hostile intent and subject to constant incitement, and with no disposition to settle down as cooperative loyal citizens. The same may be said about indemnification by Israel. If war is the order of the day, it was quite legitimate to assume that the money would be used for the purpose of preparing the destruction of Israel, and not for resettlement.

Surely in this world and age of ours, the way to solve refugee problems is not revanchism. What Pandora boxes would be opened if all the nations whose members fled from homes during armed hostilities, were forced by marching armies to leave their homes or were expelled by *ukase* (tsarist decree) were to resort to war to right the wrong or merely to wreak vengeance. To mention only the case of the Germans who had formerly lived in Poland and Czechoslovakia, the case of India and Pakistan and other such instances. The Arab refugee problem is intractable not because no solution can be found through their resettlement and absorption elsewhere in the Arab countries, but because of the implacable Arab refusal even to consider such a possibility lest this assuage the burning acuteness of the political problem and blunt the edge of the refugee issue as a political weapon.

It would be cruel cynicism not to recognize the motive power behind Arab intransigence. And whatever the amount of trouble, suffering and tragedy caused to the Jews in Israel by Arab attitudes, it does not behove the victor to mock the vanquished and to trample under his feet the fallen foe, who fought as well as he could for a cause in which he passionately believed. It is not just simple malice, an over-large dose of original sin or unalloyed greed for power and territory that eggs on the Arabs. Even among the most self-centred Israelis there are few who deny that the Arabs have a case. Only their deep intuitive certainty of the justice of their own cause coupled with Arab total denial of the existence of any Jewish case sometimes prevents them from giving due allowance to the other side. The tragedy of the Israel–Arab conflict is that of a clash of rights. One is reminded of the noble statement made by the late Dr. Weizmann before one of the innumerable Committees of Enquiry that the Palestine issue was a problem which could be solved only on the lines of least injustice.

The Arabs are a proud race enamoured of the memories of their period of glory from the days of Mohammed till the thirteenth century. They woke up late from the lethargy which overtook them some time between the Mongol invasion and the establishment of Ottoman rule. They were then at the end of World War One seized by the urge to win or rather recover their place in the family of nations. Like late-comers they were in a great haste. They were also torn between visions of unearthly glory projected into the distant past and imminent future on the one hand, and the inexorable facts of actual weakness, underdevelopment and vast misery on the other; between the proud wish to assert their own authentic and peculiar identity, and the realistic, but also envious, desire to appropriate and utilize all the achievements and levers of power developed by the West. In this dilemma the Arabs never quite found a firm ground under their feet, unlike, for instance, the Japanese or Chinese. Add now the tensions between the dream of a united all-Arab Empire and the recalcitrance and refusal of the existing entities to give up their separate existence and freedom of action and commit harakiri. In this feverishly self-assertive mood, not based on any real inner strength and solid achievement, even shunning sustained and protracted effort necessary to build up concrete and solid assets, the Arabs became too prone to put all the blame on imperialism, although in comparative terms the brunt of imperialism was felt much more heavily by other races. The Arabs had for centuries been subjugated by the Turks and not by the Europeans, and apart from Algeria and Egypt, where the period of foreign rule lasted two-three generations, the span of time between the arrival of the imperialist powers in the Near East and the achievement of sovereignty by the Arab States was relatively brief.

World support for Zionist settlement for which Arab consent was not obtained nor sought, and then the establishment of Israel which, as a result of the Arab armed effort to prevent it, resulted in the plight of hundreds of thousands of refugees, assumed in the eyes of Arab nationalism the dimensions of a mortal injury and trauma, especially as it came from the hands of the Jews whom they had been accustomed to despise as second-class citizens and a non-martial race of infidels, although, in all fairness, they had not persecuted them systematically. The Palestine issue became the symbol and focus of all Arab frustrations. Their sense of grievance blinded them to the historic rights, the background of tragedy behind the Jewish aspirations, the ardour and high idealism motivating them and the constructive achievements resulting from them. It made them unable even to conceive that the civilized world as such could be deeply and disinterestedly anxious to see Jewish statehood restored after two thousand years and a revived Jewish civilization prosper in the ancestral home, even at a good deal of inconvenience to their own selfish interests. For when all is said and done, what lasting gains has Britain got out of the Balfour Declaration and what concrete advantages may the U.S. derive from her involvement? The Arabs would see in the Jewish aims nothing but a deep-laid plot and unholy alliance between Zionism and imperialism. They could not thus explain to themselves the repeated defeats at the hands of a tiny nation, which in 1948 numbered only 600,000, but as a combined operation of the greatest Powers on earth with Israel as their spearhead.

In brief, Israel became a dangerous neurosis to the Arab world. Hypnotized by Israel, the Arabs could no longer treat anything, however remote from this particular and to some extent marginal issue, on its own merits. Unable to settle down to deal with urgent needs and crying evils in their midst because of the claim that the destruction of Israel was the condition sine qua non for both Arab unity and social-economic reconstruction, the Arabs would waste endless energy and vast resources on this obsession, instead of getting on with their plans for melioration and social-economic progress. The most modern means of communication were harnessed to stimulate and excite morbid feelings and dangerous illusions among the half-literate.

The student of Arab opinion and Arab thought is often horrified to watch the growth of the anti-Israel obsession to the point of having become the cornerstone of a kind of systematic Manichean metaphysic with the Jew as devil incarnate, and of a whole philosophy of history stretching back to the beginning of time. ‘Abbas Mahmud al-‘Aqqad, one of the most prominent Egyptian writers, defines Zionism as "the evil quality which struck root in the Hebrew tribes and has made them hateful and despised wherever they are or come to. We mean their aggressiveness, presumption and selfishness." And Q. Zurayq, a distinguished historian of the University of Beyrouth, warns that "the forces which are at the disposal of Zionism all over the world, will, if only they take root in Palestine, endanger the independence of all the Arab countries and become an eternal standing threat to their very lives . . . will subject the Arab world to their will, will stifle Arab vitality and prevent any progress and advance of their civilization, if the Arab world will be allowed to survive at all." Of the one hundred and twenty Arab writers on the Israel–Arab conflict, thirty base their argument on the Protocols of Zion and seem to be accepting lock, stock and barrel its demonology, only replacing the myth of Jewish-Communist-Capitalist conspiracy by the myth of Zionist-Imperialist world plot.. One is no less horrified and indeed dumbfounded to see Soviet Russia, and horribile dictu Eastern Germany, giving sustenance to this type of neo-racism, with all the incalculable consequences it may have.

Under Ottoman despotism the Arab masses had for centuries lived in a state of complete political apathy and social subjection. Almost overnight they gained political awareness. But in view of the absence of any tradition of channelled and orderly popular self-expression and institutions of self-government, no wonder that any turn of events would be answered by them with an eruption of mob excitement and mob violence. Here was a tremendous temptation to politicians of the demagogical type to outbid each other in their anti-Israel zeal and fanatical agitation. Lacking a realistic appreciation of their own strength and of the power of the adversary, the Arabs gave themselves up to dangerous day-dreams of campaigns of total destruction, visions of imminent conquest by way of a simple walk-through, relishing images of fire and slaughter. They were kept at a pitch of excitement by the belief that Israel was only something provisional, able and indeed destined to be done away with sooner or later, and not something that has come to stay and could not be removed from the face of the earth, both because the Israelis would never let themselves be annihilated and because the world would never allow it.

This state of things did not start with Nasser and was not created by him out of nothing. Nasser's role consisted in focussing all the morbid sentiments into a compact ideology and the disparate and sporadic activities aimed at making life for Israel impossible into a systematic and sustained long-range policy, and above all the spring-board for the unification of the Arab world under his own leadership. Nasser's long-range policies were not allowed to mature. It was Syria, a country which has experienced some ten revolutions, coups and violent changes of government within a period of eighteen years, that became the chief irritant in the Middle East, more precisely on the northern border of Israel, and made the conflagration inevitable. Political instability, the long-standing claim to be the powerhouse of revolutionary-nationalist ideas in the Arab world, finally the exceptionally favourable strategic position of the Syrian outposts on the high ridge above the valley of Hula and the Jordan, where Israeli settlements form sitting targets, were calculated to conceal the intrinsic weakness of Syria, with not much of an army and a shaky economy, and endless internal strife.

The Syrians were determined to force the hand of their Arab sister-countries, and indeed of their powerful non-Arab patron in the North, confident that the real job would be done for them by others. They lustily engaged in incessant shelling of Israeli settlements and sniping at farmers pushing the plough, and in training and sending saboteurs across the border, in preparation for what they loudly proclaimed to be the people's guerrilla war after the model of Algeria and Vietcong, entirely oblivious of the incongruity of the analogy.

The Arab–Israel conflict assumed in the course of years the dimensions of an international irritant of the first order. That was inevitable in a world in which great Powers angling for positions viewed every case not on its own merits, but from the vantage point of their global strategy – how is this or that issue or move going to help us and harm the other side. This hub at the vast continental crossroads, with rich material wealth in the form of oil in the immediate background, has, as it were, been created to invite foreign manipulation. It was indeed too great an enticement to the local protagonists in the desperate tug of war not to seek alliance, collusion and plot with one or the other of the contenders. The seething little volcano, never ceasing to threaten eruption, was always in danger of sweeping into the vortex the vast power alignments, even against their better judgment, but just because of situations getting out of hand and leaving committed parties with the prospect of losing allies, interests or prestige, if they do not come to the succour of their respective clients. In his speech of resignation, Nasser invoked the threat of Israeli military action against Syria, but also stated explicitly that Moscow revealed to him the alleged secret plan of Israel, hinting at encouragement received from that quarter. Bogged down in Yemen, frustrated by the monarchial regimes of Saudi Arabia and Jordan on the one hand, and seeing a great chance in the ferment in Aden and the southern tip of the Arab peninsula on the other, Nasser seems to have resolved to play for the highest stakes: the campaign against Israel was to become the lever with the help of which the Yemen deadlock would be broken, and the reluctant Arab countries would be swept into the all-Arab war under his own leadership, and South Arabia galvanized into open revolt. Here was the unique chance of uniting the Arab world by way of a sudden breakthrough. And whatever the degree of complicity of Soviet Russia, the historian may surmise that the shrewd policy-makers at the Kremlin were not oblivious of the fact that here was the historic chance of shoring up, without the loss of a single Russian life, while posing or let us say acting as champion of the cause of Arab national liberation and unification, an empire of which the tzars had never dreamt, stretching from Iran to the Straits of Gibraltar, from Turkey into the Indian Ocean and Africa, with all the oil wells and strategic points in that vast area, and effecting a most decisive change in the balance of the world power. Nasser sends his divisions to the south-eastern border of Israel. Israel begins to mobilize. The conflagration seems imminent. Precisely at this moment the Secretary-General of the United Nations, the world body set up to keep peace and prevent its violation in any way, gives the order to the fire-watching brigade established on the Israeli–Egyptian border to keep the two protagonists apart to fold up and go home, an unheard-of demonstration of the ineffectiveness of the U.N. as guardian of peace and protector of the weak. Encouraged by U.N. capitulation, Nasser proclaims the closing of the Straits of Tiran to shipping from and to Israel, an action which Israel, strengthened in that resolve by world opinion and international law, had for years repeatedly stated it would regard as a casus belli A few days later guns begin to roar on all the frontiers of Israel. The state of half-peace half-war maintained by international machinery or if one prefers international pretence and make-believe was shattered, and the world found itself suddenly on the brink of a universal catastrophe. This time the world had a lucky escape. The swiftness of the Israeli victory took everybody by surprise, and faits accomplis were established in too decisive a manner to be undone, except by a deliberate resolve to start a world war.

No one can tell whether this dreary pattern of infiltration, sabotage and sniping on one hand, and military foray and armed raid on the other, with or without the ritual of going through the motions at the United Nations, resolutions blocked or vetoed, at all events abortive, and with the world press pouring its excited comment for or against, will not again one day – in the near future – erupt into a conflagration which may be so violent and so prolonged as to make another such lucky escape impossible. The world just cannot allow this to happen. And if intrinsically far more important and more vital trouble spots such as Berlin, Kashmir, Korea, Cuba (one shudders at the mention of Vietnam) appear to have been at least temporarily neutralized, it is not beyond the wisdom and the power of men of goodwill to remove that international irritant on the eastern shores of the Mediterranean. Surely that state of half-peace half-war must not be allowed to go on. In view of the permanent danger of its erupting into total war, there is no alternative to total peace.

In the first place, the world should make every effort to cure the Arabs of the morbid illusion that Israel was only as it were an accident, an episode, and destined to disappear, if only the Arabs knew and succeeded in doing the right thing at the right time, and allying themselves with the right allies. It has furthermore to be brought home to the Arabs that Israel was no one's instrument, not a function of some wider designs, not a bridgehead to any imperialist aspirations, but an end in itself, an interest all of its own, and that also other nations view Israel in that light, because they recognize the right and are convinced of the importance of a Jewish State in the family of nations. And because they are acutely aware of the unimaginable wrong and danger in any attempt to undo the fact of Israel's existence.

The way to alleviate Arab neurosis on the point of Israel is to impress these facts upon the Arabs so as to make them receptive to issues and aspects which in their self-absorbed fixation they are just unable to notice and grasp and adjust themselves to. They will then succeed in seeing Israel in its right proportions, indeed even themselves – as having done all in their power to save their honour and standing among the nations, and it may be hoped become disposed to make a new start. There is no dishonour in recognizing also the rights of others, and in acknowledging that the world's demand from the Arabs to recognize Israel as a rightful neighbour is infinitely less injurious to the survival, prosperity and power of the Arab world and Arab civilization as such than the order to Israel to cease to exist – addressed to the people of Israel, Jewry and the world as a whole.

The Israelis have no more ardent wish than to withdraw Israel from the vortex of global rivalries, than to be spared the role of a plaything in the confrontation between the super-Powers. Once relieved of the nightmare of mortal peril, inspired by a sense of greater security, it would feel free to make concessions and meet its adversaries half-way. There would just no longer be the justification for that agonizing feeling that not an inch could be yielded in that deadly tug of war, which allows no relenting.

Once more, there is no alternative to total peace. All may be gained from it, everything stands to be lost without it. Total peace in this area is a world interest. It should be an encounter face to face across the table between the protagonists themselves in good will and good faith, with the Powers acting not as big bullies, but as friendly and disinterested bearers of a world mission, the object of which is to extinguish embers and to widen areas of cooperation in the world, instead of confining the nations into warring camps, with the H-bomb lurking behind.

First published in *International Problems*, the quarterly of the Israeli Institute of International Affairs, as "Political Doctrine and Problems of Developing Countries," Jerusalem, Nov.–Dec. 1967, VI (3–4), pp. 60–68.

Israel and the Arab World – A View from Within

The Six-Day War of June, 1967, was a display of incredible vitality, fighting spirit, and sheer talent, and it activated a new sense of destiny in the Israeli soul. The achievement of "natural frontiers" and the reincorporation of ancient places surrounded by the halo of piety and glory were felt by many to represent an inevitable historic fulfillment. All at once Zionist became immensely meaningful again.

But meaningful in what sense? By Israel having obtained the longed-for goal of peace on the basis of a genuine recognition by its neighbours as a natural and integrated component of the area? Or by having conquered all of the promised territory and imposed its presence with superior force on an irreconciled foe?

The former was the prevailing mood in the early days after the war. People did not think of "reaping the fruits of victory." They wanted to believe that "this time the Arabs have learned their lesson" – that they cannot destroy Israel. "I do not want any Arab territory" – I was told in a private conversation 2 or 3 days after the victory by the late Prime Minister, Mr. Levi Eshkol. He was happy that "at last we have something we can bargain with," meaning conquered territory for peace.

There is likely to be much argument in the future between historians whether Israel was to blame for not coming forward on the morrow of its triumph with a bold, imaginative and magnanimous offer, instead of waiting for the famous telephone call from Cairo (and Amman), or whether the Arabs deserved condemnation for closing all the avenues of a give-and-take through the Khartoum Conference resolution, which repeated all the traditional litany of grievances and reiterated with additional vigour all the vows and bans of "never, never."

One is constantly told by Israeli Ministers that the government has passed on innumerable messages to the other side, with sufficiently clear hints for its imagination to grasp that a favourable bargain could be got. Much the same is being said by Hussein and to some extent even by Nasser. Unfortunately, what one side considers as the absolute minimum for its security is seen by the other as a pistol held at its head. There is then also the obsessive conviction that diplomacy consisted of bazaar haggling, and what is a far-reaching concession from our point of view becomes to the adversary at once a point of departure for asking more. The Israelis insist on the bitter experience of Arab hostility, the Arabs decry Israeli effective and victorious expansionism. In its paranoiac self-centredness neither side gives any thought to the fact that if you seriously mean to start negotiations you have first to think what would be acceptable and what was not acceptable to the other side. Since that is not done by either side, both are able to repeat with good conscience that there was no one to talk to on the other side and no one to whom you may give up anything.

In the event, every impediment which stood in the way to any form of reconciliation before 1967 expanded into an immovable blockage, and both sides, each in its own way, succumbed to what appears to be an incurable neurosis. Nasser may not have actually planned the June war. He may have just glided into it, egged on by Syrian recklessness, the success of each consecutive step in undoing the result of the 1956 Suez war, and the mounting pressure of Russian and his own collaborators who first took Israel's reaction to Syrian provocations for preparations for a U.S.-Israel collusion à la 1956, and then, when the crisis mounted, interpreted Israel's initial hesitations as a paralysis of will, and a corroboration of the exaggerated Soviet reports about the demoralization in Israeli society. Did not Heikal triumphantly proclaim that the Arabs had Israel in their net already? And so by the end of May 1967 the great day of reckoning seemed to have arrived.

For decades the Arabs had been obsessed by memories of past glories and prophecies of future greatness, mocked at by the injury and the shame of having had an alien and despised race injected into the nerve centre of their promised pan-Arab empire, between its Asian and African halves, just at a time when the colonial powers had started their great retreat from their colonial possessions in Asia and Africa. To ease their feelings of humiliation the Arabs would attribute all the Zionist successes – Jewish settlement, the victories of 1948 and 1956 – to the machinations of Western imperialism. Israel as the agent or spearhead of the Great Powers became thus the peg to hang upon all the frustrations encountered by the Arab peoples in their anxious and jealous effort to skip centuries of social, economic and cultural development, and catch up with the well-established and self-assured western old-timers. The effect had been to make them almost incapable of setting their minds to anything else, or of seeing anything on its own merits and as unrelated to the central grievance. Everything had, as it were, to be suspended until that wrong could be redressed.

To make a virtue out of a vice, the Arabs developed the vision of an extreme misfortune turned into the lever of an ultimate fulfillment: in the course of preparing for the joint total confrontation with Israel, the Arabs would create the sinews of their future empire, and the victory over Israel would almost automatically – as in the case of Italy in 1859–61 and Germany in 1870–71 – ensue in a pan-Arab empire, an Arab nation one and indivisible, which had also incidentally achieved its social revolution by wresting the rich oil fields from the feudal sheiks and turned them into the rightful inheritance of the nation as such.

It is easy to imagine the shock of the 1967 defeat, which not only destroyed all these calculations and schemes, but also underscored the humiliation by the fact that Israel's victory was this time manifestly single-handed, and unlike the 1956 Suez (or Sinai) campaign could hardly be attributed to Imperialist aid.

The anti-Israel obsession gave rise to a kind of systematic Manichean metaphysic, the focus of an entire philosophy of history, with the Jew as the devil incarnate from the days of patriarch Abraham himself till his assumption of the role of the lynchpin of an American-Imperialist-Zionist world-plot against the Arab world, the Socialist Commonwealth, and all colonial peoples.

By an unspeakably tragic irony the Zionism of Jewish exiles marching to the tune of "*Oh if I forget thee, Jerusalem*," not only created an Arab Zionism, propelled by a similar sense of exile and dream of a return to that very Jerusalem, but in imparting the mad obsession with a world-wide Jewish conspiracy to the Islamic world, which however contemptuous of, and unfriendly to, Jews had in the past not known that essentially Christian neurotic preoccupation with Jewish deicide and the Protocols of Zion, from the dire results of which the Jews sought refuge in Palestine.

The Right to Exist

Nothing highlights so much the intractable character of the conflict than the fact that what to the Jews appears a *condition sine qua non* as well as a crowning achievement is to the Arabs something utterly unthinkable – the ultimate humiliation: to sit down and negotiate a peace in a direct give-and-take. To the Israeli Ministers, most of them persons of sound horse sense and warm humanity, although in some cases afflicted by a good deal of self-righteous incomprehension of the Arab cause, such an outcome seems so logical and natural. But there is more to it. Deep down in the Jewish soul there is the conscious or unconscious tremendous anxiety to do away with that which had plagued their existence for two thousand years in the Diaspora – the lack of simple, unreserved recognition of their right to exist as of right, and not on sufferance. Was not the essence of Zionism the deep longing to be a nation unto the nations in the family of nations? Nothing could therefore be more galling and frustrating than the fact that Israel was the only State in the world to which its neighbours refused the very right to exist, and whose frontiers were hermetically closed even when they were not ablaze. For ultimately all turns upon this point: the presence or absence of a readiness to recognize the State of Israel, which amounts to saying the will for peace or the will for war. If the former were there and convincingly demonstrated, questions of borders, refugee settlement, guarantees against the guerrilla activities, would become secondary and likely to fall easily into their place. If the latter were paramount, then there would be only one categorical imperative "kill him before he kills you": strategic borders become then all-important, readmission of refugees is tantamount to the introduction of a Trojan horse, even the signing of some sort of document on non-belligerency by the Arab Governments only a ruse for gaining a breathing spell for another round, in preparation for which the guerrillas would be encouraged to conduct softening-up operations deep into the neighbourhood of Tel Aviv, indeed, if possible, into its very heart.

The Arab Neurosis

The other day I fathomed something of the depths of Arab neurosis. A group of prominent Arabs and Jewish intellectuals who had been meeting together at fairly frequent intervals were discussing for the nth time "the problem" in an atmosphere of accentuated mutual courtesy and in the common conviction that History had decreed that we have to live together or we shall perish together, meaning – I hasten to add – by living "together" not a bi-national State but separate Jewish and Arab States, so as to enable each people to express itself freely as God has created it – a distinct entity – without any wish for, or opportunity of, patronizing the other, and with no reason to fear of being swamped by the numbers or the superior competence of the other side. A Hebrew University (of Jerusalem) professor addressed the direct question to our Arab interlocutors whether any one of them knew a single example in history of victors withdrawing before the vanquished had even begun to sue for peace, let alone vowed day-in-day-out that they would never make peace, never recognize the victor's very right to exist, never meet him to negotiate face to face but will continue to labour with no respite for his destruction and annihilation.

"Surely you know also very well that had your leaders shown the slightest inclination to sit down with us and talk, the Jews would have been falling over each other in a stampede to meet you and you would have got out of them gains which you could never obtain on the battlefield." Turning to the soldier among the Arabs present, a former high officer in the British and later in two Arab armies, and altogether an attractive and warm person, the Israeli scholar exclaimed, "and you for one after all know that the Arabs are in no position to defeat Israel for a very long time." The man to whom these words were addressed, usually highly articulate and eloquent, sat quite speechless and his countenance showed signs of deep travail. He murmured something about honour, glory, history. He had been plainly touched on the raw. There came to my mind a recent article by Heikal in which in a pathetic *cri de coeur* he exclaimed that once the Arabs had succeeded in inflicting a single defeat upon Israel and in killing 10–15–20,000 Jews, their self-respect would be regained and – he hinted – it might become possible for them to meet the Jews face to face. It seemed like the case of the impotent who had tried and tried so many times in vain and is obsessed with the dream of that breakthrough, after which he will be able to look men and women straight into their eyes. That the breakthrough was sure to come the Arabs have the Crusaders as proof. Admittedly, it took two hundred years for the Arabs to finish off the Crusaders' Kingdom. Well, had it not taken the Jews two thousand years to come back to the Holy Land?

Fear and Distrust

There is ground to fear that a not dissimilar type of impotence is in the process of paralyzing Israel. The Arab predicament stems from resentment and rage, steeped in a sense of failure. The Jewish complex grows from a mixture of fear and distrust, on the one hand, and a feeling of power on the other. There is a deep-seated longing for peace in Israel, and there can be no doubt that were the Jews to discern some opening, a narrow chink in the Arab wall of obduracy, the great majority of them would leap forward to meet the Arabs more than half way. The grave psychological impediments which continue to pile up may prove however strong enough to stultify that urge, or at least to prevent the Israelis from detecting that longed-for "opening," even if it should begin somewhere.

That process started as soon as the Arabs closed themselves into a cage with their Khartoum resolutions. The spirit of generous euphoria began at once to give way to fear and distrust and to a hardening of arteries in Israel. If the Arabs were absolutely resolved on a war of annihilation, surely – it was said – it would be criminal negligence not to maintain the utmost precautions, stick to the present frontiers, which allow us to strike at Cairo or Damascus within seconds almost, while the Egyptian planes can reach Tel Aviv in no less than a quarter of an hour. Who can in such circumstances give up the Jordan ditch and allow the Jordanian border to be re-established at 12–14 km. from Tel Aviv? People began to recall the lessons of history, how every Arab "no" resulted in greater gains than had been hoped for from an Arab "yes." Time was on our side, no matter what pressures the U.S. may exercise – they cannot be too strong, since we are, after all, the only safe ally of America in this area, its bastion against Soviet encroachment into the Indian Ocean, and we have never asked U.S. soldiers to fight for us. One must not be scared by threats and abuse coming from Moscow, for the Russians will not send an expeditionary force against us. Nor should we be unduly upset by unpleasantness from the U.N. Security Council, which is surely dominated by our enemies and is at the same time impotent. The unrest in the occupied territories is easily manageable and the shelling on the canal or the forays of guerrillas were incapable of even making a dent in Israeli armour. All that was needed were strong nerves. The usual argument which the Israeli hawk would bring out to "demolish" the pleadings of the doves, would be "Trust the Arabs to help us out in the end."

As time went on more and more people became receptive to the romantic pseudo-religious mysticism of the various fire-eating and Bible-quoting Prophets of manifest destiny, who compare the

Zionist endeavour to a Revolution which must unfold to its last consequence. It is written in the Book of History that Israel will be restored to the fullness of his inheritance. That inheritance belonged to all generations past, present and future. And the present generation which had been singled out by the Almighty as trustee and executive had no right to give away what belonged to all the generations. The Arabs owned fourteen States, while Israel was to the Jews the poor man's only little sheep.

The Balfour Declaration and the Mandate had recognised the rights of the Palestinian Arabs as individuals, but not as a sovereign national entity. Sovereignty over the Holy Land was reserved to the Jews alone. The Palestinian Arabs who, in spite of the Israeli resolve to guarantee them their human and civil rights and to grant them equality, preferred to live in an Arab State, were welcome to emigrate.

Would such a policy not constitute an insurmountable obstacle to peace with the Arab countries? This objection the new militants would counter by saying that the Arabs would agree to peace or rather give up war only if they became absolutely convinced that they had no hope of breaking the resolve of Israel. Since any sign of weakness only encouraged them in their intransigence, Israel was bound not to yield an inch. Some extremists have gone even further than this, asserting that peace might not be desirable for Israel at all, and pointing in support of their view to the bracing effect wars have had on the nation, its pride, and its sense of unity.

There is something pathetic, at once touching and repellent, in the desperate quest of the mystical maximalists for means and ways to meet the awful, supremely ironical, contingency of the Jews of Greater Israel being swamped in no time by the higher birth rate of the Arab minority, in other words in their efforts to make good the irretrievable catastrophe of Auschwitz. Thus one of the oldest of the new militants exclaims in prophetic ecstasy: Two million new immigrants in two years! Where from? He and his life refuse to recognize any fundamental difference between the closely knit and self-sufficient Jewish communities of former Poland and Rumania, and Western Jewry, in the first place American.

Anxious Solidarity

Somewhat exaggerating the significance of the wave of anxious solidarity which swept world Jewry in May and June of 1967, when

Israel seemed to face its supreme ordeal, they would attribute it to an ethnic group in a pluralistic society, yearning for an untrammelled national existence that an older generation of East European Jews went to seek in Palestine. Failing large-scale emigration from North America, then the millions of recruits would come from the Soviet Union seething with anti-Semitism, or from South America, menaced by Castroism or Che Guevaraism. Without voicing such sentiments openly, some hawkish mystics are almost on the lookout for anti-Semitism, such as the Negro anti-Jewish resentments (assuming "the worst the better"). If egged on by fear of persecution, Diaspora Jews will emigrate to Israel. Some even set their hopes upon a change of heart among the Jewish hippies and members of the New Left. Who knows, their surplus of idealism, when finally frustrated, could still be channelled into halutzic resolve.

A poet of the romantically nationalist persuasion, but doubtful of the possibility of enticing many Jews to immigrate, launched a delirious "appeal to the Gentiles" – Norwegians, Dutchmen, Danes, Mexicans, Frenchmen and Italians: "Let us tell them: come and partake of the wonderful adventure of building Eretz-Israel . . . We will share everything with them. We will give them our pretty daughters for their wives and their dark or light skinned women will find men here worthy of the name. We will make it easy for them to convert to Judaism, and those who will not wish to convert can live here as a sympathetic minority of Christians or atheists, tied to us in heart and soul, as citizens."

The Danger of a Rhodesian Situation

The arguments about the danger of a Rhodesian situation developing in an Israel divided into two so utterly different societies are brushed aside by the hawks: their opponents were men of small faith in their doubts about the ability of Israel to cope with any problem and moreover were propagating slanders by insinuating that Israel will not know how to treat fairly and justly the strangers within her gates. The dovish argument about world opinion the hawks would brush aside as pusillanimous and dishonourable. The Jews owe nothing to the world (as if Zionism could ever have taken off the ground without public sympathy). Had the world done anything about Auschwitz or in the days preceding the Six Day War? Any concession on Israel's right of sovereignty over the whole of

Palestine was tantamount to an admission that Zionism had always been wrong.

Apocalyptically-minded superhawks are to be found on both sides. On the Arab side they are determined to provoke Israel to expand till it bursts, till it is choked with its Arab population, saddled with such insoluble problems and so harassed by guerrillas and sabotage that it is goaded into resorting to savage repression and irrational squandering of strength to the horror of the whole world.

There are some Jewish superhawks on the lunatic fringe who also pray for an apocalypse which will somehow make the Arabs vanish into thin air through mass flight and leave Israel safe and happy for ever after, behind the Jordan river, or who knows – the Syrian desert, turned into a Chinese wall.

Accomplished Facts

On a less exalted and more mundane plane, the more sober politicians argue quite plausibly that if peace is very distant, since Hussein cannot for fear of the terrorists and Nasser would not make it, for the fear of losing his leadership of the Arab world, Israel cannot impotently leave things in suspense. You cannot stand still: you either go forward or move backward. Fortified outposts must be established, and they have to be flanked by settlements and supplied with safe and easy lines of communication – the Golan Heights, strategic areas in the Sinai, in the mountains on the West Bank and in the Jordan valley. Even those who, while insisting on strongpoints, disdain the wish to annex Arab populations in substantial numbers, go on arguing that one cannot leave two economies to go their separate and very different ways. The state of uncertainty about their future – some go one further – prevented moderate Arabs from collaborating with the Israeli authorities, while it encouraged the extremists to assist in or condone the acts of the saboteurs and terrorists. From this there is little distance to the conclusion that annexation would rebound to the good of the Arabs themselves and even help in resettling the refugees. And should by some miracle the Arabs agree to negotiate at some future date, nothing would prevent us from pulling back from the outposts in exchange for a real peace, say the moderates; what we will have annexed and integrated into Israel will remain ours – is the hope of the hawks. Accomplished facts create laws, theories of international law do not establish facts.

This divided mood between the yearning for peace and profound distrust of the Arabs – consequently disbelief in peace, and the hankering sense of obligation towards the "potential" citizens of Israel in the Diaspora – becomes the source of so much that is equivocal, inconsistent, and is likely to appear hypocritical or even cynical in the eyes of outsiders. Although the official Israeli policy is still direct negotiations with all options open, increasingly more frequent and louder are Ministerial statements about this or that point – usually territorial – not being negotiable, until you even hear that it was better to hold Sharm-el-Sheikh, the God forsaken desert around the exit to the Red Sea, without peace, than to get peace without Sharm-el-Sheikh.

The divisions in the Cabinet are deep and are openly voiced. But since the need for a real decision is made to look very distant by Arab intransigence, the protagonists are only too glad to postpone the hour of decision so as not to wreck the National Coalition. The latter, imperceptibly, turns from a means into an end, and indeed a pretext to take no initiative in the pursuit of peace.

A Palestinian Arab Entity

This mixture of hubris and fear is all pervading in Israel. One hears people say in the same breach, "We can reach Cairo within hours; we may be destroyed within half an hour if the Arab tanks break through the narrow neck of pre-June 1967 Israel north of Tel Aviv." This ambivalence may be taken to epitomize the general human condition since the intrusion of the atomic weapons, but it brings into still sharper relief the baffling ambiguity of the Jewish situation through the ages. The steep and rapid fall from blinding splendour to bottomless misery has been such a constant feature in Jewish history. This makes for obsessive over-anxiety and over-reaction, and to a neurotic determination to make the worst fears come true. One of the most discussed issues in Israel has been, for instance, the question of recognizing the West Bank Arabs as a Palestinian Arab entity, with a view of establishing an autonomous Arab State there. Some see in such a plan a way of frightening Hussein into entering into negotiations, others an end in itself and a first unilateral step towards an overall settlement with the Arab world. Strong reasons for and against such a policy have been adduced on practical grounds. There is indeed much justified doubt whether such a statelet would be viable at all. There is then the argument that it would in fact be either an Israeli protectorate or a springboard for militant Arab irridentism. With El-Fatah staking out the claim to speak for the Undivided Palestinian Nation, opposing any kind of arrangement with Israel and vowing total destruction of the Jewish State, some Israeli leaders have lately caught fright at the idea of acknowledging even in theory the existence of such a national entity as the West Bank Arabs, lest this offers the enemy a handle to proclaim that the whole and undivided Palestine was the patrimony of the indivisible Palestine Arab nation; as if the fanatical terrorist groups were really in need of additional arguments. Some Israeli leaders got themselves wantonly entangled in pernicious and self-defeating theoretical disquisitions intended to show that the Palestine Arabs were not a nation, oblivious to both how ill-befitting such theorizing sounds in the mouth of people which had fought so hard to be recognised as a nation, and to the fact that to deny a group the dignity of a nation was the surest way of establishing it as a militant one. Sterile in itself though such theorizing may be, the wounds it leaves are deep. More immediately it means shelving any plan of an Israeli initiative in setting up a Palestine Arab entity as at least a tentative step.

Intervention by the Great Powers

The Israeli attitude to the Four Powers Conference is rooted in this complex of fear, distrust and sense of power. The Israeli Government stubbornly maintains its position that, by constituting themselves into a kind of Aeropagus the Big Powers are lending implicit approval to the Arab refusal to treat with Israel. They invite, as it were, the Arabs to demonstrate through the intensification of terror and the warming up of the frontiers, that they would never negotiate, and that the situation was so explosive that the Powers must curb Israel. This vehement rejection of the Four Powers' intervention by Israel may at least partly be motivated by the understandable, clear or dim wish of the victor to be left alone with the vanquished. It is, however, the Munich trauma that is at the bottom of Israeli intransigence, or at least the not unjustified fear that the Great Powers may just patch up some hasty and precarious cease-fire in order to be able to show that they have achieved something, but will in fact leave all the embers burning, and through inattention or weariness, secure to Soviet Russia a legal standing for perpetrating trouble for both Israel and the U.S.A. Israel is strong and determined enough to defy all the Powers – the official policy claims.

If the Arab press seizes upon every hawkish declaration as conclusive proof that Israel does not want peace but desires expansion, the Israeli papers, on their part, select the most blood-curdling proclamations of Arab guerrilla leaders to show that nothing can be done with the Arabs. Both sides leave out the mitigating "ifs" and "buts" of the official spokesmen, or treat the more moderate statements of the other side as a ruse, cunning, or just pitfalls and traps.

Force as the Sole Arbiter

In brief, with so many good reasons, justifications and pretexts on both sides for doing nothing to bring peace closer, the idea that force was the sole arbiter is growing into an axiom, partial rights and wrongs having become almost irrelevant. But, as Namier said, "the dead festering past cannot be eliminated by violent action any more than an obsession can be cured by beating the patient." If anything has been proved by the fifty years' conflict, it is precisely that it is just not true that the adversary "understands only the language of force." Instead of bringing him to his knees, despair goads him on to more desperate acts of resistance or aggression. When he has nothing to lose, he can risk everything, because he risks nothing. This has been shown again and again by both Jews and Arabs, not to speak of Vietnam, Algeria and so many other cases. It would be amusing if it were not so painful to hear Jews expatiating on the special and different mentality of "our" Arabs in the way anti-Semites have not so long ago been philosophizing about the innate and unalterable, usually mean, characteristics of the Jews.

Should full-scale hostilities be resumed, there is little doubt that the Israeli troops could seize Damascus, enter Cairo, and conquer Amman in no time. But what next? Could they stay there? And even if they could, what would be the point of it? Is there any certainty that a fourth Jewish victory will at last have driven home "the lesson" to the Arabs? Few people in Israel nourish any illusions on this point. Israel may be able to win and win, and go on winning till its last breath, thereby demonstrating the truth of Hegel's aphorism about the "impotence of victory." After every victory we would face more difficult, more complicated problems. For as Nietzsche has put it, there are victories which are more difficult to bear than defeat. This ghastly realization is breeding a quite fatalistic mood: we are doomed to live for ever in a state of siege; a conclusion which comes perilously close to a denial of the most cherished dream and deepest *raison d'être* of Zionism – a safe home, and to an admission that we have exchanged a ghetto of pariahs for a "ghetto of victors."

Should this state of war between Jews and Arabs continue, which has already lasted 50 years – and who knows what type of weapons will be introduced into the area in the midst of a world changing with kaleidoscopic speed all the time, and what forces may still intervene in this region – there will be no victors and no vanquished, but mutual general destruction. Those Arabs capable of thinking lucidly, and from time to time one meets such persons, realize fully that Israel cannot be destroyed, and even if that were possible, the Arab countries themselves would be shattered beyond repair before they could succeed in striking a death blow at Israel, so that the victorious survivors would celebrate their triumph on ruins and ashes. Nor could Israel bring a suicidally determined Arab world to its knees without incurring in the process mortal, material and moral damage, and having all the values which had in the past won it the sympathies of the best of mankind completely eroded.

Reciprocal Recognition or Mutual Destruction

There is thus only one alternative to the nightmare of reciprocal destruction – that of reciprocal recognition. The very claim to the totality of Israel's inheritance does much to justify the claim to the entirety of Palestine as an Arab land, for though much as one may inveigh against the Arabs begrudging the Jews that little notch, while having themselves so much, it sounds specious in a world in which no country, no more than any individual, has divested itself of a part of its territory, its coal or oil, to make good the wants of its close or distant neighbours. Jews have been able to exist and prosper only where reciprocity was obtained. Where an exclusive claim based on superior power or supposedly higher right has prevailed, Jews have always been the first victims.

Of course, any discussion of reciprocity must take into account the fact that while the aim of the Israelis, even the extreme annexationist minority, is security, the Arabs have indicated all too frequently their determination to wipe Israel off the map, and no one can blame a people who had experienced Auschwitz for not treating threats of annihilation as rhetoric or metaphor.

But the preoccupation with security, however, natural and justifiable, so often becomes a self-defeating obsession. Which state in the world has ever enjoyed absolute security, and particularly in the age of nuclear, chemical and biological warfare? The axiom of the eternity of Arab hatred and active hostility is suicidal: if these can not be stilled, then every new defeat will exacerbate them still further, and the Arab resources in manpower and material are ultimately inexhaustible. The desperate anxiety not to allow Jordanian rule to return to Kalkilya for fear of guerrillas in the neighbourhood of Tel Aviv may – by preventing any settlement – help the most uncompromising extremists in their effort to sweep away all the moderate particularistic forces in the Arab world and to unite it, with the blessing and active help of Maoist China.

There are so many lessons in the history of victorious nations, just out of mortal peril, anxiously and desperately determined to obtain foolproof guarantees against aggression which they feared would be renewed in ten, twenty or fifty years. Through the search for the best they lost the chance of obtaining the good, and brought upon themselves much sooner than feared calamities much greater than those they wanted to ward off from future generations. One is reminded of the frantic efforts of French statesmen and generals after 1918 to obtain guarantees against German militarism, as well as of the insensate, and very soon regretted perorations of British statesmen on squeezing the German lemon till the pips burst. The allies got no reparations in the end, but they helped to conjure up Hitler. Many people who hurled abuse upon Lord Lansdowne for his famous letter to the *Daily Telegraph* pleading for a negotiated give-and-take peace with Germany in 1917, came afterwards to muse ruefully how much better a place the world, and their own country, would have been, had the advice of the former Foreign Secretary been heeded – in all probability a world without Mussolini and Hitler, and without Stalin.

Security in the Atomic Age

The Israeli army has shown itself so many times more than a match for all the combined Arab forces that one is taken aback by the fears that if this or that is given up or not made secure, Israel is signing its own death warrant. Furthermore, should Arab hostility never relent, but continue to mount, and with it its military ability, what frontiers will ultimately be of any avail? And what kind of security could there be for a country with such a large and determinedly hostile minority within its frontiers, be those wide ditches and high mountains – in the age of jets and missiles! So any measure of real security is in the disposition of the protagonist. In other words, in dismissing its grievance and urge for revenge, and with the obligation towards the potential Jewish settlers in Israel, could one really justify the certainty of continued actual warfare, with all the suffering and unknown disasters in store, for the sake of a hypothetical need for refuge, which might arise if, God forbid, the world is again plunged into the barbarism of the 'thirties and 'forties, a state of affairs which would in all probability spell universal destruction?

Hopes for Peace

The quest for therapeutic means to replace force hangs upon the by now very thin thread – the anguished hope that there is a fundamental disposition in favour of peace, though terribly inhibited and handicapped by neurotic impediments and overstrained susceptibilities. Which means that nothing should be done that might provoke or hurt these, and everything to gently enable the buried better self to assert itself. One clutches at the hope that sufficient and sufficiently influential people in Egypt and in the other Arab countries realise the utter futility and dangerous consequences of renewed war; that they have become aware of the fact that if the present state of war is continued the dream of restored Arab glory, with the common cause of Palestine as the cement and a lever of pan-Arab nationalism, will reach a sad consummation in Soviet advisers in every Government office and technicians in every Arab factory, and in every army unit, difficult though it be to imagine two races and civilizations less congenial to each other than Communist Russia and the Moslem Arabs.

One should perhaps try to remind the Arab intellectuals of historical parallels. In the sixteenth and seventeenth century Spain was bled white, went bankrupt and sank into torpor and impotence at the end of eighty years of war against Holland. Catholic-Monarchic Spain could not bring itself to recognise or to treat, except for cease-fire arrangements, with heretics and rebels, and usurpers of parts of its Empire assigned to it, after all, by the Pope himself in 1496. In the end the proud Spaniards were compelled in 1648 to sign a treaty with a Holland which had in the meantime grown from a handful of desperate rebels and fugitives into a world Empire, the first financial power in the world, and culturally the most advanced country in Europe.

What misfortune has the burning but constantly frustrated desire of the Italians to demonstrate martial qualities and win resounding victories brought upon that so wonderfully gifted, sophisticated and generous nation. The Italians seem to have at last learned their lesson and cured themselves. Both nations, the Arabs and the Israelis, would do well to take to heart the resigned words of wisdom spoken by a thinker who has grown white in the quest of justice, passing through the whole spectrum of ideas: "past injustice cannot be made good. The sufferings endured by earlier generations obtain no redress."

"Total Peace" a Myth

The Arabs cannot get a "just" peace, and the Jews are unable to obtain a "total" and "true" peace. All that can be hoped for at present is – stemming of the tide in the hope of its gradual ebbing away. The hope that the Arabs will come cap in hand to sue Israel for peace is no longer cherished even by those who had still not long ago believed – or still believe – that time was working in our favour, and laid store on accomplished facts. Were even a directly negotiated and formally signed Peace Treaty attainable – the Israelis themselves say – the Arab leaders who will have put their signature to it would be assassinated the next day, and the Arab Ministers would in any case, like the Germans in 1919, sign it only under duress and with mental reservations and hostile resolve in their heart. By refusing to have anything less than that, and thus perpetuating and perhaps intensifying the present tensions to a boiling point, may we not be helping the guerrilla organisations which, however insignificant their military achievements have been, have nevertheless raised a flag, created a myth, and become a focal point for the hopes and the activities of the young, and done incalculable harm to the image of Israel in the world?

Any arrangement with the Arab governments at this hour, even one short of a Treaty negotiated face to face and signed amidst handshakes in the blare of television lights, would implicitly be based upon the one common interest of all sides concerned – Israel, the Arab governments, the U.S.S.R., and the U.S. – in preventing the contingency of a total triumph of the extremists in the Arab world and the incursion of China into the area.

But the sands are running out fast. The chance may be lost for that detente and de-escalation, which a common interest not so much in positive peace as in the avoidance of further dangerous complications may bring about in an unacknowledged way leading to factual cooperation, notwithstanding the continued incantations about the unforgotten wrongs suffered and eternal rights possessed by the Arab people. It is today highly unpopular in Israel to recall that such a situation has existed between Israel and Egypt for some ten years after Suez. Admittedly it did not prevent the 1967 explosion. But where is the proof that this must happen again? And have we not shown a supreme ability to meet such a contingency? Why despair of the genius of the Israeli army in the future? There are no more pressing, and in the long run more decisive imperatives, than these two – the checking of the growth of the guerrillas, and the resettlement of the refugees through a concerted action, internationally supported and financed. The success on these two issues would take the sting out of the terrible imbroglio, and enable both sides to slide slowly into peace should the hope of first establishing the formal peace as a prelude to the particular remedies prove vain.

Of course, if Israel be prepared to go to such lengths to save the susceptibilities and irrational obsessions of the Arabs, it is surely entitled to expect the Arabs to offer some alleviations to the Israeli deep-seated fears and passions, like the unity of Jerusalem (with some autonomous status for the Arab community in it), some modifications of frontiers, the right to hold on to strongpoints if not forever at least for some years as guarantees, till the need for them has become superfluous in the eyes of all, and of course total freedom of passage through the straits.

If stemming the tide and defusion be the aim, should we not take another look at the Four or Two Powers Conference on the Middle East, and instead of savagely looking at it as a conspiracy, perhaps try to utilize it in making it easier for the other side to come forward with a minimum of loss of face?

Sense of Proportion

There are liberals in Israel who though aware of the immense difficulties and pitfalls of an imposed settlement, endeavour not to lose their sense of proportion. They recall that hardly ever has such an intractable conflict as the Israel–Arab imbroglio been resolved without the Great Powers Concert intervening and laying down the law. Their intellectual integrity is rather offended – when they think of the treatment of Palestine Arabs in the past by the incantations of some Israeli ministers about the right of the parties directly concerned to determine their own affairs without the tutelage of outside powers – "the Middle East is no one's protectorate." They do not expect the powers to become angels, forgoing their own interests, or eunuchs impotent to defend them, but set their hopes on the mutually contradictory interests of the Powers cancelling themselves out into some reasonable compromise.

In Search for a Face-Saving Formula

The State of Israel came into being in 1948 through Soviet-American agreements; the Suez crisis was resolved in 1956–57 because the two super powers wanted it to be. It is said that in the early days of Israel Ben-Gurion would instruct a diplomat going abroad to "do everything possible to please the Americans and nothing to displease the Russians." That balance could not be maintained for long. Soviet support for partition in 1947–48 was an isolated episode. Although it was greeted with jubilation by Zionist left-wingers, to whom consistent Soviet hostility had been a source of deep chagrin, the motive of the Russians, as soon as it became unmistakably clear, had been no change of heart in regard to Zionism. Nor can any such change be expected so long as the U.S. and the U.S.S.R. are locked in rivalry.

It is impossible under any circumstances for Israel to adopt an anti-American attitude or even to defy American wishes for any length of time in a vital matter. The reasons are too obvious to need elaboration. This is well known to the Russians, and from it they draw extreme conclusions. Russia is surrounded by American bases, and it is very important for her to have allies and friends and bases behind the American bases – in other words, in Syria, Egypt, Iraq. The Russians think in quantities, and thus conclude that even if Israel could be weaned away from America, the strategic value of the large Arab territories, not to mention the oil they contain, makes the Arab world a much more worthwhile ally. The Soviets ask themselves also the simple question: who pays for it? He who pays has the say. Since totalitarian regimes would never allow, in fact could not even conceive of, a group of their own citizens advocating a foreign policy which differs from, or is not dictated by, the government, they are bound to conclude that through the intermediary of American Jewry, Israel is of course an American puppet and agent.

There are other considerations behind Russian policy as well. Insofar as it has been stirring up Jewish sentiment among the Russian Jews, making this "indigestible" group still more difficult to digest, Israel is resented by the Soviet Government as a nuisance and an irritant. The social achievements of the Israeli Labour movement, far from impressing the Bolsheviks, evoke contemptuous hostility: how dare a tiny country like Israel presume to build socialism better than Russia itself! Similarly the demand to permit emigration from Russia to Israel must appear as an anti-Soviet device, implying as it does a vote of no confidence in the achievements and nature of the regime.

Thus, while not motivated by conventionally anti-Semitic convictions and aims, the Soviet Union is almost "objectively," to use its own language, led to adopt policies which, given the murderous hostility of the Arabs and the role of Israel in the post-holocaust period of Jewish history, amount to a definite threat to the survival of the Jewish people.

Particularly horrifying is the Soviet-Arab sponsorship of an updated version of the "Protocols of Zion": the Zionist-American-Imperialist world plot, operating not only against Arabs, Asians, and Africans, but also against all the socialist regimes, causing economic difficulties, student unrest, Catholic intransigence. We have travelled a long way from the revolutionary universalism of Marx which recognised neither Jew nor Greek nor Gentile, but only workers and capitalists.

And yet, there is a glimmer of hope that the spectre of China and the inexorable compulsions of modern technology and warfare may still work to bring about a Russo-American agreement to resolve the Arab–Israel conflict once the Vietnam imbroglio is out of the way. As a very great power, Russia finds it extremely difficult to do nothing for the Arabs beyond replacing the arms they have lost, and to take Israeli defiance lying down. At the same time there can be no doubt that the Soviet Union will never risk a nuclear war over the Middle East, any more than the United States will. This may induce the two superpowers to search for a face-saving formula for a Middle Eastern settlement.

Understandable as their anxieties are, the Israelis would do well to pause and reflect whether it be the long-term interest of Israel to be irretrievably tied up to America in the way South Vietnam, South Korea or Western Germany are. It is not only a question of the image of Israel in the eyes of the world, especially the Afro-Asian nations, with whom Israel must live and trade in amity. A great power finds it easier to change allies or abandon clients than a small isolated State to win new protectors. The Israelis would be well advised not to bank too much on the "special relationship" between Israel and the U.S. Nothing would be more dangerous for them than to act on the assumption that they have America in their pocket. The Suez War had shown that they did not even have American Jewry in their pocket. The only hope of a peaceful settlement in the Middle East lies in an American-Soviet agreement, and not in the preponderance of Israeli armies backed by the Sixth Fleet.

For the Israeli liberal to be able to come out against the rising tide of anxious and militant intransigence and press his case with any effectiveness, the condition *sine qua non* is that the Arab leaders wish in their hearts to be more gently or more forcefully cajoled. For when all is said and done Israeli hawkishness is really a function of Arab obduracy and hostile intent. Without some clear and convincing proof that Nasser was prepared to be coaxed, the Israeli liberals would be powerless Don Quixotes. Worse, they would be decried as faint-hearted defeatists, capitulationists, traitors. They would inevitably be reduced to watching fatalistically and impotently the great cruel ironies working themselves out in a seemingly inexorable manner: Heroic exertions and astonishing talents of a so hard-pressed a nation, with a deep yearning for peace and justice, beating in vain against an unattainable goal, and suffering horrible haemorrhage in the process; a society which started off with so much socialist idealism and constructive resolve becoming reduced to the position of a beleaguered city, wasting its substance on arms and the best years of the flower of its youth on destruction; a freedom-loving society doomed to engage in the squalid business of spying, policing, suppressing, putting behind bars school girls; a rational people swept by morbid passions and neurotic obsessions;

a nation whose deepest desire has been to escape the fate of being not an end in itself, but a function of the existence of others, a problem, a liability, an impediment, an undesirable presence, compelled to treat a neighbouring people in that very manner; a barrel of powder – which all the Powers are most anxious to prevent from exploding – catching fire through some untoward "Sarajevo accident."

Some console themselves with the hope that there is a Hegelian *List der Vernunft* hidden in all that, and that like Holland, as we mentioned before, the nation would come out greater and better from this ordeal. The twentieth-century experiences are bound to have an inhibiting effect on such expectations. Yet one does not dare not to reflect from time to time that most problems are in fact never solved. They are survived, outlived, by-passed, slowly shaken off out of weariness, driven out by more urgent and more pressing ones. "It is," writes R. H. Tawney in one of his purple passages, "the tragedy of a world where man must walk by sight that the discovery of the reconciling formula is always left to the future generations, in which passion has cooled into curiosity, and the agonies of peoples have become the exercise in the schools. The devil who builds bridges does not span such chasms till much that is precious has vanished down for ever."

First published in *The Jewish Quarterly*, Vol. 17, No. 3–4 (63–64), Winter 1969.

Domestic and International Politics – A Presentation

I will define myself as a hawkish dove. When I am being visited by one of my more mystical moods I experience a sense of awe at the thought that there has come into existence – if I may use the expression, which has somewhat bad associations – a kind of nexus, Jerusalem-New York. It is as if Providence had arranged it in advance for restoring the Jewish civilization, and I stress this word civilization, of Central and Eastern Europe, from where I hail. I came to Israel, or Palestine, as it then was, at the age of seventeen and a half, from Poland.

That Jerusalem, as it were, is confronted by the most powerful Jewry ever in what is at present the capital of the world, New York. Now this holds out very great possibilities but also very great dangers. The Hebrew language has got a very fine play of words and sounds – *siku'im ve sikunim.* The prospects are very splendid; the dangers are mortal. That has been a feature of Jewish history for a very long time, perhaps though its history. On the one hand, the blinding splendor; on the other hand, the easy and rapid fall into the abyss.

Especially in this century it is a frightening thought to what extent this occurs, and a physical sense of doom is like a shadow following Jewish life and accompanying it throughout the century. I'm alluding to the Holocaust, and I'm alluding also to our own position here.

Now, the relationship between Israel and America again confirms the rule of *plus ça change plus c'est la même chose*, and brings into relief again the serious relationship between the permanent and abiding and the innovative and the changing, showing that the abiding and the permanent is more potent, perhaps, than the deliberate resolve to bring about a change.

Now the relationship between Israeli and U.S. Jewry is such that if, God forbid, a catastrophe were to overtake the State of Israel, American Jews might not be immediately affected in their daily lives, in their economic situation, and in their social relations. But, I believe, I fear to say, that the blow to their self-respect, to their Jewish self-assurance, would be so grave that it is quite legitimate to doubt whether as an entity they would be able to survive for long.

Now if, God forbid, misfortune were to befall American Jewry – and you can use your imagination and find associations – well, need I tell you that Israel's existence would be put into mortal jeopardy, and I leave it to your imagination to go on. So here again we have the demonstration of the collective fate, of the mutual dependence.

Now, after this introduction, I want to say a few words about American Jewry as I got to know it in the course of my visits. And then I shall come to the problem which has exercised our minds this morning, the Jews of the Right or the Left in the world, in America, and particularly in Israel in the present constellation. Now, when I was visiting professor at MIT, I was asked to participate in a dialogue, an Israel–American dialogue in Boston, and there were opposite numbers, distinguished Harvard professors, none of them present here. And the subject was – we flogged that "dead horse," if I might say so – Jewish identity. And my friends the Americans were trying very hard to define Jewish identity: Being a Jew meant being progressive, humanitarian, tolerant.

One person improved on all that. He said: "I will give you an example of what it means to be a Jew. My son the other day came home and said: 'Daddy, I have become interested in Buddhism, and I think it is a very fine religion.' And so I, his father, said: "Yes, and in the time to come when everybody will be free to choose his religion as he chooses his philosophical system, that will be the time of Jewish identity'."

I confess that I was somewhat at a loss to know what to say to all this. Now, of course, it is very difficult to generalize about American Jews, like America itself. Whatever you say about American Jews is true and false at the same time. The exceptions, reservations, are so numerous that it is very difficult to say something that would stick.

I have met American Jews who said to me: "When I have to vote for Congress, or to make any decision, the first thing I ask is: Is it going to help Israel or not?" And I have met other Jews who were demonstrative in their display of indifference to Israel. So the spectrum is very wide. But to one who is deeply committed to Judaism, to Zionism, as I claim to be, I was, of course, interested in the Jewish essence, and the thing that struck me was that there is an inflated feeling of Jewish self-awareness among American Jews, as I could observe also among Jews in Europe many years ago. They are very fully and painfully aware, they are acutely conscious of being, if not a problem, at least a phenomenon.

But I use the word "inflated" really because there are precious few contents to fill that awareness. They identify themselves, as it were, through mediations, through reflexes, through reactions rather than in positive terms. Why? Because, and this has been brought up already, there are no spiritual, cultural contents to American Judaism. The religious establishment has little prestige, offers little inspiration. Zionism is too politicized. And something else also. I always remember a very fine saying by Martin Buber: "Zionism started as the passion of the poor. It is before our eyes becoming the hobby of the rich. Woe unto it." And that is what is happening in America.

And then there is another element, the crass and dismal materialism of America and American Jewry. And Jews, the young Jews, become uncomfortable because of being comfortable – like, let us say, the Russian intelligentsia at the time of the Czar. They have, as it were, to justify themselves. They feel guilty that they are happy, comfortable.

Now all these things militate against any growth of positive Jewish contents. Also – and here I blame the Zionist establishment in Israel and elsewhere – the mistake that is made by Zionist propagandists is that they believe that they can still address a highly sophisticated, hypercritical, superbly educated youth in the same way they were addressing, thirty or forty years ago, sentimental ladies in the Middle West. And they believe – I have experience of this myself – that you can offer the young only sweet lemonade. No self-criticism; Herzl has to be presented as an angel; Zionism has to be presented as the acme of idealism and purity. Things which, of course, cause the young and critical to smile and to react with angry contempt.

Now, the situation of American Jewry. I was struck today by the observation made by one of the participants that there is now a possibility of a new kind of pluralism in America, that is to say each ethnic group being able to cultivate its own identity and its own culture and so on, as a recognized thing, and not in any way as separatism. This presents rather good prospects to American Jewry, precisely because it is so highly cultivated by now. Most of the Jewish youth go to the university, and some of them become professors. And because they are thoroughly compact and closely-knit groups, there is a possibility of spiritual revival as, for instance, in Germany, where the Jews, although they were deeply immersed in German culture, nevertheless, between the two wars and before, were able to create, cultivate and develop a style of their own in literary pursuits, in Jewish self-awareness – indeed, as I admit, a somewhat too spiritualized, too rarefied culture. But then, the Jews are a nation of intellectuals, and intellectual life is also life to those who are committed to it.

Now I want to address myself to the subject of Left and Right. As some people here know, I am not a Leftist, not in my outlook, not in my ideas. I always felt uneasy in olden times when Zionism was being identified, especially by Left Zionists, with the progressive forces, just as I feel uneasy now, very uneasy indeed, when people of a certain persuasion try to depict Israel as the bastion of the free world, fighting against Soviet barbarism, and so on. I feel very deeply disturbed by this. Although I am a universal historian, not a Jewish historian, I think that the only way, and the authentic way, of presenting Zionism is as a phenomenon *sui generis*. That is to say, its reality, its significance, its place, its value, is not derived from being identified with either of the two camps.

About Right and Left. Let me start with the Left. The Left is silly; the Right is stupid. And I shall try to develop this point in application to our issues.

Some of you may remember, or be aware, that Herzl actually had ideas of coming to terms with anti-Semites, even after he had become a Zionist. That is to say, he wanted to come to them and say: "I admit that there are too many Jews in Poland, or in Rumania. It is not good for the Jews and not good for you. Let us make an agreement. We shall evacuate them, and you help us to get a Jewish State." And there were others – Jabotinsky had certain ideas in that direction.

Unfortunately the twentieth century has shown that with real anti-Semites there is no deal; there is no bargain at all, at least as far as Jews are concerned. I remember early in the war, World War II, I had a discussion with somebody very high up in the Zionist establishment in London on this very issue, and he said something which stuck in my memory. "No," he said, "with anti-Semites you cannot come to terms, to make a bargain with them. In order to help Jews, one has to wish them well, and anti-Semites do not wish the Jews well, so it excludes any bargain, any arrangement."

I was stuck this morning by Prof. Gordis saying that to him liberalism, if I quote him rightly, is the idea about a compatibility, or the harmony of human aims; I think that is a wonderful definition. It presupposes a fundamental natural or logical harmony between us. I'm afraid I don't believe in it. Although I am a Jew, I am deeply aware of the problem of original sin, which is a Catholic idea, as we all know, but still I can never get rid of it. I went to a Catholic school. And also, as a historian, I have been bitten too much by the realization of the massive contradictions, the unbridgeable differences between classes, races, nations, and so on.

However, after having said that, I want to say with all the emphasis that I am able to command: One must not yield to that point of view, especially at the time of the atom bomb, because the assumption of the unbridgeable differences means that force is the only solution. And force in an atomic age means a war to death. That is one thing, and another is that where the great, profound and unbridgeable differences have been resolved by force, the Jews, historically, have been the first victims, the first and the earliest victims. There are some things, some policies, some ideas, which Jews, out of a sense of Jewish taste and propriety and, I should say, shame, cannot embrace, cannot espouse, without being untrue to themselves, without undercutting their own moral position, and without also worrying about the possibility of bringing about the necessity of rewriting Jewish history from the beginning to the end.

Now let us be concrete. What do we mean when we refer to the Left? It has been said that, first of all, it is universalism, in the sense that free rational choices take precedence, or are more real, than the deterministic effects of blood, race, history, tradition. Now, such attitudes have enabled the Jews to prosper; they have made possible social mobility. They ignored the peculiarity of Jews, I hasten to add. This was often very good for Jews as individuals, but bad for the Jewish entity, and there was a kind of dichotomy about it. One may remember that at the time of Napoleon there was a famous controversy between two great rabbis. And the idea was: Yes, if Napoleon wins, there will be light for the Jews, but it will be bad for *Yiddishkeit*. If the Russians win, there will be bondage for the Jews, but the *Yiddishkeit* will remain safe and prosper.

The major difficulty about the Left has been that it operates with ideas of vast, disembowelled, abstract forces, which ignore peculiarities, the details, the concrete data. The Left is very often brought to a readiness to sacrifice the concrete Jews, the concrete Jewish situation, for the sake of some abstract universal idea. That has happened more than once. And to us Jews, to me as a Jewish nationalist, the survival of Jews and Judaism is an end in itself which cannot be bargained away for anything, and cannot be a kind of condition for other achievements.

Now I turn to the Right. What is the difficulty with the Right? Why, as my friends from Harvard have quite rightly stressed, has the Right never been congenial to Jews? The Right starts out in fact with authority, authority coming from above. The Right is impatient, contemptuous and fearful of change. In modern times the Jews have always embodied change, novelty, experiment. Why? Because change, of course, threatened privilege and established rights.

There is something else. The Right has always, in one way or another, been popularist, believing in glorifying the direct instinct, the unerring certainty of the blood, and has always been contemptuous and suspicious of sophistication, analytical reason, and so on. And again and again, almost invariably, the Jew became to them the embodiment of those threats to tradition, to national certainties, and so on. The Right, then, is not a congenial partner to Judaism, hasn't been and cannot be.

I want to say something about a subject which has not been touched upon, except by way of a little sniping from a certain Israeli. I want to say something about the moods in Israel and their effects on American Jewry, and the image of Israel in the world. Some people may know that I belong to the Opposition in this country, but I want to put on record, with all sincerity and emphasis, that the record of Israel for the last three years as far as freedom of expression, freedom of opposition is concerned, is peerless. It is very difficult to imagine a nation so hard-pressed, so beleaguered, so in danger of physical extinction, not only tolerating but encouraging such a wide variety of freedoms, discussions on touchy matters, not excluding high strategy, sometimes bordering on revelation of secrets. Oh, there is occasional barking from some quarters, but it doesn't amount to anything.

Another thing I want to say is this. With all the love for peace, the hatred of war, that many of us feel, we also have to remember that the world outside Israel, friends and very often good friends, are naturally in a hurry to get this trouble out of the way. They want a peaceful world, and this is a running sore. And so, out of inattention, unwillingness to enter into the difficulties, the almost intractable issues, they may patch up something in order to appease their own conscience, in order to be able to show to the world: "Well, we have solved the problem." But they leave the fire burning, and the victims will be us, nobody else. So the seeming stickiness, the rigidity, if you will, of the Israeli government – and I am not a government stooge, as you may know – has to be understood, and it should earn a measure of sympathy.

And now, after having said this, I want to say something else. We are witnessing in this country an unpleasant polarization of attitudes, as could have been foreseen. The dangers, the times, are giving rise to feelings of ardent nationalism, a sense of manifest destiny, and attitudes, if not of superiority, at least of a mystical character: Israel is the will of God. This country belongs only to the Jewish People, has been promised only to the Jews and to no one else, and the Arabs have no right except as individuals, and that force and might will resolve this issue, and so on.

And this sudden imagery is being too greatly bandied about. It reminds me, too much for my liking, of chauvinist theories and patterns of thought in Europe, and also of the mythology of nationalism in the age of cavalry, and not in the age of jets. Now, this extreme attitude, if you like, of mysticism or mystification, naturally breeds a reaction, a revulsion.

It is always dangerous for a nation to develop a complex about being utterly alone, utterly unique. There is a Zionist publicist who is trying very hard to show that the Jews and their problems are so unique that they cannot be compared to anything else in the world. I am always tempted to say: "It may be right for someone to say I am unique, I am unprecedented, and so on, but the trouble is that perhaps the man on the other side will say: Perhaps you are not so unique, perhaps you are a monster." So all this emphasis on uniqueness is a dangerous thing.

And something else. Once you begin to overemphasize this problem of uniqueness you create a dangerous image of the Jews as a strange tribe which is not an essential component in the sum total of the civilized achievement, of mankind as a whole. However, the Jews should be presented to Jews and non-Jews as a special, accentuated, terribly intense sample of the general human situation; and that the uniqueness of the Jew consists of having been exposed in history, the guinea pig of history. Even the problem of religion and state is uniquely Israeli, and yet it is a sample of the human situation.

And this brings me to my final point. There is a danger in adopting narrow nationalistic attitudes in Israel – and I am a Jewish nationalist, let this be quite clear and quite plain. But if we bear in mind that the Jewish youth, and the Jewish intelligentsia, throughout the world live in a different atmosphere, in a different frame of reference, the effective way of estranging them is precisely by adopting chauvinistic attitudes.

And the best way of winning them over is the other way – the other way of . . . well, human values, human solidarity, and so on. And finally, we must recognize the urgent need not only to appear but to be determined upon peace, that is to say, to struggle for an understanding with the Arabs. We must accept the idea that this country, in one way or another, belongs to the two races: there is no exclusive claim, because if there is an exclusive claim to the totality of Israel, we thereby offer an argument to the other side, to the totality of Palestine.

We must remain aware of a tragic clash of rights, and to use the expression of the late Dr. Weizmann, "this is a problem which can be resolved only along the lines of least injustice."

I wouldn't be a Zionist, I wouldn't be in Israel, if I didn't believe that the greater measure of justice was on our side; and less injustice would be done to the Arabs by enabling Israel to exist, to live and prosper – and vice versa.

In the eyes of the world, in short, we cannot, we must not, appear as a belated version of exclusive militant nationalism which in Europe, at least, is at present, I hope, an extinct volcano.

First published in *Congress Bi-Weekly*, Vol. 8, Nos. 2–3, February 26, 1971, pp. 39–42, the 8th Annual American–Israel Dialogue, on "Reciprocal Rights and Responsibilities of American and Israeli Jews."

Reflections of an Historian in Jerusalem

Ideological history creates it own nemesis. It is born out of a deep craving for salvationist certainty and finality, for a total answer to all riddles and ills. When hopes fail and saviours are shown to be idols with feet of clay, nations, movements, parties are plunged into desperate confusion; they feel let down and deceived, become ashamed of their credulity, doubtful of their own judgment and horrified by yesterday's enthusiasms. A crisis of identity sets in. Men find it impossible to come to terms with their immediate national past and their own self-image.

Hardly a nation has been spared such a crisis in our own day. Germany has its Hitler to live down and all those traditions, aspirations, values, images, and symbols in German history which paved the way for the Führer. Present-day Italy is haunted by the twenty years of Fascism. France has difficulty in shaking off the nightmares of 1940 and Vichy. Less than forty years after having buried the Tsarist past and all its works, and twenty-five years after almost the total leadership of the October Revolution had been tried, sentenced and executed as criminal traitors, the Russians (and with them the world-wide Communist movement) were suddenly told that for a whole crucial generation of untold suffering they were ruled not by the iron laws of scientific socialism, but by a paranoiac tyrant. The East European nations, which gained their independence at the end of World War I and in the short inter-War period were intoxicated with nationalist exaltation, have now to abjure their national, largely anti-Russian myths and to resort to all kinds of mental acrobatics to recast their history.

Even countries which like Britain and the United States have not suffered violent revolution have had their self-image, national myths and self-assurance deeply shaken in this generation. Britain has – in the unkind words of the late Dean Acheson – lost an Empire, and has not yet found a role. An Anglophile foreign historian recently confided his present difficulty in teaching English history – he has been so used to extol the British genius for government by consent, the continuity and excellence of British institutions, and the peculiar British combination of freedom, cohesion, and efficiency. The United States has still to recover from the traumatic shocks of Viet Nam and Watergate.

One wonders how much of the anarchic spirit animating the rebellious students and the various radical and terrorist groups – and to what extent the present revival of anarchist ideology – is due to the passionate, contemptuous urge to kick fallen idols, to tear up sham and mask, to punish hypocrisy and destroy all establishments, with all their claims, pretence, decorum and sacred cows, their *arcana imperii*.

In one of his more purple passages, Joseph de Maistre writes of

> "that nation of five or six million perched on the bare rocks of Judea, the proudest of cities in Proud Asia, which resists all shocks which would have pulverised a nation ten times more numerous, braves the torrents of centuries, the sword of conquerors and the hatred of peoples, astonishes by its resistance the masters of the world, survives finally all the conquering nations and shows still after forty centuries its deplorable remnants to the eyes of the surprised observer."

In the middle of the eighteenth century the eminent Rabbi of Prague, R. Ezekiel Landau, defined the unwritten contract between the Jews and their Christian neighbours by stating that "taxes are our rent for being permitted to live amongst [the nations] . . . They have possession of the land, and we are only sojourners. . . ." The older contemporary of Landau, Rabbi Johanan Eibeschuetz of Metz, reprimanded his congregation for engaging in "worldly vanities, idle talk, stories about wars," gaping at passing musketeers and pikemen. "These things befit rulers and their underlings." Jews should mourn the destruction of Jerusalem and recall the calamities which befell their ancestors in the days of Nebuchadnezzar and Titus.

The world was soon to witness the beginning of a terrific nuclear explosion – to borrow an expression of Lewis Namier in another context – of long bottled-up human energies of an intense and purposeful race. The fission resulted from the violent contradiction between an immemorial, hermetically closed tradition and a sudden irresistible leap into a world of constant change, of ever-precipitated motion, all the time advancing towards unity and at the same time tormented and torn by fissiparous pulls.

In a number of countries, the Jews became both the leaven and the pioneers in the phenomenal conquests of capitalism and also the inspirers and leaders of revolutionary commotions. They stormed their way into the sciences and arts, from which they had till then kept clear and for which they had for so long been thought to possess no aptitude. At the end of a century-and-a-half, they suffered the most horrible blood-letting that a people has ever suffered from the hands of a world power bent on the conquest of the globe; as part of that campaign a crusade was proclaimed against the Jewish invasion. It absorbed and funnelled in the process all the old prejudices and all the modern ill-will against Jews into a murderous machine. In their desperate effort to withdraw from the storms of history into a safe refuge, it soon seemed to the Jews that the focus of international conflict had been transferred with them into that would-be retreat.

As if to make up for centuries of despised and persecuted sectarian existence, the most theocratic of communities gave birth to the most effective of the revolutionary and atheistic transformers of man's consciousness in modern times – Karl Marx and Sigmund Freud. The most clannish of peoples produced such fierce practitioners of revolutionary internationalism as Marx, Rosa Luxemburg, and Leon Trotsky, as well as some of the most restless and enterprising promoters of international communications, agencies and media. As if in defiance of Rabbi Tam's dictum that "anything new is forbidden by the Torah," Jews have, in the last two centuries, been in the forefront of every *avant-garde*, pioneers in every new experiment, novel fashion and indeed craze, from psychoanalysis and nuclear research to hippyism. In the West where a liberal atmosphere offered their small communities considerable facilities, Jews eagerly embraced the ideas of individualism, society based upon contract, social mobility, *carrière ouverte aux talents*, in brief the type of liberalism which denies relevance to ancestry, blood, tribal and national traditions, religious allegiance.

In their desire to become integrated into the society around them, many Jews, such as Karl Marx's father and Heinrich Heine, embraced Christianity, if only nominally. Those who, with all their striving for equality and admission, were held back from baptism by too deep or psychologically too compulsive an allegiance to Judaism, or were too honest and too proud to take the step without conviction, reinterpreted Judaism as a message of the brotherhood of all men born in the image of the One God, Father of all, and depicted the role of Jews in history as that of carriers of the prophetic ideals of social justice, charity, and eternal peace. They went to great lengths to reform the prayerbook and liturgy, to cleanse them of references to beliefs and practices which were held not to be in conformity with the "spirit of progress," such as references to animal sacrifices or to the exclusiveness of the Jewish nation and to the dream of the return to Zion. The Jewish religion was made into a humanitarian, ethical, and as abstractly universal a creed as possible; and the Jews were enjoined to become model citizens of a liberal, tolerant and benevolent modern state.

Moses Mendelssohn, friend of Kant, rationalist but strict observer of the Law, described the Jewish religion as embodying figuratively all the essentials of natural law and the commands of natural morality, with the severe ritualistic commandments obligating Jews alone – in order to train them for their universal mission in an especially strenuous discipline. Under the influence of Romanticism, Mendelssohn's successors in the field of *Wissenschaft des Judentums* devoted themselves to painstaking scholarly study of the Jewish religious tradition. They were motivated by the conscious or unconscious wish to depict by comparative method how the Jewish tradition grew out of a collective psyche and peculiar circumstances in the same way as the Christian denominations; and to reject the disparaging descriptions of Judaism as a tissue of absurdities and superstitions, peculiar to a fanatical, solitary sect.

The immersion in the ancient sources brought Heinrich Graetz, the greatest modern Jewish historian, close to a Romantic conception of the Jews as not merely a religious community, but as a *Volk*. He thereby caused much displeasure to many of his contemporaries, Jews and non-Jews. The violently nationalistic and anti-Semitic Treitschke was roused to put to the Jews the sharp alternative of either becoming Germans in everything or – if they chose to consider themselves a *Volk* – to pack up and go to Palestine. In his pamphlet against Treitschke and in the defence of the Jews and their equality, Theodore Mommsen gently advised his "beloved Jewish pupils" to take the final step in their endeavour to identify themselves completely with German culture – the conversion to

Christianity, at least for the sake of their children. It was their duty to free them from the tiresome and hurtful ambiguities which they themselves had to endure.

It was in the wastes of windswept Lithuania, under the influence of the reawakening of the subject and history-less nationalities of Eastern and Central Europe and of the Hebrew translations of historical novels on the Hasmonean period written by German-Jewish authors, that Hebrew novelists such as Mapu and poets like J. L. Gordon (who called himself very mistakenly, "the last bard of Judah") took up Biblical themes in an entirely new spirit. They dwelt with loving nostalgia on the splendours of the court of David and Solomon, the wars of Israel, the dramatic reigns of the Kings of Judea. This was heady wine to the oppressed and deprived Jewish masses in the miserable townlets in the backwaters of the Romanov and Habsburg Empires. Yet the greatest Jewish historian after Graetz, Simon Dubnow, was not captivated by Biblical Romanticism. He wrote his voluminous history of the Jewish people in the spirit of the Nationalities ideology which at that time was espoused by radicals of the dominant as well as of the subject races in that part of Europe. The Nationalities doctrine taught that a country belonged to the ethnic and cultural groups which inhabited it, and not to any dominant nationality. The significant components of a multi-national Empire were not atomised individuals, but these ethnic and cultural groups, *i.e.* the nationalities living on its territory. The Jews were one of them, equal to every other, and not a "guest people" soliciting tolerance from a "host nation." Like every other ethnic group, they were entitled to linguistic, cultural, educational and communal autonomy, and to financial help from the State to maintain their institutions. In fact, the Austro-Marxist theory of Otto Bauer and Karl Renner about personal and cultural autonomy of each ethnic group, which was to embrace all its members wherever they might be dispersed, recalled the Jewish *kehillah*: the ancient communal self-government, which the Jews would set up and get recognised as soon as they settled in a country, and jealously guard, even when they had forsaken their distinct tongue, Hebrew, Aramaic or later Yiddish, and retained little of their peculiar folkways.

Dubnow applied this criterion to the whole of post-Exile Jewish history, and he remained a secular non-Zionist Jewish nationalist to the day of his martyrdom at the hands of the Nazis in Latvia as a very old man. He was a tragic witness to the dismal failure of his seemingly only too rational conviction that having lived for well over a thousand (nay, nearer to two thousand) years in Europe, having spun their tradition and buried their dead in its lands, the Jews had every right to be regarded as natives and as a part of the civilised landscape.

Zionism combined most of the features of the two most potent and the most history-minded of modern ideologies – Nationalism and Socialism. It harked back to a glorious, distant past. It strove to restore those glories of old by a revolutionary act of self-emancipation from the miseries and indignities of an evil present and by rebuilding from scratch a free and independent existence in the original home. It thus lovingly reaffirmed one part of history and passionately rejected another part of it.

The Socialist aspect was present not only in the resolve to establish a society that would be a model of rational planning and social justice. It was to be found also in the bitter, on occasion almost anti-Semitic critique of the Jewish role in the European economy throughout the ages, in the condemnation – sometimes with scant regard to objective historic causes and circumstances – of the allegedly Jewish penchant for the unproductive, demeaning, and demoralising occupations of money-lender, middleman, tradesman, and in the Tolstoyan and Russian Social Revolutionary apotheosis of labour, toil, rustic pursuits, closeness to nature as healthy and morally superior. A normal social structure, a society of toilers and peasants, a new civilisation and morality that would revolutionise Jewish existence – these became the battle cries of Labour Zionism. A strictly Marxist gloss was added by the emphasis upon the need for a normal and healthy class war unhampered by the irritant of anti-Semitism which interfered with the pre-ordained class struggle both of Jews and non-Jews.

The vision of the breakdown of capitalism and of the violent revolutionary confrontation between the bourgeoisie and the proletariat had its parallel in the haunting fear of Zionists or – with the more daring, or more fanatical, spirits – the expectation of some apocalyptic crisis which would engulf Jewish life under the blows of mounting mass anti-Semitism. There were, long before Hitler, voices warning of the coming of a St Bartholomew's Night which would send the Jews fleeing from Eastern Europe to Palestine.

Under the impact of Nazism some Zionist historians were driven to lay down a kind of law that precisely in the places where the assimilation of Jews had gone farthest and Jews had achieved the highest measure of culture, wealth, and influence, there was no escape from ultimate catastrophe: Alexandria, Spain, Germany. Needless to say, such views were bitterly fought by assimilated liberals who accused Zionists of "defeatism" and of offering a rationale for anti-Semitism. Socialists condemned them for creating "bogeys" and fostering "chauvinism," and for deserting the general battlefield by giving in to black reaction and diverting the attention of the Jewish masses from the general struggle on behalf of a revolutionary ideology.

Zionist historiography glorified the Messianic movements in Jewish history. Where older historiography saw only delusion, downright deceit or mass psychosis, Zionists lovingly sought hints and signs of a national ideology, of emancipatory aspirations, and links in a perennial undying tradition: the dream of the Return to Zion. Similarly – and not uninfluenced by modern psychology, especially Jung and the contemporary preoccupation with symbolic and mythological aspects of culture – Kabbalah and Jewish mysticism (which had received short shrift from liberals and rationalists as the raving and ranting of diseased minds) came to be seen as the esoteric language of a repressed, rebellious tradition and of powerful life forces which were straining to break out of the harsh discipline of rabbinical scholasticism, and had a liberating impact on their practitioners by preparing them for emancipation from their sectarian mentality. Similarly, too, Hassidism with its overflowing emotionalism and pantheism was treated with affectionate approval as an expression of vitality and a manifestation of a people's peculiar genius.

The Six-Day War had the electrifying effect of making all Jewish history up to date look like one long preparation for the phenomenal victory. Biblical descriptions of the conquests of Joshua, the battles of David, the victories of the Maccabees, all acquired a vivid reality. It was hardly possible not to feel a tremor of awe at the way in which the promises given to Abraham, Isaac and Jacob, and the prophecies of the seers, appeared to have come true, with Israel having miraculously come into its full and undivided inheritance and, at long last – it was confidently hoped – security. Tiny Israel seemed to have emerged as the strongest military power over a large area comprising three continents, and as one of the few countries in the contemporary jaded world with a sense of purpose and overflowing with self-assurance. What a miraculous change after Auschwitz!

The greater was the shock of the Yom Kippur War in 1973. It was not only that the unthinkable looked for a few days possible: the abyss was wide open. Israel was made to feel the cold wind of isolation, when country after country cut off relations, as if to add insult to injury. The loneliness was in due course intensified, when a succession of international forums began to treat Israel as an outlaw and pariah nation. The fondest hope of Zionism – to revolutionise Jewish existence by securing equal and recognised status as a nation among nations in the family of nations – was being systematically shattered. It was an old story all over again: the nation that dwelleth alone. . . . The State of Israel seemed to have become the collective Jew of the ghetto, whose very right to exist was questioned, whose claims to equal treatment were not taken for granted, who was held to have to earn his right to exist by special exertions, by some special atonement, through being better than others. Of all the nations which defended their vital interests against majorisation by UN bloc voting, Israel alone was being bullied to forgo them. Of all the States from which refugees had fled, Israel was the only one to feel the brunt of relentless pressure to take them back. Overnight would-be-imperialist Israel was reduced to beggary, while mortal enemies, pledged to destroy the Jewish State, had surfaced from being objects of pity into the position of the bankers of the world. Theirs was now a power which could hold the planet to ransom and extort exorbitant pay for the life-blood of its economy, and make the proudest nations court its favour.

Vast historical developments partly unconnected with Jews, on the one hand, and tragic ironies besetting Jewish fate in this century on the other, combined to create an entirely new setting for Jewish history, and yet to push it back upon the old paths. The re-emergence of the old-new races of China and India and of the extra-European and non-Christian States all over Asia and Africa brought into the councils of mankind civilisations which had never known anti-Semitism, never persecuted Jews, never been obsessed with "the Jew." They were free of the morbid oedipal complex of Christianity towards the Jew – the parents of its religion, yet murderer of its Saviour. They had never been haunted by the image of Judas Iscariot, nor did the word Jew conjure up to them the figure of Shylock.

But their record was empty of Jews. And without the knowledge of the Bible and familiarity with the sad story of the centuries-old tension and conflict between Church and Synagogue, between persecutors and persecuted, no wonder they were entirely deaf to the sound of the magic names of Zion and Jerusalem, to the myth of Zionism. They lacked any sense of guilt, unease or obligation towards the Jews or appreciation of their unique fate and contribution. To them the Arab version of Zionism – as an imperialistic venture overrunning an Arab land on the morrow of the exodus of the white man from all over Asia and Africa – sounded plausible, especially when national interest (or the Moslem religion) drew them closer to the rich Arab world. Moreover, Israel stood condemned as "the satellite of the United States."

To many Jews it looked like an act of Providence that, on the eve of the destruction of the millennial Jewish civilisation in Europe, there should have come into being in the most powerful country in the world the most powerful Jewish Diaspora of all time – and that the government of that power should not only be in need of the Jewish votes and financial backing, but also be saturated in Biblical lore, suffer from a sense of shame at not having opened its gates to Jews escaping from mass murder, share very tangible interests with Israel, and admire its prowess and dynamism.

This became a scandal in the eyes of the Left. The Left had no mind for memories of Auschwitz when passionately preoccupied with the favourite historical schema of Imperialism on one side and colonial oppressed nations aspiring to freedom and progress on the other (even if that version was occasionally tarnished by Soviet strategic and imperialist interests). The reversal of alliances was a heartrending development to a good many Jews and Israelis who had so firmly believed in the natural alliance between Jews and the Left (and all progressive forces). Few could bring themselves to believe in the possibility of a genuine and lasting understanding with the Right, whose views, temper, mentality and past prevented genuinely friendly feelings towards Jews from striking root.

The only dependable ally of Israel was the Jews of the Diaspora. And they were deeply shaken and bewildered by what to some seemed a terrible change in the position of Israel, from the carrier of the banner of world Jewry and its proud shield into a heavy and possibly permanent burden. At the same time, they realised that they just could not evade their responsibility for Israel. What enemies decried as an international conspiracy was nothing but the closing of ranks of a sorely tried people, with long memories and reflex reactions in face of danger. The destruction of Israel was sure to deal a mortal blow to corporate Jewish existence all over the world, and a catastrophe that might overtake US Jewry was certain to doom the State of Israel.

This is, in my view, the background for the emergence of the Masada complex, or the complex of Samson, in the days after the October War. The Masada complex is indeed a striking example of the vicissitudes of historical consciousness, of the fortunes of a historic myth, and the changes in the self-image of a nation. As is now universally known (partly thanks to Professor Yigael Yadin's celebrated excavations on the rock), the last remaining group of Zealots to escape death and captivity at the hands of the Romans refused to lay down arms, and entrenched themselves on the precipitous craggy mountain of Masada in the Judean desert. With certain defeat staring into their faces, they preferred self-immolation to falling into the grasp of a heathen enemy. The men slaughtered their women and children, and then committed mass suicide. The only source to teach us of the event is the tale in Josephus, the Jewish general who despaired of victory, went over to the Romans, and then wrote his famous history of the Jewish War. The speech of the Masada leader before the act of suicide (as recorded by Josephus) is, like other speeches in ancient historiography, an exercise in rhetoric. It is, strangely enough, couched in terms and abounds in images which are wholly alien to Jewish tradition. It extols the love of freedom and honour and the beauty of heroic death. Apart from very general digressions about divine choice and gentile enmity, it contains no references to Jewish law, lore, writings, or beliefs. What is no less astonishing is that – as one young Israeli historian, Benjamin Kedar, has recently pointed out – no Jewish source (Mishna or Talmud or any later sage or scribe) makes reference to the macabre episode or to Josephus's account of it, except for a mention in Josiphon, a tenth-century compilation. The event found no echo in Jewish writings or consciousness till 1927, when under the impact of the pogroms in the Ukraine, following the Bolshevik Revolution, the Hebrew poet, Itzhak Lamdan, wrote a very powerful epic poem of which the key sentence is: "*Masada shall not fall again. . . .*"

In contrast to the total oblivion into which the tragedy of Masada had fallen, generations of Jews have ever since been brought up on the story of Rabbi Johanan ben Zakkai. The Rabbi was a most distinguished spiritual leader in Jerusalem. Realising that the fall of the holy city was imminent, he asked his disciples to smuggle him out of the beleaguered capital, as a corpse on a bier, so as to deceive the Zealots. Upon reaching the Roman lines, he asked to be taken to the Commander. Granted an audience, he begged the Roman general to allow him and his pupils to proceed to the little town of Yavneh, south of Jerusalem, and to establish an Academy there. The request granted, Yavneh in due course became the most important seat of learning in Palestine. The legend of Yavneh was handed down from generation to generation as symbolising the metamorphosis from political statehood to spiritual confraternity. It was an example of the survival of the soul after the death of the body (the corpse!), and as proof of the eternity of Judaism which, as an idea, was more immune to destruction and more authentically Jewish than earthly institutions and power. Paradoxically, it was left to some of our contemporaries in Israel (among them one aged historian, whose life-style and achievements qualify him much more to be a follower of the Rabbi than of the Zealot leader), to condemn Rabbi Johanan ben Zakkai for acting like a "fifth columnist" and cowardly breaking the solidarity of his embattled people.

No less remarkable is, of course, the hostile attitude of the rabbinical tradition to the Bar-Kochba uprising against the Romans in the second century. The leader of the uprising is in some references called Bar-Koziba (son of the lie), notwithstanding the fact that he was supported by one of the greatest Rabbis of the age, Akiva, who perished in the memorable execution of the ten martyred sages.

Similarly, the feast of Channukah has no record in the Old Testament, nor has the Book of Maccabees of the Christian Apocrypha been included in the Jewish canon, and its Hebrew and Aramaic originals have been lost. The religious zeal of the first Maccabees in fighting idolatry was dimmed in the eyes of the Rabbis by the Hellenistic culture of their Hasmonean descendants; and the feast of Channukah, celebrated in modern times as a commemoration of a war of national liberation, was treated by the Rabbis as a feast of the miracle of the lights.

That the Rabbis did not have it all their own way, and that there was another tradition which suffered suppression, is shown by the fact that, when the Patriarch Judah I tried to abolish the fast of Ab (because the occasion was used by agitators to incite the people against Rome), he was resisted and overruled.

Masada has now become the place of pious and patriotic pilgrimage. The bones of the fighters and their families have been exhumed and given a State funeral. Units of the army are taken there for the swearing-in ceremony. Few pause to reflect that the almost Wagnerian fascination with death and suicide is utterly non-Jewish. Judaism glorifies life and survival above all. Little thought is given to the fact that Masada was never accepted by past generations as a way of living or dying, and that, at bottom, the cult of Masada could become a morbidly defeatist preoccupation. Instead of inspiring courage, a will to fight, a faith in victory, the sepulchral myth may lure men to death by fostering the conviction of an inevitable end. It may become a self-fulfilling prophecy.

The examples of the Poles, the Irish, and other defeated fate-ridden but rebellious nations is enough to show what a magnetic impact defeat, and its associated images of heroic death, may exercise. The sober historian can hardly help treating the three great Polish uprisings – of Kosciuszko in 1794, of 1830, and 1863 – as anything but hopeless ventures from the start. They were hardly inevitable events, and their results were utterly disastrous. They sealed the fate of that unhappy nation for generations. Yet a fighting nation needs myths and legends, heroes and martyrs; and it cannot afford to treat them as lighthearted, excitable men who died in vain.

The bloody protest for a glorious thing,
They shall be spoken of among their people,
The generations shall remember them,
And call them blessed.

The crisis of identity in Israel is, thus, producing a far-reaching polarisation on the two extremes of the ideological spectrum. The crystallisation of a type of Integral Nationalism at one pole is being answered by a decline of Zionist faith and a scepticism verging on nihilism on the opposite side. The two extremes, with their lunatic fringes, represent small numerical minorities. But they are highly articulate figures of an activist temper confronting a perplexed public and are significant as symptoms and portents.

Anyone familiar with the French variety of "integral nationalism," or the Slavophile version of it, will be ready with a slogan for the Israeli phenomenon: the power of the dead over the living. The present generation, which has been singled out by Providence to liberate the fatherland in its historical boundaries – so runs its argument in the current all-important grand debate on the future frontiers of Israel – has no right to renounce any part of the nation's patrimony. This is an organic whole and belongs to all generations, past, present and future. Just as every generation is subordinated to the perennial imperatives, values, and aspirations of the immortal nation, so is the individual to the totality, to its interests and aims.

What, then, is that authentic legacy of a history of 3,500 years, spun over several continents, influenced by such a variety of civilisations, and affected by such a multitude of factors, situations, changes? The Orthodox militants have of course a *prima facie* unanswerable answer: the Jewish religion. Without paying any heed to the time dimension and to evolutionary change, they call "authentic" unchanging Judaism literal fundamentalism as it was practised in the ages of an utterly apolitical, sectarian, and ritualistic seclusion in Eastern Europe, many centuries after the canon had been codified in the Middle East in very different circumstances. This they combine with persistent evocation of the eternal enmity of the Amalekites and the Edomites and the persecution suffered through the ages.

The tribal ingredients of Judaism of the Bronze Age are overstated at the expense of the later strictly religious, metaphysical, humanist, and universal elements. Resentments and consolations, and dreams of revenge – hopes of deliverance impotently nursed for centuries in eschatological visions on the far margin of society – all are now summoned in connection with political programmes, territorial claims, resort to arms and coercive procedures. Politicised and militantly nationalist Orthodoxy is courted by the devotees of secular integral nationalism who set great store by anything that deepens national self-awareness and intensifies the sense of destiny. Religious myths and symbols are to them part of a sacred national tradition, the expression of the nation's genius, and thus objects of adoration. They welcome, above all, the passionate motivation that activates the nationalist wing of Orthodoxy. The emphasis upon the absolute and transcendental sanction of political aspirations appears as an infusion of ardour and self-assurance.

Few of the political nationalists are strict in their observances. Still fewer would wish to be pressed to render account of their religious beliefs. The integral nationalists of Israel may be compared to Maurice Barrès and Charles Maurras who were not interested in the authenticity of the stories of the Gospel or in the logic of the religious canon. In fact, they disbelieved all of them. But they admired the hierarchical discipline maintained by the Catholic Church. They saw in authority from above the secret of social cohesion and national grandeur, and in the Catholic past of France a vital part of its historic personality.

Israelis at the opposite pole are deeply worried by the spread of a mood which has elsewhere invariably overflowed with violent anti-Semitic accents. The theories which offered it a rationale treated the Jews as an "alien" body which the national organism must reject, since the Jews had no share in the national heritage, and were incapable of entering into its spirit. The addiction of Jewish intellectuals to analytical scepticism – their ironical attitude to collective myths and symbols, their tireless questioning of all accepted beliefs, their association with cosmopolitan ideologies such as liberalism, socialism, and pacifism – made them appear a dangerous solvent.

Liberal or Left-wing Israelis, as well as the religious elements of purer spirituality in the kibbutz and university, are dismayed by the spread of mythological patterns of thought and behaviour, the rhetoric of a holy war at a time when the enemy is playing with the equally dangerous slogan of *jihad*, and by a mystical nationalism which threatens to breed collective solipsism and to foster an authoritarian temper. Not a few secularists are swept on into positions quite beyond the defence of freedom of choice and individual rights, and in some cases into conflict with basic tenets of liberal Zionism itself. They are being thrown back into what Friedrich Meinecke called *Weltbürgertum*: a pre-political cosmopolitanism, and an abstract natural-rights moralism. They become sceptical about the reality of collective entities staking out juridical and political claims. They develop a deep sense of guilt towards the Palestinian Arabs. In their irritability a few go so far as to lose sight of the tragedy of the clash between rights. They torment themselves by obsessively dwelling on the phenomenon of Palestinian Arab

Zionism, and taunt the Zealots of Israel with the name of "Jewish Fascists." Each side provokes the other to go much further than it originally intended.

Notwithstanding some noisy demonstrations, neither the religious nor the secular integral nationalists have so far given cause to suspect their allegiance to parliamentary democracy and to the rule of law. But the appeal to a superior, impersonal, eternal sanction against the vagaries of mortal men conjures up both the image of an élite claiming to represent and embody the only authentic form of Judaism and of activists usurping the right to take coercive action to impose their ideas on the unruly and the faithless. Fears of such a development are inevitably aroused by the implication of the passionate resolve of both the national-religious Zealots and the believers in integral nationalism to annex territories inhabited by an alien, unwilling, and hostile Arab population in the name of a transcendental right and sanction.

Horrified and incensed by what seems to them nihilistic and treasonable undermining of the nation's morale at the moment of its supreme test, the nationalists utter menacing hints about the characterless and poisonous enemy within, possessed by a death wish and too demoralised to feel the unquestioned obviousness of the national interest and imperative, but perplexed by the case of the implacable enemy. Are there any Arabs – they ask – who give the slightest thought to the Jewish case? Are there any who feel any respect for the Jewish phenomenon or have any understanding for Zionist motivation?

The deep cause of this polarisation which is calculated to determine the very shape of Israeli society and Jewish mentality for a long time, goes back much further than the Six-Day War or even the Yom Kippur War. We are, again, at Auschwitz. Among the six million Jews who perished in the ghettos and death camps of Eastern Europe there were at least two million potential citizens of Israel, who represented the best of Jewish manhood and had a total commitment to the Zionist idea and to liberal democracy at the same time. The State came into being too late for them.

And there was no substitute for them. The Oriental Jews who were hastily brought into nascent Israel, admirable as their qualities and potentialities otherwise are, not only lacked the modern skills and techniques, but came from an environment which did not foster dedication to abstract causes and did not encourage a spirit of self-reliance and voluntary cooperation with others.

There is another fact of immense importance. The deepest motive force of Zionism and its strongest justification in the eyes of world opinion was originally the Jewish plight, the sufferings of homeless millions. The "final solution" has removed from the world press not only news about pogroms and persecutions but, indeed, the very expression which in bygone days was never absent from public debate – "The Jewish Question." The desperate Jewish need gave to the Zionists their irresistible courage and determination to disregard Arab opposition, their ardent faith in the rightness of their cause and their conviction of its utter urgency. Not only has the "Jewish Question" by the most tragic of ironies ceased to haunt the world; most Gentiles have, in the meantime, become used to the image of the well-to-do, established, and influential Jewish communities in the West; and they are not much affected by Soviet policies on Jewish emigration or towards the Jews in the USSR.

Zionist philosophy and apologetics have, as a result, been more and more driven to resort to argument from history, from historical rights and divine promise, on top, of course, of the insistence on the needs of Israel's security and the danger of annihilation facing it. The ear of world opinion – especially in the Third World and in the Communist bloc – is not exactly attuned to the argument from historical rights.

Not a few Israelis have grown more and more confirmed in their farouche, not to say paranoiac and solipsist obsession with their own righteousness and with the old implacable and immutable hostility of the Gentile world. Mystical nationalism offers itself in these circumstances as a narcotic and a shield against confusing circumstances, inner uncertainty, and the bad will of an uncomprehending wicked world.

Owing to the fact that for centuries they formed there the only middle class, the Jews of Central and Eastern Europe constituted (before 1939) not merely a religion and an ethnic group, but a variegated and vital civilisation. Religious distinctness may have been its root; but in modern times it became one facet of Jewish life among others, to some of overriding importance, to others of only marginal significance, or almost irrelevant. There was a separate language, a rich Jewish culture, a flourishing literature, a wealth of traditions, customs, habits, a network of autonomous institutions, a particular economy and social structure, and a proliferation of ideologies and parties. With the tragic, sudden disappearance of that civilisation, the Israeli leaders woke up to the fact that in this secular age and in face of the growing atomisation and assimilation of the Jews in the Western countries, the only remaining focus of Jewish cohesion was the synagogue.

They were seized by a frantic anxiety that liberal legislation on such matters as for instance, civil marriage, was calculated to lower the barriers and expose the unity and the very survival of Jewry to mortal danger. Israel must not show a bad example and make it easier for young Jewish men and women to "drop out." Hence the irksome restrictions in such matters as civil status, Sabbath observance, dietary laws which often cause inconvenience to many, intense misery to some, and wide-spread indignation. Yet these restrictions are despairingly defended by politicians who are by no means ordinary opportunists and who, in their younger days, had sometimes been militant anti-clericals and even now do not themselves observe any ritualistic precepts. Only they do not stop to reflect whether, instead of preventing backsliding (which they fear so much), illiberalism may not rather foster it among those Western Jews whose attachment to liberal values and modes of life is very deep and who in fact owe their welfare and remarkable success to them.

The most history-ridden and history-obsessed people thus finds itself torn between solipsistic self-apotheosis, which comes from an idolisation of history, and the self-rejection which is the result of a denial of the past. Although it is certain that a reasonable settlement of the Middle Eastern conflict will stem the drift to the extreme, the question of Israeli (and indeed Jewish) identity, which has become so acute in the middle of the fourth millennium of Jewish history, will remain an open and tormenting issue. Nor is there any prospect that Jewish anxiety about Jewish survival, ceaselessly threatened from outside and undermined from within, is going to be stilled by a Messianic solution. Too great a charge put on History by appointing it to the role of saviour carries with it its own nemesis.

First published in *Encounter*, May 1976.

Sadat's Peace Initiative and Its Aftermath

Sudden and unexpected historic events which appear to be a turning point – a sort of *deus ex machina* – are not capricious acts which their authors and heroes decide to carry out in an arbitrary manner or on the spur of a momentary inspiration. Such events must be viewed as the end of long processes which ripen slowly, without people noticing, or being able to follow the developments. A simile from the field of physics might be apt: For example, the turning of water into ice, or conversely, into steam. In such a case, the change is absolute. Things do not work that way in biology. Sometimes a new species emerges as the outcome of a mutation, at other times as an accidental result or of a genetic "mistake," so to speak. But whether such a species will survive and continue to exist depends on all its ability to adapt itself to its environment and to the conditions of the battle for survival. Which is to say, it has to be able to survive in objective circumstances. Imagine that, suddenly, but in actuality as the result and at the conclusion of a long process, or as a function of an unexpected constellation (unexpected to the contemporaries), a new alternative arises, a propitious hour arrives. Whether the chance becomes an opening for a new reality depends on the ability of the actors and those who must take decisions to assess it correctly, and on the strength of their resolve to seize it. And the question as to whether this will turn out to be the beginning of a new, continuous, desirable and constructive course rather than a passing episode or a stillbirth depends again on people and on circumstances.

Sadat's peace initiative looks to me as the climax of a process. It became clear to him, beyond all doubt, that the alternatives in the Arab–Israeli conflict were either a true peace or a bloody war whose outcome was wholly incalculable, and which the Egyptians were not capable of waging. He decided therefore that there was no escape from an accommodation through peaceful ways. First he placed his trust on American arbitration, or even on American pressure. But it seems that when the American-Russian agreement faded out through the influence of the "Jewish lobby," Sadat concluded that he could not depend on the United States and that in any case, reliance on a third party that would bring the two sides of the conflict together meant an endless dragging out of the process. And then only did the daring decision ripen. He wanted, of course, to push Israel into a corner. If he were met by an Israeli rejection, he would always be able to tell the world: "Look, I did the impossible, but there was absolutely no response from their side." But it seems to me that there was an additional factor at work which gives great credit to the man Sadat. When he confronted the possibility that only the sword could bring a decision, a fearsome worry rose up in him and he felt a deep-seated need to examine and ascertain for himself if in truth there was no escape from this terrible nightmare. He then made his daring jump. The welcome extended to him by the people of Israel convinced him that indeed there was another way.

I said Sadat acted neither suddenly nor capriciously, but under the stress of circumstances. But that does not detract one whit from his great merit. Not everybody would have been capable of sorting out the components of the situation in such a clear and analytic way, to draw the firm conclusion and to find the strength within him to shock, to surprise, to embarrass, to alienate and to infuriate so many factors.

Who could at all doubt the reality of the immense leap which Sadat made from Khartoum and the Yom Kippur War all the way to Jerusalem, to the Knesset, and all the way to a declaration on Israel's right to exist in security?

The longer a dispute between nations continues, the more complicated, entangled and insoluble it proves. As a result of the accretion of mistakes, errors, shocks, traumatic happenings and indeed the hardly avoidable escalation and brutalization of the conflict, it becomes more and more impossible for either side to come to any decision. In a meeting between the two heroes of the drama, such as took place in Jerusalem last November, the Gordian knot can be cut, its components reduced to the first simple data and the few available alternatives. The springs which move the entire mechanism seem then revealed. The issues are, as it were, on a razor's edge. A monumental simplification results.

Given the technological means of our day, such a meeting has an immense power to galvanize things. The media add the element of dramatization which has a tremendous impact. The whole world is a witness and participant. This exerts enormous pressure and poses a great challenge to the heroes of the drama to decide and to act. And when one adds to this, as was actually the case, manifestations of chivalry, generosity of spirit and of a readiness to understand and to spare the susceptibilities of the other side – all of these contributed to bring about in a population, which has for so long laboured under a stifling sense of hopeless impasse and in the shadow of the spectre of war, a catharsis, a release of pent-up strains and fears and a loosening of repressions and inhibitions. There was an opening up of new vistas and sunny uplands and a welling up of deeply buried forces and resources.

Modern psychology and the contemporary historiography which has been influenced by it lay bare the neurotic elements in the lives of individuals and societies that are behind the paralyzing suspicions, fears, obsessions, which suppress our power of decision. Discovering things as they are here and now and seeing and assessing the immediate concrete situation are hampered and distorted so frequently by the compulsive impact of memories, whether conscious or subconscious, or experiences, images, beliefs, trials and nightmares, of the past. And so it happens that as individuals and as peoples we do not deal with the matter at hand, tackle the concrete situation in its true proportions, but struggle with associations rooted in the past. Such behaviour is called neurosis.

In our case we have those aggregates of mutual hatred, of wars, of terror and reprisals; the nightmare of Auschwitz and the trauma of Munich haunting us, the plight of the refugees and the legend of the Crusades stirring up the Arabs; the Divine promise and the commandment to remember Amalek sustaining the Jews, and the vision of the restored glories of Islam and Arab power inspiring our adversaries – all these have brought about a demonization of the conflict. Each of the sides in the conflict imagined the other as the devil incarnate, and we were all hypnotized, both Jews and Arabs, by an atmosphere of "if a fellow is out to kill you, rise up earlier in the morning and forestall him." What Sadat's visit has done is to contribute so much to a humanization, in the place of the demonization, of the conflict, to a thawing of the neurosis and to a rationalization of the dispute.

Neurotic fear is always a bad adviser. It brings out the hastiness of extremism, and it prevents rational, sober evaluation of the ever-changing components. It beclouds analysis of the long-ranged constants of security. It dulls vigilance for opportunity. It engenders apocalyptic sentiments and raises a compulsive longing for a test similar to Massada or the one that Samson underwent. It spreads mystical modes of thought. When in an exacerbated mood, we seem to hear only the categorical imperative – the challenge of martyrdom. One no longer relates to the circumstances of the here and now or to needs of the future.

In his day Bismarck spoke about voices from above which were heard not once and for all time only in the early dawn of history, but continued to speak to us anew from the din of historic occurrences, through the fluttering of wings or in thunder and lightning. In the vast emotional upheaval in the days of the Sadat visit, the attuned ear could discern signals sent by Providence. To decipher them we must strain all our faculties. Do they say, "Here is a propitious hour. Here is the end of a rope which, if you seize firmly, can bring you to an accommodation based on compromise"? Or, "Here is an opportunity for you to deepen the rift in the Arab world and to continue avoiding hard decision by sophisticated evasiveness, to gain time so that you can create 'new facts' so that it will be possible for you to hold on to the territories, in a situation of neither peace nor war?"

It is incumbent upon the historian to warn his listeners that there is a danger in thwarting those high and uplifting expectations of a breakthrough. Should this yearning for peace be frustrated by the walls closing in again, the outcome could be soul-destroying indeed. It could breed Sabbatean moods of various and different kinds: crippling despondency and lack of faith, or vain delusions and an itch for nihilistic adventure.

All those who care should master the courage for a sober, and even agonising reappraisal of the data of the situation, and for a deep probe of their consciences. And if there are leaders, and there are such, who are committed to positions or sworn to hard and absolute stands, they must listen to the voice of the people, which has the power and the right to bind to and to absolve from oaths and vows.

Perhaps because I want peace as badly as I do, it seems to me that if we continue with the same openness which we showed when Sadat was in our midst, and we also demonstrate this in deeds, then just as Sadat's visit to us caused emotions to well up and thoughts to soar high, something similar may take place in the Arab world, certainly in Egypt. And as to the world, I am convinced that we will be in a very strong position as we will be in the eyes of moderate

Arab public opinion, if we accept the principle of withdrawal from the territories that were occupied, and while proclaiming that we do not want to rule over a hostile, alien population, in the throes of national passion, we insist on our moral and legal right, nay duty towards the principle of self-preservation – to oppose the setting up, in the wake of our retreat, of a state dominated by a terrorist movement pledged to destroy us. The world will understand this position of ours.

The immense historical significance of Sadat's visit and what came immediately after it found its expression in Sadat's words in the Knesset: "You want to live together with us in this area of the world and I say to you in all sincerity, we accept you with blessing amongst us. We accept you in security and with tranquility." The response of the Israeli public was so overwhelming that it crowded out and obscured all of the concrete hard demands that were presented to Israel. That the President of Egypt did indeed intend to achieve this impression comes out clearly from his comment, one that he repeated many times, that 70 per cent of the conflict was of a psychological nature.

Let us not forget that such a large proportion of Jewish history in the *Galut* was determined over the generations by the refusal of the surrounding environment to take the Jews as they were for granted, and to recognise the very legitimacy of their existence. The harbingers of Zionism saw their goal as the creation of a free and independent state in the ancestral land, recognised as an equal member in the family of nations. It was therefore such a galling and exasperating experience for the Israelis to have to face the fact that we were the only country in the world with which its neighbours were not merely interlocked in conflict, but absolutely determined to deny the right to exist, nay to destroy us. The Arabs did indeed succeed in isolating Israel in the international arena. They turned the State of Israel into the "Jewess among the nations," as a French-Jewish historian put it.

A sincere recognition of our right to existence and our right to security by the Arab world would not yet of course be an answer to all the problems, nor a guarantee against all dangers. Yet it is a precondition to any kind of normalisation of our existence and of our status. No technical measures, no political arrangement, no pledges of non-aggression will prove effective without it.

As we confront the chance to achieve such a recognition, we must think about the future and not rummage in memories and accounts of the past. The most talented of Russian statesmen at the beginning of this century once spoke a sentence which we must memorise: "In politics there is no revenge, there are only consequences."

First published in *The Jewish Quarterly*, Vol. 26, No. 1 (95), Spring 1978.

Part Four

Intellectual and Political Debates

The Argument between Arabs and Jews

An Exchange between Arnold Toynbee and J. L. Talmon

London, 3 July, 1967

Dear *Professor Talmon,*

I have just been staying with my son Philip and I have read your paper "For Total Peace in the Middle East" which Isaiah Berlin passed on to him. I believe, like you, that this is the moment for everyone of goodwill and good sense to make an all-out effort to get total, genuine, and lasting peace there. I believe there is a real opportunity for this, if we seize it now. I am just back from the United States, and, three weeks ago, I stuck my neck out by writing, for the United Press International, an article saying this, and making some concrete proposals for bringing it about. The United Press tell me that my article has been reproduced pretty widely in the U.S. press, so a copy of it may come into your hands some time, but, as there is no time to lose, I am writing to you now direct.

I feel a responsibility for doing anything I can to help towards getting a permanent peace now. I have a number of reasons. (1) I am British, so I have a share of responsibility for my country's past actions. (2) As a young man during the First World War, I was working as a "temporary Foreign Office clerk" on Middle Eastern affairs, particularly on British war-time commitments in the Middle East, so I know the history of these from the inside. (3) I am known as a Western spokesman for the Arab cause, and it is therefore just possible that what I say in public now might have some influence in the Arab World, though it is perhaps more likely that the Arabs might write me off with the verdict that I am no friend of theirs after all. Anyway, I believe that the truest act of friendship that any friend of either the Arabs or the Israelis can do for them at this moment is to try to help them to see that the facts make genuine peace a prime interest for both parties. (4) Being now an old man, with grandchildren, I feel what Johnson and Kosygin seem to have felt when they met. One's grandchildren symbolise for me, in a concrete way, all the future generations of the human race – 70 million unborn generations who might be deprived, by our generation, of their right to life if we, in our time, were to stumble into an atomic third world war. (5) Thinking also in terms of the present, I want to see something done now which, besides saving the world from an enormous catastrophe, will reduce present human suffering in the Middle East to a minimum. I should have been as much horrified at genocide of Jews in the Middle East as I was horrified at it in Europe. I also think it very wrong to treat any people, living or unborn, as political pawns, instead of treating them as suffering human beings whose alleviation ought to have priority over any political considerations. In discussing the Arab states' policy with my Arab friends, I have always pointed out to them that West Germany's post-war policy towards refugees from Eastern Germany and from east of the Oder-Niesse line has not only been humane, but has paid dividends to Western Germany, economically and therefore also politically. Israelis should look ahead for their grandchildren.

Now about the facts that each side has to face and about practical possibilities for a settlement.

In your paper, you, yourself, have put your finger on the fact that Israel has to face. A series of more and more sensational victories in successive wars does not, in itself, give Israel the vital thing that she wants and needs: that is, real peace with her Arab neighbours. So long as Israel has not mutually agreed permanent frontiers, but only a military front, always smouldering and periodically flaring up into full-blown hostilities, Israel has to stay constantly on the alert and cannot concentrate her energies on her own internal development, which is, and always has been, her real objective. She has demonstrated now conclusively that, in war, she can always conquer more Arab territory without any foreign military aid; but, the more of this that she occupies, the more she will become militarily overextended, and the larger the proportion of her limited and precious manpower she will have to keep unprofitably mobilised. The Arab World has the same passive military advantage as Russia and China have: there is virtually no end to it. So Israel's overriding interest is genuine peace; even the greatest military victories will be fruitless unless they can be converted into that.

The Arabs have to face the fact that Israel has come to stay; that a three-times repeated experience has shown that they cannot defeat her; that the Soviet Union is not going to go to war with the United States for the Arabs' sake; and that, in the unlikely event of the Arabs becoming, one day, able to destroy Israel, the United States would not let this happen.

I need not dwell on your psychological analysis of the present-day Arab state of mind. It is masterly; you have shown a power of sympathetic understanding by which you have entered into it imaginatively. This is very important and very encouraging, because Israel, as the present victor, holds the initiative. The party that has suffered injustice and has been humiliated is the one that is the more sensitive and that therefore needs the more delicate handling. The Palestinian Arabs have suffered injustice. To put it simply, they have been made to pay for the genocide of Jews in Europe which was committed by Germans, not by Arabs. The Arabs as a whole have been humiliated, because, in the establishment, first of the Jewish National Home and then of the State of Israel, the Arabs have, as you point out, never been consulted. It has all been done over their heads. They have been treated as "natives," with no more than sub-human rights. For a people with a great, but no longer actual, historic past, this is infuriating. The present Arab and present Chinese states of mind have the same explanation.

So I would plead with Israel to make the first move towards achieving the total genuine and lasting peace which is the supreme common interest of Israel, the Palestinian Arab refugees, and the Arab states. For Israel publicly to make the first move would be magnanimous as well as far-sighted. I suggest that Israel should now propose that the two sides should make the following simultaneous declaration:

> "The Arab states and the Palestinian Arab people pledge themselves to recognise, *bona fide*, the existence of Israel with the intention of making a permanent peace with her, and they also guarantee to negotiate permanent frontiers with Israel on approximately the 1948 armistice lines. Israel pledges herself to accept these agreed frontiers *bona fide*, with the intention, on her side, of making permanent peace, and she also undertakes to take the initiative in bringing about a satisfactory permanent settlement of the problem of the 1948 refugees."[1]

If both sides would give these reciprocal pledges in a formal agreement of the kind that used to be called "preliminaries of peace," this would open the way for a negotiated treaty about details, and then things that have so far been impossible would become possible, *e.g.*:

1. In the conversion of the 1948 armistice lines into permanent frontiers, there could be minor rectifications, so long as these offset each other fairly on balance.
2. There could be a mutual opening up of communications that are vital to both parties. Israel could be assured of a right of way not only through the Straits of Tiran but through the Suez Canal too. Egypt could be assured of a right of way, across Israel, to Lebanon, Syria, Jordan, and Saudi Arabia, thus removing the "Polish corridor" irritant of Israel's having split the Arab World in two by extending from the Mediterranean coast to the Gulf of Aqaba. Syria and Jordan could be given a free port at Haifa, with a right of way to it, and Jordan could be given a second one at Jaffa.
3. The 1948 Palestinian Arab refugees could (a) be given monetary compensation for the loss of their property situated in Israel; (b) be given an extra indemnity for having been forced, as innocent victims of the conflict between Israel and the Arab states, to spend twenty years as refugees; (c) be given the option of either returning to their former homes on condition of becoming loyal citizens of Israel (as the Galilaean Arabs have been during the present crisis) or else being settled on good land outside Israel; (d) a fund could be raised for the refugees' resettlement, whether inside Israel or outside it. I am sure the majority will opt for resettlement *outside* Israel; but for Israel to offer the choice of returning home (on condition of their becoming *bona fide* loyal Israeli citizens) is psychologically very important for producing a change of heart among the refugees. If Israel appealed to the world to help her raise a fund for these four purposes, money would pour in.
4. Water for irrigation: in the London *Times* a few days ago, there was an important letter from Edmund de Rothschild about this, followed up next day by a long and constructive article by a desalination expert. They make the point that, even though desalination has not yet been made possible at

an economic price, it would pay the world to subsidise it for the use of Israel and Jordan. This would (a) make it no longer necessary to pay a pittance to the refugees; (b) in combination with the Jordan water, it would supply abundant water for *both* Israel *and* Jordan, and would therefore make it unnecessary for them to contend with each other over their respective shares of Jordan water.

The future of the Old City of Jerusalem is a question of special urgency and danger. It is of crucial importance that Israel should not take unilateral action for annexing it. This would not be valid in international law; it could not be accepted by the United Nations; it would make genuine peace between Israel and the Arabs impossible; and it would arouse the whole Muslim World, and probably a large part of the Christian World too, not only against Israel, but against the Jews in general. It might seriously prejudice the diaspora's position in many countries.

Moreover, possession of the Temple area (the Muslims' Haram ash-Sherif) would be an embarrassment for Israel. She would have either to refrain from rebuilding the Temple or else she would have to demolish the Dome of the Rock and the Al Aksa Mosque, which would really be unthinkable. Of course, Israelis and all other Jews must have free access to the Wailing Wall. I like the Pope's proposal for an international trusteeship for the holy places of *all* religions in Palestine. But any change of sovereignty here would be most provocative unless it were freely negotiated in exchange for some equivalent *quid pro quo*. For instance, Jordan might conceivably say to Israel: "Cede to us the fields, now in Israel, that belong to villages on the Jordan side of the frontier, and then we will cede to you the south-west corner of the Old City of Jerusalem, up to the western face of the Wailing Wall." A bargain on these lines would be all right, but unilateral action by Israel would be disastrous.

Well, I am writing this to you, and am sending copies to Isaiah Berlin and to a friend of mine in Baltimore, Maryland, Rabbi Agus.

I am now an old man, and most of my treasure is therefore in future generations. This is why I care so much, and why I am writing this letter to you.

Please make any use of my letter that you think useful. I am not marking it "confidential."

Yours sincerely,
ARNOLD TOYNBEE

JERUSALEM, 18 JULY 1967

Dear *Professor Toynbee*,

I expressed to you by wire my first deeply felt reaction to your letter as soon as I finished reading it. I wish to apologise to you now for the ten days delay in sending you the detailed reply which I promised in my telegram. This was the last week of term at our University, teaching having been resumed at the end of June, after the interruption caused by mobilisation and war. I had also wished to show your letter to friends at the University and to a few persons in government circles for their comments. Finally, I needed time to ponder over what you say and sort out my own thoughts in the light of the feelings and ideas which animate the people of Israel at this moment.

May I say at the outset that I have reason to claim that I voice the sentiments of most Israelis in the appreciation of the moral fervour and sense of urgency which motivate your letter. I speak however only for myself when I deal with your concrete proposals and offer my own suggestions. All the same, I know for certain that a very strong volume of Israeli opinion shares my views on the practical prospects of an Arab–Israeli settlement; and I do not think I exaggerate if I add that, given the proper response from the other side, the suggestions voiced in the second part of this letter may easily become acceptable to the vast majority of the people of Israel, and – Israel being a genuine democracy – to its government.

You list a number of reasons for your feeling of "responsibility for doing anything [you] can to help towards getting a permanent peace now." I would add one reason which you do not mention, but which to me outweighs perhaps all those enumerated by you, for in a sense it contains them all. I seemed to hear in your letter the voice of Arnold Toynbee who in the *Study of History* had been speaking to me not just as the architect of a colossal edifice, but, if I may say so, as a prophet who stands in awe before the mystery of Time and is engaged in a passionate quest for overriding purpose and redeeming significance in History. Some of us who are living in "permanent and anguished intimacy with the mystery of Jewish martyrdom and survival" could not help responding to these "Judaic" ingredients in your work, and therefore felt especially pained by what to us, Jews and Zionists, appeared as a failure to accord to Judaism and its contemporary mutation, Israel, their due place in your scheme of civilisations emerging and falling, vast spiritual forces shaping and dissolving them, all that supposedly leading to some salvationist denouement in the end, but now suddenly faced by the mortal danger of total and meaningless destruction.

I welcome, therefore, most heartily your letter as some kind of opening to a friendly and fruitful dialogue. And it is not in any spirit of polemic or out of a wish to put into your mouth things which you did not say in your letter, but out of deep respect and genuine inner need, that I feel compelled to make these few, general comments before I come to your suggestions.

Zionism did not start with Hitler, and to us, therefore, the emergence of Israel could not be summed up in the statement that the Arabs "have been made to pay for the genocide of Jews in Europe which was committed by Germans, not by Arabs."

Just as we would not base our right to exist as an independent state in the Middle East solely on our right of conquest and demand of the Arabs simply to bow to that fact of nature (or history), so we could not possibly subordinate the immemorial aspiration of the Jewish people, admittedly much quickened by the rise of nationalism in the world at large, and made unbearably urgent by murderous persecution, to the exclusive resolve of the Arabs. Whatever the degree of our imaginative understanding of the Arab resentment at not having been consulted on the Balfour Declaration and the Palestine Mandate and for having had their objections overridden by the UN and their armed resistance to partition (the solution contrived to meet a clash of rights) overpowered by the Jews in 1948; and whatever the measure of our embarrassed sympathy for the terrible plight of the Palestine refugees, we could not put into question the very basis of our existence.

It is probably too much to ask – in this fallen state of mankind – of a nationalist movement to see the point of the other side and to make concessions to it readily and altruistically. Many as may have been the Zionist sins of commission or omission in this respect, every one of their attempts at a compromise had all along been met by Arabs with the absolute and implacable refusal to recognise any Jewish claim. This was bound to lead to the half-despairing, half-defiant reaction that since nothing could be done with them, it had to be done in spite of and even against them. Arab intransigence has proved a disastrous policy to the Arab interests. Every crisis culminating in armed clash cost the Arabs more and more, and weakened their position still further, which again deepened Arab neurosis on the point of Israel.

Wounded pride of a race with glorious memories is not an ignoble feeling. But an obsessive sense of injury and self-pity are conducive to sterile self-centredness and stultifying misanthropy. Where would we Jews have been today, had we never ceased to remember all the scores and been reliving all the humiliations we had suffered at the hands of every possible nation with which we had come into contact throughout our long history? What would have happened to the persecuted and maltreated of our race, had we behaved like the Arab States towards the Arab refugees: "May they suffer and rot, for it is all the doing of the Jews, and we must not make it easier for the enemy, but should on the contrary keep that sore running." Is there no hope of breaking this vicious circle – the source of so much misery to the peoples of the Middle East, and now threatening to engulf the whole world in an unspeakable catastrophe?

A man greatly revered by both of us, my late teacher R. H. Tawney, wrote:

> It is the tragedy of a world where man must walk by sight that the discovery of the reconciling formula is always left to future generations, in which passion has cooled into curiosity, and the agonies of peoples have become the exercise in the schools. The devil who builds bridges does not span such chasms till much that is precious to mankind has vanished down them for ever.

Surely enough blood has flowed down the chasms for the reconciling formula to be evolved and accepted at last. It is infinitely sad that *homo sapiens* should be so slow-witted, and that his reason should be so dominated and twisted by irrational drives and intractable aversions that only an overwhelming shock and inexorable *faits accomplis* are able to make the sweet voice of reason heard.

I entirely agree with you that on the morrow of the third Arab–Israel war in twenty years, the most self-absorbed nationalists on both sides should be ripe for the acceptance of the fact that galling as it is not to be able to attain one's supreme goal in its undiminished totality, that is the way the jealous gods will it. It may be hard upon the Arabs impelled by a vision of a pan-Arab Empire from Iran to the Atlantic to find the Jews planted on the Eastern shore of the Mediterranean. But the war to the bitter end advocated by the extremists, while most unlikely to wipe out Israel, is sure to bring, at once, the Arab States under Soviet domination, with Russian "advisers" and "technicians" in every office and regiment: a strange consummation of the dream of an Islamic renaissance. Even those no longer very numerous Jews who are still capable of becoming intoxicated with verses on the vastness of the Kingdom promised by the Almighty to His children have to wake up to the fact that God has played them an unfair trick in putting so many Arabs on the banks of the Jordan and scattering so many more in the countries around. The Israelis may defeat them again and again, but only to find the promised "rest and inheritance" removed further and further, and themselves condemned to live by the sword instead of walking by the spirit, to be a Sparta and not the combination of Jerusalem and Athens – the fondest dream of the noblest among the prophets of Zionism.

There is in fact no need to persuade Israel of the desirability and necessity of peace. All the effort is required on the other side. As to the actual terms envisaged by Israel, these would be a function of Arab readiness to recognise Israel and make a genuine peace with her. The graver our fears, the stiffer the guarantees we think necessary for our survival and security; the greater the confidence the Arabs are able to inspire, the more lenient are our terms likely to be.

You single out two items as all-important and indeed all-embracing: refugees and frontiers.

Only yesterday I was deeply impressed by a person whom I was always inclined to consider something of an extremist exclaiming with heat, "But we should pawn all we have to the tenth generation to solve this terrible problem of Arab refugees!"

I feel sure that, on this, all but one of your suggestions would be met: monetary compensation, extra-indemnity, participation in an international fund for resettlement. The difficulty would frankly be the suggestion of an Israeli offer to the Arab refugees of 1948 of the choice of returning home. You consider this as more important for its symbolic significance by expressing the certainty that the "majority will opt for resettlement outside Israel." As you know, we have made such an offer to the 1967 refugees who, seized by panic (out of implacable hostility to Israel or out of a desire to be with their own next of kin) crossed to the East Bank of the Jordan during and since the recent hostilities. We do not know yet how many will avail themselves of the offer to return to the West Bank. While I can see the human and symbolic significance, indeed the duty, of allowing such an option to the recent refugees, I doubt whether there is a case for doing the same in regard to the refugees of twenty years ago. It would not only create very grave problems for Israel. It would also impose upon the refugees, transplanted into realities quite different from those they knew a generation ago, strains and stresses which they would be spared if resettled in an Arab land or overseas. This does not mean that we shall not be prepared, as we have been in the past, to allow reunion of families or make special consideration where warranted.

This world should become one and a fit place for men and women of different races and religions to live together. Yet I cannot help remembering to what extent precisely régimes which claim to be inspired by a universal creed which subordinates racial peculiarity and national self-assertion to proletarian solidarity and universal brotherhood, have found no other solution to their nationalities problem but in the expulsion of millions of women and children, and in the annexation of vast territories to which their historic claim bears no comparison at all to the strength of the Jewish claim to Palestine. Even in such advanced and rich countries as Belgium and Canada racial conflict is assuming a virulence which baffles all observers. Incidentally, in absorbing some hundreds of thousands of Jewish immigrants or refugees from the Arab countries, Israel has carried out something of an exchange of populations.

As to the territorial terms, again, I and many like me hold the realistic opinion that territory densely populated by Arabs is not only not an asset to Israel, but a liability which even from the strategic point of view outweighs the supposed strategic advantages of what is called "more defensible frontiers." But there are reservations. Israel is entitled to security, and while I do not wish to be an annexationist, I could not consider the 1949 (you say by mistake 1948) armistice frontiers as sacrosanct, and would think rectifications for which you make an allowance in your letter to be justified and indeed indispensable on those trouble spots like the Syrian ridge, the Sinai border, the Straits of Tiran. But I hasten to add that if other effective guarantees for our security could be devised – by way of demilitarisation, international force (not one always exposed to be sent unilaterally packing), international government – I dare say there would not be any insistent pressure for far-reaching territorial changes. The Gaza strip cannot remain an Egyptian enclave.

Israel has repeatedly offered Jordan free access to Israeli ports on the Mediterranean, and although I cannot see the necessity for Syria, which has good ports of her own, of free access to Haifa, surely in an atmosphere of good neighbourly relations this request, like the question of a right of way for Egypt through Israeli Arab territory to the other Arab States, would not present an insurmountable obstacle. But for this, free passage for Israeli shipping through the Suez canal is a precondition.

The question of Jerusalem is a point *sui generis*, and on this our opinions are likely to differ. Of one thing I can assure you: there is no person or group of persons of any standing in Israel, even among the ultra-orthodox, who would dream of rebuilding the Temple and destroying Muslim or other sanctuaries. The whole matter is not worth a moment of your anxiety. At the same time, public opinion in Israel is so unanimous and determined on the retention of Jerusalem that no government would survive a week if it showed signs of giving in on that. I invite the historian Arnold Toynbee to weigh the pros and cons of this issue in historical perspective and with the historian's detachment, difficult as it is to treat this loaded problem in that way.

If Israel is prepared, and indeed is most anxious, to submit all holy places to international administration and supervision exercised by the accredited representatives of the various religions, Christian and Muslim, with extra territoriality guaranteed, why should there be all that fuss about sovereignty over the areas which do not contain any holy places? In what way was the Hashemite dynasty of Jordan, whose rule over Jordan resulted from a pure post-World War I accident and indeed a British embarrassment, a more trustworthy guardian than an Israeli government, which (as you hint) has hostages in all the Christian nations? The Jordanians have not left a single synagogue standing in Old Jerusalem and paved the road with tombstones from the ancient cemetery on the Mount of Olives. Are we not faced here with a residue of that unhappy, age-long special attitude to the nation of deicides, whose inferiority to Christendom (and Islam) must be made especially manifest, and the members of which must never be allowed to rule or command the members of the true and triumphant faith? Internationalisation? I seem to detect signs that the Vatican has by no means made up its mind on the desirability of a Jerusalem run by the UN, in which pagan, communist-atheist and Muslim, not to speak of Protestant powers, constitute the vast majority. Finally, may I recall the tremendous agitation against the incorporation of Rome, the capital of Christendom, the seat of the Holy See, into the Kingdom of Italy in the nineteenth century. It requires an effort of imagination today to visualise a situation in which Rome is not the capital of Italy, but the free state of the Pope or an international city.

This brings me to my last and most immediately practical point: how to go about getting peace.

Like very many Israelis I fervently desire an early arrangement with King Hussein of Jordan. In order not to lose myself in too sanguine illusions I would say no more than that this solution appears to me to be the least impossible of all solutions talked of. The Israelis have genuine respect and a sneaking affection for the brave little King, and one can hear expressions of almost sympathetic regret that he would have made the terrible blunder he did. Incidentally, the total absence in Israel of any hatred or contempt for the Arabs as such is best illustrated by the fact that the spate of songs and poems of war and victory has not produced a single hate hymn; and never has any note of abuse crept into radio or press. There have been only minor cases of plunder which received prompt punishment, although in the heat of firing and sniping there seems to have been some unnecessary destruction of houses. The people left homeless were soon provided with shelter. I believe it is our interest to come to terms with Jordan and that Hussein stands to gain no less than we from such a settlement which would return to him most of the West Bank, except Jerusalem, its immediate vicinity and a few strategic points elsewhere, while ensuring to Jordanians some form of free access to Jerusalem and the Holy places of Islam. I believe, like you, that the international community, especially the West, would be enthusiastically ready to offer very large sums and sponsor a joint international venture, with Israel and Jordan as partners, designed to resettle the refugees, execute those public works of irrigation and desalination you mention, solving thereby not only the refugee problem, but restoring Hussein to his former position. A common stake in joint prosperity would thus be created. Would Hussein dare to take such a step alone? Objectively speaking, Egypt and Syria can afford not to conclude any arrangement with Israel and play the part of the intransigent patriots; Jordan just cannot exist without it. Hussein had been for so long cruelly vilified and ill-used by the more powerful Arab

States. In the war he and his army have acquitted themselves very honourably and the sacrifices made by them have been infinitely greater than those by other Arab States. So he has done more than his share to fight for Arab honour.

It is quite possible that once the shouting against Hussein for having come to terms with Israel had died down, the other Arab States would tire of their excitement and get down to their internal affairs and gradually slide into some modus vivendi, or even follow Hussein's example fairly soon.

Now I am going to stick out my neck with a good many Jews just as you in your words stuck out your neck with your Arabs. I dislike the idea of a separate little autonomous Arab State in the West Bank of Jordan which would be a camouflaged Israeli protectorate. Not only because I doubt its economic viability, am apprehensive of the crushing financial and administrative burden it is sure to impose upon Israel, fear its irredentism, and the grave security problems arising out of it. I recoil from the idea of Jews lording it over others. It is at variance with the image of Judaism I cherish, and the example of other nations makes me fear the dangers to the moral fibre, the psychological balance, and spiritual values lying in wait for a master race.

I pray that we shall not be compelled to assume that role, which may happen if an arrangement with Jordan proves impossible and the other Arab States refuse to establish peace with Israel.

You speak movingly of your grandchildren. I understand you well. I am a younger man and I have two small children. When I look into their eyes, I think of the million Jewish children whom the Nazis separated from their parents, starved to death and killed in the gas chambers. At such moments my heart goes out to all the children of the world, Arab, Vietnamese and all others, and I feel like crying aloud: "Never, never again."

Yours sincerely,
J. L. TALMON

First published in *Encounter*, October 1967.

Note

1 The repatriation of the 1967 refugees was taken for granted in this letter. – *A.I.T.*

An Open Letter to the Minister of Information

HAKIRIA, JERUSALEM

The Honorable Mr. Galili,

I recently read an account of your speech at the United Kibbutz Conference in which you stated: "We do not consider the Arabs of the land an ethnic group nor a people with a distinct national character."

Likewise, I read similar statements and other reports presented at the above-mentioned conference. One encounters daily, strange, stupid and even infuriating statements. If one were to spend time answering them – and they are numerous – one would have to devote oneself entirely to this task. I do not happen to belong to this category of people who have nothing better to keep them occupied. However, on this occasion, I have decided to answer your statement with an open letter. In doing so, I am driven by my sense of duty toward you as a Minister of Information, toward the issue that concerns all of us – the future of the State of Israel – and also toward myself, as the problem interrelates with the field of study to which I have devoted my life.

I have recently returned from a long trip after spending one year and a half outside Israel, mainly in the United States. During this time, I worked as a research fellow and a visiting professor at three esteemed academic institutions. I also had the opportunity to lecture on the problems of Israel and the Middle East within my field of study at more than twenty universities all over America. This provided me with an excellent opportunity to become acquainted with public opinion, to test the opinions and feelings of students and intellectuals, and to observe political developments. America, today, has seven million students in addition to hundreds of thousands of professors, and undoubtedly, you are aware of the influence of those students and professors on public opinion, political and economic issues, and even on security decisions.

As my letter relates to our Israeli problem, I would like to mention that I had the honor of delivering the opening speech at the

Conference of American Professors' Association for Peace in the Near East. The word "clarification" does not mean "monologue" but "dialogue" in which one side, in an effort to convince the other of the righteousness of its opinions, is forced to understand the psychology of that other side, to distinguish between acceptable and ineffective claims, and to stir either support or enmity. If this is the meaning of "clarification" then some credit might be attributed to my experience in this respect. Furthermore, as the topic of discussion related to ideological matters and the definition of nationalism, my academic research in ideologies and socio-nationalistic movements for the last thirty years is worth mentioning.

However, I am not writing to you merely to discuss a problem that outrages me, but because your above-mentioned statement presents me with a difficult choice that weighs on my conscience, and promotes a clash between two kinds of loyalties – my loyalty to my conscience and that to my government's policy. Only a few days ago, I received an invitation from The Center for Study of Near Eastern Problems at Harvard University to lecture on "The Spiritual and Cultural Depths of Israel." My speech will be one in a series of discussions on the problems of the Middle East. The suggested topic – "The Spiritual and Cultural Depths of Israel" – implies moral aspects as well. This will force me to touch indirectly upon the topic raised in your statement if not to discuss it directly. Even if I try to avoid the issues – which is not really possible unless I exercise deceit – it is certain that there will be people who will raise the question and demand that I take a stand. Furthermore, there may be among those present some who have read your statements and may use them as arguments, especially as the members of this Center carefully follow everything that is being said and done in our area. I, personally, have come across them in two newspapers placed within parentheses, suggesting that you intended them as official policy statements.

In the eyes of the world and mine as well, the problem of recognizing or not recognizing the Palestinian Arabs as a people with the right of self-determination is considered to be the crucial problem according to which we will be judged as to whether we are searching for reconciliation and peace or expansion, whether we respect the rights of others or ignore them. This will be the measure according to which will be decided the democratic and moral nature of our state. Those who say that our recognition of the rights of the Palestinian Arabs will only shake our right to exist as a state are totally misinformed. The reverse is the truth, as recognizing the right of others lends moral support to our claims, while denying them their rights deprives us of every moral right – at least in the eyes of non-Jews. To those, we cannot advance the claim that God has bestowed upon us a "Koshan" over Jenin and Nablus.

You, sir, could have argued with more accuracy that the Palestinian Arabs form a part of the large Arab element for scientific, geographical, historical, and economic reasons and may thus not be justified in obtaining recognition as a separate ethnic group. Hence, that it is not a huge sacrifice for the gigantic Arab world to relinquish its sovereignty over a small portion of the vast areas under its jurisdiction. Or you could have said that it would be more practical for all the West Bank inhabitants to go back to Jordan. Had you expressed anything of the sort, you would have avoided the loud challenge and insult that filled your recent statement.

It is possible to argue that what non-Jews say is of no consequence – yet, under *such* circumstances, we should stop talking vacuously about the necessity of "clarification." Moreover, we should then actively withdraw from being a nation within the family of nations, and retract to a state where we can be a closed, isolated, religious sect with no partnership in the general destiny of humanity and no feeling of obligation toward it. In such a case, we would have no right to complain to the world or expect any help from it.

I am deeply aware of the fact that your statement seriously endangers both the possibilities of peace in the area and Israel's reputation as a state. It likewise endangers the vital interests of this state and the status of Jews in the world. Moreover, it can cause the alienation of some important Jewish groups in the world, and will as such be regarded as a sin against morals, good taste, understanding, and academic integrity. It utterly contradicts examples from history and offends the sensitivity of the staunch supporters of humanity and justice in the world.

I beg you, sir, to instruct me how to overcome this problem. I do not wish to discredit my government's policy in front of a group of strangers (members of the Study Center at Harvard) some of whom have held or will be holding important positions in America's political nerve center. Yet, at the same time, I cannot deceive myself and justify or even defend a stand which I consider immoral and also underlying a tragedy. Should I refuse the invitation? Such behavior will only be interpreted as cowardice and escapism.

Please instruct me how and in what manner I should answer

arguments that are bound to come up as they have frequently done in the past. Those who have brought them up are neither evil nor can they be dismissed as haters of Israel. On the contrary, they have been friends of Israel, and in some instances, of the Jewish faith. They argue: You are right when you refused to withdraw from your present positions (cease-fire lines) before starting negotiations or even realizing peace. Throughout history there has not been an instance where the victor withdrew before the defeated at least started to negotiate with him. Your demand to be accorded secure and recognized borders is also a preliminary matter, and your insistence on free navigation may well be a just one. Your stubbornness concerning Jerusalem and the Golan Heights is understandable and is subject to discussion. It is not even possible to rebuke your government for protecting its people against terrorism, gun-fire at night, and bomb explosions in populated areas. We will support you if you are afraid of terrorists' activities even after arriving at an agreement with the Arabs which does not include the elimination of these organizations. It is even possible to understand you when you revolt against the Big Powers' attempt to impose a settlement concerning your very existence without your participation, though History is full of such solutions under similar circumstances. The Jewish national home itself and the establishment of the State of Israel were a result of one of these agreements among the Big Powers imposed on the Arabs.

That is what they generally say, then they proceed to ask: Don't you see that your refusal to recognize the Palestinian Arabs as an ethnic group and a people with its own distinctive and nationalistic character means that you are actually saying that they are unimportant natives with no identity, i.e. with no rights under these circumstances? Why are you puzzled, then, when Arabs, or their friends, describe you as imperialists as long as you do not recognize the principle of mutual rights and instead seek expansion? They continue: Some words are more painful than physical blows and, man may remember them longer – or may even find it more difficult to forgive those who inflicted the injury. Moreover, by using such logic, are you not transforming yourself into a foreign relations employee in the service of Arab extremists just as Mr. Shukeiri and some Arab propagandists served Israel in May, 1967, when they called for the annihilation of the state?

What do I say, sir, when confronted with facts like these? Should I say that a man belonging to a certain nationality is entitled to make decisions and issue statements concerning a people and judge whether they do or do not form a nation? This, sir, is taking place in the last third of the twentieth century, some two hundred years after the advent of nationalism, keeping in mind that such a decision is an absolute right of the people concerned. Moreover, a claim of this sort about the Palestinian people seems to be a devilish irony precisely because it is issued by a socialist and a member of a people – I am one of them – who fought bitterly twenty years ago against the allies and others who denied them this same right.

Anti-Semitic Polish employees wrote the word "Jew" – "ZYD" – with a small "z" which indicates that Judaism is a religious sect, as a capital "Z" would have indicated a nationality. The Polish extremists also refused to use the word "Ukrainian" and called the Ukrainians "Rusinis." The German nationalists, prior to 1913, called the Poles in the Eastern Reich areas "Wassen-Polaken," while the Rumanians were called "Woolkhaim" by their persecutors. The Hungarians refused to use the word "Slovac" – the Czechoslovakians were ruled by the Hungarians for 1,000 years – and the Germans used expressions like "Bohemian" and "Moravian" but never "Czechoslovakian." Finally, even Russia, under the Tzars, changed the name of Poland to "the land on the Vestula." Did this help to change nations in any way? And do we want to join this aggregate of dictatorships who persecuted our people?

In addition, I would like to seek your advice as Minister of Information, as to what to answer the educated and intellectuals of the world when they ask me: Why should not the Arab who reads Minister Galili's words, join the terrorists? If you steal his nationality away from the Palestinian, what else does he have to lose? Or do you assume that he has no sense of nationalism or concept of honor? Did not the Haganah and Stern resort to terrorism when the British wanted to force you to forgo the establishment of a separate political and national entity?

Yes, I am seriously asking you, sir, what should my answer be? Again, I emphasize the fact that I am not making up or inventing these questions. Rather, in keeping with my intellectual integrity as a historian, I try to look at all aspects of every problem and avoid being transformed into a liar and a propagandist.

Will you instruct me what to say to a wise, good-hearted, non-Jew when he says to me: Your claim that your security requires the assimilation of a million and a half Arabs, who do not want you and who harbor the deepest enmity toward you, only indicates that your state will not last. What kind of security can you gain when 40 per cent of the residents of your state are your enemies – add to this the fact that their national increase is greater than yours, all this at a time when bitter nationalistic struggles are taking place in ancient, rich and socially stable states like Cyprus, Canada, Belgium, and Great Britain. This is all accompanied by bombs, bullets and all sorts of violence and destruction.

This non-Jew will proceed to say: Israel will not only be unable to survive but will not deserve to, neither will she have the right to ask for assistance for, in this case, she will merely be a police state pursuing a persecution policy not unlike that of Rhodesia.

What should I say? And what should my colleagues, who are multiplying in number and who think like I do, say? Please do not accuse me of weakness in my Zionist beliefs or brand me as a Jew insensitive to the righteousness of our common problems and our aims. If selfishness – even were it to be viewed as Holy Nationalistic egoism – and non-recognition of other people's rights are signs of health and deep-rootedness, while sensitivity and self-criticism, in this field, should signify sickness, I prefer to be among the sick, and do not envy the "healthy" for what they have.

I hope that you are not tempted to denounce our Zionist and Jewish loyalty or to throw at us accusations such as "cosmopolitan," "decayed," and "non-rooted," – as it is enough for me here to hint at where, when, and who invented the terms "rooted" and "real" on the one hand and "cosmopolitan" or "nihilist" on the other. It was my destiny to bury myself for twenty years in this kind of filthy literature composed by evil people and haters of Israel.

I met an educated American girl at one of the better universities there who has relatives occupying top positions at both the Foreign Ministry and in the field of education in Israel. She argued: It is indeed a disturbing experience for one to discover the impotence of Israelis to understand that the world should not say Amen to everything they like or do. Even if what they like is their soul's desire and is likened to the love of the most dignified and beautiful of all women – a love that has been unequalled since Adam and Eve – Israelis should not feel that everyone is called upon to give up their vital interests in order to help the lover get his desire.

Did we not know this for a fact twenty years ago and yet have persisted in ignoring the rights of the Arabs while the world stood and watched? (Some Israelis say: If we have no right over Jenin, then this means that we have no right over Tel Aviv.) A big difference should be kept in mind between *then* and *now*. At that time, millions of Jews were being persecuted, lived in constant danger, and had no homes of their own. Their souls longed for Zion and they had no place else to turn to.

Our tragedy, Mr. Galili, is that those Jews do not exist any more. In the past, nations supported us because of the disasters that befell us and not because we possessed historical rights. Romanticism (the dream of Israel) had to slow down out of necessity, thus in spite of our miserable conditions, we agreed to the 1948 Partition Plan. Tactics alone did not constitute the sole reason for our agreement. We regarded the resolution as a just solution for the clash between two rights. This clash and its solution were described by Mr. Weizmann as causing the least possible harm. The agreement was a victory for justice among nations, although, at the time, some people showed reservations and hidden thoughts. (A reference to the demand voiced by some Israeli leaders to reject the resolution and occupy *all* of Palestine in 1948.)

Nowadays it is difficult for us to entice Jewish immigrants to this country even when we promise them grand apartments with modern ventilation and furniture. Only one third of the Jews who leave Poland come to Israel. We dreamed of immigration from Russia long before the possibility of border expansion was raised. Non-Jews in America, France and Britain today, see very rich Jews around them leading a grand life and advancing into top positions. One more thing has changed: the age of imperialism has ended, and do you, sir, believe, for one second, that the United Nations, in its present composition, would have decided on establishing a Jewish state?

The Zionist dream is the most idealistic among the available nationalistic samples in history. Statements like yours contribute to the destruction of this dream and force the world to hate it. Only by recognizing the rights of the neighboring people (the Palestinians) to live as they choose, to be independent or to unite with Jordan, can the justice of our cause be recognized.

Mr. Galili, how can I disprove the New Left claim, when it is argued that here is the case of one nation stepping on another and transforming it into a tool to uphold its existence, and laud its aims, security and development. It is as though these people were not the creation of God, and were not entitled to their own objectives. Such things smack of supremacy and racism.

Your answer may well be: The situation is quite the opposite. The Arabs are the ones who deny our right to exist and threaten us with annihilation. Well then, are we supposed to follow suit? And what virtues remain then for our cause?

Historical allegations are meaningless. Historians with whom I am familiar remind me that Italy had to give up Nice, the birthplace of Garibaldi, hero of the Italian Renaissance when it gained its independence and unity in 1860. It also had to give up Savoy, seat of the royal family which liberated Italy. One can hardly mention Germany without speaking of Königsberg, birthplace of Kant and the city that witnessed the crowning of the Kings of Prussia. And were not most Polish heroes and poets born and raised in districts annexed to Russia after World War II? Did not the Germans, especially the Social Democrats in the Weimar period, believe that their major objective was to unify all German-speaking people like Austrians, Swedes and others? And did not Marshall Foch at the Versailles Conference, claim that the security of France demanded the Rhine as a natural border, repeating what generations of French politicians had said before?

The feelings of these people were strong, deep and full of enthusiasm, yet, the world did not respond. It should not surprise you, Mr. Galili, to hear that the public polls in America showed that only 9 per cent of the people advocate extending help to Israel in the event of an attack by a communist country – less than those who showed willingness to help Rumania, 13 per cent; Kenya, 21 per cent; or Thailand, 25 per cent.

You may inquire, how dare I compare our pure and dignified movement to that of the Germans, Italians, Russians, and the like? My answer is: Research has shown that every individual and every people feels that it is unique. To a certain extent this is a *fact* especially from the subjective feelings of those directly involved. Who can delve into the depths, personalities, or even heartbeats of others? Yet spectators cannot avoid searching for similarities in others – however large or small those similarities are – as a group with a common denominator. It is more difficult to decide what are the more significant: those that unite or those that divide.

Human beings do not accept exaggeration either from individuals or from nations. Generally, people understand and sympathize with a poor, tortured individual or nation – but their feelings change when the subject turns almighty proclaiming his greatness, strength and righteousness. "What is important is that our army is very strong. All the world recognizes that" (Dayan's statement). No one who has studied history, gathered a little information about conflicts among peoples, or is familiar with class struggles, will naïvely believe that anthems and oaths can solve deep and conflicting problems among nations Everyone recognizes the meaning of force as there exists an infinite number of examples of powerful, proud occupied nations who have toppled overnight from the peak to the bottom and from there to the deepest abyss. There is not one example of a people that has obtained an everlasting treaty through its Minister of "History."

There is a basic discrepancy in a motto which becomes a disease and which states that Arabs do not understand except the language of power and will even never surrender or agree to peace unless placed under desperate conditions. Only the few have taken the trouble to discover that the opposite may be true, and that, if we place the Arabs under such conditions, they might decide that they have nothing more to lose and, hence, may resort to Samsonic behavior.

I do not know of one instance where a nationalistic movement has stopped because it has been dealt a blow or brought to the brink of despair. There are countless examples of nationalistic movements which, after verging on exhaustion and nearing death, have retrieved their ranks and regained new strength. Our own people is a living example of that.

In Israel today, I see two contradictory stands: the first – basically a defeatist attitude – advocates that we squeeze as much as we can from the Arabs as they are determined to refute our very existence, and it is not to our advantage that they do so. In my view, this defeatist attitude will, on the practical level, only signal the resumption of endless fighting and total destruction. As for the second group, they believe that the time for reconciliation is now, and may prove to be the last chance. Therefore, we ought to make it easier for the moderate Arabs who sincerely and publicly declare their readiness to accept a settlement imposed by the Great Powers. We should further simplify matters for them either by taking a step to spare them humiliation and possibly help them escape assassination, or else we could agree to an international peace conference where delegates from other nations can join in the discussions. This has been repeated over and over again in the history of conflicts among nations. We can take advantage of the fear of the Big Two of a nuclear confrontation between them and also of their joint fear of

China which is bringing them closer. All this can be attempted without slowing down our military preparations, even *after* arriving at an agreement.

We, the children of refugees, purposely belittle the urgency of the refugees' problem. Nevertheless, we go back and repeat in the tone of "real" politicians with vast experience that we constitute the best army to protect American interests in the area, and that America depends on us much more than we depend on her. We pretend to know her interests more than she does herself – and yet, we are shocked by the Russian and the New Left reaction to this boasting.

Everyone who knows America, however little, and is aware of her techniques and policy, must realize that our own attitude is immature. This is becoming clearer by the day. Such claims may have been relevant forty or fifty years ago with respect to Great Britain. Today, how does an Englishman feel after losing his Empire together with the Suez Canal, the Middle East, and India, when he assesses his country's blunders in those areas? Starting with the Balfour Declaration and ending with the sad and shameful termination of the Mandate, what is this Englishman's regard for his country's shameful role?

When I served in the Jewish Diplomatic Service toward the end of World War II, those who were my superiors – some dear old Jews who aged in the service of people either by waiting patiently in passageways or exhausting themselves in pursuing ministers of state – taught me that anyone who helps bring about peace among nations contributes to Israel's peace. Today, some of our leaders scream: "Danger! The Russians may give in to the Americans and the two may reach an agreement." There are those who panic every time they hear of an improvement in the possibility of peace in Vietnam. Should the Big Powers agree – knowing that without their agreement in 1947–48 Israel would not have been created disregarding the changes that have taken place in Russian policy since – and find a solution, "we are unwilling to discuss it (Golda Meir); we will not even bother to examine its contents."

Many are those who rejoice when they see a fist shaking in the air, especially when it is a woman's fist. But, as Queen Victoria said: "This does not amuse me." I do not view this as an incentive to Jewish pride, for I need no compensation for an inferiority complex resulting from exile. For, even in exile, I did not feel as an exiled Jew and I do not envy you, sir, if you find it necessary to sell this trade to nations. You may have to beg for it from Jews when this game of "anger" clearly becomes useless and demands no justification.

Power, power, almighty power! What is essential is that our army is very mighty and the world knows it. Were we not brought up on the motto, "Not by force, but by spirit"? Did we not grow generations without tiring; boasting about class equality, recognition of other people's rights, and campaigning for the rights of the weak? Did we not always revolt against being transformed into a tool for others? Have we not revolted against being called parasites? Nowadays, power has become our absolute aim and we consider the neighboring people as instruments to fulfil our divine interests. This may be the real "Munich" committed by the Jewish people against its own past. A more harmful "Munich" than giving up Jenin or Jericho. The results will even prove worse for Austrian Jews – for why should nations henceforth grant equality to Jews or why should they allow Jews to occupy high positions? Moreover, if the stand of American Jews grows weaker or if they perish – God forbid – would Israel then be built on the tragic plight of the largest Jewish community in history?

It is also my duty to mention one other danger, which is alienating the good and the educated young Jews from Judaism. This is as serious as complete annihilation. I still clearly remember the farewell words of an educated Jew, a genius of this generation and a spokesman for the American Left: "Don't put us in a position where we are forced to choose between our loyalty to the human ideals we are fighting for and our loyalty to Israel. Remember always that everything has a limit and don't alienate us from you – don't force us to disintegrate."

Y. TALMON

First published in *Ma'ariv*, September 1969; translated into English and published as *A Letter to his Establishment by an Israeli Intellectual* by the Arab Information Center, New York 1969).

The Mideast War – A Rejoinder

Dear Professor Amit,

May I start my reply to your Open Letter (*NYR*, November 29, 1973) by pointing out the differences in our approaches, yours as a scientist and mine as a historian. Dialectical thinking seems to be alien to you. Nor do you appear to have much feeling for the dynamics of historical events and situations. This is at the root of our present disagreement. A government statement, an official handout, a conference resolution, and a sentence in a minister's speech are treated by you not only at their face value but as if they were components of a chemical experiment and data in a physical process.

Our statement presented the Yom Kippur War as a war for Israel's very existence and spoke of the Arabs' basic desire to destroy the state of Israel, whereas you refer to Arab declarations which in your view indicate no such intention, but rather a desire for political settlement. You fail to see that even if these were meant seriously and sincerely when they were made, once the guns began to roar a new and very different dialectic was created by them from that in peace time. War develops a momentum and a dynamic of its own. Do you really believe that had the going proved to be good and the Egyptian tanks had broken through in the direction of Tel Aviv and the Syrian troops reached Tiberias or Haifa – as seemed quite possible when we were drafting our statement – past conciliatory Arab statements would have halted the élan of success, the sweep forward, and the fury of the more determined, the more ruthless, and the more extreme? There would have been nothing to stop the Arab victors at the 1967 borders and to prevent wholesale massacre, not to speak of the liquidation of the state of Israel.

In face of the stark fact of imminent mortal danger to the homeland created by so much idealism, toil, and sacrifice, on the morrow of Auschwitz and of the unspeakably tragic end of over a thousand-year-old civilization in Central and Eastern Europe, what relevance had all that careless talk of one's own loose-tongued and excitable politicians, the occasional lack of restraint, tact, prudence, or foresight by government, the mystique of manifest destiny which turned the heads of some Israeli scribes, to which you refer, and all of which have hardly made any significant, lasting, and irreversible change in the position of the territories occupied since June, 1967?

In the hour of the supremely dangerous surprise attack, the grimmest diagnosis of Arab intentions, the vital importance of defensible borders, the fate in store for us had we had no strategic depth to delay the attackers assumed terrible reality. You seem to have been so strongly affected by the experience of the anti-Vietnam War stand of the intellectuals in America that you have become oblivious to the abysmal difference between what was at stake for the US in Vietnam and what was at stake for the Israelis in Israel: a matter of a great power's prestige and perhaps ideological commitment as compared with the physical survival of the Yishuv, indeed, in my opinion, also of Judaism as a corporate entity in the Diaspora, since the destruction of Israel was sure to deal an irreparable moral blow to Jews all over the world.

You give the impression of one of those left-wing intellectuals who can find all the excuses and mitigating circumstances for the nastiness of foreign governments but can never free themselves of the worst suspicions regarding the leaders of their own country.

You grow eloquent about the traumatic experiences which inhibit the Arabs from meeting the Israelis face to face, but you seem to give hardly any weight to Israeli traumas, fears, suspicions, and blockages which make them deeply apprehensive of the Arab refusal to talk to them, and which consequently hinder them from agreeing to a total withdrawal to the June 4, 1967, borders and from accepting a Palestinian state on the West Bank run by the Palestine Liberation Organization, pledged to wipe out the state of Israel through indiscriminate terror, boycott, and sabotage, as distinct from a Palestinian–Jordanian federation which Israel favors.

You rightly deprecate annexationist declarations and moves by Israeli leaders as contradicting the statements on Israeli readiness to negotiate without prior conditions, but you take no exception to the Arabs' relentless insistence on the prior acceptance of the principle of total withdrawal from all the occupied territories, as if that were not a precondition. You furthermore appear to assume that the conflict only began in June, 1967, and that it was only the Israeli refusal to give up the territories then acquired that stood in the way of a peaceful solution. Surely the Six Day War was only an explosion of a deep-seated and prolonged crisis, and it is not enough just to sweep away all that happened after June 4, 1967, to cure it. You hardly mention Israeli anxiety to secure defensible borders and guarantees for its continued existence, and do not give a thought to the nature of the desired peace settlement.

I do not see any reason to retract the view which I expressed in 1968, that had the Arabs shown any sign of readiness to recognize the state of Israel as a datum, a fact of nature and history, and demonstrated it in the only convincing manner in which such an attitude can be proved – namely by responding to Israeli requests to meet face to face, to negotiate all and everything with no preconditions – the Israeli government would have come forward to meet them more than half way, and Israeli public opinion would have overwhelmingly accepted a reasonable compromise. I have referred in one of my articles to the private conversation I had with the late Prime Minister Eshkol only a few days after the Six Day War, in which he told me, "I do not want Arab territory. At last we have something to offer to the Arabs: territory in exchange for peace."

Our government communicated this attitude to the American government a month after the war. It was the implacable No of the Khartum Conference, sustained and made painfully persuasive by guerrilla action and terror, that caused so many people in Israel to despair of the possibility of a peaceful settlement and to turn all their attention to strategic considerations. It was this No that fortified others in their mystical belief that God was hardening the heart of Pharaoh and inspiring His people to fulfill their destiny by recovering the totality of the promised land, and that finally goaded those on whom the triumph of Israeli arms had too intoxicating an impact to dream of some kind of imperial action on a minute scale. This never became the unanimous resolve or the general mood of the population, or indeed the policy of the Israeli government, whose gravest sin was actually *immobilisme.*

Like other "peace mongers" in Israel, including the present writer, you seem most reluctant to remember that for every single conciliatory Arab statement one could quote hundreds of hair-raising and blood-curdling threats and torrents of abuse in the Nazi style. And when examined critically with the help of philological Arab scholarship, even the Arabs' moderate utterances turn out to have shades of meaning which are by no means reassuring. For instance, they speak not of peace, but of non-belligerency; not of recognition of the state of Israel, but of recognition of borders. All in all, until the Yom Kippur War, what the Arabs had really been promising, when one discounts empty phraseology, amounts to: you first get out, get back to your June 4, 1967, borders, and then, then . . . . Would any state in the world have thrown away all the cards it held against a hardened adversary, whom it had so many reasons to distrust, for merely a most ambiguous expression of intent?

Then, then . . . is explained as meaning that even if we, in this case Egypt, make a declaration about ending the state of belligerency or even patch up some settlement, Israel will still have to restore "the legitimate national rights of the Palestinian people." The official Arab spokesmen prefer not to elaborate the point. But the guerrilla leaders never tire of proclaiming that they envisage not merely the establishment of a Palestinian state on the West Bank of the river Jordan, not just permission for Arab refugees to return to their old homes, or compensation for losses sustained and resettlement wherever possible, but after our return to the 1967 borders, Israeli withdrawal to the 1947 (as distinct from the cease-fire of 1949) borders, then the "total liberation of the soil of the Palestinian homeland,"[1] (which of course means the dismantling of the state of Israel), some add the "repatriation" of all the Jews who came to Palestine after 1948, and, in another version, since the November 2, 1917, Balfour Declaration on the Jewish National Home.

There is now a cease-fire, although unfortunately the guns are not yet quite silent. The process of peace-making has at an agonizingly late hour been started, and all men of good will must pray and labor for the success of the shaky and fragile enterprise. A dialectic quite different from that which became operative on the day of the Egyptian and Syrian attacks has now been set into motion. I can again take my bearings, as before Yom Kippur, from a perspective which makes the Arab–Israel conflict appear as a tragic clash of rights. Both sides are laboring under deep stress: the Jews were driven by homelessness, Holocaust, a great historic vision, and an unconquerable urge for national self-expression in their ancestral home, and the Arabs had their dream of restored greatness and glory frustrated by alien newcomers, repeated defeats on the battlefield, a grave refugee problem just at a time when the European powers were making their exodus from Asia and Africa.

To repeat a famous sentence by Dr. Weizmann, this is a problem which can only be solved on the lines of least injustice. Both sides have a case, and there can be no solution which is capable of offering full satisfaction to both sides. Any resolve of either side to achieve such complete satisfaction for itself is sure to perpetuate war, untold misery, and growing barbarization, and to lead to irreparable disaster for all concerned, including the two superpowers.

Since on both sides there are men in the grip of neurosis, engendered by deep resentments, injured pride, fears, suspicions, rancorous spite, it is the duty of all thinking and responsible people to do all in their power to combat hawkishness, hysteria, and wild talk in their own camp and carefully to spare susceptibilities in the other, and to try to alleviate the malady by dispelling specters and nightmares, by reducing things to their right proportions, and showing to men driven by furies where all this may lead. This is why, with all the terrible awareness of the ever-present contingency of annihilation, I have been urging my readers in Israel not to succumb to this kind of neurosis, lest the obsession become the cause of a self-fulfilling prophecy. Each side lives in genuine fear of the other. Rather asymmetrically, the Israelis fear Arab resolve completely to destroy them, the Arabs Israeli ambitions to overwhelm them in a very sensitive part of their domains.

Mutual fear is the cause of ceaseless escalation. It is therefore most imperative to break, at some point, this vicious circle: Israel by renouncing territorial claims beyond what is absolutely vital to its security and the Arabs by genuinely accepting Israel, and the world by offering and persuading the contending parties to devise guarantees that would give a greater feeling of security to both sides. The practical arrangements, including the territorial settlement, will emerge as a function of mutual trust shown in free negotiations by the Israelis on whom this war has had a sobering effect and by the Arabs who have come out of it with a greater self-assurance and a sense of regained honor.

J. L. TALMON
The Hebrew University, Jerusalem

First published in *The New York Review,* January 24, 1974. In the November 15 issue appeared a statement on the Mideast War signed by twenty-one members of the Hebrew University in Jerusalem. In the November 29 issue Prof. Daniel Amit of the Hebrew University replied in the form of an open letter to Prof. Jacob Talmon, one of the signers of the statement. This essay is Talmon's rejoinder to Amit.

Note

1 From the Aims of the Political Program of the Palestinian Revolution adopted by the 11th Palestine National Congress, Cairo, January 12, 1973, and confirmed now in the secret resolutions of the recently held top-level International Arab Conference in Algiers, which designated the Palestine Liberation Organization as the sole representative of the Palestinian people and granted its full support to past PLO decisions.

"The Homeland is in Danger" – An Open Letter to Menahem Begin

Dear Mr. Prime Minister,

"He hoped that it would bring forth grapes, but it brought forth sour grapes." It is now 33 years after the UN General Assembly's vote to establish a Jewish state and 32 years after the young state's soldiers, in the War of Independence, repulsed the Arab armies that threatened its existence. And it is now 14 years since our unprecedented victory in the Six-Day War, and two years after the historic breakthrough of Sadat's visit to Jerusalem. Yet, today we see that the State of Israel is the "Jew among the nations" – isolated, an outcast without legitimacy in the eyes of its enemies, and a nuisance to its friends: its people divided over the all-decisive existential question, its economy on the brink of ruin. . . .

It seems that the rule of law and order has collapsed and that the government is too feeble and cowardly to implement its own decisions or to withstand the pressures of various interest groups. The government encourages the growth of extraparliamentary groups who defy the state and seek to impose their will upon it by force, bringing the dream of a renewed Jewish statehood to derision. We witness with horror a massive emigration of our nation's citizens, among them many *sabras* [native Israelis]. We are also witnessing the heart-breaking spectacle of the Russian "drop-outs" – redeemed from bondage with help secured from the largest superpower – immigrants who seemed to symbolize a miraculous resurrection of the dead.

Among the Arab population, there are signs of an organized rebellion instead of the reconciliation envisaged on the basis of the autonomy plan, which was to supplement our treaty with the largest Arab nation. Hardly less alarming is the rampant assimilation of Jews in the Diaspora, only one generation after the Holocaust. What has produced this deterioration? Our task here is not to examine its immediate causes, but to try to understand its structural foundations.

Between the two world wars, the term "lost generation" was widely used in countries that had fought in the First World War. The term referred to the millions of young men who had fallen in the war, but especially to those who came from the elite, whose casualties – because of the unconventional and destructive method of fighting – were disproportionately high. A great many graduates of Oxford and Cambridge were lost in that bloodbath – and so were many of their equivalents in other nations.

One survivor, former English Prime Minister Harold Macmillan, devotes many heart-rending pages in his memoirs to express his sense of being one of the few survivors out of a large and closely knit fellowship. Contemporaries and historians of the 1920s and 1930s who seek to explain the poor quality and lack of imagination of politicians, the cowardly policy of appeasement, and the inability to halt the great economic crisis attribute all this to the absence of the lost generation.

But this catastrophe was nothing compared to the Holocaust that befell our people during the Second World War, resulting in the elimination of Jewish civilization from Europe. Those who were born and educated there before that catastrophe find it impossible to imagine the Jewish streets of the East and Central European cities that were destroyed, the silence of the *shtetlach* of the Pale of Settlement, never again to be broken by the sound of prayers coming from the *Bet Midrash* and the *hadarim*. . . . Silenced are the youth of the Hashomer Hatzair and the Betar who once sat around campfires that are now extinguished. Silenced are the prayers of lamentation, the women's "Don't cast us away when we have become old, when our strength has left us, do not abandon us," during the Days of Awe. Gone forever are the street debates between Zionists and Marxists. Gone are the Jewish girls who once greeted the coming of spring on the eve of Passover. Their strong will to live and their faith in the coming national and social revival were destroyed by suffering, humiliation, endless horror, and, finally, death.

My reader will forgive me for being so cruel as to commit to paper what many know but cannot bring themselves to utter: the melancholy truth that the Zionist national liberation movement achieved its goal at the very moment that it lost its standard-bearers. The winds around Auschwitz and Treblinka carry away the ashes of two million potential citizens of the State of Israel, people imbued with intense and genuine Zionist sentiment and the firmest Jewish roots. We shall never be able to replace them.

Yet, the state's first years counterbalanced some of this loss. They witnessed a great explosion of Jewish energy, intelligence, vigilant tension, and feverish activity. We all were summoned to build new foundations, and to absorb hundreds of thousands of immigrants. But the loss was felt later – once the first exuberance began to subside – about two or three years before the Six-Day War.

The very important result of the Six-Day War victory was that it appeared to many as a compensation for the martyrdom of the Holocaust, as a sign that the nation had heroically overcome its tragedy. Indeed, for many, this victory was a testimony to the great change that had taken place in our people – a people that only yesterday had been led like sheep to the slaughter and was now conquering empires.

Many among the Orthodox had difficulty accepting the Holocaust within the scheme of Providence and Jewish history, for they could not see the death of more than a million innocent Jewish children as punishment for sins of the whole Jewish people. What kind of sin would justify such punishment? They did not like to speak or think about the Holocaust. I remember Zalman Aranne's impassioned cry to the Orthodox representatives in the Knesset: "I will never forgive you for not having produced a second Book of Lamentations after the Holocaust!" After the Six-Day War, therefore, the Orthodox were much relieved, for now they could argue that the Holocaust had been the "birth pangs of the Messiah," that the Six-Day War victory was the Beginning of Redemption, and the conquest of the territories the finger of God at work – all proof that the vision of renewal and God's promises were being fulfilled.

The non-Orthodox nationalists soon caught this fever. A while ago, our Foreign Minister Yitzhak Shamir gave a perfect demonstration of this mentality when he said that our generation was not "entitled" to give up Judea and Samaria and the Gaza Strip – implying that these territories were the heritage of all generations of Jews, past, present, and future. Our generation, singled out to be the trustee of this heritage, does not have the "right" to let these sacred lands slip out of our hands.

Is this an eternal belief that will never falter or waiver? Is it loyalty to an ideal vision that no enemy, no suffering, no catastrophe will ever overcome? Or is this merely the characteristic, which the Jews may have bequeathed to other monotheistic religions – namely the need to subordinate oneself to an idea, to a vision of perfection, to an ascetic and ritualistic way of life – instead of treating life as it really is, as did the Greeks, for example, who perceived reality as a challenge and sought to extract from life and nature all the possibilities inherent in them, in order to expand the mind and give pleasure to both body and soul? In short, is it a compulsive drive that makes us deny our essential human nature? Or is this perhaps the sign of a tragic inability to live with the fact of the Holocaust and the reality it has left us with? Is it our inability to adjust to them and, consequently, a detachment from what Freud called "the reality principle"? Is it an escape into a world of mythological thought-patterns and emotions whose classical example may be found in Sabbatianism? What is the meaning of that widespread determination to return to where we were in 1939, and to go from there to the farthest reaches of our emotion, as if the ghastly bloodletting had never taken place and Jewish reality and global realities had remained unchanged?

The extent of our Six-Day War victory encouraged this trend. It made us forget that, in Nietzsche's words, "there are victories that are harder to bear than defeats," and that victory in battle is by no means proof of true and enduring strength, unless it is supported by other components, such as an adequate economic infrastructure, a homogenous population, appropriate geopolitical factors, favorable world opinion, a network of alliances, political experience, and more. For commitments or aspirations that exceed one's objective ability to carry them out are a trap. Pursuing policies that harm the vital interests of other important states – flying in the face of accepted values, of an age – give rise to an opposition that will undercut such political initiatives.

I have never doubted that we reached a turning point when the government of Israel in the summer or fall of 1967 (right after the Six-Day War) abandoned its declared policy that Israel has no territorial claims and is willing to return all occupied lands in exchange for peace. I regard this disavowal as a fatal error, a denial of the UN resolution on partition arrived at 20 years before that – and of the principle of partition itself. I believe this disavowal reopened the Israeli-Arab conflict, after the family of nations had recognized the solution that was reached as a stable and accepted fact of political life, despite the friction, the incidents of terror, and the general bloodletting. This new policy was a grievous error, and it had no chance of success.

There are some who argue that the Khartoum resolutions closed all the doors to peace. I am not an expert in these matters, but people whose opinion I respect claim that close inspection of these resolutions reveals more flexibility than was generally perceived. It is reasonable to suspect that there were those in the Israeli leadership and public who were relieved when the Khartoum conference created this impression, and when the "telephone call" from Hussein never came. I do not believe that the National Unity government and the Labor Alignment had a Machiavellian determination not to budge and not to give up one inch of captured territory. The majority, in fact, recoiled from the idea of total annexation. Yet, at the same time, it was unable to relinquish the territories for Zionist, political, and strategic reasons. There was also the evidence that our military superiority was unshakable, that the PLO's terror was bearable, that the Arab population was passive, Egypt had broken loose from Russia, Hussein was liquidating the terrorists, the Arab countries were as usual fighting among themselves, and America was not exerting pressure – on the contrary, it was supplying us with great quantities of aid and weapons. So why move?

You never know what can happen in the Middle East, and since politics cannot long endure inactivity or deadlock, and since the indecisive usually let themselves be dragged after the resolute, the government and the moderates had neither the strength nor the conviction to oppose partisan attempts to establish settlements, spontaneously, or with the support of sympathizers inside the government who provided half-hearted assistance or accepted whatever the settlers did as a *fait accompli*, or acted out of electoral considerations.

I remember a meeting initiated by then-Foreign Minister Abba Eban in 1969 between senior professors of the Hebrew University (of Jersusalem) and the leadership of the Ministry of Defense. I was asked to express my opinion. I said that as a historian whose diagnosis, like that of a physician, must not be influenced by personal interests, I did not know of any instance where a conflict as complicated and tinted with emotion, irrationality, fears, and feelings of vengeance was ever solved without the involvement of a superpower, alone or in concert with other powers, to offer advice, mediation, and sometimes to impose a solution. In a talk a few days ago with one of Israel's most talented and important diplomats, we agreed that history would not absolve the United States from the fault of not entering into the arena long before 1973. This should have been its responsibility as the leading superpower of the period.

Despite the usual boast of liberated nations of having achieved freedom solely by their own courage, there is almost no example in history in which a national movement did not require the active aid of at least one great power – whose support flowed from self-interest, or from historic or ideological sentiments. Naturally, support from abroad only comes once the people themselves have risen in revolt and proved their stubborn resistance. The Greeks in the nineteenth century were perhaps the first to succeed in kindling world opinion against their enemies by the use of a great myth. All the bravery and martyrology of the Irish and the Poles, however, did not help them in the twentieth century; no great power was prepared to tangle with Britannia, "ruler of the waves," or to risk tampering with the balance of the three great northern powers who regarded the dissection of Poland as basic to their alliances.

In recent years, our status has been that of rebels against the international system. Nothing is easier than to win applause for fulminations against the wicked gentiles, the stupidity and selfishness of the nations. Yet, all these accusations, though not groundless, do not explain our condition or advance our cause.

Every national liberation movement is initially a kind of rebellion against the international order. International law is usually on the side of the states that are in power. It consecrates existing authority and the status quo. Rebels seek to change things, if necessary by force; they try to move borders, to upset the balance of power. But every liberation movement that attains independent statehood expresses – by the very act of joining the family of nations – its willingness to accept the rules of the international game by fulfilling two conditions: a readiness to accept international law and proof of its ability to maintain law and order within its own borders regardless of the nature of the regime.

In the last two or three years, the State of Israel sometimes has given the impression that it is far from scrupulous in its observance of the first condition, and that it is incapable of fulfilling the second. The doctrines proclaimed by Israel's official spokesmen, or by spokesmen in good standing with the government, are directly opposed, or unacceptable, to the family of nations. Situations are created that are reminiscent of the stand of revolutionary France, which, by proclaiming the principle of the people's sovereignty, denied the obligations taken on earlier by the French kings vis-à-vis other kings at a time when they embodied the sovereignty of their states. Yet, France still demanded that the foreign kings' commitments toward France continue as valid obligations, since these other states had not yet liberated themselves from the monarchical yoke.

We claim, similarly, that the West Bank and the Gaza Strip are not conquered territories and that therefore the restrictions of international law do not apply to us, particularly with regard to settlement, confiscation of land, and so forth, since we consider these lands to have been "liberated." This claim, by the way, has a long and respectable history; for the term "occupation" went out of fashion with the French Revolution and every conqueror since has proclaimed himself a "liberator." The extremists in Gush Emunim, on the other hand, use religious sanctions in order to justify their activities in the territories.

There is nothing more contemptible and harmful than the use of religious sanctions in a conflict between nations. It is doubtful whether the young man from Gush Emunim who made the Elon Moreh appeal had any idea of the Pandora's box he was opening when he argued, crudely but in a seemingly honest manner, that he and his comrades wanted to settle in the place they had chosen not for reasons of security but because God had commanded the Children of Israel to inherit the Land of Canaan. Wars of religion cannot be resolved by compromise, by "give and take a little"; and this young man was provocatively inviting a Muslim declaration of *Jihad* and a Vatican pronouncement that since the Jews had rejected Jesus they were no longer the "chosen people" and thus God's promises to Abraham were now invalid.

A religious claim is valid when it relates to matters between people and their creator – to prayer, fast, atonement, faith, and ritual. It does, however, inspire opposition if it disregards others' claims and assumes the right to impose its way, or to harm the rights, freedoms, and interests of others. A religious claim will give a strong impression of hubris, an ambition of mastery, if it tries to subordinate the believers of one religion to those of another. It is one thing for the believer to remain within the boundaries of debate over passages in his holy books and theological commentaries; it is quite another if behind him stand tanks, planes, missiles, soldiers, and police, ready to use direct or indirect violence.

An influential American journalist told me recently about "a dialogue of the deaf and dumb" he had held with members of Gush Emunim who had attempted to persuade him that theirs was a holy war. The non-Jew pressed them: "What does the use of tanks and planes, the occupation of territories and political rule, have to do with religion?" "Don't you understand," they replied, "for us, religion is total, and religious commandments and political practice are interdependent." This kind of Khomeinism is likely to return us to the days when millions were ready to join the Crusades to slaughter millions of others in order to keep them from going to Hell, in their own way, and to the early militaristic days of Islam when Holy War was declared against non-believers desecrating the name of God and thereby insulting the believers. This is just like Qaddafi of Libya, who dreams of an Islamic Europe and feels an obligation to aid all, including terrorist anarchists, who seek to shake the foundations of Western civilization.

After hundreds of thousands had been killed, or had died of hunger and plague, and entire nations had been destroyed, Europe grew tired of religious wars. Shrewd people realized that before the believers would have a chance to arrive in Heaven, the zealots on all sides would have turned the earth into Hell. They resolved to separate religion completely from politics, just as they had once separated religion from science. Claims such as those of Gush Emunim sound to the international community much like that biblical passage – "Sun, stand thou still upon Gibeon, and thou, Moon, in the Valley of Ayalon" – would sound in an astronomers' debate.

In the eyes of most of the earth's people – that is to say, the cultures that do not know the Bible, the Covenant made between God and the Jewish people, or even our historic right to the Land of Israel – all this is not binding. The Christian nations, inasmuch as they still have attachment to the Bible, usually treat the biblical stories (so – we must admit – do most Jews) as allegories produced by primitive tribes who had not yet reached a high level of abstraction.

The term "historic rights" does not connote a *Kushan* (certificate of registration), a term that characterizes the special link between the Jewish people and its unique cultural and religious contribution to civilization – the spiritual bond between generations that connects the dispersed people to its ancient origins. There is also the fact that throughout centuries of wandering, the Jews have been unable – because of historic memories and universal hostility – to strike roots as citizens and, no less important, to create a political entity in any other territory. Therefore, when the age of self-determination had come, this people found itself persecuted, slandered, outcast, and homeless. It surely seemed natural that it would be promised a home, located in the territory with which it was historically identified and where it would live as a normal nation.

But it is a far stretch from this point to the sanctification of political frontiers that have gone through so many changes in the history of all nations and all times. Even in the age of Jewish political rule in the Land of Israel, large portions of the country were either settled by other ethnic groups or controlled by foreign rulers. What place do Acco, Jenin, Halhul, or Gaza have in Jewish history, compared with Toledo, Vilna, Odessa, and Warsaw? No matter how frustrating it might be, we cannot expect the international community, whose guiding principle is the right of every nation and tribe to self-determination, to treat the Arabs of the Land of Israel, the Palestinians, as a group of bandits who have broken into someone else's home while the owner was away, and are now illegal squatters who must leave this place to make room for the returning owners, or settle for the status of second-class tenants with whatever autonomy the owner, now ruler of the land, deigns to grant them.

It is accepted among historians concerned with nationalism that continuity and the creation of a collective way of life are the foundations of nationhood; a historian does not ask who were the first settlers, for most of those have since been lost or have migrated. One might argue that the Palestinians did not develop a collective consciousness, language, culture, or specific political framework of their own; or that neither the great Arab civilization nor humanity in general would lose anything if a twenty-third Arab state was not established. But once the consciousness of a "we" arises in an ethnic group that is in conflict with settlers alien to themselves, those arguments cannot cancel the fact, undesirable as it may be, that there may well occur a head-on collision between two national movements. We have long preferred to disregard this fact.

Mr. Prime Minister, with all due respect to you as head of the government and as a fellow historian, permit me to make an observation, on the basis of decades of study of the history of nationalism. However ancient, special, noble, and unique our subjective motives may be, the desire, at the end of the twentieth century, to dominate and govern a hostile foreign population that differs from us in language, history, culture, religion, consciousness, and national aspirations, as well as in its economic and social structure, is like an attempt to revive feudalism.

The question is not a moral one. The idea is simply not feasible, nor is its realization worth the price – as France learned in Algeria. The Soviet analogy is irrelevant: we have neither the material strength nor the requisite spiritual and moral toughness. The only way to bring nations to exist together in our day, ironic and disappointing as it is, is by separating them. God Himself, nature, and history divided the Land of Israel before it was ever divided by human decree. It may well be that the most powerful force that can impel individuals, classes, and nations to act in the modern era is the determination to oppose the hereditary humiliation of an inferior position, arising from the subjection of one people by another. Political inequality leads invariably to social and economic inferiority, since the ruling nation, motivated by feelings of tribal solidarity and fear "lest they multiply and become mightier," will try to restrict the growth and power of the subject population, denying it access to office, responsibility, and sensitive positions and, of course, to any activity defined as "subversive." The combination of political subjection, national oppression, and social inferiority is a time bomb. Voltaire is said to have remarked that all men are born equal but that the population of Timbuktu has not yet heard the news.

But by now they have heard the news, and since then the world has not known a moment's peace. Whoever speaks of the need for one people to rule over another for security reasons leads his audience astray. To do so is to sit deliberately on a volcano; it is a source of insecurity and perpetual alarm. The rebellious hostility of a subjected population, particularly if it is supported by millions on the other side of the border, neutralizes any degree of security provided by holding on to this hill or that stream, a strait or marsh, in an age of long-range missiles and bombs. There is something repulsive in the kind of cynicism or naïveté that claims that settlements are needed to create conditions of coexistence, while everyone knows that for the Arabs each settlement is another sign of dispossession and gradual conquest. The Jewish image suffers as a result of such double-talk that does nothing to enhance our security or honor.

The world is not naïve. It does not believe the claim that a few trailers on a rocky mountain will block the path of a modern army or deter it. Historians remember very well what happened to the Maginot Line, the Siegfried Line, and even the Bar-Lev Line, and how the assurances of the war minister of Napoleon III that the French army was "prepared to the last button" were proven false – or claims that this or that natural barrier would save a nation from destruction. This does not mean that bargaining over borders is impermissible, particularly if such a change will not lead to domination over a foreign population more numerous than it was in the age of feudalism. In the modern age, it is not land that is inherited but the consciousness and will of the people living in it.

Any talk of the holiness of the land or of geographic sites throws us back to the age of fetishism. One of the greatest living Orthodox rabbis in America once told me that he does not know of one authentic holy site in the Land of Israel except for the Wailing Wall. "I even have my doubts about the Cave of Machpelah," added this rabbi, who refuses to give any support to political rabbis.

Your concept of autonomy, Mr. Prime Minister, is an anachronism – a device to lull foreign public opinion. Anyone who has taken a look at the history of the multinational empires of the Hapsburgs and the Romanovs at the end of the nineteenth century will shake his head at this idea exhumed from the historical junk pile. The last word on Otto Bauer's and Karl Renner's Austrian experiment with autonomy was said at Sarajevo – the inauguration of the greatest international catastrophe till that day. The days of autonomies in the frail states that were erected on the ruins of the Czarist empire were short, hard-pressed, and without glory.

The idea of "personal autonomy," which you took over from the Austrian Marxists, was never proposed by them as an end in itself. Its aim was to supplement and realize territorial autonomy. It was intended for ethnic groups living outside their "homeland." Now, if you apply these ideas to our situation, who can guarantee that the Arabs on our side of the Green Line will not also demand "autonomy' – if it is going to be a permanent condition in the territories?

It is hard to believe that any population would agree to this sort of "autonomy" without a legislative assembly of its own, or that such people would settle for a mere "administrative council" subordinate to the executive authority of an alien sovereignty. History abounds with examples of such legislative assemblies ending up by declaring their independence. When this happens here, will we use our soldiers to disband such a legislative assembly, and will we then put its insurgent leaders on trial for treason?

Let us keep in mind that those who designed this sort of "autonomy" for the national minorities of the Austro-Hungarian Empire argued, and some believed, that the empire's territory was not the sole possession of the dominant nationality – but that it belonged equally to all the ethnic and national groups that lived within its boundaries. And let us keep in mind that this belief engendered strong opposition to the recognition of one dominant language (German) or even of a *Verkehrssprache* in the Austro-Hungarian Empire. This notion stood in sharp contrast to the concept of an "autonomy" that is graciously granted to minorities by the sovereign people – a people that conceives of itself as the sole sovereign. In our case, we are speaking of a sovereign people that holds on tightly to the ownership of land, to sources of water, to rights to unrestricted settlement – while permitting the national groups to which it has graciously given "autonomy" the right to care for the sewers, to immunize their children, and to maintain elementary schools while unable to determine the content or spirit of what is taught in those schools.

Giving a minority autonomy makes sense – if it is intended as an interim solution for a specified length of time and as a chance to find out if the two nationalities in question can pass the test of coexistence, and can live together as neighbors, in peace.

There are those who say, "But our vital security interests make it imperative that we hold on to our sovereignty over *all* of the present territories of the Land of Israel; and settlements in the territories are crucially needed for our defense." We have already heard from two of your ministers of defense and from some generals that this just is not the case. Such claims (as the thinking majority of the country has known all along) are mere rationalizations for the pursuit of other goals. On the contrary, these settlements are at present destructive of our vital interests and of our Zionist goals – and especially of peace with our neighbors, which is the precondition for achieving all other goals.

To focus solely on the dangers to security arising from the loss of the territories is a grave demagogic error. It sounds strange indeed when it comes, as it usually does, from those who never tire of repeating what a big power we are, and how we are the only secure bastion of the U.S. and of the entire West in the Middle East.

If we are so vulnerable that our entire security depends on a few kilometers of barren hills, what kind of bastion can we possibly be to anyone? This argument from "security" surely must raise doubts in our allies' minds as to our ability to survive at all; and it must make them wonder if it is indeed worthwhile to give us the aid we are constantly requesting in order to guarantee our security. When an Israeli minister and a former general [Arik Sharon] rebukes the American Jewish leadership for keeping silent during the Holocaust, he creates panic lest Israel is on the brink of destruction. Such foolish remarks make it easier for American Jews to understand why Russian immigrants are leaving Israel, and why so many Israelis, too, are emigrating to the U.S. So, for all the noise and tumult surrounding the settlements issue, who, really, are the defeatists – and who are the "brave patriots" who know no fear?

Israel, obviously, is surrounded by enemies prepared to drown it in a sea of blood. Yet, has not Sadat given proof that there are other Arabs, too, who for one reason or another are ready to accept our existence? This now is a fact – for whatever reason. Perhaps it is because such Arabs have concluded that they cannot annihilate us by force, and perhaps because they hope that the State of Israel will destroy itself through its own internal contradictions and its economic weakness, and perhaps because of apathy among Jews in the Diaspora.

It is indeed dangerous to argue that the State of Israel is incapable of defending itself without holding onto the captured territories (granted, of course, some minor rectification of some borders will have to be made for authentic reasons of security). For this implies that Israel cannot exist at all. Is the River Jordan as wide as the Volga or the Mississippi? Are the mountains of Nablus as high as the Himalayas? Does anyone remember the slogan that Sharm el-Sheikh without peace is better than peace without Sharm el-Sheikh? Let us face it, Mr. Prime Minister, the real danger to the existence of the State of Israel lies in continuing the Sisyphean attempt to defeat the Palestinians: whoever cannot see now the grave threat of a binational war is blind.

Those of us who speak out against the settlements are opposed by your supporters who ask, "Is not settlement the life-blood of Zionism? What is the difference between Degania in 1913 and Eilon Moreh in 1980? If we don't have the right to settle now, then what gave us the right to do it then?" In considering these arguments, we should remember that history is a record of change. History does not stand still or repeat itself exactly; it is the record of interrelationship and objective change – and the presence (or lack) of human wisdom. Loyalty to a historic tradition is not expressed in a neurotic dependence on past models. It is expressed in frank acknowledgement, with the necessary flexibility, of new and unexpected situations, while preserving the essential core of that tradition, which may take different forms at different times.

History's fuel is not to be found in abstract ideas or utopian desires for adventurism, or in romanticism – but in brutal force that cannot be withstood. Without this force the caravans of history would not be on the move. And if the enthusiasm of the avant-garde succeeds in moving it a bit, it will be stopped when the power runs out. Who has not heard of revolutions or uprisings that were attempted too soon or too late, before or after a change in the supporting factors inherent in a revolutionary condition, in a crisis, or in a particular international constellation?

And here we all remember Marx's poignant remark that history has a compulsion to repeat itself – in situations that may seem similar but are in reality radically different. "History repeats itself, the first time as tragedy, the second time as farce." This remark is now relevant to the present analogy that compares "the towers and the stockades" in the Galilee of our founding days with the improvised colonization of today. But our modern activists are not the pioneers who built roads where there were none, who outmaneuvered cruel enemies and avoided the danger of annihilation. Today's settlers in the territories rely on our army's tanks, helicopters, and planes. They come to demonstrate our presence, to display our force – *not* to plow, to sow, or plant. These settlements are more than a desperate attempt to hold onto the territory of our homeland. They are a political act and its principal purpose is to determine who will rule or, as the settlers put it, "to show the Arabs who is the boss here. . . . to put the Arabs in their place."

Such settling, it seems to me, is tantamount to conducting a kind of war. It will be very difficult to prevent the situation from turning into a head-on collision between two peoples in a land that suffers from "agrarian famine." This process resembles the agrarian wars in Ireland, between colonizing English noblemen and Irish tenant farmers, or Prussia's policy concerning the Polish peasantry within its territory. It is the same wretched discrimination, extortion, robbery, fraud, and repression, on the one hand – and agrarian rebellion and military repression, on the other hand. It is an unfair struggle between two nations when one side can rely on military power, and the other must hold on with its bare teeth and fingernails to its impoverished, tired, arid land. The same holds true when we contemplate the struggle against a foreign invader and a repressive regime. Who is not ashamed when confronted with the wretched sight of Bedouins being driven out, having to move on, again and again, from place to place – "for famine was in the land, and there was no pasture for the sheep. . ."? And all this is done in the name of preserving the nation's laws – as if the Bedouins were accustomed to living in Holland or Switzerland, as a brutal and arrogant general once said.

For all the shame and pain we feel over the harm done to us by our neighbors because of anachronistic perverse policies, our fear should be greater over what these acts will do to us, to the Jewish people, and to our dream of social and moral justice and renaissance. For this dream was one of the vital and beautiful aspects of Zionism, setting it apart from other national liberation movements. The desire to dominate, Mr. Prime Minister, leads to perpetual fear and mistrust of the subjugated people and creates terrible temptations that are stronger than any subjectively good intentions.

This situation of perpetual terror and counterterror, retaliatory raids and protective strikes unleashes aggressive and evil impulses that the rule of law barely manages to control. In such an atmosphere nothing positive can develop, there can be no vitality, no joy in living. Do you remember Jean Jaurès's famous answer at the time of the Dreyfus affair to those who saw no reason for socialists trying to save a bourgeois officer from other bourgeois officers? "If we allow evil and aggression and violence to run wild," said Jaurès, "then the whole earth will be corrupted, until it will no longer be fit for socialism." Now, in our country, such corruption is no longer a masochist's bad dream; it is a reality, and it is strangling us. And this is not the product of a government that enjoys tyranny for its own sake – but of a weak government that pretends to be strong and is forced to camouflage its weakness with trickery. This weakness is promoted by zealots who have lost all sanity and common sense and who receive their funding at the expense of tens of thousands of young people living in poverty, all because everything is dedicated to the pipedream that the settlements will be able to prevent the establishment of a PLO state and stave off the opposition of world opinion.

Could the settlements really prevent the establishment of a PLO state – and how are they to assuage world opinion?

Most of our people either oppose or have strong reservations about the settlements. Needless to say, world public opinion universally denounces the current policy as a violation of international law and, indeed, as a unilateral provocation that makes the idea of negotiation seem ridiculous. From this follows the conspiratorial pattern in which these settlements are established, and the way they are fenced in, "for military purposes." The seizure or purchase of land, "for public use," proceeds much in the same way. This is not the way a sovereign, law-abiding nation should operate, nor is it the way of a society whose openness, until now, has always been one of its most admirable qualities.

So it has happened that a government whose leaders were reared on slogans of Jewish pride and honor is now turning our state into an underground movement, using arguments and excuses so blatantly deceitful that they inevitably conjure up in the gentile imagination the figures of the contemptible scheming Jews of traditional anti-Semitic folklore. One of your [former] cabinet ministers [Ezer Weizman], Mr. Prime Minister, has already publicly commented that "we are succeeding in making ourselves hateful to the whole world."

Since the government, for one reason or another, is unable or afraid to initiate its own settlement policy, an avant-garde of passionate zealots has emerged that proclaims itself the protector of the national destiny. These people consider themselves destined to operate in the territories without regard for a cowardly government or for our laws. For these zealots believe that our courts have no jurisdiction when it comes to faith. Indeed, these zealots consider anyone who opposes them as nothing less than traitors.

The result is contempt for the courts; disregard for governmental decrees; scorn for the rule of law and the rights of others – in short, wanton lawlessness in the guise of ardent patriotism. All this is happening while this movement's fifth column within the government succeeds in suppressing the voices of opponents. This century has suffered much, and the Jewish people more than most from similar groups of a "nation's finest," which always claim they are saving their country, in the name of a divine sanction that allows them proudly to trample on the laws of a democratic society and on human morality.

And so these zealots speak of "the need of the hour," in order to whip up nationalist feelings and to exploit sources of religious mysticism – to fight, in the spirit of the old-time Zealots against any form of wicked "Hellenization." And so they aim to suppress the spirit of pluralism and of skepticism, and to strangle any criticism at home or abroad. In short, our latter-day zealots are determined to adopt the doctrines of integralist nationalism whose French prophet, Maurice Barrès, once defined truth as the angle of sight of the French national interest. The same imperialistic brand of nationalism flooded Europe at the beginning of the nineteenth century, and everywhere it made hatred of the Jews its emblem.

Instead of being a nation that is experiencing a renaissance, a nation that is courageous, and proud to be a member of the family of nations, we are manifestly returning to a mentality and a system of actions that rather befit an isolated and diaspora-bound religious sect. Is it not the way of a sect to remain insistently on the margins of history and to isolate itself from the world? Such a sect, however, is also capable of becoming an armed band of guerrillas, fighting with the instruments of modern technology – according to the patterns of a well-known Master Race.

The Romantic movement of the nineteenth century gave rise to modern Zionism and the modern idea of a national revival of the Jewish people. The goal of a return to Zion, of course, had been alive among the Jewish people ever since our exile from the Land of Israel. It sustained us through centuries of dispersion. Over the centuries and throughout the Diaspora Jews have prayed, and still pray, for this return, night and day.

Modern Zionism was one of the last movements to espouse national liberation. It flowered late in the tremendous wave of movements that fought for national freedom after the French Revolution. Almost every suppressed people then began to struggle for liberation – from the Eskimos to the natives of Papua, from the Basques to the tribes of Baluchistan. The driving force behind these movements was, and still is, the concept of human dignity, and of the right of every ethnic or national group to freedom and self-expression. This aspiration captured the imagination of the subjugated nations. And so the search for identity and the desire to express it led national groups to an exploration of their roots. Many began to make a cult of their past, for this was how they could emphasize their uniqueness. Such heralds and prophets of political nationalism as Moses Hess, Leo Pinsker, Theodor Herzl, Max Nordau, and even Ze'ev

[V.] Jabotinsky did not draw their inspiration from religious experience or even from Jewish history; at least, not in the beginning. They were stirred by the concept of human dignity. They wanted to heal the injuries to Jewish pride, and yearned for the Jewish people hereafter to be spared all humiliation and persecution; it was their burning desire to see the Jewish people in freedom – a member of the family of free nations. These early Zionist leaders were moved to take a more active role in Jewish life by this general awakening of interest in ethnic roots, dignity, and liberation. Even the Zionism of Rabbi Kalischer and Rabbi Alkalai was aroused by the wars of liberation that were being fought by the Greeks, the Serbs, the Hungarians, the Romanians, and the Bulgarians. Moses Hess was inspired by the vision of the resurrection of Athens and of Rome – which he believed to herald, inevitably, the resurrection of Jerusalem.

The Jews were, so to speak, the "last to arrive at the feast" among the movements of national liberation. During the "Spring of Nations" of 1848, the Jews were the only national or ethnic group that did not experience a national awakening. The Jews, however, enthusiastically greeted the revolution as a victory for the ideal of the brotherhood of nations. Many emancipated Jews saw the revolution as a sign that the hour had now come for the Jews to give up their unique status of "chosenness." But then, around 1880, there rose up a murderous wave of mass anti-Semitism – ironically, just at the moment when it seemed as if the dream of human rights had triumphed throughout the world. This fearful wave of anti-Semitism deeply shocked the sensitive, assimilated, European Jews.

At this very time, in Eastern Europe, after the liberation of the serfs, millions of impoverished peasants and aristocrats flowed into the Jewish towns and cities. Thus the Jews faced a situation of danger precisely when their religious security had substantially weakened and their snobbish feelings of cultural and intellectual superiority over their "boorish neighbors" were on the rise. The combination of these two trends moved hundreds of thousands of young Jews to join the revolutionary, or nationalist, movements – or to leave their homes and emigrate to America.

This is not to say that Zionism lacked faith in God's promises, and in the hope of redemption, or that it did not derive sustenance from prayers that speak of the return to the land of our fathers; but these were not the sparks that lit the great fires of political Zionism. On the contrary, it was the Jewish people's religious life that received new sustenance through these Zionist, and political, developments. It is quite reasonable to claim that the Jewish religion actually prevented the vision of redemption from being turned into a historical and political concept. The Jewish religion served as a substitute for redemption; the reliance on Providence, on the Messiah, and on miracles, exempted Jews from acting in the here and now. The religion, in a way, even prohibited them from doing so, for the law could be observed and the feelings of longing expressed anywhere in the world . . . and is not today's enthusiastic Zionism-by-proxy of millions of Jews in the Diaspora proof of this? It is no coincidence that Jewish orthodoxy was from the first suspicious of and even hostile to Zionism. Like the Catholic Church, it viewed nationalism as a serious secular competitor to religion and, to a certain extent, as the sin of hastening redemption without waiting for the Messiah.

Some people argue that it was not solely an internal dialectic – but rather the persecution of the Jews that was the principal reason for the rise of Zionism and for the sympathy extended to it by the best of the gentiles. These people, indeed, are saying something that is elementary to the historian: no matter how great the power of ideas or ideology in the shaping of history may be, the progress of history in the end is determined by various forces, and by various kinds of distress. It is enough, for example, to recall the periodic ebb and flow in the movements of immigration into the Land of Israel in order to demonstrate that this is so. Let us compare, for instance, the wave of immigration in the 1920s with the huge waves of emigration today, during Israel's statehood.

Mr. Prime Minister, you should not regard these meditations as an attempt to defend the creation of a Palestinian or a PLO state. I am not concerned here with the rights of the Arabs regarding whose past and culture I have little knowledge or interest. I am concerned with Israel's security and welfare. And I am concerned with the quality of the people and culture that make up Israel. I have no doubt that the attempt to rule a million and a quarter Arabs against their will may result in corruption and make our beautiful dreams of national and spiritual renewal seem ridiculous. I am convinced that the annexation of the territories will not only fail to increase our security but will also weaken our ability to defend ourselves against hostile neighbors and international opposition.

In a debate with Arnold Toynbee, right after the Six-Day War, I spoke in favor of what later became known as the "Jordanian orientation." I do tremble at the thought of flag-waving PLO brigades streaming into the occupied territories, firm in their belief that they are taking only the first step toward the complete destruction of the State of Israel. . . . Is it possible that our intransigence could destroy any chance – as it has done in the past, when we were in a position of real strength – of accepting another possible kind of settlement, such as an agreement with Jordan, on the basis of partition?

There will be no alternative to a PLO state if we continue systematically to ignore the Jordanian option, or other possibilities that many seem to fear more than a PLO victory. Nor will we find salvation in an "information" campaign, which solely consists of denunciations of the PLO as Nazis – if we do not put forward a constructive plan that is based on reasonable compromise. Our generation can point to numerous counterparts of the PLO for acts of terrorism, both near and far. We can also point to endless examples of decent men who were terrorists until they became cured of their frustration and reached positions of responsibility – such as Kenyatta or Mugabe. It will not be helpful to continue seeing all the good in ourselves and all the evil in others.

All those who are not blinded by zealotry are bound to be very unhappy when they realize the terrible acts that have been committed by Israelis – individually and collectively – sometimes in retaliatory raids, sometimes in protective strikes, and sometimes because we have thought it a *mitzvah* to take vengeance on the helpless. Clearly, the PLO has its sadists. And there is indeed the possibility that a PLO state might turn into a Soviet satellite; but who can guarantee that this will not happen to any of our other Arab neighbors? We must avoid pushing the Arabs into a position where they will feel they have suffered so much humiliation that they might as well use all their strength to die with the Palestinians. . . . And yet, we must use our defensive capability to repel all who threaten our existence and seek to destroy us. Ironically, we have worked hard to convince ourselves that there is no possibility of compromise; that the Arabs are implacably resolved to annihilate us, and that we must therefore act accordingly – because we despair of any possibility of peace, or of international guarantees of borders, or of demilitarization arrangements, or of other solutions. I am afraid, Mr. Prime Minister, that this attitude is likely to become a self-fulfilling prophecy.

We should talk with anyone who is prepared to talk with us and, by doing so, is prepared to recognize our existence and our right to be here, and who is willing to declare so on the eve or in the course of the negotiations. I also would not insist on such solemn declarations as a condition for a dialogue. We Jews have learned in the Middle Ages to treat such declarations more like bargaining chips than obligatory expressions of practical intent. In those days, people already distinguished clearly between the sphere of the kingdom of mercy and the eternal sacred values – by which only God, kings, and saints were able to live – and the Vale of Tears where most mortal sinners are bound by laws by which we somehow manage to live. "The Heavens belong to God, and the Earth is mankind's." Let us admit that politics and political arrangements belong to this lower sphere. Let us also admit that it is permissible, and perhaps even desirable, for the sake of aesthetics and conscience, to pay lip service to lofty principles at the beginning of any agreement – so as to alleviate our conscience and to be able to get down to the necessary compromises and pragmatic agreements. Just as humanity cannot survive in laboratory conditions or sustain itself solely on pure substantiality – so we, too, cannot exist in the realm of purism and sheer elevation.

We invite much trouble when we cling to principles as if they were the word of the Living God and, in doing so, we fall in with the fundamentalist zealots. The most famous document in England's diplomatic history was written by Castlereagh, the Conservative counterrevolutionary, and not, as was thought, by the Progressive Canning. It was a response to an invitation to join the Holy Alliance, and it said that England would never undertake any blanket obligations – in this case, to put down rebellions wherever they might occur. England would, instead, deal pragmatically with situations as they came up, and consider each case on its own merits. Some people who once studied law, and who still respect what they then learned, even though they never practiced the legal profession, love to make declarations of rights every other day. This strikes me as political folly. In life, and certainly in political life, we are not interested in narrowly defined rights or principles, but in the conflicts between opposing rights that are in need of compromise, and that require a profound understanding of the prevailing circumstances.

If we accept that the State of Israel and its people now live under a state of siege and are completely isolated; and if we also accept for a moment that Jewry in the Diaspora is eventually bound to disappear; then – given the country's present economic strangulation and its moral and spiritual disintegration – it appears that the Six-Day War was one of Nietzsche's "victories that turn into defeat." The attempt to hold onto the captured territories has turned out to be not the sacred mission that will bring about our redemption and the climax of our history – but a trap, whose burden we cannot withstand without corruption and perhaps even collapse. The world refuses to accept the Revisionist version of Zionism, Mr. Prime Minister, and we do not have the power to force it on them. Nor do we have the strength to establish the "Iron Wall" that Jabotinsky hoped would somehow force the Arabs to accept our existence without losing their self-respect.

Jabotinsky, in contrast to his students, admitted that if "our faith is deep, so is theirs." He refused to believe that they would sell "their country's future" for a mess of pottage; he believed that "any people without exception would fight against the colonization of their country at the hands of people of a different race who come from another country." Balfour was very aware of the contradiction between taking away the right of self-determination from the Arabs of Palestine – and doing so in order to grant the Jewish people a national home. Nonetheless, Balfour was convinced that it was right to ignore the protests of 700,000 Arabs in order to rectify an old historic injustice. At that time, the enlightened world agreed to apply unusual principles to the case of a people that had made a unique contribution to humanity, and had suffered persecution as had no other people in history.

In our situation today, in contrast to what generations have considered our unique gift to humanity – the idea of the rule of the spirit rather than the rule of force – we are using that rule of force. We now are using the rule of force to implement our historic rights; rights that, in their present interpretation, are holy neither to the gentiles nor to most Jews. And so we no longer can expect the world to look upon our rights as so pressing that they ought to cancel out the rights of the Palestinians to self-determination. Without the foundation that is represented by the writings of our prophets, we are nothing but a peculiar band of tribes that has given nothing to humanity except a lot of trouble, and that is now asking to expand at the expense of another people and to subordinate this other people's freedom to its own security needs, real or imaginary, as well as to its self-interest. . . .

Mr. Prime Minister, the policies of your government are turning the

State of Israel into an underground sect; they invite the Jews of the Diaspora to disavow liberal values that have not only made it possible for them to reach positions of unprecedented influence – but values that represent a philosophy to which they are deeply committed. The chauvinist sectarianism that your government is encouraging (and so the version of East European religious orthodoxy to which it has granted special rights while denying such rights to all other forms of Judaism) not only fails to bring our people closer to Judaism; it also harms our people's unity and alienates them from Judaism and from the State of Israel – for the majority of our people will not agree to go back to ghetto life.

The future of Israel and of American Jewry is interconnected. Should, heaven forbid, Judea fall a third time, the Jews of America and of the world will have suffered an overwhelming blow. There would be paralyzing despair, breakdown, and a massive departure from Judaism. Should something fearful happen to American Jewry – despite the calculations of our millenarians who regard anti-Semitism as fuel for Zionism and a supplier of Israel's immigrants – an isolated Israel would not be saved from such a huge conflagration. The future of the entire Jewish people is totally dependent on close cooperations between Israel – as a culture-creating, open, and liberal society – and Diaspora Jewry, particularly American Jewry, some of which today is part of the elite of humanity.

It is not often that a historic problem of a people reaches so dramatic a point that we can characterize it, without exaggeration, with such slogans as that of the French Revolution's "Our country is in danger; help us whoever can!" – or the Russian revolutionaries' call, "Now or never!" You will agree with me, Mr. Prime Minister, that we have reached such a point in our history. Our people now are divided into two camps.

The first camp is convinced there is an international conspiracy to create a PLO state that will be controlled by the Russians and will seek to destroy Israel, and therefore it is imperative to speed up and intensify the settlement process and to pursue an uncompromising policy, inspired by "courageous activism." This camp believes that only thus will catastrophe be averted.

The second camp believes that the moment has come for us to make peace with our neighbors, and that the effort to expand our borders and to force our rule on the population of the territories will dispel all chances for peace, and create dangers for our country from which there can be no salvation.

The adherents of this second camp, Mr. Prime Minister, view your historic achievement of peace negotiations with Egypt as an ambiguous success, while your supporters, the adherents of the first camp, hope that the Camp David agreements, by putting an end to any threat from Egypt, will grant us a free hand to rule over the occupied territories. Your adherents believe that this will lead to the completion of the territorial homeland, that it will grant "personal autonomy" to its Arab residents – confirming Israel's sovereignty and our people's right to settle anywhere within this homeland's borders.

Your opponents, however, are fearful that the other parties to this treaty will continue to view this agreement and the proffered autonomy as nothing but a stage on the way toward guaranteeing a separate Palestinian entity. And your opponents are afraid that the differences of opinion on this issue will intensify the conflict between the Arabs and an Israel that is now weaker as a result of its withdrawal from the Sinai and its oil fields.

I have attempted here, Mr. Prime Minister, to draw your attention to the serious structural changes that have occurred during the decades since the Holocaust in the Jewish population centers that gave birth to Zionism. I have referred to the lack of an effective Zionist response from the Diaspora in the form of mass emigration to Israel. In addition I have tried to outline the recent developments in the larger world, such as decolonization and its ideological and political consequences. I have tried to point also to the rise of civilization and peoples who have no ties to the Bible and feel no obligation toward the Jews. I have also spoken of the important changes that have occurred in the position of the Arab world, thanks to its near-monopoly of the oil resources, which are so vital to our industrial civilization, and of the declining military clout and spiritual strength of the Western nations who are so close to us in tradition and spirit. We must be aware, of course, of the alliance between the Communist ideology (now transformed into the ideology of an imperialist power structure) and the national liberation movements. This alliance has led to the political isolation of the Jewish state and has succeeded in distorting the image of Israel and its historic and moral significance in world public opinion.

Tragically, our victory in the Six-Day War has led our people to a loss of a sense of proportion regarding the strength of the State of Israel, and has shifted too much of our focus upon military matters, away from other significant factors vital to a democratic society. This focus on the military has diverted much of our attention from the nation's economic and social problems – which have to be solved *before* there can be any effective military strength.

So we won on the battlefield but were not strong enough to force our enemy to make peace with us. And the more Israel increased its weaponry, the more dependent it became on American aid and support. Meanwhile, the Palestinians – termed "refugees" in the U.N. Resolution 242 – succeeded in obtaining recognition as a people.

Our refusal to treat the Palestinians as a collective entity has diminished Israel's legitimacy in the eyes of the world. And now our people are divided over the meaning and interpretation of the proposed "autonomy." Is it home rule, with selected clerks performing duties that are essentially controlled by the Israeli government? Or is it self-rule, based on partition into two *autonomous* sections, with autonomous authorities in each of them?

Those Israelis who do not believe that the government's autonomy proposals are acceptable to the Arabs of the world are now asking that you preserve the possibility of reaching a real peace settlement. They ask that you preserve the chance for peace by an agreement on territorial autonomy, or even by agreeing to a Palestinian national home in exchange for effective guarantees and a federation with Jordan and a federal tie to Israel. This option seems more promising and less dangerous than the one you have proposed.

The more time passes, the more polarized become both sides, and the Israeli public, too. There is the grave danger of civil war between Jews and Arabs – and Jews and Jews.

Mr. Prime Minister, in the eyes of the majority of the nation, your allegiance to the faith of your youth, and your conviction of having a historic mission to deliver "the home of our fathers" intact to the coming generations appear more and more as an obsession. It seems to be an obsession that has no chance of realization and is a source of errors and disasters that are dividing the nation as well as the coalition that you lead. Conflicting views, frustrations, and feuds are now paralyzing the operation of that coalition. They are also destroying the people's respect for its parliamentary institutions, for the democratic process, and for our judicial system and its moral authority. This has led to the creation of extra-parliamentary groups which now see themselves as agents of the national destiny and the saviors of their people. These groups believe themselves subject only to their own law and rules. . . .

There comes a time in the life of a politician when he must weigh whether, in changing circumstances, he will be an asset or an obstacle in the service of his people. More than one historian has asked in astonishment why, for instance, Lloyd George did not leave political life at the end of his extraordinary historic mission, or why Churchill insisted on remaining on as prime minister for his final term.

What should a leader do who is unable to shake off his youthful faith, even though in their hearts he and others are doubtful that it can be realized? Before him is the example of the Social Democratic leader Philip Scheidemann, the first German chancellor of the Weimar Republic. When the Allies' peace terms of Versailles were announced in 1919, he solemnly swore in an emotional address before the Reichstag: "This hand will not move to sign this disgraceful document!" And Scheidemann resigned. Others were found to sign that document.

Published in *Dissent*, Fall 1980. First published in *Ha'aretz*, 31 March 1980, as "Open Letter to Prime Minister Menahem Begin". This was the last article he wrote.

Part Five

Profiles in History

The Ordeal of Sir Lewis Namier – The Man, the Historian, the Jew

I was privileged to know the great historian Sir Lewis Namier, and to enjoy his friendship for some twelve years before he died in 1960. The more I got to know this strange combination of scholar and man, of English gentleman and East European Jew, the deeper grew my admiration – which was characterized by awe, fear, and occasionally irony. There was the historian of phenomenal erudition, whose knowledge of various cultures and languages, and whose mastery of several disciplines, led Sir Ernest Barker to compare him to Lord Acton. Further, there was the pioneer and founder of a school of historical scholarship who earned that rarest of distinctions – having an "ism" affixed to his name in his own lifetime. There was also the man of culture and imagination whose words – spoken or written – were charged with the meaning achieved by individual observation and richness of expression. But above all, there was Namier himself.

If he was a monumental figure, there was also something infantile about him. His fondness for the saying of a philosopher, a deceased colleague, that the idea that man ever grows up is a childish notion, often made me gaze at him inquiringly. He was a tall man, sparely but powerfully built, and he talked as if it was natural for him to make himself heard and for others to listen. His egocentrism, which was proverbial, came partly from the familiar self-absorption of the artist who innocently rides roughshod over the feelings of those around him, and partly from deep-seated problems that robbed him of flexibility and real assurance. He had a strong sense of mission, and yet was pathetically in need of approval. But praise, in turn, would again give him pain – the embarrassed pain of the perfectionist who feels he is unworthy and lives under false pretenses. Any stimulus, friendly or adverse, could evoke an exaggerated response in the man, and throw him off balance. Thus his affection and warmth would almost submerge those whom he liked, but he was capable of the most implacable, indeed paranoic hatred.

But beyond the meaning of Namier's behavior, there was the deeper meaning of his character, one that was reflected in his work as it was in his life. In the Introduction to his second major work, *England in the Age of the American Revolution* (1930), there is a revealing passage on the role of landed property in the growth of English liberty. After a rhapsodic reflection on the social significance of the stately homes of England throughout the ages, Namier concludes as follows:

> The relations of groups of men to plots of land, of organized communities to units of territory, form the basic content of political history; social stratifications and convulsions, primarily arising from the relationship of men to land, make the greater, not always fully conscious, part of the domestic history of nations – and even under urban and industrial conditions ownership of land counts for more than is usually supposed. To every man, as to Brutus, the native land is his life-giving Mother, and the State raised upon the land is his law-giving Father, and the days cannot be long of a nation which fails to honor either. . . . There is some well-night mystical power in the ownership of spaces – for it is not the command of resources alone which makes the strength of the landowner, but that he has a place in the world which he can call his own, from which he can ward off strangers, and in which he himself is rooted – the superiority of a tree to a log.

Then, suddenly, and for no apparent reason, the flow is interrupted by a powerful *cri de coeur*: "Only one nation has survived for two thousand years, though an orphan – my own people, the Jews. But then in the God-given Law we have enshrined the authority of a state, in the God-Promised Land the idea of a Mother-Country; through the centuries from Mount Sinai we have faced Eretz Israel, our Land. Take away either, and we cease to be a nation; let both live again, and we shall be ourselves once more."

These two passages express Namier's two most deep-seated emotions – an agonized, envious love of historic England, and a tormented passion for Zion; or one may put it more abstractly – the outsider's need for roots and the wanderer's yearning for an anchor.

These passages were written in the 1930s – when a Central European Jew would curse Hitler by asking that God might make him a Polish Jew without a passport, and when almost every part of the world was considered as a possible refuge for Jews or as a possible site for a Jewish state, except the repeatedly promised Jewish National Home. However, Namier's reaction was not merely a temporary response to the Jewish fate in the 1930s. The intense interplay between the need for roots and the yearning for an anchor was a constant that determined not only Namier's character as a man and his work as a historian but also gave a further dimension to the meaning of his life. There is a famous remark of Keats that the story of a man of any worth is a parable, and may thus serve as an allegory. Namier's "story" richly bears out this notion. Unique as his life was, it also can be seen to represent the lesson of the Jewish predicament in modern times, specifically of those talented and ambitious young Jews from Eastern Europe, who tried to take by storm the new, alien places they had come to in the West, and who had to pay a heavy price in spiritual torment for their brilliant successes.

Namier's fate was to be always and everywhere an outsider, a resident alien rather than a full-fledged citizen and participant. His parents were landowners in Eastern Galicia, and their deepest aspiration was to enter the Polish Catholic nobility. They hid from the boy the fact of his Jewish origin. When at the age of nine he learned the secret, he experienced a shock whose effects he would continue to feel throughout his whole life. He was filled with bitterness against the parents who had deceived him, and his suppressed rebellion against them was full of potent implications for the future theoretician of conservatism and the poet who celebrated the glory of the traditions that are passed on from father to son. This sense of not belonging fully – neither to Judaism nor to Catholic Poland – was further intensified when he met with the refusal of his Polish friends to accept him, in spite of the burning Polish patriotism he felt at the time. It was, indeed, the experience of overhearing anti-Semitic sneers at his parents' desperate attempts to elbow their way into the Polish gentry that eventually made him a dedicated Zionist.

England was kind to him when he arrived in London in 1908 after a spell of Vienna and Lausanne. He stayed for a while at the London School of Economics, attracted by the Fabianism of its faculty, even though the Fabian temper was so different from the romantic nationalistic socialism of Pilsudski's Polish Socialist party. He then went to Balliol College at Oxford. Balliol, in those days very fashionable, was the recruiting ground of British cabinets and diplomacy, and enjoyed the patronage of one of its most illustrious sons, the Liberal Prime Minister Herbert Asquith, later Lord Oxford. There, Namier (or Bernstein-Namierowski, as he then was) hobnobbed as an equal with young men who were to become famous, like T. E. Lawrence and Arnold J. Toynbee. Among his Jewish contemporaries at the College was Leonard Stein, future secretary of the World Zionist Organization and president of the Anglo-Jewish Association. (His lately published *History of the Balfour Declaration* is likely to remain the definitive study of that much-debated document which contains in a few lines the most controversial and vaguest promise of all time.) Another Jewish contemporary was Leonard Montefiore, of the famous Anglo-Jewish patrician family, a rather shy though witty man, almost cynically apologetic but at heart zealous in his work for non-Zionist Jewish causes.

Bernstein-Namierowski must have seemed an exotic and overbearing figure to the Fellows and undergraduates of the college. On one occasion, when they as yet hardly knew each other, Namier appeared at the door of Stein's rooms, and announced in his heavy accent: "I have come to discuss with you the Jewish question." Similarly in the course of a visit to the Montefiores' country home, young Namier sitting down one morning to breakfast announced that he intended to open a discussion of the problems of the Jews in Rumania. Upon which Mr. Claude Montefiore, the fastidious and wealthy scholar and theologian, editor of the Synoptic Gospels, abruptly barked out at his guest: "Now, Bernstein, you will eat your egg, and there will be no discussion either of Rumanian Jews or any other subject." Dr. Toynbee remembers how Namier would regale him and those who would care to listen with the intricacies of the nationalities' struggle in the Austro-Hungarian Empire. From the start he had to dominate others by acting as their teacher and mentor because he was incapable of feeling accepted simply as a member of whatever group he was in.

In 1914 Namier volunteered for the British Army. He served for a time in the Foreign Office Intelligence Service,, and was brought to the Versailles Peace Conference to advise on the problems concerning the old Hapsburg Empire, Poland, and Eastern Europe generally. There is reason to believe that he played some part in the rejection of the Andrassy note – a last attempt to ward off the dissolution of the Hapsburg monarchy through a separate peace with the Allied Powers. Although he was listened to on questions relating to the future of Poland, it is not true, as some Poles and above all the anti-Semitic Roman Dmowski claimed, that Namier initiated the Curzon Line scheme. It is true that he was against the inclusion of the territories inhabited by a Ukrainian and White Russian population into the new Poland: an arrangement which, while it flattered the Polish ambition to undo in part the 1772 partition, became an incubus upon the artificially inflated body of the new republic.[1]

The years following the First World War were exceedingly difficult in both his personal life and scholarly career. He did not turn at once to an academic career, but tried his luck in business, representing British firms in Vienna and then in the United States, without much success. (He needed the help of friends to complete his first book, which he wrote as a private scholar.) His first marriage turned out disastrously, and ended in divorce. These miseries were followed by years of solitude and study and were acutely unhappy ones.

One outlet he found was his Zionist activities, into which he threw himself with devotion. However, the leaders of the Zionist movement, and still more the delegates to the Zionist Congresses, viewed him with suspicion. He did not belong to any of the factions, his ways were strange. His pedantic insistence on the niceties of formulation and protocol, his close contacts with the English world, his lack of flexibility, and finally his unclear religious affiliations made him appear as an outsider to the ordinary Zionist from the Pale, someone to be appointed but never elected, a useful technician but not a representative. For a time he served as political secretary of the Zionist executive, but his deep wish – in which he had the support of Chaim Weizmann – to be elected member of the executive was never fulfilled. On one occasion two renowned Zionist leaders pulled him up sharply by reminding him that he was no more than a secretary and should know his place.

It was as a volunteer backroom boy in the kitchen of history that Namier made his contribution to the Zionist cause. He and Mrs. Blanche Dugdale, the niece of Arthur Balfour, were the chief draftsmen of the Jewish Agency. The infinite pains Namier would take to eliminate a superfluous word or to dig up the most telling and most idiomatic adjective became a legend, and a source of much mirth. However, Namier also played a considerable role as go-between in obtaining the Ramsay MacDonald Letter, which in fact cancelled the Passfield White Paper of 1930. Thanks to his friendship with Professor Copeland, the author of the famous 1937 Report of the Peel Commission (the first official British document to bring up the idea of a Jewish state in a partitioned Palestine), Namier was able to exercise a direct impact on matters of high importance.

For a time he served as deputy to Weizmann on the Anglo-Jewish Committee for Refugees from Germany, and took part in the struggle against the anti-Zionist notables (or "barons" as they were sometimes called) of Anglo-Jewry. On the eve of World War II, Namier returned to active Zionist work on a full-time basis. Criticizing Weizmann for his feebleness, he took a militant stand at the St. James Conference which resulted in the publication of the ill-fated White Paper of 1939. A British patriot, he nevertheless insisted on the need of a forceful and even threatening policy toward His Majesty's Government.

The Jewish world and the Zionist masses knew little of Namier's work, and this lack of recognition weighed heavily upon the historian-diplomat. Apart from his devotion to the Jewish people, Namier relished political action, a trait not uncommon in historians. Theodor Mommsen, for example, could never forgive either himself or the German people for his not having become a statesman. It is a moot point whether scholars of this type take up historical research and teaching as a substitute for making history or remain in the academic field (with occasional forays into the world of politics) because they cannot overcome their inhibitions.

In any case, Namier's Zionism was of a special kind. It was above all a passionately sentimental reaction to the humiliations inflicted upon the Jewish people in the last generation. His essays of wrath and pride on the Jewish question are among the most moving of all Jewish writings. But for all its intensity, Namier's Zionism had little connection with Judaism. He knew no Hebrew literature, he hated the Jewish religion, especially the religious parties in Zionism. He kept aloof from the ideological struggles between the various Zionist factions, although he had a definite predilection for the Labor leaders. Namier's Zionism was political, untouched by any cultural Ahad-Ha'amism. It was a romantic nationalism in the tradition of Mazzini and Pilsudski – the vision of a historical breakthrough conceived in messianic terms. He was too conditioned by the spirit of Polish patriotism to rule out military means for the achievement of Zionist ends. In later years – sophisticated as he was – he would proudly wave a newspaper which praised the Israeli infantry as the best in the world and which prophesied that the Israeli army would be in Damascus twenty-four hours after the start of hostilities if another war were to break out.

One day while visiting with him I began to lament the lost glories of the Mount Scopus landscape, to which he remarked that he had never set foot on the former campus of the Hebrew University. I expressed astonishment that he had never found time in the course of his numerous trips to Jerusalem to visit Mount Scopus before the road to it had fallen into Arab hands. "I would not shake hands with traitors," he said. "Traitors?" I murmured with raised eyebrows. "Well, Magnes," came the reply.

Once Namier was asked by a friend of his youth, a Gentile Polish historian, whether he would settle in Palestine after the Jewish state came into existence. "No," he answered, "I would not be able to feel at home there. Everything will be rough and ready, with no roots, with no organic cohesion, so provisional. No, I could not."

It was a typical remark. Lewis Namier was considered by many an incurable snob. Not only was he always seeking the company of the well-born, but he never tired of talking – both to those who were interested and those who were not – about his intimate contacts with dukes and lords, and about his week-ends in the great ancestral homes of England. With what delight Namier would roll off the names of all the members of this or that clan, the dates of their marriages across the centuries, the vicissitudes of one or another family estate. Yet to me, at least, none of this sounded like braggery – partly because of Namier's way of treating his own person and all that affected it as somehow of objective significance, and partly because of the deep romantic strain in the homage he paid to aristocracy. Other great Jews – among them Benjamin Disraeli and Ferdinand Lassalle – have displayed the same pathetic longing for ancient lineage. This is the way of some outsiders, who always sit on the edge of the chair, trying to experience a moment of communion with the "unbought grace" of the deeply rooted and the self-assured, those who have never known the need to present credentials.

Namier was much less eager for friendship with those famous for their intellect than he was for intimacy with men and women whose names could be found in Burke's Peerage. With them he met on a plane where the question of competition did not arise. In their eyes, he was a kind of glorified jester whom they genuinely admired and liked, and they appeared to his imagination – as they had to

Disraeli's – as living symbols. Not that such exceptionally shrewd and penetrating men as Namier and Disraeli were unable to see through this duke or that marquis and realize that he was after all a dullard. In their heart of hearts both men, capable of exquisite irony, would even mock their own passion as climbers. But in every aristocrat they saw the values which he was supposed to represent in all their splendor – the idea of nobility and chivalry, the chain of generations. Furthermore as outsiders weighed down by the sense of squalor attendant upon the struggle for recognition, these two Jews of genius and heart yearned for a loftier reality above and beyond their concrete circumstances. No wonder that Namier and Disraeli became the greatest poets of the glory of British aristocracy after Edmund Burke, who indeed belonged to it as little as they.

Namier's historical research may be classified under four headings: the social-political structure of England in the eighteenth century, the 1848 Revolutions, the twilight of the Hapsburg Monarchy, and the international crisis leading up to World War II. His writings under the first heading are concerned with the stability of a society with deep historic roots and unshakable sense of continuity. Under the second heading, he explores the discrepancy between the ideological will to total revolution and those forces and habits which resist change and in the end prove their superiority. Under the third and fourth headings, he finds lessons in decline and fall. It may be said that all four inquiries are variations on one and the same theme: cohesion versus disintegration.

To this extent, Namier's work, like that of every great historian and true artist, was also a veiled spiritual pilgrimage and even a way of working out a personal predicament. But however strongly subjective the imprint may be, the work must nevertheless retain objective significance. Thus the first question to ask is what is objectively novel about Namier's contribution? What does "Namierism" stand for? The best answer is provided by Namier's masterpiece, *The Structure of Politics at the Accession of George III*, which was published in 1929 when he was already past forty.

In this book Namier broke away from the prevailing Whig interpretation of English history which presented the struggle between George III and the opposition as a stage in the perennial conflict between liberty and tyranny. According to that view the Court lacked the power in the second part of the eighteenth century to challenge the authority of the Commons in open battle, and it therefore resorted to intrigue and corruption in an attempt to drain the parliamentary system of any real content. The results were not late in coming – the weakening of fiber lost Britain the American colonies. Namier decided to eschew any attempt at another panoramic view of the political scene, and resolutely ignored accepted categories such as ideology, party, general tendencies inherent in the march of history, or socio-economic determinism, which are so often merely a cloak for prejudice and the refuge of lazy or fuzzy minds. Instead he embarked upon a fabulously microscopic examination of the composition of the successive Houses of Commons under George III: where did the M.P.s come from, what was their family background, into what families did they marry, what and how much did they own, what was their education, what schools had they attended, who were their friends, what prompted one or the other to take up politics and stand for Parliament, in what ways did each one get elected? Namier followed up this investigation with questions on the circumstances of the emergence and of the fall of governments, the process of crystallization of parties, groups, and factions, and other such matters. He even went so far as to consult graphologists about the handwriting of an obscure eighteenth-century squire, and he would discuss the utterances, the lapses, and the style of a Hanoverian politician with a psychoanalyst. This method of research came to be called the biographical method, and was adopted for the great collective *History of Parliament* which Whitehall and Westminster initiated and over which Namier was invited to preside.

The picture which emerged from Namier's examination of the eighteenth century was of a political system run by a network of powerful families with the help of followers, or rather retainers, who were dependent on them. From this point of view the Court was only one of the great families, although the most important. Its ways and means of obtaining support were not appreciably different from those used by the territorial magnates, except, of course, the Royal patronage exceeded in scope any rewards that even the richest aristocrat could offer. On the other hand, the King could claim with a good deal of justification that he, if anyone, embodied the national interest, while the noble clans represented only their own self-interest.

On the face of it Namier may seem to arrive at a rather cynical conclusion: the governance of a selfish oligarchy without any idealist aspirations. But that was not what Namier meant to convey. What was to him most important was that the tradition of political independence, of a direct and active share in local and national government which the nobility and gentry succeeded in preserving for centuries, became a model to all classes of the nation. English liberty, then, was not the result of an uprising against existing institutions, but the concomitant of the assurance and stability which removes all fear of arbitrariness on the part of government or individuals. The monopoly of the ruling classes was not destroyed in one blow but rather the privileges and powers of the aristocracy were gradually extended to all. Class after class, as it were, won its spurs. Further, in England, immunities, privileges, liberties, and political rights were rooted originally in the ownership of land. They constituted one of the ingredients – alongside others – of the family patrimony, as inviolably the hereditary possession of the landowner as the chattel or the house or the land itself, and thus they were not something conceded by the legislator that could also be withdrawn. They were property pure and simple. Hence their strength and permanence.

Namier has one further reason for viewing the land as the matrix of liberty. For him, it is the focus of integrated ways and habits which make the man who lives by them feel self-assured and firmly fixed. Otherwise, outside the organic web of custom, man is a lonely and weak creature, hesitant, swayed by many conflicting influences, and a prey to tyranny.

From these premises Namier reached a somewhat disconcerting conclusion for an orthodox Zionist. He condemned the nationalist movements inspired by the idea of the unity of language and race – that is to say, those movements which rested on a personal instead of a territorial basis. Too conscious of the English example – which has hardly any relevance to conditions on the European continent, especially Central and Eastern Europe – Namier attacked linguistic nationalism as a pernicious solvent which destroyed the social-political cohesion that had crystallized in the dynastic empires over the course of centuries. Societies were turned into hordes, clusters of groups into human dust. Since it was impossible to separate the interlocked races who made up the mixed population of these empires, the national conflicts which began to break out in Central and Eastern Europe around 1848 assumed the character of racial wars being fought to the death. In that atmosphere, charged with hatred and warlike postures, the tender plant of liberalism could take no root. And the drama came to an end in the Second World War in race massacre, mass expulsion, and, at the very least, in the transfer of millions of people from one country to another.

The cry "away from Namier and Namierism" was raised two or three years before the historian's death. Critics began to point out the weaknesses of Namier's method. One-sided, certainly, was his concentration upon political history, in spite of his strong awareness that politics is a function of social realities. Namier was not interested in economic transformations or social structure or class struggle in themselves. His concern was with how politics are made. In this respect the corrective offered by him remains important: a country is run not by the masses or classes or great individual leaders, but by closely interlocked groups of men. Namier set out to portray through the biographies of individuals a group mind and a political style.

The most telling objection against Namier was that he took the mind out of history, that by dwelling too much on how and by whom intrigue is consciously or unwittingly cooked up, he forgot the existence of great causes that stir men's minds and hearts, and of leaders who are able to inspire and, when endowed with vision, to impose a pattern on generations. There is some substance in that criticism, but it seems to me that one issue is wrongly put. In a certain sense Namier was in fact obsessed by the question of the role of ideas in history to the point of its having a tragic meaning to him. He was haunted by the mysterious discrepancy between conscious ideas and unconscious urges in the hearts of men and masses, between the image we have of things and what things really are. Far from denying the potency of political and social ideologies, he was frightened by their power to disturb, and he was inclined to regard them as the neurotic symptoms of a society, as traumatic visitations. Experiences of early childhood dominate men for all their lives like demons: instead of adapting themselves to a given concrete situation, men cannot help going again and again through the motions which had been summoned up by that earlier fateful situation. The French people could not shake off the trauma of the French Revolution for over a hundred years. Although objective conditions would have frustrated any attempt to restore feudalism even in its mildest form, the left never ceased to dread the restoration of the *ancien regime*. And although the revolutionary volcano of 1793 had been extinct for a long while, the right saw in every insignificant riot the specter of the Red Terror coming back, and out of this mortal fear came the bloody massacres of 1848 and 1871.

Namier sums up his viewpoint as follows: "Human society is not an organism capable of unconscious growth; at every stage thought and theory intervene, more often impeding than promoting readjustments imposed by circumstance and achieved in practice . . . a neurotic, according to Freud, is a man dominated by unconscious memories, fixated on the past, and incapable of overcoming it: the regular condition of human communities. Yet the dead festering past cannot be eliminated by violent action any more than an obsession can be cured by beating the patient. History has therein a "psychoanalytic" function; and it further resembles psychoanalysis in being better able to diagnose than to cure."

How else is one to explain the attacks of collective madness that sweep a nation – for instance, the "Great Fear" that swept France in 1789, to which Namier liked to refer; or the strange vacillations of popular sentiment toward heroes and creeds – if not by psychological projections or displacements, and the externalization of unresolved inner conflicts? The organic cohesion of historic continuity is the most constructive factor, whereas ideas act as solvents or as paralyzing forces, and any attempt to transform "the way of life of a nation, its *moeurs*, by an act of will or an edict . . . [is] . . . expressive of intellectual hubris. . . ." For Namier, the ideologue lacked the saving wisdom of self-knowledge; he was duplicitous and dangerous: "self-deception concerning the origin and character of his seemingly intellectual tenets enables him to deceive others; the intensity of the hidden passion sharpens his mental faculties and may even create the appearances of cold, clear-sighted objectivity."

In Namier's later years, of course, a traumatic memory of Nazism and Bolshevism was always at the back of his mind, but there was also the suspicion that recourse to ideas is an expression of some neurotic choice. He believed in "instincts and modes of thinking much deeper and much more cogent than any conscious reasoning." Characteristically Namier concluded his essay on "Human Nature in Politics" (a review of a new edition of Graham Wallas's famous book of the same title) with an aside against those who since the end of World War II have been complaining of a "tired lull" and the "absence . . . of argument on general politics." To him this absence "seemed to betoken a greater national maturity," and he could "only wish that it [might] long continue undisturbed by the workings of political philosophy." The best state of affairs is characterized by a situation in which "practical solutions are sought for concrete problems, while programmes and ideals are forgotten by both parties."

If all attempts at consciously directing the flow of events are doomed to frustration and impotence, are we to conclude that history is propelled by predetermined and uncontrollable forces? In one place Namier gives a blood-curdling answer to this question. "Those who are out to apportion guilt in history . . . judge the collisions of planets by the rules of the street traffic, make history into something like a column of motoring accidents, and discuss it in the atmosphere of a police court. But whatever theories of 'free will' theologians and philosophers may develop with regard to the individual, there is no free will in the thinking and actions of the masses, any more than in the revolutions of the planets, in the migration of birds, and in the plunging of hordes of lemmings into the sea."

Namier's achievement and reputation as a historian did not win for him the regard he most desired, and his academic career was marked by much the same frustration and disappointment that attended his work as a Zionist. After the publication of *England in the Age of the American Revolution*, he was given the chair of Modern History at Manchester University which he held from 1931 to 1953. He never grew attached to Manchester; his heart was set on returning to Oxford, which he loved in the spirit of Cardinal Newman or Matthew Arnold. However, Oxford continued to keep him out. When the Regius Professorship of Modern History fell vacant in the late '40s, there were rumors that Prime Minister Attlee did not appoint Namier because he would not have a scholar who was both a Zionist and a Tory. However, what is more likely is that Oxford, like Cambridge, though fond of eccentrics, is frightened of men who do not converse at ease but instead hold forth and grant audiences. Namier's manner was such that the faculty of Oxford could feel no more comfortable with him than could his Zionist colleagues.[2]

Yet in the end this lonely and neurotic man won his fight for acceptance, and some measure of peace and happiness came to reward his years of toil and torment. Namier was invited to give the Romanes Lecture, the highest of the honors that Oxford can bestow; and shortly after Harold Macmillan's election as Chancellor of the University, he awarded his old friend an honorary doctorate. Namier's second wife, the former Julia de Beausobre, brought joy into his life. A daughter of the Russian gentry and deeply committed to the Greek Orthodox Church, she had suffered in Soviet prisons and concentration camps; her first husband had been executed by the Soviets, and her only child had died in prison (an experience movingly described in her book, *The Woman Who Could Not Die*). To her Namier symbolized the people chosen by God for some mysterious calling, like the Russian people. It is possible that her influence accounts for Namier's having begun to believe – or having tried to persuade himself to believe – that Christianity was nothing but a kind of Jewish Protestantism, and that Jews should forget all animosities toward Christians and become proud of their offspring. (Curiously, this was also Disraeli's conviction.)

It may well be that the most solemn moment in the closing phase of his life was Namier's address to the Modern History seminar at the Hebrew University in Jerusalem, when he came for the last time to Israel in connection with a scheme for the publication of the Weizmann papers. It was one of those exhilarating spring days, before the khamsins from the desert have tarnished everything with that dusty brown color and when in a riot of Van Gogh sunshine every rock seems to be bursting with flowers and every hill calls hosanna. The reception hall of the Sherman Building was packed with teachers and students. Lewis Namier rose to his feet. His voice trembled and tears rolled down his cheeks as he began with the Hebrew "If I forget thee, O Jerusalem. . . ." It was not a lecture in the ordinary sense. Without a scrap of paper in his hand he gave us his testament as a scholar, recalling his early beginnings, his later successes and failures, issuing warnings, giving advice and encouragement to the young. The words were simple, but the things he said came straight from his deepest personal experience. One felt an intimation of the tremendous seriousness of the historian's quest, and one was touched for a moment by the majesty of life, when wisdom becomes indistinguishable from goodness and the same as beauty.

First published in *Commentary* 33, 1962.

Notes

1 Namier was later to play a certain diplomatic role in the Second World War, serving as a semi-official liaison officer between the British Foreign Office and one of the Allied governments in exile. Yet I have only recently been

given proofs of the extent to which the British Foreign Office distrusted him in that role, even though it had no connection with Zionist or Jewish issues.

2 There can be no question of discrimination in Namier's case, for in recent years Oxford has awarded some of its most important and sensitive chairs to Jews, a number of whom came to England in middle life: Sir Isaiah Berlin (Chichele Professor of Social and Political Theory), Max Beloff (Gladstone Chair of Government), David Daube (Regius Professor of Civil Law), the late Sir Francis Simon (Physics), Sir Hans Krebs (Nobel Prize winner in Medicine), Herbert Fraenkel (Colonial Economics), Edgard Wind (Art), not to speak of A. E. Goodhardt, Master of New College.

Andrei Sakharov's Odeal

The phenomenon of Andrei Sakharov is a paradigm of the eternal dilemma of Antigone – the conflict between the law of the state and one's sense of natural justice, between the call of one's fatherland and the voice of one's conscience. In its peculiar metamorphosis in our age, this dichotomy between loyalty to one's country and duty to mankind is also bound up with the awesome tension between the eternal search for discovery and application of scientific truths and the moral responsibility for the sacredness of life and the survival of civilization.

Sakharov exemplifies the position of an intellectual vis-à-vis politics; he must be seen in the context of Russian tradition on the one hand, and of Western values on the other. We must also examine the significance of Sakharov's public stand on behalf of the Jews and of its bearing on the struggle of the State of Israel, and this from two points of view: Soviet realities and policies as they relate to them, and the present alignment of world forces in this hour of wrath for our people, which is also a testing ground for mankind.

Since the emergence of totalitarian regimes in the wake of World War I, there has been no example of an individual's revolt against the regime as momentous as Sakharov's. The extent of the present confrontation is measured by his personality, the world-wide attention he has attracted, and the issues. Sakharov is fighting alone. He holds no official position, there is no organization or party behind him, and (according to the accounts of my informants who have left Russia) most of the intellectuals there have strong objections and not much sympathy for this man who has managed to cast off the inhibitions and restraints that silence the others.

Sakharov's strength lies in both his scientific eminence and his prophetic stance: "I can bear it no longer!" This fact is of general historical significance when we recall that apart from the hunger demonstrations in Posen, Berlin and Danzig, the standard bearers of all revolutionary uprisings and opposition movements since World War II have not been workers but highly motivated intellectuals – the intelligentsia in general. Even if we do not shut our eyes to the sometimes awkward, even perverse excrescences accompanying these phenomena of opposition and revolt, it must be said nevertheless that they have in the main been an expression of resistance to the suppression of the spirit and tokens of a struggle for freedom. In our days history is being stood on its head (as, according to Hegel, it should be!).

But we should be in error if we analyzed this phenomenon as a clash between force and spirit and as nothing else. In our time, to be sure, as in the past, although to a lesser extent, the spirit represents a mighty force. It is one of the ironies of history that while technological and socio-political centralization is constantly strengthening the monopoly of power held by the State, this very power is to an ever increasing extent bestowed upon it by the exertions of scientists and men of intellect. The regime depends on them; it is sustained by them. And although it would seem to be easy to suppress or neutralize such a relatively small group, it would mean killing the goose that lays the golden eggs.

I have said that the Soviet intelligentsia does not consider Sakharov its chosen spokesman; in fact, it opposes him. But it is one thing for people to identify themselves actively with a person's deeds, which sometimes seem to overstep bounds, and another to remain indifferent and hostile to him when he is being persecuted for objectively representing their fundamental interests and basic ethos, and for embodying the immanent desires of the group, indeed of the whole society.

Neither the despotic regimes of the past, nor the ideological totalitarian dictatorships of the present century, have been based on coercion, bayonets, police and spies exclusively. The old despotism relied on the aura of divine right, sanctified taboos and the sense of awe surrounding it to restrain rebels from raising their hands against God's anointed and his aides. Modern tyranny depends on a pervasive faith in an all-embracing, omnipotent and exclusive ideology as a guideline that there can be no deviation from and that must not be questioned. The scientist's commitment to rational methods and the very effectiveness of his contribution rest on a critical approach, on casting doubt, on the revision of accepted dogmas, on an ever-changing shift of perspective, on the admission of the provisional character of every statement, and the recognition of the ambivalence of all phenomena.

The great achievements which inspire the scientists with a sense of power and a consciousness of their own importance also stimulate their resolution, courage and ability to fight for rational methods. And this is at least a partial answer to the question many have asked: how was it possible that what was inconceivable in the days of Stalin, such as the phenomenon of Sakharov and the emergence of various opposition groups, became feasible under his successors?

Communist dogma regards the Communist Party not as an association of men presenting itself to serve the people and promising to withdraw when it is no longer wanted, but as the oracle of history – an essential part of the ideological pattern. Moreover, "scientific" Socialism as such is held to be unfolding in a way similar to the hierarchy of the Catholic Church. The truth of the dogma of the infallibility of the leadership of the Communist Party appeared in its own day vindicated by the victory of Stalin over his rivals, and even more convincingly by his triumph over Hitler, and reaffirmed by the duration of his regime and by his seemingly total immunity from all opposition – overlooking the instruments of oppression and revolutionary terror employed, which Communist theology does not, of course, see as invalidating "dialectical" inevitability.

The turning point in the attitude of the intellectuals toward the political leadership came after the deadly blow against the Stalin cult delivered by Khrushchev at the 20th Congress in 1956, which brought to light in all its amplitude the capricious, sadistic character of Stalin's regime. It gave scientists and intellectuals a greater feeling of self-confidence, since it coincided with a series of remarkable scientific breakthroughs. Moreover, that was the time when the Soviet regime was growing visibly weaker, partly because of the system of collective leadership. All this opened the eyes of intellectuals and led them to distinguish more and more clearly between the dogma of the unique mission of the Community Party in fulfilling the Communist ideal and the self-aggrandizing ambitions of the ephemeral men who claim the crown of prophecy and also the crown of leadership which under a Communist regime are inseparable.

The moment of truth in Sakharov's life came during a banquet held to celebrate the first successful experiment with the hydrogen bomb. He made a speech in which he expressed his pride at this achievement and at the same time his fears of the terrifying possibilities it entailed. It was his belief and hope, he concluded, that those called upon to produce this powerful weapon would have some say in the ways it was used so that it would not bring an end to mankind: "Our handiwork shall never burst over the cities."

Sakharov reported that the head of the military establishment, his tongue loosened by drink, retorted that it was not the scientists who were the owners of the monster they had created, but the political-military establishment, and its members would decide when, where or whether to use it. "Your task, scientists, is to perfect the instrument – the way it is used is none of your business." At that moment Sakharov's eyes were opened, it seems, to the situation of scientists in a totalitarian regime.

Sakharov, his friends say, is not a man easily overcome by the sort of attacks of divine madness that would turn him into a monomaniac. According to his acquaintances whom I talked to, he is rather naive, a slow thinker, who nourishes his thoughts for a long while, but doesn't change his mind once it is set. To say that he is naive simply means that in his straightforward manner he says what he means. And when the spirit moves him, he becomes indifferent to approval or disapproval, public opinion, prevailing fashion, personal interest, or prospects of success. This is a sign of genuine greatness. One of his hostile critics wrote that "he plays the fool"; one might add "Christ's fool."

When Sakharov started working on the hydrogen bomb he was anxious to serve the USSR. A patriotic Russian, a faithful Communist, he wanted to help his country and defend it from hostile powers.

After his eyes were opened, he became increasingly critical of Soviet policies; more and more he began to protest the misguided ways of the Soviet regime before the world forum.

He not only condemns the actions of his government to its face, but even requests foreign governments to put pressure on it – as in the case of the Jackson amendment and the U.S. policy on détente – and to impose conditions and limitations on it.

Sakharov has indefatigably pointed out "the tragic dangers that will ensue from the disunity and egoistic shortsightedness in Western countries and from their under-estimation of the cunning of their totalitarian enemies" and "the lack of a clear understanding of the ever-present global threat latent in totalitarian states." The internal policies of the leaders of the USSR were inseparable from their international schemes and as such – granted the immense power and the sustained dynamism of Russia – were of overriding concern to all mankind. Human rights were, in any case, never an internal affair of a single country.

Even in the most liberal countries there is a general acceptance of the rule: "My country right or wrong." This is hardly questioned even by dissidents. The problem is much more severe in Soviet Russia because of the prevailing siege complex, the dogma of the never-ending and never assuaged hostility of the capitalist world, the myth of the imperialist conspiracy and the idea that it is the mission of the Soviet Union to be the standard-bearer of a salvationist world Communism. In addition, there is the deeply rooted tradition of secrecy and suspicion in Russian diplomacy – a legacy of centuries.

A totalitarian system, and especially the Bolshevik régime, fortifies itself by the existence or even the creation of an atmosphere of emergency. It must be able to point to internal and external enemies, it needs the myth of secret conspiracies lying in wait, working incessantly underground, the Jacobin "complot" in the French Revolution, in order to justify the unrestrained rule of a terrorist dictatorship at home, and policies of unbridled opportunism, subversive methods, and a treacherous Machiavellism in foreign policy. The Communist regime regards itself as engaged in perpetual rivalry with the capitalist world for the soul of man. Each of them is competing for a proper image, is bent upon strengthening and intensifying morale within its own country while destroying the enemy's spirit.

Paradoxically, the Soviet regime came into being by way of national treason, committed, it is true, in the name of the categorical imperative of redeeming the world proletariat. Throughout World War I, Lenin called on the workers of all the combatant countries to turn the imperialist war of nations into an international civil war; he exhorted the workers and peasants of Russia to oppose the war effort, to sabotage it, to turn the guns against their officers and rulers – words which were interpreted by the soldiers in the trenches as a call to desert, to return home in order to divide up the estates and property of the landowners among themselves. Support for the country's war effort or opposition then became the yardstick, the shibboleth: "For us or for our Foe [the Tsar]."

Lenin condemned all shades of opinion that justified a national war of defense, the Social Revolutionaries and the Mensheviks within Russia and the workers' parties outside Russia, and denied them the title of Socialists and the right to participate in the Workers' International. For him the War was the apocalyptic crisis of the capitalist regime and bourgeois civilization, and the birthpangs of the world revolution on the ruins of the sovereign bourgeois nation-states.

The international revolution, passionately proclaimed, intensely desired by Lenin, was regarded by him as the condition *sine qua non* for the success of the revolution in Russia to such an extent that – upon his own reiterated admission – he would never have dared to order the final assault to bring about a revolution in only a single country, and a backward and ruined one at that, had he not had the certainty that it would be followed by revolutionary uprisings in the neighboring countries, above all Germany.

But that revolution never happened – for the Bolshevik Party there was no alternative but to elevate absolute and unconditional devotion to the "Socialist" fatherland to the dignity of the supreme categorical imperative not only for the citizens of the Soviet Union, but for Communists the world over. Otherwise, in view of their failure to bring about a world revolution, the disloyalty of the Bolsheviks to their country during the War was likely to be interpreted as a fatal error, indeed a crime. At the time of the Nazi invasion, there was again no choice but to resuscitate traditional Russian patriotism.

Sakharov has turned upside down Lenin's precept of the primacy of the policies of the regime. The day of the exclusive sovereignty of the nation-state – he claims – is over. It is no longer possible in the era of nuclear weapons, in the light of the dependence of the small states upon the supplies and arms from the superpowers, in the face of ecological dangers confronting all mankind, and the threat of famine and strangulation on a global scale. None of these problems can be solved by egoistic policies conceived through narrow and hasty assessment, and for the short term.

From this point of view, the worst menace is the dogma of inevitable ideological struggle between states, and the atmosphere of tension and military preparedness that this engenders. In the face of weapons with a power of inconceivable destruction, there is no goal, no aim, no ideal that can justify the price of its employment as a weapon of war.

Sakharov does not uphold any specific socio-political or philosophical doctrine. His views can be summarized as follows: he is fighting for an open society, a free exchange of ideas, for public discussion of internal and external issues; he demands that human rights be unconditionally honored and internationally protected, and he staunchly refuses to see them as an internal affair of the single sovereign state. He calls for a sense of individual and governmental responsibility for the future of mankind, and preaches an internationalism that will ensure global cooperation against the dangers confronting humanity, such as squandering natural resources, an uncontrolled birth-rate, and technological advances which are likely to bring incalculable socio-economic military and moral perils. He calls for a reduction of armaments by putting their production under local, public and permanent control by international agencies and for an end to ideological and psychological warfare. He is a strong believer in the principle of international interdependence; he insists that the existence and rights of any people or group must not be subordinated to the ideas, interests, power or self-glorification of another; the universal aspiration to secure the equality of all has in any case made such an attempt unworkable in the long run – the resentment of the subjugated turns into revolt. The chain of rebellion and suppression proves to be utterly corrosive, wasteful and self-destructive to both sides.

These are ideas of western liberalism. But while describing himself as a "confirmed evolutionist and reformist," Sakharov tries to win people over to his way of thinking in the spirit and style of the nineteenth-century conscience-stricken Russian intellectuals, the prophets of the revolution, men like Herzen, Chernyshevsky, Dobrolyubov and Tolstoy, in whose ears there always echoed the injunction: "Cain, where is your brother Abel?"

Sakharov does not attack Marxism, Communist ideology or collectivism frontally. It was not his original intention to refute them. But the rejection is clearly implied in his contention that they have become obsolete and reactionary.

In the chapter entitled "The Liberal Intelligentsia of the West: Their Illusions and Responsibilities," from his recent book, *My Country and the World*, there is a sentence that speaks of a "totalitarian socialism (which may be called pseudo-socialism) which by nature of its inherent quality of immanent stability, and the inertia of fear and passivity . . . is a kind of historical dead-end from which it is troublesome to escape." The postscript of the book, written only in June, 1975, entertains far-reaching demands, including "legislative confirmation of the right of Soviet republics to secede, and the right to discuss the question of secession"; a "multi-party system"; public discussion of constitutional proposals; and finally, demands with revolutionary implications for "partial denationalization" of all types of economic and social activity, probably excluding heavy industry and major transportation, "in the area of services, in retail trade, education and medical care . . . partial decollectivization of agriculture."

What is the crux of the debate between Sakharov and the Soviet establishment? It cannot be maintained that Bolshevism, in theory, had ever advocated dictatorship as a permanent system of government based upon total and endless subjugation of the individual and society by the State. Bolshevism prophesied that following the abolition of private property, the removal of inequality, the nationalization of the means of production, the liquidation of the remnants of backwardness, prejudice, class egoism, capitalistic aggression – by a temporary dictatorship of the proletariat – there would emerge in the foreseeable future a complete consensus of opinion. Such unanimity would resolve the contradiction between freedom and equality – when all are in agreement, all are free and equal – and there would be no need for any kind of coercive rule – government would gradually "wither away."

Although Sakharov does not openly call for free elections and parliamentary government, he implies that the provisional conditions that allegedly necessitated and justified dictatorship are no longer relevant. The Soviet man and the Russian people have grown up and no longer need custodians or coercion. They only hinder the potential, the abilities and the initiative of the citizens. The long dictatorial regime, continuing without any control, has confirmed its role as that of an oppressor and a hindrance that stifles and erodes society. Sakharov deplores the "chaotic situation" in Soviet industry and agriculture.

As the Dubcek episode in Czechoslovakia has proved, such criticism must call into question the principle of the monopolistic power of the Communist Party, a principle on which no Communist government can yield without virtually committing suicide. It may repeatedly declare its faith in détente, but in order to maintain its monopolistic rule, it must again and again reiterate that Communist achievements are still being endangered by subversive ideas, foreign agents, or simply by powerful evil-doers sustained by alien ideologies. And thus, paradoxically, an ideology whose starting point was a rationalistic belief in the natural goodness of man and in his capacity to improve, has come to adopt an attitude of inordinate suspicion, contempt and oppression towards man.

Sakharov's views on freedom of emigration are of particular interest. "The question of the freedom to choose one's country of residence has become a touchstone [for the entire process of détente]." It is indeed so. Soviet spokesmen do not tire of proclaiming that complete social justice has been achieved in their country and that everybody there is assured of happiness. It follows that anyone who wishes to emigrate, is *ipso facto*, expressing his disbelief and contradicts the statements of the government by showing his dissatisfaction. Moreover, if everybody is free to choose the country of his residence, why should he not be free to choose a government to his liking?

Russian tradition is anti-individualistic and anti-liberal *par excellence*, with scant interest in law and jurisprudence. In classical Russian socio-political thought the individual did not appear as a subject with rights, able to claim his due, as an owner of chattels, as a freeholder. If a peasant, he belonged to the village commune holding its fields and meadows in common; if a serf of a landlord, such as one of the souls of Gogol, he was owned as a transferable property. And even when a landlord, he held one of the ranks in the system of ranks in the service of the Tsar.

In Russian literature man was depicted as an object of love and compassion, but also given to sin and suffering. This attitude concealed in itself a large measure of contempt. He who wishes to show compassion, who is ready to forgive, to bestow good deeds, is motivated by a hidden craving for ascendancy because he expects that the object of his noble graciousness would be weak, weighed down by a sense of debt and guilt.

No one can ever be sure of his rights without what Montesquieu has termed the certitude, the conviction that there are things that will never happen to him, and other things that are sure to happen – a trust that constitutes the guarantee of freedom. And where there are undefined and undetermined human relations, which cannot be properly measured, and like love, compassion, mercy and charity are preferred to legal norms, there we have obfuscation, and willfulness. Wherever the rule of law does not prevail, institutions are weak, unable to develop, distrusted. Instead there is the glorification of the hidden inner light, the intentions of the heart.

It is no wonder that not a few of the Russian prophets of compassion so easily developed a disregard, a profound suspicion, contempt and indeed a manifest hatred of man. It is sufficient to recall Pobedonostsev, Katkov, Leontieff, not to speak of Dostoyevsky. All of them were intoxicated by the idea of original sin.

There is no need to impose, consciously or unconsciously, forced historical analogies in order to perceive the continuity of the patterns of thought and behavior in the evolution of Russia from the Tsarist times to the Communist regime, against which Sakharov has risen in rebellion.

The mystique which permeated and sustained the Tsarist empire was derived from Russia's being for so long the only Christian-Orthodox power in the world. After the conquest of Constantinople by the Turks and the establishment of Ottoman rule over all the other Greek-Orthodox nations, Russia stood out in the eyes of the faithful as the guardian of true Christianity. She was regarded as the Third Rome, heir to Italy and Byzantium, not merely a political and military power, but a Light unto the Nations, leader of all the believers in authentic, pristine Christianity. It was Russia's mission to deliver them from the Turkish yoke and also from heretical Catholicism, and to bring them under the rule of God's deputy on earth – the Tsar, who was at the same time the head of the State and the Church.

In the West such a unity of Church and State was never brought about. The ensuing dualism turned out to be the main factor which ensured freedom in the West. The Western Church was never in a position to subordinate the state and to establish a theocracy, and for centuries, the State was not strong enough to absorb the Church and to subjugate it to lay authority.

Tsarist Russia, asserted the Slavophiles, was not just a great power pursuing policies to its own advantage, but a bearer of good tidings, of a redemptive mission to all mankind, while the West, the heir of Rome and the apprentice of Roman Catholicism, was being eaten away by the cancer of selfish individualism. Pagan Rome (and, in the course of time, the Jews) bequeathed the West the doctrine of the sacredness of private property, *ius utendi et abutendi*, with no thought to humanity or to the community, and with the mercantile worship of mine and thine, written contracts, hair-splitting legalities – all signs of distrust and materialistic utilitarianism. In contrast to this was the spirit of love, trust, absence of written documents, of any felt need for guarantees or sanctions – the mutual affection and trust that characterized the relations between the paternalistic Tsar and his subjects, and the ties between members of the village commune. The very clamor for written agreements, a constitution, separation of powers, individual rights, as customary in the West, was regarded by the true Russian as a sign of alienation and apostasy, of nihilism and the spirit of rebellion. Again, the doctrine of boundless love co-existed with arbitrary despotism on the one hand, and servility, deceitfulness and bribery on the other. As a consequence life in Russia was a fantasy permeated with hypocrisy and mendacity. The Soviet version of this phenomenon caused Sakharov to rebel and to become a prophet.

There is a considerable difference between Sakharov, a liberal upholder of the rule of law and of free institutions, and Alexander Solzhenitsyn, who is deeply rooted in the Slavophilic tradition. In the view of the latter, the wicked Soviet regime has corrupted all that was good in Russia to such an extent that the best institutions have become powerless, and that only through a change of heart and a return to the true Christian-Orthodox faith will it be possible to redeem and to resurrect Russia. Solzhenitsyn stands in opposition to totalitarian ideologies, but he is ready to come to terms with a dictatorship, if only it will leave freedom of the soul intact. His attitude to Western liberal democracies is cool; this explains in no small measure his love-hate feelings for the Jews. He is bothered by Judaism, finding it difficult to reconcile the messianic Jewish message with that of the Russian people.

The Russian revolutionary movement in the nineteenth century aimed first and foremost at freeing the enslaved Russian people from their veneration of the Tsar, God's anointed and from the compulsive grip of religious dogma, including all kinds of taboos, prejudices and superstitions. Contemptuous and rude defiance of all symbols, decorum, customs and images, terror, bloody attempts on the life of the Tsar and leaders of the aristocratic regime – all these were used as exercises in defiance to undermine the edifice. In this context it is easy to understand the revolutionaries' extreme philosophical materialism, utilitarianism and nihilism as well as their crude and uncouth approach to art and literature.

The underlying reasons behind these approaches was the conviction that the distinctions between the material and spiritual world served as a justification of the division of men into two exclusive groups: those convinced of their own superiority, on one side, and, on the other, the coarse ignorant masses destined to remain forever outside the pale of culture, hewers of wood and drawers of water.

Hence the teaching that all men were prompted by selfish interests, sought pleasure and wished to avoid pain. Egoism was masked by lofty, idealistic talk. Even a mother who sacrificed herself for the sake of her child did so because it brought her pleasure. Justice must come before aesthetics, and was prior to all cultural strivings.

The revolutionaries strove to redeem the ignorant, oppressed and hungry masses and to compensate them for the generations of bondage and exploitation. But at the same time they were painfully aware that the backward and enslaved masses were not capable of redeeming themselves – they would not dare to do so. The masses were in need of leadership. But was it not in itself pride and arrogance to be ready to propose oneself for the leadership, to put oneself at the head? At whose prompting?

A solution to this conflict of conscience was found in the idea of a vanguard leadership, putting all its soul and body into Revolution, sacrificing itself for the sake of the people. The image of such a revolutionary hero became known as "the new man," the prototype of "the man of the future," an advance copy of tomorrow's race: Rachmetov in the greatly influential novel by Chernyshevsky, *What is to be Done?* (*Tch'to dielat?*) which so deeply impressed Lenin that he used it as a title of his most popular pamphlet. Rachmetov, who never stops preaching that all human activity was prompted by selfish considerations, tortures his body by all sorts of ascetic practices, sleeps on a bed studded with nails, and abstains from all pleasures of the world in order to be better prepared to assume the burdens and afflictions of a leader, ready to sacrifice himself for all who are oppressed. A vanguard, however idealistic in its origins, invariably tends to degenerate into a clique upon gaining power, much to mankind's misfortune.

Sakharov represents this awareness which was long ago acknowledged in the West. And at the same time being a Russian and imbued with the Russian tradition, he repeatedly asserts, as I was told by one of the Russian immigrants who knew him well, that he is only able to fight for others, for the sake of his fellow men, and not for his own interests: "Cain, where is your brother Abel?"

Sakharov himself is possessed by a stricken conscience, a feeling of guilt. But he turned the sense of original sin into a feeling of apocalyptic awe in the face of the spectre of impending doom, and into the intellectual's sense of responsibility for saving humanity.

"Thermonuclear warfare has already become a dark reality of modern times like Auschwitz, the Gulag, and famine," writes Sakharov. "Perhaps I feel it more acutely than other people, since for over twenty years I was in contact with that fantastically terrifying world." Although he has not participated in secret military work since 1968, "the psychological experience of those tense decades is still alive in me. And I feel that this entitles me, and in fact obliges me to put my thoughts in writing. . . . Not for a moment can I forget that all this time hundreds of thousands of workers, thousands of talented engineers, and scientists from many fields of specialization are working and expanding and perfecting systems" to wipe out mankind and to destroy all that is on this earth.

How does Sakharov's attitude to the Jewish people and to the State of Israel appear to us in the present world situation, at a time of the greatest calamities that have overtaken the Jewish people since the destruction of the Second Temple?

In my view, it confirms once again the contention that we, the Jewish people, can breathe freely, more or less, only in the climate of liberalism. Jewish civilization in Eastern and Central Europe is ten, in some countries indeed fifteen centuries old. (A few months ago I was told by the noted scholar, Professor Scheiber who keeps alive the spark of Jewish learning in far-off Budapest, cut off from all contact with world Jewry, that an inscription about a Syndicus Judeorum was found in Hungary dating from the third century, from the days of the Emperor Alexander Severus – five or six centuries before the Magyars poured out of the Asiatic steppes and invaded Hungary!) Jewish civilization came to an end in countries in which liberalism had never taken root, and which in modern times were carried away by a wave of extreme nationalism focused on biological determinism. With all its weaknesses, faults and crimes, the main values of the liberal tradition were not entirely wiped out in the West even during the severe test of the momentous ideological confrontation, and across the ocean, within the greatest power of all time, there emerged a Jewish community of unequaled strength and possibilities in the framework of a liberal society, contractual nationhood and ethnic and cultural pluralism.

In the Roman-Hellenistic period, of all the people who were conquered by Alexander the Great and by Rome, only one culture retained its independent identity in a world of nations entirely absorbed by Hellenistic, by Roman, and in the course of time by Christian civilization – Jewry. From then on and until today Jews have never been able to flourish under a biological or ideological exclusiveness. Even if it does not proclaim explicitly its anti-Jewishness, there is no room in such a regime for Jewish non-conformism, for universal Jewish unity, and for a specifically Jewish foreign policy.

There are increasing signs that an old constellation is forming anew, this time in relation to the State of Israel. In the nineteenth century, Jewish emancipation served both as a test and a milestone. The inclusion of the Jews within the scope of general equality of rights became a touchstone of the victory of the liberal-democratic tenets, a sign of the acceptance of the principle of human rights. Their exclusion was proof of the unshaken potency and paramountcy of the idea of the Christian state, hierarchical social structure and authoritarian modes of thought.

Countries of the Third World, with a past devoid of the Jews and also of the liberal tradition, and the Communist countries which have denied liberalism and refused to acknowledge the uniqueness of the Jewish phenomenon, lack the openness, the generosity of spirit, the tolerant wisdom, the awareness of the destiny and of the peculiar contribution of the Jewish people. They experience therefore none of the feelings of shame, gratitude and indebtedness towards it that move the hearts of the peoples in the West, and that Sakharov has become the spokesman for in the East. "I regard [Jewish immigration to Israel] as a phenomenon that has meaning for all mankind and is of basic importance in the tragic thousands-of-years history of the Jewish people." Such sentiments cause the followers of Western liberalism to act with instinctive, almost reflexive recoiling to any voice or hint demanding the liquidation of the State of Israel, whatever their egoistic calculations may be, or whatever uncomfortable thoughts about that or other manifestations of Israel's policy they may have.

The State of Israel and the Jewish people are once again in that siege mentality. Public voices proclaim that the entire world is aligned against us; some spread slogans that the world was ruled by nothing but force, and that the only response to brute force was force. Such sentiments are calculated to justify the doctrine that in an hour of emergency accepted norms do not apply and are not binding. Here lies the danger that our enemies will drive us into an attitude, and force us into a situation which will cause us to forfeit the moral case which puts us in a special light in the eyes of liberals such as Sakharov. Our moral justification, however, is in the long run the sole guarantee of that enduring sympathy, which does not depend on fleeting circumstances. Such a sympathy is a basic condition for the readiness to stand by us, to help us and to offer aid in need.

The example of Sakharov ought to serve as an inspiration and challenge to Israeli intellectuals to safeguard the spiritual fiber of this tortured and bewildered nation. They are called upon to comfort it, to strengthen it, to prevent it from shrinking into the mood of an isolated sect, full of resentment and rage, steeped in bitter thoughts and dreaming of revenge. It is necessary to inspire the people with the feeling of pride at being heirs and descendants of one of the most ancient, noble and vital civilizations in history, a highly significant strand in the tapestry of universal history, a fellow member of the family of nations that is struggling for the dignity of men, for the right of all ethnic and cultural entities to free expression, and for the creative unity of mankind.

First published in *Midstream*, February 1977. This essay was presented as an address to the Israel Academy of Sciences and Humanities at a celebration in Sakharov's honor when he was awarded the Nobel Prize.

Bibliography of J. L. Talmon

1. *The Origins of Totalitarian Democracy*, London: Secker & Warburg, 1952.
2. *Political Messianism: The Romantic Phase*, London: Secker & Warburg, 1960.
3. *The Myth of the Nation and the Vision of Revolution: The Origins of Ideological Polarization in the Twentieth Century*, London: Secker & Warburg, 1981.
4. *Romanticism and Revolt: Europe 1815–1948*, London, Harcourt: Brace & World Inc., 1967.
5. *The Unique and the Universal: Some Historical Reflections*, London: Secker & Warburg, 1965.
6. *Israel Among the Nations*, London: Weidenfeld & Nicolson, 1971.

The above list provides first edition publishing information. These books were translated into many languages and excerpted in numerous journals. For a list of Talmon's publications, see: Ya'akov Talmon, *The Riddle of the Past and the Cunning of History*, Bialik Institute, Jerusalem 2000, pp. 416-422. [Hebrew].

Index